Tears and

The Winged Wheel Story

Arnie Gibbons

Winged Wheel Publications

CW00660793

Tears and Glory: The Winged Wheel Story

First published 2008 by Winged Wheel Publications
102A Cole Park Road
Twickenham
TW1 1JA

Copyright © Arnie Gibbons 2008

The right of Arnie Gibbons to be identified as the author of this work has been asserted in accordance with the Copyrights, Designs and Patents Act 1988.

All Rights Reserved. No part of this publication may be reprinted or reproduced or utilised in any form or by any electronic, mechanical or other means, now known or hereafter invented, including photocopying , scanning or recording, or in any information storage or retrieval system, without permission in writing from the publisher.

A CIP Catalogue record for this book is available from the British Library

ISBN 978-0-9558455-0-5

Production credits:
Cover design: Rachael Adams www.scrutineer.co.uk
Copy edit: Graham Russel

Photo credits: Evening Post (EP), Bill Taylor (BT), Dave Armstrong (DA), Wright Wood photos courtesy of John Somerville (JS), Alf Weedon photos courtesy of Retro Publications [www.retro-speedway.com] (Retro), Bryan Horsnell (BH), Reading Museum (RM)

Printed in Great Britain by Cromwell Press, Trowbridge, Wiltshire

To Reg
who made it happen

and

Pat and Bill
who kept the Racers going when many would have thrown in the towel

and not forgetting

Geoff and Denny
proud wearers of the Winged Wheel

Winged Wheel Publications

102A Cole Park Road
Twickenham
Middlesex
TW1 1JA

Rachel Adams
Scrutineer Publishing
45 Stanley Road
BN1 4NH

Tel (020) 8744 9269
e-mail: arnie_gibbons2004@yahoo.co.uk

13 June 2008

Dear Rachel,

Tears & Glory – The Winged Wheel Story

After many months of waiting I am delighted to finally receive printed copies of my history of Reading Speedway. Although the heart of the book is the chronicle of Reading Racers 40 years on track, I have included the results of my research into speedway in Berkshire before the historic meeting against Nelson on 17 June 1968.

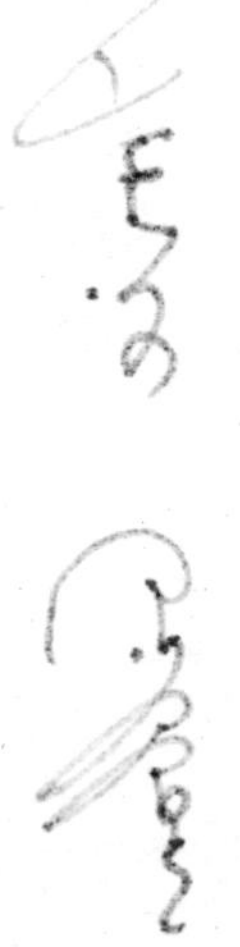

little bit of Reading's social history and the ebbs and flows of the sport. And finally I've flavoured it with a few personal observations and experiences.

I have never even thought about writing a book before, and as a novice I found many people helped enormously.

Your contribution is greatly appreciated.

The complimentary copy of the finished product is enclosed as a token of my gratitude.

With grateful thanks

Arnie Gibbons

Contents

Foreword by Pat Bliss	6
Introduction	7
Reading before 1968	9
California Dreaming	12
Lloyd Goffe	27
An Undiscovered Venue	29
Reading 1968–2007	30
Appendices 1– 6	238

Foreword

The question I have been asked so often in the past two years is: 'do you miss the speedway'?

After it being so big a part of my life for over 25 years there is only one answer - of course I miss it and especially the company of the many friends we made amongst the riders, officials, track staff, promoters and the supporters. I truly believed when we moved on and BSI came in with such a blaze of publicity that we were leaving Reading in safe hands but alarm bells certainly rang when they changed the name - it's good to know that the Racers are now back.

My Father was the real driving force behind the team for so many years and few can forget him standing quietly on the centre green, his pipe in mouth, and the Racers loved him for it. He missed very few meetings, home or away, and I often think of him saying that the journey home from the far-flung away tracks never seemed so long when we had won! It is in no small part due to his presence that Reading kept on an even keel for so long and why no rider ever turned down a booking with Reading without a very good reason. They all knew that Bill's word was his bond and that they would have no problems at Smallmead.

I think Reading must have held more testimonials, both for ten and twenty years service, than most other clubs and I take this as a huge compliment that 'once a Racer always a Racer'. Very few riders asked to leave and the dreaded points limit was usually the reason for this.........and often they came back too!

To try to name individual riders would be unfair. We have fond memories of so many over the years, and they all brought something of themselves to the team. We have stayed friends with them all and still keep in touch with many. From the League winning 1980 team when I personally first became involved to the current Racers seven we have had more good years than bad. We spent many happy hours reliving these times, and although we had years when nothing seemed to go right these were just a part of the sport and even these had their merits.

We have always had the best 'back room' staff at Smallmead and still keep in touch with most of them, they were the backbone of the club and although over the years we unfortunately lost some old friends we also made new ones and none will be forgotten. Their recollections of the antics that went on behind the scenes could easily fill another book.

I give my thanks to all the people who have been involved in Reading speedway over the years: to the riders who have entertained us, the officials and track staff who have worked so hard with us, my family who have always been involved and to the supporters who have followed the Racers through thick and thin.

Pat Bliss
March 2008

Introduction

It all started due to Pauline Rowe's altruism. She attended Tilehurst as a St. John's Ambulance Brigade volunteer and her son (and my friend) Andrew dragged me along to watch the speedway in October 1970. I was hooked and couldn't wait for the start of the next season. That love has endured even though I moved away from Reading 25 years ago. Two decades exiled in the Midlands and the lows of the period from 1994 to 2003 haven't deterred me from following the Racers.

It's been a bumpy ride, from the heady excitement of 1971 and the triumphs of 1990 to the agony of the 2006 Elite League play-offs, via 1977's injustices and the despair of sitting on the steps of Hackney hospital on the night of 16 July 1982.

When Reading Museum announced that they would be mounting a display last summer I offered some of the items I have accumulated over the years. This resulted in me getting involved with planning the display. During one of these meetings I commented that the 40th anniversary celebrations marked the appropriate time to produce a book celebrating Reading speedway and its ups and downs.

Andy Povey turned to me and said: "well, you should write it". So thanks to Andy for encouraging me to start the project and to Brendan Carr at Reading Museum for his enthusiasm in organising the Reading speedway exhibition.

No sooner had the idea been planted in my mind than Reading's very existence seemed in doubt. Without Mark Legg and Malcolm Holloway this book would have been an obituary – Reading speedway's continued existence is down to them. Thanks, guys.

I have enjoyed reading many books in the existing speedway library, none more so than Jeff Scott's *Showered in Shale*. I must thank him for his encouragement throughout this project and practical help on the technical side.

I quickly concluded that I couldn't tell the story of Reading speedway without going back before 1968 and looking eastward to California. A number of people provided me with assistance – Les Hawkins in particular helped me greatly.

In telling the story of Reading speedway I have attempted to put it in the context of the wider landscape of speedway's decline and the changing world.

I have used a wide variety of source materials but *Speedway Star* remains the publication of record for the sport. I am grateful to the magazine for permission to quote from it. Their statistics compiled by Bryan Seery and Dave Welch are my primary source of data, but I have used a number of other sources notably the many publications of Peter Oakes.

In most cases averages mentioned in the text are for official fixtures and include bonus points except where stated or clearly implied by the context. For a definition of official fixture see Appendix 1. At the end of each season the principal riders and their averages in official fixtures are listed. All riders who made ten or more appearances are included. In some cases riders with less than ten matches have been listed, these are printed in brackets.

The *Reading Evening Post* have assisted, not just in their coverage of the Racers over the years, but also by allowing me access to their picture archive.

While I have kept a speedway diary for 16 of the 40 years covered by this book my memory is fallible, and I would like to thank veteran supporters Pete Butler and Mick Napier for their input and feedback.

Some facts are easier than others to check. It is amazing how many riders have two or even more dates of birth, but it is attendances and transfer fees that give the greatest difficulty. These are impossible to verify, but I have used figures quoted in the press at the time, as they give a sense of the size of crowds and transfer fees. Hence where I have quoted figures these should be taken as estimates and heavily qualified as to their accuracy.

I have also found the following websites particularly useful:

- www.readingspeedway.com
- http://www.speedway.org/history/ (Anders Aberg)
- www.rlach.republika.pl/ (Roman Lach)
- myweb.tiscali.co.uk/intspeedway/ (Brian Collins)

I know footnotes are not to everybody's taste, but I have used them principally to cite sources and to include personal commentary.

In addition to those already mentioned I would like to thank (with apologies to anyone I've left out): Dave Armstrong (photos), James Ashford (at the *Evening Post*), Robert Bamford, Pat Bliss, Nick Dyer, Reg Fearman, Ross Garrigan, Bryan Horsnell, John Hyam, Norman Jacobs, Bob Smith, Barry Stephenson, Bill Taylor (photos), Stuart Towner.

Arnie Gibbons
January 2008

Co-promoter Malcolm Holloway and Team Manager Tim Sugar at the Reading Museum open day in September 2007 with the 1990 League Championship Trophy. (RM)

Reading before 1968

Most sports are not invented, they evolve. Speedway's creation myth pinpoints the invention as the responsibility of Johnnie Hoskins at West Maitland, New South Wales, Australia in 1923. It is fair to say that a sport that was recognisably the one we know today evolved in Australia in the 1920s. There is also little doubt that Hoskins, a great self-publicist, played a significant role in that development.

There are similar debates about the origins of speedway in Britain. High Beech, February 1928 is the event that is usually pinpointed as speedway's first appearance in Britain. The principal rival claimants are Droylsden (near Manchester) and Camberley, just 20 miles from Reading. Both staged events in 1927 that bore some similarity to speedway. The first Camberley meeting[1] on May 7 took place on a quarter-mile sand circuit with the riders racing clockwise. Female pioneer Fay Taylour was among the competitors along with members of the Reading & District Motor Club.

The timing of speedway's arrival in Britain was fortuitous, as another sport arrived in the country just a few months before. After making its first appearance at Belle Vue (the current home of the Belle Vue Aces) in 1926, greyhound racing took hold the following year. This meant stadiums springing up across the country that would soon play host to speedway tracks as 'dirt-track' racing became the new craze.

After the First World War, Reading expanded, and the town seemed like ripe territory for a greyhound track. In 1931 a group of entrepreneurs formed the Reading Greyhound Society Ltd and purchased some land. The site in Tilehurst on the Oxford Road was an ideal location. It sat opposite the Pulsometer Pumps Engineering Works and was served by a tram that ran up the Oxford Road and terminated close by. Although there was housing nearby the area still felt like the edge of town, with plenty of green fields in view.

Prior to completion of the stadium a spokesperson for the company (a Major McEnnery) said: "It is proposed, with the assistance of the speedway authorities, to build a dirt track and hold dirt track meetings as well". On 14 November 1931 the stadium opened with a crowd of 4-5,000 for the initial greyhound meeting.

The following spring, motorbikes came to the Tilehurst stadium. A meeting promoted by the South Reading Motor Cycle Club (SRMCC) took place over the Whitsun holiday weekend on Monday May 16. Photographs from the event in the following week's *Reading Chronicle* clearly show that racing took place on a grass surface. The only rider named in the photos is an F. Mathews. The 'speedway' pictures shared a page in the *Chronicle* with highlights from the Emmer Green church fête.

The following week the *Chronicle* carried the announcement that the Reading and District Motor Club (R&DMC) would be staging 'grass speedway' on Saturday June 11, promising that it: "will be extra specially good and exciting."

The results of the June meeting were covered in the *Chronicle*. There were four classes:

- 4-lap 350cc final: W. B. Wakefield, R. C. Halls, Roper
- 4-lap 500cc final: Roper, Wakefield, C. B. Ballard
- 6-lap championship final: Ballard, J. Keene, F. Mathews
- 6-lap handicap final: F. W. Clark, Halls, Ballard

The R&DMC had run a rival grasstrack meeting off Scours Lane very close to the Tilehurst stadium on the same afternoon as the SRMCC meeting in May. This may have been a spoiler. The *Chronicle* and the *Standard*'s reporting of the two clubs' activities before the war suggests that they did not always see eye to eye. Both clubs provided members with a mix

---

1 An account of this meeting can be found in *Five-One* magazine, February 1996

of sporting and recreational events for motorbike enthusiasts. For example in 1933 the *Reading Chronicle* advised SRMCC members to: "meet at Whitley Pump 6 p.m. Saturday next for run to Stamford Bridge to witness the England v Australia Test match". The R&DMC dated back to 1910 (give or take a year); its founders included a Mr F.J. Deacon[2].

Further meetings were contemplated but did not materialise. By 1933 the initial bubble had burst and speedway had settled down to a core of more professionally run tracks. There were no longer queues of people wanting to open new tracks, and interest in Tilehurst as a venue waned.

The two motor cycle clubs remained interested in speedway, and looked east to Longmoor. For the next quarter of a century this became the centre of Berkshire's speedway activity, better known by its post-war alias as California.

Reading's local papers, the *Standard* and *Chronicle,* reported on the racy events of the era, such as the 'pretty ankle competition' at the Huntley & Palmers Recreation Club Gala, and like today's local papers were much concerned with crime. One report was headlined 'Six Tons of Bovril Stolen'. Then in July 1936 the news broke of a further attempt to stage speedway at Tilehurst.

The R&DMC planned a grass meeting at Tilehurst stadium with a view to laying a 380-yard cinder track if successful. An emergency general meeting of the club at the Elephant Hotel in Market Place (next to the Westminster Bank) approved the proposals providing sufficient members came forward to guarantee the 'rent' demanded by the stadium owners. After nine months the *Reading Standard* revealed that a meeting (on grass again) would take place on Whit Monday 1937. However, as two greyhound meetings took place on that day it seems certain that the event didn't take place.

After the Second World War, austerity was the watchword of the day. It wasn't just food and clothing that was rationed, entertainment was too. With people desperate for something to contrast the dull daily grind speedway flourished. In 1946 over 600,000 people went through the turnstiles at Wimbledon. The 12 league teams reported an aggregate profit of £160,000 (equivalent to £4.5 million today). Seeing the opportunity to profit from the sport's new-found popularity, dozens of applications to open new tracks reached the speedway authorities. By the start of 1951 the number of league teams had risen from 12 to 37.

Potential new applicants had to overcome two hurdles. The first was to get a licence from the Speedway Control Board, but permission was also required from the Home Office. The Government feared that leisure activities might undermine industrial production and frowned on weekday tracks in particular.

The list of applicants for 1947 makes interesting reading. Among those granted permission were pre-war venues such as Harringay (the original Racers) and Southampton, and new tracks like Cradley Heath. Among the unsuccessful applicants were Charlton, Crewe, Peterborough, Yarmouth, Staines and Reading.

The following year Reading again appeared on the list of 18 applicants for a licence to stage speedway. Among the hopefuls were Leicester, Worksop, Poole, Coventry, Romford and Leeds.

Come 1949, and again Reading failed to get a licence, unlike Swindon and Oxford. Swindon, originally granted an open licence, replaced Hull in the league mid-season.

A rare opportunity for Reading citizens to see a top speedway star came at the Reading Conservative Fete at Denton's Field, Bath Road in 1949. As well as a demonstration of skills by Bill Kitchen (winner of 11 National League championships with Belle Vue and Wembley) and George Wilks, a grasstrack event entertained the crowds. Participants included California

---

2 From a report of R&DMC annual dinner in the *Reading Chronicle* (31 January 1913). It is probable that F. J. Deacon was related to Herbert Deacon, California rider and chairman of R&DMC in 1939.

regulars Bill Newell and Maurice Leonard.

All went quiet for the next few years. Crippled by a punitive level of entertainment tax the sport shrunk to a hardcore of ten league tracks and a handful of open-licence venues by 1958. The formation of the Provincial League by Mike Parker and Reg Fearman in 1960 initiated the third golden era of the sport.

By 1963 the Provincial League was well established, while the top division (still called the National League) struggled to retain enough tracks willing to carry the heavy cost base of top division speedway. In Parliament the legalisation of off-track betting would play a major role in bringing speedway to Reading.

Clapton Stadium Ltd, owners of the Tilehurst Stadium since 1932, needed to review their business as attendances were hit by the liberalisation of the betting laws. They decided to concentrate on Slough, and allowed their other two stadiums (Reading and Clapton) to become prospects for re-development. After being acquired by the Greyhound Racing Association (GRA) in 1966 all three stadiums eventually fell into the clutches of property developers. Clapton had staged speedway before the Second World War as Lea Bridge.

In the short term, the stadium owners were keen to replace the expected loss of income due to off-track betting with other activities. The first stock car meeting took place on 3 July 1962. Promoters Speedworth also ran stox at other venues with speedway connections such as Aldershot and Ipswich. A tarmac stock car track was laid in the stadium, that looked much as it had done before the war. The Grand Opening ceremony (following 'God Save the Queen', as was customary in those days) was conducted by Split Waterman.

'Split' (real name Squire Francis) twice came within four laps of becoming World Champion. In 1951 he lost a run-off to Jack Young; and in 1953 he went into his last ride unbeaten but dropped points to Olle Nygren and eventual winner Freddie Williams. Both these performances came while riding for Harringay Racers. A hard-riding and colourful character, Split's career started at Wembley in 1947 and was drawing to a close in the colours of Ipswich by 1962. Split became the first big speedway star to race at Tilehurst – not on a bike but in a stock car – when he competed in the evening's consolation race. (Incidentally Waterman is the uncle of record producer Pete Waterman of Kylie and Pop Idol fame.)

Another connection with speedway arose from the presence of Johnnie O'Connor, the stock car announcer/commentator. He had been the announcer at California, and a rider on the fringes of the Poppies team, making one Southern Area League appearance in California colours.

A few weeks after opening, Reading Council pointed out that there was no planning permission to run stock cars. A retrospective application was hurriedly submitted, but the Council refused planning permission. A public enquiry in 1963 resulted in planning consent being granted by the Minister.

With motor sport in situ, Tilehurst naturally became the subject of speculation that it could be hosting speedway next. When Southampton closed in 1963 the National League faced the prospect of having to run with just six teams. After failing to coerce Provincial League champions Wolverhampton to move up, the lower league severed its links from speedway's control board and ran 'black'.

The National League promoters, desperate to supplement their numbers looked for a new venue, and in February 1964 *Speedway Star* reported that their eyes had alighted on Reading as a possibility. In the end West Ham joined the National League, but just eight months later Norwich closed and once again Reading came close to joining the speedway community. King's Lynn became the new home of the Norwich Stars. They joined the British League in 1966 a year after its formation from the unification of the National and Provincial Leagues.

The next mentions of Tilehurst as a potential venue would finally lead to fruition.

California Dreaming

1 Longmoor

Nine Mile Ride runs from Bracknell in the east to California Country Park, a couple of miles south of Wokingham, in the west.

According to Wokingham Borough Council: "California Country Park is set within 100 acres of rare ancient bogland and lowland heath. It offers a wealth of walking and wildlife watching opportunities for visitors." Today it offers a sedate and peaceful experience. The park café, called 'California Dreaming'[3] is about as noisy as it gets. Its past is more lively.

The central area of the site, Longmoor Lake, was dug out in the 19th century for brick making. In 1931 Alf Cartlidge developed the area into a leisure resort. An advert in the 1933 *Reading Standard* promises: "Berkshire's best bathing resort – fed by mineral springs acknowledged by medical authorities to be beneficial to health," and children's entertainments.

After the Second World War, Alf and his son Norman Cartlidge developed the park further. Berkshire's "lakeside pleasure resort" offered swimming, boating, monkeys and bears, a miniature railway, cooked teas and dinner dances in the large ballroom amongst its many delights. But above all it offered speedway; the following account describes the joys of a Sunday at California-in-England during the early 1950s.

> *"One of our very happy memories is of this time when our whole family would attend speedway, or as we called it, the 'dirt track' racing at California. Mr Cartlidge, the owner at the time, ran quite a successful leisure park, a miniature zoo, and a train running around the site. There were boats on the lake and swimming was allowed.*
>
> *"But back to speedway. This was the most popular event on a Sunday afternoon. The crowds would pack all around the track – many climbing up nearby trees. It was always quite a thrilling spectacle, to see these chaps on their racing motor-cycles, whizzing around the track."*
>
> From Ken Goatley's *Wokingham, Town of my Life*

Speedway at California has its origins to the 1930s. Motorcycling activity at the site evolved, with the first recorded activity being scrambling. The *Reading Standard* (which became the *Evening Post* in 1965) reported on a scrambles meeting at the site on 22 May 1932. Further references to activity in 1932 are hard to find, but *Speedway News* (10 June) reports that Stamford Bridge speedway supporters club were planning a visit to California, and that the scrambles track was among the facilities available to the fans.

Moving forward a year to 1933, and Reading was just recovering from the excitement of biscuit week in 'biscuit town' when speedway arrived.

The first speedway type meeting at California took place on May 28, promoted by the South Reading Motor Cycle Club. Advance publicity described it as the first "dirt-track" meeting. Winners of the four categories were: 350cc scratch: Jeff Keene – unlimited scratch: Herbert Deacon – GP race: H. J. Hitch – unlimited handicap: Bushby. A one-lap track record of 20.6 seconds was set by P. Gardner. These races would have been rolling starts, as it wasn't

3 And already we have a link to Smallmead and modern day speedway, thanks to the Mamas & Papas who sung both 'California Dreaming' and the Smallmead signature tune 'Monday Monday.' How a song with the chorus: "Every other day of the week is fine ... but whenever Monday comes you can find me a-cryin' all of the time" became so cherished by Racers fans remains a mystery.

until the following month that Crystal Palace promoter Fred Mockford piloted an invention new to speedway – the starting gate.

Three more meetings were held in 1933 with Johnnie Walker and Jeff Keene proving to be the top dogs.

In 1934 Reading & District Motor Club took over promoting meetings at the track, and continued to organise events there until the Second World War curtailed activities. The club was run by the riders. H. Deacon was chair and club captain, and H. Norman secretary in the years immediately before the war. Norman rode regularly in 1935 and 1936 finishing fifth in the 1936 club championship. Top riders Goffe, Boyd and Walker all served on the committee for a period, and site owner Alf Cartlidge occupied a position as vice-president.

The author explores the site of California speedway. The concrete starting grid can be seen in the foreground; the posts on the right mark the position of the safety fence.

A typical meeting consisted of three or four competitions each consisting of four to six heats followed by a final. Most of these were scratch races, but there was generally a handicap to liven up the day. The meeting would typically be rounded off with a consolation race, and a race for the fastest riders of the day.

A record crowd of over 2,000 turned out for the second meeting of 1934 to watch George Newton (later to be a participant in the very first World Final two years hence) give an exhibition of broadsliding. In September the club championship, a 16-rider 20-heat event, went to track record holder Johnnie Walker. Fred Tuck (who made his name with Bristol) came second and J. Bourton third. In joint fourth were Deacon and K. L. Goffe. Born in Woodley, Kenneth Lloyd Goffe went on to reach the World Final and become the most significant Berkshire-born rider in speedway's history.

During the season, three team matches were staged. Although the track was known as Longmoor, the team rode under the Reading banner. In the first of these (July 15), Oxford went down by a single point: 27½ – 26½. After Newbury couldn't raise a team a second match against Oxford ended in a home win, as did the visit of Hounslow. Walker topped the score charts in all three; Bourton and Goffe achieved paid maximums against Hounslow.

None of the visiting teams had speedway tracks of their own, and many of the riders lining up were Longmoor regulars. In the second Oxford match Reg Vigor appeared for the visitors.

In August 1935 a fresh daily local paper, the *Evening Gazette* hit the news stands. Unlike the *Chronicle* and *Standard* – which only carried ads on the front page – the *Gazette* featured news. Early editions were largely taken up by Mussolini's invasion of Abyssinia and had a similar layout to the pre-tabloid *Evening Post* that reported Reading Racers exploits half a century later. To promote the newspaper, Longmoor's club championship received sponsorship from the new newspaper. The trophy went to Reg Vigor after a three-man run-off with J. Forbes (a participant in 1933's opening meeting) and rapidly improving Lloyd Goffe. Deacon scored 11 points from his first four rides, and a fall in the wet conditions cost him the title. Instead he finished joint fourth with reigning champion Walker.

Oxford were beaten twice more in 1935 and a couple of later meetings featured sidecars. A sense of how informal meetings were can be gathered from the inclusion of a spectators' race in the final meeting of the season. Prior to the event the *Reading Standard* informed dirt track fans that: "there will also be a spectators' race open to anyone mounted on a machine fit for the road. Mudguards must be fitted but lamps may be removed[4]."

At the beginning of the season the track was enlarged to 400 yards before being reduced to 310 yards in October. No less than six riders broke or equalled the track record during the year: Goffe, Deacon, Tuck, Walker, Vigor, and Forbes.

By 1936 Longmoor was hosting speedway on a regular fortnightly basis. Meetings started at Easter and continued to the end of October. The R&DMC AGM reported aggregate attendances for the year of 25,000, making the average attendance just under 2,000. Most meetings consisted of scratch races and individual tournaments with the notable exception of a challenge against Barnet on September 27. Boyd (11) and Vigor (10) top scored as Reading beat Barnet 41-31 avenging a 48-23 defeat at Barnet earlier in the month. The Barnet team at Reading included Archie Windmill and Charlie Appleby. Reading also rode a challenge match at Dagenham, losing 40-29. Top scorers were Jim Boyd and Reg Vigor with 9.

Speedway pioneer Jack Adams, a member of the 1929 West Ham team, was a regular at California from 1934 to 1939. (JS)

The big names at Longmoor clashed in the penultimate meeting of the season – the club championship sponsored by the *Evening Gazette*. Reigning champion Vigor went through the

4 *Reading Standard* 25 October 1935. Now just imagine the health and safety issues that would be raised if a similar race were proposed today!

card to retain his title. Fast-improving Boyd (who first appeared at Longmoor towards the end of 1935) beat Jack Adams in a run-off for second after both riders scored 12 points. Goffe (11) could only manage fourth. Adams had been a member of the West Ham team in 1929, the first year of league speedway. Also in the field were two new riders who would still be part of the California set-up after the war – George Bason and Billy Newell.

Boyd established a new track record at Longmoor on 30 May 1937 and remained the sole holder of the track record until the outbreak of war. He went on to become a professional speedway rider. Born in Maidenhead in 1913, he made his Southampton debut in July 1937. In 1938 his scoring increased and he was rewarded with a Division Two cap against 'the Dominions' at Hackney. The following year Southampton moved up to Division One and he found the going tougher.

After the war Boyd found himself at Belle Vue where he stayed until a May 1949 move to Division Two Walthamstow. 1947, his best season at Hyde Road saw him finish 21st in the National League point scorers' rankings. At Walthamstow he became the club's all-time top scorer topping their averages in 1949 and 1950. Arriving after the season's start in 1949, Boyd found himself outscored by Charlie May. After three seasons Walthamstow closed and Boyd moved on to Oxford where he topped scored in 1952 and 1953.

Boyd dominated Longmoor events in 1937. Goffe had moved on to West Ham, and after making his Provincial League (effectively Division Two) debut for Bristol Vigor ceased to be a Longmoor regular.

Vigor performed sufficiently well for Bristol to warrant a call up by his parent club – Wimbledon. After breaking into the 1937 Wimbledon team the Tooting-based 22-year-old was keen to defend his Longmoor Club Championship title. On September 19 Vigor was keen to ride, but rain caused the meeting to be postponed.

Two weeks later when it was re-staged the meeting commenced with a minute's silence and the singing of 'Abide with Me' to mark the passing of a local hero. The previous Monday Vigor had crashed at Wimbledon while making his seventh National League appearance and died three days later. The *Evening Gazette* agreed to donate the original trophy to Vigor's mother. Wimbledon promoter Ronnie Greene joined a record crowd of 4,000 who witnessed Jim Boyd take the title with a 15-point maximum. Johnnie Walker (14), and Billy Newell (12) joined him on the rostrum, with Jack Adams just missing out on 11.

At the following meeting, riders competed for the California Cup, again over the 16-rider 20-heat format. Site owner (and honorary vice-president of the R&DMC) Alf Cartlidge presented the trophy to Walker, with Adams second and Boyd tied on third with Bason.

Away from Longmoor, the club contested a challenge match at Portsmouth in September and lost 36-26. Reading's top scorers were Lloyd Goffe and Peter Hoult with 6 points each. Hoult was still riding at California in the early 1950s. Former California track record holder Fred Tuck top scored for Portsmouth with a 9 point maximum, in what turned out to be the last meeting staged in Portsmouth's brief existence. There were no team matches at Longmoor (or California as it was increasingly being referred to) that year.

The fortnightly pattern continued in 1938. Meetings were again mainly individual competitions with two challenges in July. The first was against an Oxford club based at the Sandford 'grass-speedway'. (Cowley didn't open its doors until 1939.) A 41-30 win in this fixture was followed by a return match at Sandford in September, won 42-30 by the home team.

On July 31 Reading thumped High Beech 59-24, Boyd and Jack Adams both completing maximums. A return match at High Beech a week later saw the Essex team gain their revenge by a 61-23 margin with Boyd (10) putting up the only resistance.

Neither Reading nor High Beech participated in the Sunday Dirt-track league. Dagenham, Romford (based at Dagenham), Eastbourne, Rye House and Smallford formed this new venture. Although most fixtures never took place it is notable as the first attempt to run a training league for amateurs.

The remaining meetings at California were individual competitions. The season culminated with the Club Championship and California Cup, both run in October. The meeting on May 8 produced a rare event – a clean sweep. Boyd won both scratch competitions, the handicap and the fastest riders' race, possibly the only occasion this feat was achieved. As Boyd came close to repeating this feat a couple of times later in the season he was the red-hot favourite for the club championship sponsored by the *Evening Gazette*. After two wins Boyd suffered machine problems and ended up well down the field with just 6 points. Johnnie Walker (15) won the meeting from Jack Adams (12), and Sid Lewington (11). Bason and Newell finished in the top half of the field along with a new name – Jack Peck.

At the next meeting Adams improved on his second place, lifting the California Cup.

California put on a similar programme of fortnightly meetings in 1939. Johnnie Walker won most events, with Boyd his closest rival. Boyd went through the card on June 25 scoring 18 points and lowering his own track record to 69.2. Newell, Adams and L Shepherd were among the more successful of the other competitors. Newer faces included Peter Robinson (a post-war professional with Southampton, Plymouth, Oxford and Liverpool), Arthur Flack and Stan Tebby. Speedway arrived at Cowley this year and in July the two clubs met. The aggregate win went to Oxford; after a 47-37 win in the home leg the Reading team went down 49-33 at Cowley. The bulk of Reading's points came from Adams and Sid Lewington.

Newell won the California Cup on August 20, from Boyd and Lewington. The following meeting on Sunday September 3 had to be postponed because of the declaration of war on that day. The *Reading Standard* found space on page seven to run the headline: "War declared against Germany," and carried photographs of children evacuated from London to Reading over the weekend. Although Reading FC beat Southend 1-0 on the Saturday cinemas and the greyhounds at Tilehurst ceased. After a week or so the cinemas re-opened and on September 13 greyhound racing resumed.

While the papers carried announcements about how to apply for petrol coupons, plans to carry on with speedway at California were made. A meeting took place on September 24. Lloyd Goffe (still generally referred to as Ken in the local press) made his first appearance on track at California for three years. The highlights of the meeting were his encounters with fellow National League rider Jim Boyd. Walker, Adams, Lewington and Deacon were among the competitors who turned out to perform in front of a poor crowd. Several of the regulars were missing, competing in a meeting held on the same day at Cowley stadium, Oxford. That meeting featured Newell, Peck, Flack and Bason, among the California regulars.

There is no evidence of any further meetings at California during the war. Almost nine years would elapse before racing resumed at California. Speedway during wartime faced two major problems: the availability of riders and petrol rationing. With its rural location the latter problem would have been particularly challenging. Only Belle Vue and Rye House ran a significant number of wartime meetings.

The sandy soil surface of the 310-yard racetrack meant that events at Longmoor tended to fall between two stools – neither grasstrack nor speedway. Early meetings were fairly consistently described as sand-track racing, but soon the terms 'dirt track' and speedway crept into local coverage in the *Reading Standard* and the *Chronicle*, and programmes referred to speedway racing.

Speedway News tended to regard Longmoor as closer to grasstrack in nature. In part this was because right up until 1954 meetings were staged as club events under the auspices of the Auto Cycle Union (ACU), without the oversight of the Speedway Control Board (SCB). Other amateur tracks such as Rye House and High Beech were licensed in the same way but because of their more traditional surfaces considered to be 'proper' speedway.

For example in its obituary of Reg Vigor, *Speedway News* noted that he: "came to the front as a grass-track rider at New California, near Wokingham. Here he won a much coveted cup two years in succession." Similarly Cyril May[5] writes about Lloyd Goffe's 'speedway debut' at Crystal Palace in 1936 having already acknowledged his two years of experience at Longmoor.

For a contrary view George Bason, whose California career spanned 20 years, said: "Prior to the outbreak of war in 1939 closed circuit racing on dirt and grass tracks was enjoying a terrific boom. Most tracks billed themselves as speedways, but the only circuits that really qualified for the title were Dagenham, High Beech, Rye House, Oxford, Arlington and Longmoor (now known as California)"[6].

Ultimately when California was licensed through the Speedway Control Board in 1954 it became an accepted part of the speedway scene. However, all that had fundamentally changed was the way it was administered. There is no evidence that the track surface in 1954 differed in any major respect from that in the pre-war era. If it was good enough to be called speedway in 1954 then it should be accepted as speedway in its earlier life.

2 1948-53

In 1948 speedway was still booming. Three divisions accommodated 29 teams. Wembley rode most of their matches at Wimbledon having been temporarily evicted from the Empire Stadium for the Olympics. As a result New Cross won the league title, the only time in the first eight post-war seasons when the honour didn't go to Wembley. The Racers (of Harringay) boasted the world's best rider in Aussie Vic Duggan.

Speedway enjoyed the limelight and the year culminated with the release of 'Once a Jolly Swagman', a film with a cast list headed by Dirk Bogarde. Other actors appearing included Thora Hird, Moira Lister, Sid James, Cyril Cusack and Renee Asherson.

Few tracks offered facilities for juniors or amateurs. Rye House provided regular opportunities for novices like 15-year-old Reg Fearman, but the league tracks generally offered no more than the odd second-half novice race. The demand for additional amateur racing (licensed by the ACU, not the SCB) led to California re-opening.

Dirt track racing, to use the description on the programmes of the era, returned to California in 1948. The first of four meetings, promoted by the California Motor Cycle Club, took place on August 8. The meeting secretary was Norman Cartlidge, son of Alf who was in the process of expanding the activities at California. The weather didn't look too kindly on the venture, with two of the meetings abandoned midway

California-in-England
TELEPHONE EVERSLEY 2256
Berkshire's Lakeside Pleasure Resort
Near WOKINGHAM Berks.
for
CATERING
LARGE OR SMALL PARTIES
LARGE BALLROOM
AVAILABLE for ALL Occasions
DANCES RECEPTIONS
DINNERS ETC.
FULLY LICENCED RESTAURANT
Next time your Club is in the district ask
YOUR SECRETARY TO BOOK FOR TEA
Plain or High Teas . Luncheons
Dinners or Suppers
MENUS ON REQUEST
For the Kids!
Swimming Pool, Lake, Boating, Monkeys, Bear
Lion, Swings, Miniature Railway, Ices, etc.

An advertisement for California leisure park taken from a 1950 California programme.

---

5 *Speedway Star* 17 November 1973

6 *Speedway Star* 4 October 1958

through due to rain. Between newsprint shortages and the extensive coverage given to plans for the development of Bracknell new town there was little space for coverage of California speedway.

The following year a longer season of racing took place. For the next five years meetings were a mixture of individual competitions and team challenges, usually between made-up teams. Some of these had intriguing titles like Meteors v Vampires and Muckspreaders v Moonrakers. Only in 1950 did California ride matches against teams identifiable with other tracks. Opponents in 1950 included Rye House, High Beech and Eastbourne (away only).

The major individual event of 1949, the California Trophy, held over three rounds, went to Bill Newell. Plymouth had provided Newell with a regular team place in National League Division Three racing the previous two years. Earlier in the season Jack Peck set a new track record in the first round of the event. Peck, a farmer born in 1916, went on to make a few appearances for Aldershot in National League Division Three the following year. Trevor Davies and Gerald Jackson were the other top names that year. Jackson went on to complete 18 seasons shared between Rayleigh, Wimbledon and Hackney and made his England debut in 1958. Also appearing on track were Roy Bowers, Stan Tebby, Maurice Leonard (the father of Brian Leonard) and Jack Griffin.

In 1950 there were two individual meetings and the following year three. All of these were won by a single rider – Trevor Davies. Despite his dominance at California his professional career was fairly modest. The Welshman signed to West Ham but only made a handful of National League appearances.

The first of these five wins came in a meeting where Davies broke the track record three times. In the final meeting of the 1950 season (a 44-40 defeat v Rye House) Davies lowered the record again only to see Ron How post an even quicker time.

How started riding at Rye House the previous year and was quickly signed up by Harringay. He went on to become one of the top English riders of the era. After four seasons with Harringay and nine with Wimbledon he finished his career with two years at Oxford. He reached nine World Finals and represented Great Britain in four World Team Cup Finals, including the competition's first-ever staging in 1960.

In 1951 Davies regained a share of the track record, equalling How's time of 66.8 in the second meeting of the season. Davies came away from this meeting with the April Trophy and added the Whitsun Trophy and Festival Trophy to his haul.

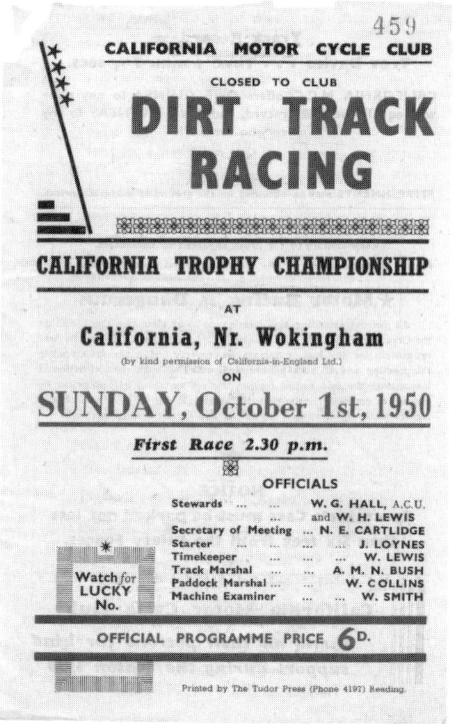
459

CALIFORNIA MOTOR CYCLE CLUB

CLOSED TO CLUB

DIRT TRACK RACING

CALIFORNIA TROPHY CHAMPIONSHIP

AT

California, Nr. Wokingham

(by kind permission of California-in-England Ltd.)

ON

SUNDAY, October 1st, 1950

First Race 2.30 p.m.

OFFICIALS

Stewards ... ... W. G. HALL, A.C.U. and W. H. LEWIS
Secretary of Meeting ... N. E. CARTLIDGE
Starter ... ... J. LOYNES
Timekeeper ... ... W. LEWIS
Track Marshal ... ... A. M. N. BUSH
Paddock Marshal ... ... W. COLLINS
Machine Examiner ... ... W. SMITH

Watch *for* LUCKY No.

OFFICIAL PROGRAMME PRICE 6D.

Printed by The Tudor Press (Phone 4197) Reading.

Trevor Davies won the 1950 California Championship. He received the trophy from Lloyd Goffe.

The Whitsun Trophy required a run-off with the improving Roy Bowers. Two young prospects who became California regulars in 1951 were Ron Sharp and Jimmy Gleed. Among the older competitors Arthur Flack produced several good scores, and Maurice Hutchens, a rider with Southern League experience at Saint Austell also featured at the top end of the score charts.

By 1951 the post-war boom was over and tracks could no longer absorb the massive burden of entertainment tax. Sheffield and Southampton both closed down mid-season and California put up admission prices to 1/9d. Of this 8½ old pence went to the Treasury in tax. Despite a reduction in entertainment tax the following March, speedway continued to struggle.

In 1952 California only ran four meetings. These did produce a major new talent, following in his father's tyre tracks, in the shape of 16-year-old Jim Tebby. The younger Tebby recalls[7] going down to California in the winter of 1950/51 to watch Danny Dunton and Ron How practice, before taking his first practice laps.

California stalwart Pete Mould's career also started at the track this year. Sharp, Gleed and Bowers continued to learn their trade while veterans such as Billy Newell and Stan Tebby continued to enjoy their Sunday speedway. The father and son pairing of Stan and Jim Tebby partnered each other in a best pairs meeting in June.

From the start of 1951 to the end of the 1953 season the number of league clubs in the three divisions had shrunk from 37 to 27. Biggest casualties were London club New Cross who pulled out part way through 1953. With fewer team places available opportunities for juniors to break into the sport became increasingly limited. The idea of a Sunday training league for novices and amateurs began to circulate, but no concrete proposals emerged.

With meetings approximately fortnightly California's 1953 season was a more substantial one. Jim Tebby won the opening meeting from Ron Sharp and then went on to set a new track record of 66.0 in the next meeting. This track record still stood when the track was lengthened before the following season, but it continued to be noted in programmes as the track record even after the change. To further confuse matters it was incorrectly listed as 65.0 from 1954 onwards.

Tebby continued to be the form rider throughout the year, also winning the California Trophy in October. Although signed up to Harringay he didn't get to ride for them as national service prevented him from competing regularly in 1954 and 1955. By 1956 Harringay had been consigned to the history books and Jim signed for Oxford. A long career, spent mainly at Wimbledon followed and Tebby finally retired wearing Newport's colours in 1975. He is one of a handful of riders to have ridden at Smallmead, Tilehurst and California.

Tebby's father Stan continued to ride and pre-war star Newell spent his last year as a California regular. They were joined by another veteran George Bason. Bason won the Whitsun Trophy in front of a crowd that included Ronnie Moore and Barry Briggs. He also won the Lloyd Goffe Trophy and tied for second with Jimmy Gleed in the California Trophy. The final meeting of the season (a four-team tournament between teams with the imaginative names of red, blue, white and yellow) featured a match race between Bason and California's favourite son Lloyd Goffe. Although now retired from British speedway, Goffe claimed victory.

Like Goffe, George Bason graduated from grasstrack to amateur speedway. He first appeared at California in 1936. After the war he took up professional speedway principally with West Ham, Southampton and Liverpool. Southampton marked the most successful period of his career, with the Bannister Court track record among his achievements. He retired in 1950, but after a brief return with Swindon in 1952 he re-appeared at California in 1953. Along with Phil Bishop he was styled the last of the leg-trailers. These two riders continued to be involved with the sport organising and riding in meetings on the continent right up to the 1960s. Bason also gained a reputation as one of the sport's top tuners.

Other names making regular appearances on the California bills in 1953 included Reading

---

7 *Speedway Star*, 23 November 1957: "Jim Tebby has plans for 1958". Danny Dunton rode for Harringay; later in his career he rode for Oxford and went on to promote there. He was one of the five original co-owners of Allied Presentations Ltd when the company launched speedway at Tilehurst.

Racers first team manager – Dick Bailey, and Wimbledon junior Gil Goldfinch.

3 Southern Area League

The winter of 1953/54 produced many upheavals. The track length changed as the white line was taken out, increasing the track length from 310 yards to 334 yards. The system for licensing amateur tracks changed. Instead of being run as clubs affiliated directly to the Auto Cycle Union, tracks like Rye House and California were directly licensed by the Speedway Control Board. This paved the way for the formation of the Southern Area League. Long-established training tracks at Eastbourne, Rye House and California, former Southern League Aldershot and newer tracks at Brafield (in Northamptonshire) and Ringwood made up the league.

The California Motor Cycle Club continued to be the promoting organisation. Secretary Jack Griffin (a California rider earlier in the decade) fronted the operation. California became the 'Poppies' after the California poppy, the state flower of California. It is yellow/orange in colour and not a source of opium! The race jackets featured a red poppy enclosed by a 'c' on a dark green/red background.

The name of the new league caused some confusion. Over the winter it had started as the Amateur League before changing to the Metropolitan League. A month after the season began it changed again, transforming itself into the Southern Area League (SAL). The race format chosen involved eight-man teams in 14-heat matches. Riders would be paid 7/6d per point. (For comparison Division Two pay rates were 24/- a point.)

In their opening meeting at home to Ringwood the Poppies lost 45-38 despite leading 37-35 with two races to go. A fall by George Bason robbed him of a maximum and left Gil Goldfinch as top scorer on 11. Dick Bailey ended the meeting with a fractured skull.

In the next two matches Jimmy Gleed and Peter Mould made their league debuts. Mid-way through the year Wimbledon junior Bob Andrews and local discovery Ross Gilbertson joined the team. In July Aldershot closed down bringing Tommy Sweetman and Eric Hockaday to California.

These six riders plus 1954 ever-presents Goldfinch and Sharp became the central figures of California's SAL existence:

- **Peter Mould** – born in Richmond, Surrey in 1928 and contracted to Rayleigh, his career was principally confined to California and Aldershot in 1957.
- **Jimmy Gleed** – a log merchant who was mechanic to Lloyd Goffe before he tried out at California. Gained National League experience with Saint Austell (1952) and Southampton (1953) and came out of retirement to ride for Poole in the Provincial League's first season (1960).
- **Ron Sharp** – first rode at a Rye House training school where he became a protégé of George Bason. Signed to New Cross but never made a league appearance for them. Continued riding in the SAL and second-halving. Injury and the decline in tracks meant he didn't get a regular team place until the Provincial League era, when he rode for Stoke and Long Eaton.
- **Gil Goldfinch** – on Wimbledon's books for over a decade, eventually becoming a regular team member in 1960. He arrived at California in 1953 with three years experience at amateur tracks High Beech, Eastbourne and Rye House. He last rode for Long Eaton in 1963.
- **Bob Andrews** – started second-halving at Wimbledon as an 18-year-old in 1953. A Wimbledon regular from 1956 to 1964 he reached heat-leader status in 1960 and won five league titles with the Dons. He made three World Final appearances (plus one as reserve) and in 1969 left pundits eating their words when he and partner Ivan Mauger won the first

staging of the World Best Pairs Championship. He represented England, the country of his birth, in the individual finals, but after emigrating, he donned New Zealand's colours in the pairs event. His career in Britain finished in 1972 after spells with Wolverhampton, Hackney and Cradley[8].

- **Ross Gilbertson** – from Berwickshire, but based on the South Coast. Graduated from cycle speedway via grasstrack to speedway at California. Rode for Poole for all five years that the Provincial League operated (1960-64), becoming their top scorer. A plumber by trade he came out of retirement to ride in the British League Division Two for Romford, Canterbury and Eastbourne. He retired in 1973 by which time he was over 40.
- **Tommy Sweetman** – another Wimbledon junior and another rider with a background in cycle speedway. He started at Aldershot and later in his career rode for New Cross, Wolverhampton, Exeter and Hackney. In his best season (1966) he topped Exeter's averages and received an international call-up for England.
- **Eric Hockaday** – an accomplished cycle speedway rider, started at Aldershot. A professional stunt motorcyclist, he went on to ride for: Coventry, Oxford, Rayleigh, Exeter, Leicester, Stoke, Cradley and Sheffield.

A second home defeat (to champions Rye House) followed, but after their mid-season strengthening three away wins (including one at Rye House) raised California to second place in the league. Over the season Goldfinch topped the California scorers list with Gleed second.

There were three individual events staged. The Whitsun Trophy went to Goldfinch after a run-off with Bason. Mould finished third with four wins and a fall in the wet conditions. Later in the season former World Champion Tommy Price presented the California Championship trophy to Jimmy Gleed. Gleed won from Andrews after the two met in their final ride and Andrews fell. Finally the Handicap Championship went to former California regular Roy Bowers.

Peter Mould, the all-time top scorer for the California Southern Area League team. (BH)

In National League Division One, Wimbledon replaced Wembley as top dogs going on to win seven championship titles in the space of eight years. North of the Thames Harringay Racers became the latest big name team to fall by the wayside. While the National League's two divisions continued to shrink the SAL announced before Christmas that all five teams that finished 1954 would be starting again. Rumoured additions at Brighton, Rochester, Weymouth and Saint Austell didn't come to fruition.

Once again California finished runners-up to Rye House Roosters. This time they were in

8 Visit http://bobandrewsspeedway.tripod.com/bobandrewscontents.htm for extensive details about Bob Andrews's career.

with a shot at the title, but a home defeat to the Roosters in September ensured that the league trophy would stay in Hertfordshire.

Before the 1955 season started California announced a largely unchanged squad, but promised one major new signing. This turned out to be Roy Bowers who appeared in the first two meetings of the season before Rye House objected that he had too much experience for the SAL. He had been a Division Two regular at Yarmouth in 1953, but couldn't find a team place in 1954 after Yarmouth decided not to run. After being denied the opportunity to ride for California Bowers signed for Division Two newcomers Weymouth – but they closed after just a few matches leaving Bowers on the sidelines. A physically striking rider, due to being completely bald, he went on to spend five years with Oxford and finished his racing career at Swindon in 1965.

California fielded a very settled team. Top scorer Peter Mould and Tommy Sweetman rode in all 12 league matches. Gleed, Goldfinch, Gilbertson, Hockaday and Sharp only missed a single match leaving Bob Andrews with two missed matches against his name. All scored well, only Gilbertson (the least experienced member of the team) didn't top the score charts in at least one match.

Captain Ron Sharp finished joint third in the SAL Riders Championship won by Rye House's Mike Broadbank. These two clashed in the Silver Sash at California in June. The newly inaugurated match race title went to Broadbank, who was presented with the sash by double World Champion Jack Young. Later in the season Pete Mould successfully challenged for the title. Andrews and Sweetman also made unsuccessful challenges.

Goldfinch won the Whitsun Trophy (after a run-off with Mould) and the Supporters' Handicap Trophy, while Eric Hockaday took the California Championship. California also staged two qualifying rounds of the SAL Riders Championship on successive Sunday's. The second one was technically Brafield's home round but their track was unavailable. Curiously Brafield's Colin Goody won both meetings! In the first he tied with Tommy Sweetman, the following week he finished a point clear of Mike Broadbank.

The Poppies league season started with a 61-23 win at Eastbourne, the largest by any team in the six-year history of the SAL. Goldfinch (full) and Gleed (paid) remained unbeaten by a home rider. The previous Sunday's home programme advertised a supporters' coach for this meeting making pick-ups at Camberley, Reading, Wokingham, Maidenhead and Slough. Home meetings were promoted as being easily accessible from London (train from Waterloo and bus from Wokingham station).

A change of management distracted attention from the racing during July and August. This manifested itself publicly in the pages of the *Speedway Gazette*. Earlier in the season a comment about the lack of facilities provoked a response from club secretary Jack Griffin. He placed much of the blame for this and problems with track maintenance on Norman Cartlidge. Clearly affronted after involvement with California speedway stretching back to 1936 Cartlidge responded in robust terms[9].

This letter revealed in considerable detail the financial operations of California speedway. Patrons paid grounds admittance of 6d (2.5 pence) and this along with teas money went to California Leisure Park. Separate admittance to the speedway cost 1/- (5 pence) and this along with takings from programmes (6d) belonged to California MCC. Out of this the club paid prize money, advertising and other costs. The club paid no rent; California Leisure Park were responsible for maintenance of the track.

When the dust settled, and after an emergency general meeting of the California MCC Jack Griffin handed over to Norman Cartlidge. As well as owner of the California Leisure Park, Cartlidge was a motorcycle enthusiast. In 1951 the *Wokingham Times* reported that he

9 *Speedway Gazette* 16 July 1955, letter headed : "California ... a Second Opinion"

received a plaque awarded for completing the Pioneer Run (from Tattenham Corner to Brighton) on a 1903 Featherstone Thorough motorcycle.

For team manager Fred Millward, a Wimbledon supporter since 1928 and mechanic to Billy Newell at pre-war California, it was business as usual.

Crowds were healthy, the 1956 Astorias annual reported that "crowds of 5,000 were not uncommon at Rye House and California". This seems a gross exaggeration, the lack of banked terracing would have made it difficult to accommodate that many at California and accounts of those who were involved at the time tend to corroborate this.[10]

California track staff pose for the camera – on the far left is Bryan Horsnell, for a more recent photo of him turn to 2005. (BH)

While the SAL quickly announced plans for 1956 their senior colleagues continued to grapple with their shrinking numbers. 1955's innovations – guest riders and tactical substitutes – hadn't stemmed the tide and amalgamation began to appear on the agenda. In the end they ran with two divisions of just seven teams. With the closure of Wembley at the end of 1956 consolidation into a single division became inevitable. In 1957 just 11 teams competed in the National League.

Meanwhile the SAL had its own problems. When Brafield fell by the wayside and plans to resuscitate Ringwood (they had pulled out mid-season in 1955) fell through, the three remaining SAL clubs acted quickly. They created a team without a home: the 'Southern Rovers'. The Rovers raced their 1956 home matches at neutral venues. California staged a Southern Rovers fixture against Eastbourne. Ex-Poppy Eric Hockaday registered a maximum for the Rovers who won 47-36. Although not ideal it kept the league going.

A second threat to the viability of the SAL came from a totally different direction. The Lord's Day Observance Society (LDOS) campaigned against 'unchristian' activities on

10 Further support for this view comes from *History of Rye House Speedway* by noted author Norman Jacobs. He quotes 2-3,000 for the Rye House crowds in 1955.

Sundays (and it still does). Sunday grasstrack meetings had become one of their targets. In February the ACU announced that it would not issue new licences for Sunday tracks, and in June Eastbourne switched to Saturday racing after a challenge from the LDOS locally.

In July the ACU banned admission charges for Sunday meetings. California increased the cost of programmes from 6d to 1 shilling and held a collection to replace the lost gate revenue. Clearly this was not a long-term solution and although it enabled California to continue to the end of the season it left the long-term future very uncertain.

The eight riders who served California so well in 1955 were all named as starters for 1956. Andrews gained a team place at Wimbledon and Hockaday signed for Coventry. Goldfinch and Sweetman both decided to concentrate on gaining a senior league spot at Wimbledon after a couple of California matches. While Goldfinch made several Wimbledon appearances Sweetman re-emerged in the SAL with Southern Rovers where Hockaday had also found a new home.

With four gaps to fill the Poppies team had an inexperienced look about it. Ron Walton, Ron Webb and Phil Sheppard gained regular team spots but all struggled. John Day (start marshal at Smallmead in 1975) made a few appearances, as did a young novice called Mike Keen. Another vacancy arose in the second half of the year when Ron Sharp signed for Southampton.

Peter Mould narrowly retained his position as the team's top scorer from the rapidly improving Ross Gilbertson, but the team had too long a tail and finished last in the four team league. A 42-41 defeat to Southern Rovers in a match contested for double points at Swindon doomed them to the bottom position. With Gleed and Mould missing Mike Keen showed his potential with two heat wins. Eight years later Keen finally joined Swindon and 20 years later, on a very wet night, his testimonial meeting showcased a fine maximum from Dag Lovaas.

Peter Mould won the Whitsun Trophy and finished fourth in the SAL Riders Championship (at Rye House) after finishing last in a three-man run-off for second. Jimmy Gleed won the California Championship and held the Silver Sash as did Gil Goldfinch. As well as the regular team members open meetings at California featured veterans George Bason and Stan Tebby. Son Jim (now an Oxford rider along with Roy Bowers) also put in a couple of appearances in individual meetings. Swindon junior Roy Taylor won the Supporters Handicap Trophy.

Star performance of the year by an away rider came in August when Eastbourne won 43-40 after Jimmy Heard won the last-heat decider passing Mould and Gleed. In this race he also completed his maximum and broke the track record, with a time of 65.0 seconds. This equalled Tebby's erroneous track record (set on the larger track). The real track record[11] prior to Heard's feat belonged to Brafield's Vic Hall. He set a time of 66.0 on 29 May 1955. As a result of the new track length, several new records were established in 1954; the holder at the end of that season was Gil Goldfinch (66.8).

The SAL received much criticism during the year for the increasing number of 'old hands' riding and the lack of new talent it produced. However, the contraction of the National League meant that there just weren't the team places available for both experienced and new riders. Riders like Keen, Tebby, Bowers and Sweetman always found themselves competing with riders displaced from recently closed teams. Many riders dropped out of the sport around this time. The formation of the Provincial League in 1960 encouraged some of these to return as well as finally providing regular team places for some of the 1950s juniors.

Although plans were made to run in 1957, doubts continued. A cryptic remark in *Speedway Star* (2.2.57) about speedway returning to a new garrison with a ready-made team

---

11 The records attributed to Heard, Hall and Goldfinch are based on a thorough review of California programmes from 1954 onwards. However, it is conceivable that there may have been a faster time that has escaped detection.

suggested that California's future remained uncertain. By the time that the Poppies relocation to Aldershot (just 15 miles away) was announced in March the speedway track had already been put to alternative use as a camp site serving the California Leisure Park. Unlike other SAL tracks Aldershot rode on Saturdays, thus avoiding problems with the LDOS.

The Aldershot team had a bit of an identity crisis, appearing as California Poppies initially before switching to Aldershot Poppies. Programmes were billed California Speedway, Aldershot stadium, and continued to advertise the California ballroom and leisure facilities. Norman Cartlidge continued as promoter and Freddie Millward as team manager. The team was recognisably California and continued to ride with the poppy race jacket.

Ross Gilbertson topped the list of Poppies scorers with Pete Mould and rapidly improving Ron Walton tied in second. Had injury not curtailed his season, Jimmy Gleed would also have featured among the big scorers. One newcomer, scoring just 10 points from eight appearances was Ted Spittles. The novice had shown up well in winter training at California, and knocked around long enough to win a place in the first-ever Reading Racers team over a decade later.

Eric Hockaday – won the last-ever meeting at California – the 1957 California Championship. (BH)

Crowds were not good at Aldershot and towards the end of the season hopes of a return to California were running high. The staging of the California Championship on August 5 (a Bank Holiday Monday) added weight to those hopes. Eric Hockaday won the meeting with a maximum 15 points, 3 ahead of Ross Gilbertson, Ron Walton and Phil Sheppard. Jim Tebby, Gil Goldfinch and Ted Spittles were also competing that day. A further meeting, the Supporters' Trophy was advertised, but called off with little notice. Many fans turned up at the venue only to find a notice stating that owing to unforeseen circumstances the meeting had been cancelled and there would be no more racing at the circuit in 1957.

Training recommenced at the track in June 1958 with George Bason and Ted Spittles among those present. A licence application was refused in July leaving Eastbourne and Rye House the only remaining amateur tracks. Both tracks included challenges against California in their plans. In July Eastbourne beat California 51-33. A young New Zealander scored the first maximum of his career in this match – Eastbourne's Ivan Mauger. The following month the Poppies took to the track for the final time going down 59-25 at Rye House, with Jimmy Gleed top scoring.

In 1959 the SAL re-formed, but California were not among the entrants having once again been refused a licence. Speedway became part of California's past. By the time the California ballroom burnt down in 1973 the forest had started to encroach on the speedway track.

California left their mark on British speedway. When in 1956 Wimbledon won the National League (their fourth in succession), former fastest man around California Ron How and Bob Andrews joined double World Champion Ronnie Moore in the heat leader positions. Support came from Gerald Jackson, Gil Goldfinch and Jim Tebby, all of whom owed much to California in their early careers.

But if you go down to the woods today, you're in for a big surprise – you can still see the recently re-excavated concrete starting area. A few fence posts still mark the outside of the track, and an oval of gorse bushes closely follows the perimeter of the track where the dirt built up and created ideal growing conditions.

California League Record

	Teams	*Position*	*Matches*	*Won*	*Drawn*	*Lost*	*Race pts for*	*Race pts against*	*Match points*
1954	5	2	16	9	0	7	718	617	18
1955	4	2	12	7	0	5	531	470	14
1956	4	4	12*	4	0	8	432	479	8

Note: Includes match away to Southern Rovers for double points (lost 41-42)

California – Leading Point Scorers

(League matches only)		*points*	*matches*
Peter Mould	1954-56	282	33
Jimmy Gleed	1954-56	277	32
Gil Goldfinch	1954-56	232	29
Ron Sharp	1954-56	195	35
Ross Gilbertson	1954-56	135	26
Bob Andrews	1954-55	123	19
Tommy Sweetman	1954-56	111	22
Eric Hockaday	1954-55	95	18
George Bason	1954	32	8
Phil Sheppard	1956	32	10

Note: Bonus points not included. Four matches subsequently deleted from the records are not included either. If these four matches are included then Jimmy Gleed has 308 points and Peter Mould 307.

Lloyd Goffe

Berkshire boasts few native-born riders. Burghfield's Andrew Appleton is the best known from recent years, and there have been a few others such as Brian Leonard (Newbury), Gary Tagg (Wokingham) and Barry Allaway (Reading). Lee Richardson, although associated with Bracknell, was born in Sussex. However, the biggest names to emerge from the county hark back to the 1930s at Longmoor. Pre-war track record holder Jim Boyd became a post-war regular with the famous Belle Vue Aces but Lloyd Goffe came closest to stardom.

Born in Woodley on 30 January 1913, Kenneth Lloyd Goffe developed an interest in motorbikes as a youngster. He left school at 14 to become a clerk in the office of a local firm. He continued working there until he became a full-time speedway rider a decade later. As a schoolboy he started on a wage of 8/6d (43 pence) a week; by the time of his departure that had risen to £2 8/3d.

Early in 1934 Goffe decided to purchase a bike (a 350cc AJS for £3 10 shillings) and try his luck at nearby California. He won his first event on May 21 – the Wokingham Stakes. (Runner-up Herbert Deacon went on to become chairman of the R&DMC). He quickly became a regular competitor, finishing fourth in the club championship at the end of the season. The following year he finished third in a three-man run-off for the club championship, but did have the consolation of finishing the season as track record holder.

He took up grasstracking and became very proficient, winning the South of England Grasstrack Championship in 1936 (at Basingstoke), 1937 (Salisbury) and 1938 (Shaftesbury) before concentrating on speedway full-time.

In 1936 he graduated from the sandy surface of Longmoor to the cinder surfaces of the big league tracks. His first appearance on a 'proper' speedway track took place at Crystal Palace on Whit Monday. Although only programmed at reserve for the novice event he came out and returned a score of 14 points from five rides.

He quickly found himself invited to sign for West Ham, much to the disappointment of Hackney who were also keen to sign him. He quickly started winning second-half junior races at Custom House where his opponents included Longmoor club champion Reg Vigor and Charlie Dugard (founder of the Eastbourne dynasty).

Goffe returned to California for the Evening Gazette Club Championship in October, but after shedding a chain when facing Vigor, he could only manage fourth. Although no longer appearing on track, Goffe's affection for California remained evident. As well as putting up an annual novice trophy before the war, he occasionally returned post-war to present trophies and held the position of honorary vice-president of the California MCC. In what may have been his last appearance on a British track, he won a match race with George Bason at California's final meeting of 1953.

In 1937 Goffe gained experience on loan to Provincial League Leicester. He made three appearances in May scoring 9 points. The last of these was in a 33-7 defeat at Southampton. The home team's winning margin would have been much greater had the home promoter Charlie Knott not decided to abandon the match on the grounds it was too one-sided! Knott was still promoting at Southampton when the track fell to developers in 1963.

Shortly after this Leicester folded and Goffe returned to West Ham. On June 16 he made his National League debut at New Cross, replacing the absent Bluey Wilkinson. West Ham won the National League that year, although at 6 points from 4 matches Goffe's contribution was a modest one.

In 1938 he started the year riding for West Ham's reserve team in National League Division Two before moving to Harringay in May. His debut for the Racers saw him face West Ham, and he impressed with a 5-point tally. As well as establishing himself in the

Harringay team he also rode in Division Two for Lea Bridge, scoring maximums in his first two matches at the Clapton track. In October he rode in a Division Two Test match against the 'Dominions' at Birmingham.

In 1939 his progress continued. When war brought the speedway season to a premature end Goffe stood at 30th in the list of National League point scorers. Clearly on the brink of stardom the six years of war deprived him of what should have been the peak of his career. He spent the war as a fitter in the RAF, and in 1942 married his wife Molly.

When speedway resumed Goffe ended up at Wimbledon. In 1946 he finished 16th highest scorer in the league and qualified as reserve for the Speedway Riders Championship (the nearest thing to a world championship in the immediate post-war years). After another productive year at Wimbledon in 1947 Goffe wanted a move. Harringay jumped at the opportunity and on 9 January 1948 (shortly before he turned 35) Goffe signed for a record fee of £1,350. 24 hours later Wimbledon signed a replacement – Alec Statham of Bradford – for a fee of £2,000.

As well as scoring solidly for Harringay in 1948, Goffe reached the Speedway Riders Championship Final (scoring 5 points) and made his Test debut against Australia.

At this time he lived on the Bath Road in Sonning (and he still did nearly 30 years later). A quiet, non-smoker, non-drinker, and passionate about motorcycles he also owned a garage. On track he stood out with his immaculately polished shiny leathers and his 'pre-war' leg-trailing style hence the nickname of 'cowboy'.

Despite a further decline in his league scoring Goffe comfortably reached the first post-war World Final, finishing seventh in the list of qualifiers. On the big night Goffe scored just 2 points.

Midway through 1950 he moved from Harringay back to West Ham. Shortly after Goffe experienced the low point of his career when he couldn't avoid fallen Joe Abbott in a race at Odsal that resulted in the 48-year-old veteran losing his life.

As his form declined he became more difficult to manage and in both the next two years made further mid-season moves. A fee of £500 took him to Bradford during 1951, and the following year he dropped down to Saint Austell in the Southern League (as Division Three of the National League had been renamed). The Gulls finished bottom of the league and fielded many riders including pre-war legend George Newton, Max Rech (the first Polish-born rider in British league speedway) and future California points machine Jimmy Gleed. (Gleed had spannered for Goffe before trying out speedway at California.) Making his debut in July, Goffe scored just 30 points from 8 matches before bowing out.

He continued to ride on the continent the following year, and continued to satisfy his love of motorcycles by returning to work full-time in the business.

Goffe attended meetings at Tilehurst and Smallmead. The 1976 and 1977 programme contained a constant reminder of Berkshire's best – a regular back-page advertisement for his garage in Twyford. ("The ex-England international speedway star welcomes your call".)

An Undiscovered Venue

The village of Winkfield lies three miles north-east of Bracknell, close to Ascot racecourse and Legoland. It seems like one of the last places that one might find speedway. The *Wokingham Times* headline "Speedway Racing at Winkfield – New Track Opened" challenges that perception. The report of a meeting on 17 September 1939 is contained in the following week's paper.

A reference to the 'newly formed Winkfield Motor Club' in the August 25 edition of the *Wokingham Times* indicates that plans were under way to stage an event before the war broke out. The meeting featured many of the California regulars – Sid Lewington, Billy Newell, George Bason, Jack Adams and Herbert Deacon all appeared. With his National League experience it is no surprise to find that Jim Boyd dominated the meeting by winning six races.

A further meeting planned for a fortnight later failed to materialise. A clearly annoyed reporter wrote in the *Wokingham Times* (6 October 1939) under the headline: 'Speedway Racing at Winkfield – A Protest at its Cancellation'. He described his experience:

> *"... on arriving at the Winkfield track on Sunday there were no officials there at all and only one rider. However there were quite 100 people there at 2.30 p.m. including dozens of cars and other conveyances ..."*

The big question though is – was it really speedway? In the 1930s and 1940s a number of grasstrack events were promoted as speedways. *Homes of British Speedway* (Tempus), the excellent reference work by Robert Bamford and John Jarvis lists over a hundred of these.

The meeting report identifies the location of the Winkfield track as Crouch Lane, a road dominated by farms and farm buildings. The track was described as of similar length to California (310 yards at the time) but with straights sloping uphill and downhill. It seems almost certain that this was essentially a grasstrack circuit set up in a field.

Born in Woodley, Lloyd Goffe went on to win test honours and appear in the World Final at Wembley. (JS)

1968 – The Racers Hit Pay Dirt

The story of speedway's arrival in Reading begins in 1967. Local news stories included Reading's efforts to become a city and in October the opening of the Top Rank Suite near the station. The Top Rank Suite is long gone, but Reading is still trying to gain city status.

In speedway circles former California rider Bob Andrews was contemplating a return to Britain after a two-year absence. It was a year when a new star burst onto the scene at Long Eaton – one of speedway's less glamorous venues. A new Swede by the name of Anders Michanek made his British League debut, culminating in a glorious September where a World Final debut was followed by a hat trick of individual meeting wins in just three days. The Olympique (then at Newcastle, now at Wolverhampton, and one of the few open meetings still run in Britain) was won on the Monday, followed by the East Midlands Open at Long Eaton on Tuesday, and the Brandonapolis at Coventry on Wednesday. One of the riders he faced in all three meetings was Ivan Mauger.

1967 British League champions were Swindon – and our Thames Valley rivals haven't won a league title since! But some things never change – the 1967 fixture list was issued late and not published in *Speedway Star* until May! The British League, formed from the amalgamation of the National and Provincial leagues, was now three years old. It had been a great success, and at 19 teams there was no room for further expansion.

Concerns were being expressed that there were too many foreigners in the British League. In addition to Michanek newcomers that year included: Torbjorn Harrysson, Hasse Holmkvist, Oyvind Berg, Bengt Larsson, Gunnar Malmkvist and Ole Olsen. Most teams included a couple of foreigners, mainly Australians and Swedes. Meanwhile Ted Spittles, an Oxford junior, was writing to *Speedway Star* complaining about the lack of opportunities. New tracks were needed to provide opportunities for riders like Ted, and to bring on more British talent.

Speculation about a second division grew. Suggested venues included Colchester, Bath, Barry, and Maidstone. *Speedway Star* columnists Peter Oakes and Eric Linden were downbeat about the chances of a new league taking off. Aside from the organisational issues, concern was expressed over the economic background – Harold Wilson's devaluation and Roy Jenkins's tight Budget.

Reading had last been mooted as a possible venue in 1964. The early 1960s stock car venture had run its course. Johnnie Hoskins ("the man who invented speedway", then Edinburgh promoter) and Maury Littlechild visited the track on November 21. In late December Reading were announced as certain starters with a probable Monday race night.

Five existing promoters formed a consortium named Allied Presentations. The objective was to open tracks in the new second division and pool profits ... and losses. The five were Len Silver (Hackney), Danny Dunton (Oxford), Maury Littlechild (King's Lynn), Ron Wilson (Long Eaton), and Reg Fearman (Halifax and Long Eaton). They opened three tracks in 1968. Wilson fronted Middlesbrough, Silver for Rayleigh and Fearman for Reading.

Fearman, a 15-year-old prodigy at Rye House in 1948, signed for his local team West Ham. After riding for Stoke (Hanley) and Leicester he hung up his leathers in the mid-1950s. In 1960 he returned to the track and topped the Stoke averages, as well as co-promoting with Mike Parker.

In early February the British Speedway Promoters' Association met to approve the setting up of a new league. Eight teams were announced as definite starters. These were Berwick, Eastbourne, Middlesbrough, Nelson, Reading, Weymouth, Newcastle and Newport. The last two were junior teams based at existing British League tracks. Only Reading and Berwick were completely new tracks. Canterbury and Crayford were also identified as possible competitors, subject to planning permission.

When the teams finally made it to track Newport, Newcastle and Eastbourne had been replaced by Rayleigh, Plymouth and Belle Vue II.

Work got under way constructing the 360-yard circuit at the Reading greyhound stadium situated on the Oxford Road at the junction with the Norcot Road. Incidentally just a couple of hundred yards away the country's first 'Little Chef' restaurant was opened ten years before. At the back of the stadium, originally built in 1931, ran the Great Western mainline. Where the back straight once was, there is now a road called Stadium Way. Among those working on the new track was a fencing contractor called John Poyser. It was announced that the team would be nicknamed "the Racers" and riding colours would be blue and white. The nickname and winged wheel emblem both originated with Harringay, a North London team who last competed in the 1954 National League.

Team building took place very quietly, and the septet who finally emerged as the first wearers of Reading's winged wheel were:

- Ted Spittles – best remembered for his golden boots; had been second-halving for a decade, riding a handful of league matches for Oxford in 1967.
- Stuart Wallace – born in Southampton, he made his debut in 1962 as an 18-year-old for Swindon. Rode for Southampton in 1963 and retired the following year.
- John Poyser – aged 29, lived in Oxford where he first rode in 1957, started his league career with Leicester in 1962 before moving to Hackney in 1963. Riding for the Hawks, he progressed to the point where he equalled Colin Pratt's Waterden Road track record in 1965. Eight days later he broke his thigh, and never recovered his form. Over the next two seasons he failed to reach a three-point average with Hackney, King's Lynn and Long Eaton.
- Ian Champion – came from Hoddesdon and was another Long Eaton rider, made his debut for them in 1965 becoming a regular in 1967 averaging 2.72.
- Phil Pratt – had been second-halving and riding at the Rye House training track.
- Joe Weichlbauer – Australian but Austrian born, had been attached to Cradley for whom he made his league debut in 1966 when he averaged 2.40.
- Dene Davies – a 20-year-old Australian making his first trip to the UK; at five foot four inches (1.63 m) with white hair he was a distinctive presence.

When the fixtures were published, Reading were due to make their debut at Tilehurst on June 3, with their first away fixture taking them to Plymouth on June 7. The home start was put back two weeks and the Racers made their first appearance at Plymouth's Pennycross stadium. As a result Reading were the last of the ten Division Two tracks to open. Delays in obtaining planning consent were the cause. (Although the pre-existing planning consent for stock cars would have covered the speedway, it was due to expire soon, so it needed renewing.)

The inaugural British League Division Two meeting took place at Belle Vue on 18 May 1968 when the Colts demolished Canterbury 55-23. Taffy Owen, winner of the first-ever race, went on to record a full maximum while Chris Bailey and Ken Eyre gained paid maximums.

The Plymouth away fixture was not the first time that seven Racers took to the track – that happened six days earlier at Canterbury. The Crusaders were riding at Rayleigh, but promoter Johnnie Hoskins decided to stage a meeting anyway – choosing a four-team tournament. A "Canterbury" team including three Reading riders took on "The Midlands" – a team consisting of four Racers – Weymouth and Plymouth. The meeting's top scorers were Ian Champion (riding for the Midlands) and Weymouth's Mike Vernam with 11 each. Plymouth and Weymouth tied for first place with 28 points. Canterbury recorded 24, their top scorers were John Poyser (10) and Ted Spittles (8).

The news headlines on June 7 were dominated by the assassination of US Presidential candidate Robert Kennedy the previous day. Current chart sounds included 'Jumpin' Jack

Flash' by the Rolling Stones, Dionne Warwick's 'Do You Know The Way To San Jose' and number one 'Young Girl' by Gary Puckett and the Union Gap. *Speedway Star* cost £4 4 shillings (£4.20) – for a year's subscription!

A browse of the *Evening Post* in 1968 reveals that a three-bedroom detached house in Earley cost £7,500. Job adverts stipulated the sex of employees required, and in some cases specified different rates of pay. A petrol pump attendant was wanted for an hourly rate of 8 shillings (40p) – self-service was still a novelty. A typical car, say a Morris Oxford, cost about £900 new. In Reading the first phase of the Inner Distribution Road from Chatham Street to Castle Street was under construction. Reading Football Club, still known as 'The Biscuitmen' had just completed 20 years pottering along in League Division Three (League One in modern parlance) without a single promotion or relegation.

Meanwhile, for the Reading Racers, the pay rates for Division Two's inaugural season were 10 shillings (50p) a start and 10 shillings (50p) a point. Travelling expenses were paid at 2d (1p) per mile.

When Reading arrived at Plymouth on June 7 the home team had already ridden three matches, including their home opener – a 41-36 win against Weymouth. This turned out to be the nearest Plymouth came to losing at home all season! So on first sight, Reading's six-point defeat looks an impressive start for the new club. However, Plymouth were handicapped by the non-appearance of three of their riders who broke down en route and were replaced by juniors, two of whom failed to score.

A Reading team shot, easily identified as being from 1968 due to the distinctive race jacket logo. Left to right: Phil Pratt, Stuart Wallace, Joe Weichlbauer, Ian Bottomley, John Poyser, Paul Walch. Kneeling: Ian Champion and Ted Spittles. (JS)

The first Racers on track were Ian Champion and Dene Davies. Champion won the heat in a Division Two track record of 80.2, eight seconds slower than the record established in the Provincial League days (72.0 by Jack Scott). With Davies third, Racers took a 4-2 lead which they held onto until a 5-1 in heat 7 put the Devils ahead. After Plymouth extended their lead over Reading to six, the Racers team manager Dick Bailey put John Poyser in as a tactical substitute. (At the time tactical substitute rides were available to any team that was six down and involved replacing an out-of-form rider with a stronger one who went off the gate with no handicap or double points.) The Racers first tactical was a success with the resultant 5-1 from Poyser and Champion narrowing the gap to 2 points with one race to go. The final heat was an anti-climax as Poyser and Spittles conceded a 5-1 making the final score 42-36 to Plymouth.

Scorers in that first match were: Poyser 10, Champion 9, Davies 5, Spittles 5, Pratt 4, Weichlbauer 2, Wallace 1.

After a 41-34 defeat at Berwick the gates opened at Tilehurst for the first time on Monday June 17. Promoter Reg Fearman expressed himself to be "disappointed" that the crowd was just under 5,000! And the cost? Just 5 shillings each. (Maybe some of the prospective spectators got lost in the town's new one-way system that had been implemented just the previous day.)

Nelson is a small textile town in Lancashire, that unusually was named after a pub (called the Lord Nelson Inn). Speedway arrived in Nelson in 1967 with a handful of open meetings and the Nelson Admirals were an obvious choice for founder membership of the new division. They were a less obvious choice for first opponents at Reading, but this was a result of the delayed opening, earlier fixtures having to be rescheduled.

READING
SPEEDWAY
READING GREYHOUND STADIUM - TILEHURST
OFFICIAL PROGRAMME - ONE SHILLING
1st Meeting - 1st Season
British League Division II
READING v. NELSON
MONDAY, 17th JUNE, 1968 at 7-30 p.m.

Programme from the opening night at Tilehurst.

Eventual runners-up, Nelson arrived having already credited their account with an away win at Middlesbrough. They started strongly taking an 8-point lead after 5 heats. Nelson's Fred Powell won Tilehurst's opening race, which is also remembered for the immediate impact Dene Davies had – on the safety fence. The young Australian collided with it, demolishing a substantial section and ruling himself out of the rest of the meeting. Racers fought back and took the lead for the first time via a Poyser/Spittles 5-1 in the penultimate heat.

And then the meeting turned into a farce. In the deciding heat Nelson gained a 5-1 to tie the match 39-all. Referee A. W. Day decided after the race had been run that reserve Gary Peterson was not eligible and ordered a re-run. At the second attempt Nelson's Terry Shearer was excluded for causing a three-rider pile-up. In the next re-run his Admirals team mate Gerry Birtwell was unable to take his place, and was replaced – by Gary Peterson! Peterson won the race to end as Nelson's top scorer. The final result was therefore Reading 41, Nelson 37. As at Plymouth, Poyser and Champion were top scorers for the Racers. Fastest time on opening night went to Nelson's Dave Schofield – 72.4 in heat 7.

Among the minor first-night niggles were inaudible loudspeakers – a complaint still to be heard at Smallmead to this day!

Six days later Reading drew at Weymouth; John Poyser was top scorer with 13 including 3 points from the last-heat decider. This turned out to be Racers only away point of the season.

On the other side of the ledger they dropped 5 points at home: a draw with Middlesbrough and August defeats to runaway champions Belle Vue II and bogey team Canterbury. Belle Vue II won by 3 points despite conceding a first heat 5-0 after Eric Broadbelt and John Woodcock fell. Canterbury went one better winning 41-37 with Peter Murray scoring a paid maximum in his second match for the club.

The net result was that Racers finished eighth out of ten with only Weymouth and wooden spoonists Berwick below them. However, of the ten founder members of Division Two it is only Berwick who are still racing at the same track. On a more positive note, speedway has returned to Weymouth, Plymouth and Middlesbrough (under the guise of Redcar) in the last five years.

With the league season over by mid-August and crowds still flocking through the turnstiles it was fortunate for Reading that a knock-out cup competition was held. With the benefit of home draws (in those days cup matches were held over one leg only) Reading reached the final.

The team was also aided by the signing of Vic White who had a falling out at Leicester after being replaced in his fourth ride in a Midland Cup fixture at Cradley. 36-year-old White came to Tilehurst with several years' experience and a near four-point Division One average. Like Champion and Poyser he had ridden in the 1967 Long Eaton team with Anders Michanek. His knock-out cup adventure with Reading turned out to be the end of his riding career, but he moved into management and ended up as co-promoter at Leicester – with Reg Fearman!

After three home matches, including a convincing 56-40 semi-final defeat of Belle Vue II (in which Poyser scored a 15-point maximum), Reading earned a final showdown with Canterbury. Racers went down heavily in the away leg, losing 36-60. Vic White top scored with 11 on a wet track. Despite 17 points from John Poyser, Reading also lost the home leg (in front of 6,000 fans) by 52-44. Not only had they lost the cup final but Reading had ended the year without a single win against Canterbury in six encounters. (As well as the league and cup the teams also met in the Kent/Berks Cup.)

The seven riders who represented Reading in the cup final showed only one change from the team which introduced Reading to the speedway world back in June. Vic White had taken the place of injured Joe Weichlbauer. Champion and Davies also missed several matches through injury, giving opportunities to Halifax junior Ian Bottomley. Champion's injuries were particularly damaging to Reading's cause; he averaged over 9 points a match in his first six fixtures but never regained that sort of form after returning from injury.

Poyser and Spittles were ever-present in league and cup matches while Phil Pratt missed just one cup fixture. Poyser's average put him eighth overall in the league standings, topped by Mick Handley of Crayford on 10.39. Poyser was the league's third highest scorer. His 176 points were only bettered by Dave Schofield (Nelson) and Mike Cake (Plymouth), both of whom reached 189 points. If cup matches are included, then Poyser leaps to number one thanks to the cup run. Poyser ended the season with 237 league and cup points. His nearest rivals were: Schofield 198, Martyn Piddock (Canterbury) 193 and Graham Plant (Middlesbrough) 190.

The new league had been set up to discover new talent, and Piddock and Plant were its two major successes. The story of Tilehurst's first season cannot be told without further reference to Graham Plant, the son of Wilf Plant who had ridden for Middlesbrough in the late 1940s. Graham was simply unbeatable at Reading. His record in full reads:

- 15 July: wins Stadium Trophy with a 15-point maximum, setting a new track record of 72.0 (runner-up is Dene Davies of the Racers).
- 22 July: scores a 12-point maximum as Middlesbrough draw at Tilehurst.
- 23 September: another 12-point maximum, another draw for Middlesbrough (in the North/South Cup).
- 7 October: yet again an unbeaten 15 points to win the Reading Open Championship from John Poyser.

That's 18 races, 18 wins in total. Plant also won the British League Division Two Riders Championship at Hackney from Ken Eyre (Belle Vue II) and Graeme Smith (Canterbury). Poyser, one of the pre-meeting favourites because of his past Hackney associations only scored six.

Plant's track record remained at the end of the season, although it was equalled by Poyser on 22 July. There is an unusual story to the record which Plant broke. It had been set in Reading's second meeting on June 24, an easy 50-28 win against Plymouth. The new track record holder was John Edwards, a name that features nowhere in the line-up of either team – because it was set in the second half! Edwards had last ridden for Wimbledon in 1966 and was considering a return to the sport. Sadly for Reading he decided not to.

Second-half races were usually held over three laps, and John Poyser held that record too – 54.2 seconds. The centrepiece of the second-half racing was the 'Evening Post Snowball'. Points were awarded for performances in the final, the concluding race of each meeting's programme. Over the course of the season, John Poyser ran out winner, with Weichlbauer and Spittles second and third respectively.

In September a Supporters Club was formed. Its founding chairman – Mick Smith – had watched his first speedway at New Cross in 1928. Smith remained chairman until he passed away in the middle of 1979. His son Hugh made an unsuccessful attempt to break into speedway and also had responsibility for track maintenance in Tilehurst's final years.

Attendances remained high throughout the season, regularly exceeding 5,000, similar to those at Elm Park. Reading was widely recognised as a great success. After only two meetings the *Chronicle* speculated that the Racers could be destined for Division One.

Few could have imagined then just how successful Reading's venture would turn out to be.

Team: John Poyser 9.29, (Vic White 8.59), Ian Champion 6.92, Joe Weichlbauer 6.88, Ted Spittles 6.68, Stuart Wallace 6.21, Dene Davies 5.39, Ian Bottomley 4.91, Phil Pratt 4.59

1969 – This May be the Start of Something Big

"The hunt is on ... for new tracks" wrote Peter Oakes in *Speedway Star* (20 September 1968), "If you are fortunate you strike on a Reading and find yourself on a winner". Prospective promoters were busily searching for 'the next Reading' and the question was just how many new teams would there be in 1969.

By the end of February the membership of Division Two had been agreed at 16 clubs, with Long Eaton, Ipswich, Crewe, Eastbourne, Doncaster, Rochester and King's Lynn II joining the previous season's entrants. Weymouth were the one team missing from 1968. Pay rates for 1969 were increased to 11/6d (57.5p) per point, 10s (50p) per start and travelling expenses were upped to 3d (1p) per mile.

Rochester fell foul of Kent County Council's planning committee and at the last minute an alternative venue – Romford in Essex – was found. The track at Brooklands became notorious for its concrete safety fence. This was so late in the day that the team had already taken to the track riding four away league matches as Rochester.

Weymouth riders were looking for new teams, and heat leader Mike Vernam, a Southampton-based Poole asset was revealed as Reading's first new signing in February. Vernam was a draughtsman and a former cycle speedway rider.

Two further new signings followed. Like Vernam both were British League Division One number eights. Mick Bell, a 23-year-old born in Oxford had made five appearances for his home town track the previous year averaging 4.00. Alan Jackson had more experience, making his debut for Swindon in 1965 averaging 2.00 from 18 matches. He spent the next three years at Hackney on the fringes of the team making a handful of appearances each year. His eight matches in 1968 yielded a respectable 4.40 average.

Gone from the previous year were John Poyser, Vic White, Stuart Wallace, Joe Weichlbauer, and Ted Spittles. Newly opened Ipswich benefited from the services of Spittles in 1969. The other four retired, although Poyser made a brief re-appearance for Peterborough in 1970. Mick Bell took over the role of captain from Poyser.

Weichlbauer maintained a presence at Reading – an action shot of him was on the front cover of the programme for 1969. (An advance on 1968 when the six-page programme featured two Halifax riders on the cover every week!). Joe remained in the UK working as a gas fitter. At the time this was a skill in much demand, British Gas were in the process of converting 40 million appliances from 'town gas' to 'natural gas' – a programme which lasted from 1967 to 1977.

Returning from 1968 were Champion, Davies and Pratt. This left a vacancy at number seven. In early matches this spot was left blank as Reading tried out various options. When Australian Bob Tabet top scored with ten at Long Eaton in a 50-28 away win he secured the number seven berth, and ended the season as Reading's only ever-present in official fixtures.

Two other riders fought their way into the team during the season. A Poole supporter, Bernie Leigh made his second-half debut in Reading's 1968 finale and was one of Tabet's rivals for the number seven. He made his debut against Rayleigh on June 23 gaining a paid win and a win in his first two rides and shortly after became a Racers regular replacing Ian Champion who moved to Rayleigh. Poor Champion broke a collarbone before he even made his Rayleigh debut, while riding as a reserve in Hackney's Superama.

The injured rider that Leigh filled in for on June 23 had an even more meteoric rise to stardom. Dickie May was an experienced grasstracker who first rode speedway at a Weymouth training school. In the spring he won the Weymouth training school championship ahead of Bernie Leigh. Too young to compete, and confined to doing practice laps on his own that day, was a cocky 14-year-old: John Davis. On May 12 May made his second-half debut at

Reading and within a month made his league debut. He quickly became one of the finds of the season finishing second to Mick Bell in the Racers 1969 averages and gaining international caps. The new star of the Racers had a first-class pedigree – his father Charlie May had ridden for Wembley, Birmingham, Walthamstow, Cardiff, Exeter and Southampton in the decade after the end of the Second World War.

Opening night 1969 left to right: Mike Vernam, Alan Jackson, Dick Bailey (on bike), Reg Fearman, Ian Champion (on bike), Phil Pratt, Mick Bell, Dene Davies. (EP)

Curiously both May and Leigh were born in Southampton in 1944. Although early profiles in the speedway press knocked a few years off May's age (for example 'Speedway Star Parade 1970' gave his year of birth as 1948).

This was a very productive year for new talent, among the brightest new stars of Division Two were Dave Jessup, a 16-year-old Eastbourne discovery and Australian Geoff Curtis who finished fourth in the league averages wearing the colours of Crewe Kings.

Belle Vue II were widely expected to retain their title, which they did by a comfortable margin. However, in the early part of the season they were pushed hard – by the Reading Racers.

On June 17 exactly a year after speedway arrived at the Tilehurst track, the Racers sat in second place in the league with nine wins in ten matches. Included in that tally were four away wins: at Berwick, Long Eaton, King's Lynn II and Middlesbrough. With matches in hand Belle Vue Colts were in their sights. In addition Racers were still in the cup after pulling off an away draw at Romford, one of their stronger rivals.

A month later narrow losses at Rayleigh, Ipswich and Nelson, plus knock-out cup elimination at Long Eaton (scene of the 50-28 away win which remained a record until 1976), put a dent in the Racers season.

Reading then started dropping home points. August started with a classic encounter against Belle Vue II that ended all square after Alan Jackson fell in a last-heat decider when holding a match-winning second place. Jackson sustained injuries which kept him out of the team and he never rode for the Racers again.

A month later Racers lost their unbeaten home record, going down 40-38 to Romford. This was the only official fixture number one Mick Bell missed all season. It was a big blow as Romford had emerged as the Racers main rivals for that league runners-up spot, even though Reading had won their league match at Romford on July 31.

A week before that Romford defeat, Racers suffered a much greater humiliation losing by the mammoth margin of 46 points. Crewe beat the Racers 62-16 with Mick Bell taking three second places to prevent a whitewash. One of the many unbeaten Crewe riders was Geoff Curtis, while one who did drop points was 1968 Racer Ian Bottomley. 38 years later that match remains Racers worst league defeat even though matches now contain more heats.

Racers signed off with a win at Doncaster setting a target for Romford to chase. The Bombers duly won their last three matches but needed to win 60-18 in their final match to pip the Racers on race points. Fortunately for Reading the Bombers could 'only' win by 57-21.

The closing weeks of the season saw the second staging of the Division Two Riders Championship and the inaugural staging of the Junior Championship of the British Isles (now known as the British Under-21 Championship). Mick Bell featured on the rostrum in both events finishing third in the Junior Championship, and going one better in the Riders Championship. Staged at Hackney before a crowd reported at 10,000 the latter event was won by Crayford's Geoff Ambrose. The Junior Championship was run as a second half at Wimbledon and won by Reading's 1968 nemesis Graham Plant.

International action made its first appearance at Division Two level with a Test series against Young Czechoslovakia in August and Young Australasia in September. The former was the highlight of the Division Two season, and arguably better than anything Division One had to offer. A seven-match Test series containing many exciting matches went down to the wire in a decider at Reading on 25 August.

The Czechs arrived at Tilehurst 3-2 ahead with one match drawn. Young England were six up and heading towards a victory that would have levelled the series before the Czechs upped their game in the closing heats to win 57-51. The opening heat of this match produced a new track record for Mick Bell. His time of 71.2 knocked 0.4 seconds off the time set by Martyn Piddock in April. Piddock, Bell and Dickie May top scored for the England team with 10 points each. Also riding were Mike Vernam and future Racers Dave Jessup and Peter Murray. Miroslav Verner scored a full 18-point maximum for the Czechs and was well supported by his cousin Vaclav who scored 14. Also in that team was the future colossus of Czech speedway – Jiri Stancl.

It had been a great night for Reading speedway, but it ended in tragedy. Announcer Peter Arnold suffered a heart attack while driving home to Kettering. He died in hospital six days later. Poignantly he was due to remarry the day after his crash. One of speedway's premier announcers, he was scheduled to take up the mike at the World Final in September. A memorial meeting staged at Tilehurst in October was won by John Harrhy after a run-off with Martyn Piddock.

The second series was rather an anti-climax. Young Britain won the series 4-1. Reading were strongly represented in the Young Australasia squad – 1969 Racers Dene Davis and Bob Tabet were joined by future Racers Geoff Curtis, Graeme Smith and Cec Platt.

1969 was a good year for Anzacs: Ivan Mauger won his second world title and then teamed up with ex-California man Bob Andrews for an unexpected New Zealand win in the inaugural World Best Pairs Championship, Speedway legend Ronnie Moore returned to Wimbledon after six years in retirement, and Geoff Mudge lead Poole Pirates to the Division One title.

The Racers season contained a couple of early season oddities – in consecutive matches against Plymouth and King’s Lynn II. Heat 8 of the home encounter with Plymouth was a 0-0.

There were no finishers, an event so rare it has only occurred three or four times[12] in British speedway over the last 40 years. At the first attempt Plymouth's John Ellis suffered an engine failure and was excluded for not being under power when the race was subsequently stopped. The cause of the stoppage was a second lap crash involving second placed Bob Tabet and third placed Chris Roynon (father of current rider Adam). Roynon was excluded leaving Tabet and Davies to grab an easy 5-0 in the re-run – or so most spectators thought. Instead Davies fell on the first lap and a lap later Bob Tabet fell leaving nobody standing. Curiously all three falls occurred on the fourth bend.

Five days later Racers went to King's Lynn and won 46-31. Racers rounded off the match with a 5-1 in heat 1. Yes, you read that correctly! Mike Vernam, excluded for tape breaking, erroneously took part in the re-run. Later in the match the referee realised a mistake had been made and ordered another re-run of heat 1 (but this time with Reading reserve Phil Pratt) at the end of the match.

19 May 1969 – Bob Tabet picks himself up after the fall that left the result of heat 8 0-0. The event was so remarkable that this photo originally appeared on the front page of the Reading Evening Post. (EP)

The 1969 season laid the foundations for Reading's future. May, Bell and Leigh were all to feature prominently in Racers teams of the 1970s. The rather flat-looking cartwheel design for the Racers logo was replaced by a '3-D' design more closely modelled on the old Harringay 'Winged Wheel'. This was the iconic design which only changed cosmetically over the next 36 years.

However, it did bring the first hints that there would be difficult obstacles to overcome. In the July 25 edition of *Speedway Star* under the headline 'Bombshell for Reading Fans' it was reported that the stadium may be sold for redevelopment and that both speedway and greyhounds could be kicked out. The following year the Greyhound Racing Association put in their first planning application to redevelop the site. The council turned it down, but it looked as if the speedway could be on borrowed time.

Team: Mick Bell 9.04, Dickie May 7.96, Mike Vernam 7.79, Alan Jackson 7.47, Ian Champion 6.65, Phil Pratt 6.33, Dene Davies 6.18, Bob Tabet 5.46, Bernie Leigh 5.05.

---

12 One of these was a Coventry v Middlesbrough BSPA Cup encounter in 1991 when at the final attempt to run heat 2 Rick Miller (the sole remaining contestant) was excluded for not racing. Just who he was supposed to race against remains a mystery to me and the other spectators who witnessed it.

1970 – Richard May's Rise to Stardom

British speedway suffered a terrible tragedy in 1970. On July 14 a mini-bus carrying the West Ham team crashed at Lokeren in Belgium. Six people were killed, including former Canterbury star Martyn Piddock. Cradley's Colin Pratt suffered injuries that ended his riding career.

For Reading 1970 was a disappointing year. After the strong performance in 1969 expectations had been raised. Mick Bell was recalled to Division One parent club Oxford. He wasn't replaced, but everyone confidently expected improvement from the remaining riders, particularly Richard May (Dickie no longer) and Bernie Leigh.

This expectation was fulfilled – the top three in 1970 had a combined average that was three quarters of a point higher than 1969's runners-up. However, lower down the order performances were less distinguished.

Bob Young, a 22-year-old Aussie from Sydney, was Reading's principal new signing.

Belle Vue moved their Colts operation to Rochdale which gave other Division Two teams hope that there would be a new name on the league trophy – and it wouldn't be Rochdale. Late in the day Workington were added to the league and Plymouth's licence transferred to Peterborough, who had earlier been refused admission to the league along with Workington. Prize money was increased to 15 shillings (75p) per point.

Dene Davies – although he demolished the safety fence in the first-ever race at Tilehurst he was still in the Racers team at the end of 1970. (Retro)

The Reading management picked up two riders from Plymouth: Dave Whitaker and John Hammond. A third rider, Chris Roynon, would have signed but in the end decided he needed a weekend track to accommodate his work commitments.

The Racers opening line-up included five members of the powerful 1969 team (May, Vernam, Leigh, Pratt, Davies). Whitaker replaced Tabet in the starting seven, but didn't settle and was quickly replaced by Hammond who top scored in his debut match – a heavy defeat at Nelson. The other new boy Bob Young scored paid 8 on his debut in the season opener (a challenge against Canterbury). There was every reason to be optimistic about the season.

By the middle of June all those hopes had been well and truly dashed. Racers were 15th in the league table and only Peterborough and Middlesbrough were below them. And late starters Peterborough had four home matches in hand on Reading. Not only had the Racers failed to take a point from six away fixtures, but they had lost twice at home – to Ipswich and Canterbury.

One of the few matches they did win

was at home to Peterborough. Old boy John Poyser top scored for the visitors as they went down 43-34 to the Racers. It was to be another 25 years before Reading next played host to Peterborough.

Cec Platt made his Racers debut in June when John Hammond was injured and shortly afterwards gained a permanent place with Phil Pratt moving on to Eastbourne. This didn't strengthen the team as Pratt averaged more than Platt.

Results began to improve – in early July Racers annihilated Berwick 59-19 – and then the breakthrough came with an away win at Romford on July 30. Wins followed in the next two away matches to make it three wins 'on the bounce', a feat the 1969 squad never achieved.

The Romford match was largely won due to reserves Bernie Leigh and Cec Platt who totalled 14 points between them (8 and 6 respectively) in the 43-35 win. Racers won by 10 at Long Eaton with Bernie Leigh top scoring with 9 paid 10, but this match also featured a crash which ended Bob Young's season. Finally Racers squeezed home 40-38 at Berwick with a Richard May maximum, paid 11 from Leigh and paid 10 from Bob Tabet.

Tabet had spent the season trying to regain his team place. He returned to second-halving at Reading after a short and unsuccessful spell at Ipswich. On regaining his team spot due to Young's injury he rode in all but one of the Racers last half-dozen league matches. The one he missed, a re-arranged fixture at Rayleigh, was because it clashed with his wedding.

Reading's penultimate home league match, against Bradford, generated some ill-feeling after the visitors turned up three riders short. Bradford was the new home of Nelson after they closed down mid-season. In August King's Lynn II also relocated – to Boston.

The season finished with wins in challenge matches at home to Eastbourne[13] and Canterbury. These two teams finished second and first in the league after a close three-way battle also featuring Rochdale. Although Reading finished in ninth place, bang in the middle, they were only 3 points behind Bradford in fourth place.

The main positive to come from this season was the improvement shown by the top three, particularly towards the end of the season.

Richard May had a fantastic season. After a slow start to the year he finished ninth in the league averages on 9.57. In his first ten matches he averaged 8.10, in the remaining 19 it was 10.29. June was a momentous month: Brazil succeeded England as World Cup holders; back in Britain Ted Heath's Conservatives won the General Election; and Richard May became almost invincible at Tilehurst. His record from June 1 to July 13 reads:

- Full maximum, maximum (in the Stadium Trophy), 11, full maximum, full maximum, full maximum, paid maximum.

And that dropped point came at the hands of John Louis, the season's most sensational new find. May followed this run with a confident League Division One debut for Wembley, to follow in his father's tyre tracks. Wembley had returned to league speedway at the end of May with a reported crowd of 20,000.

Another remarkable achievement for May was his hat-trick of open meeting wins at Tilehurst in 1970 – and all with unbeaten 15-point scores. In June he finished a point ahead of runner-up Vernam to win the Stadium trophy; the Peter Arnold Memorial was won in August by a convincing four-point margin over Arthur Price (King's Lynn II); and September's Reading Open was won by a single point from John Louis. On the international front May rode in 19 of the 20 matches that Young England/Britain rode. A 7-point return in the Division Two Riders Championship was one of the few lows of his season – the meeting was won by 17-year-old Dave Jessup.

Highlight of captain Mike Vernam's season came early in the year when he relieved Phil

13 My first experience of speedway. Eastbourne won the first race I ever saw with a 5-0 to Dave Jessup and Laurie Sims after Mike Vernam and John Hammond failed to finish. Richard May scored a 12-point maximum.

Woodcock (Romford) of the Silver Helmet. Unfortunately his first defence, at Nelson, saw him surrender the helmet to Alan Bridgett (Edinburgh's team manager since 1991). He also won five caps for Young England/Britain. He increased his average considerably finishing 20th in the Division Two averages, at just a fraction over 9.

Bernie Leigh hit a rich vein of form towards the end of the season, illustrated by his third place in the Reading Open. He upped his average by almost 2 points and became the first Racer to feature in a dead heat – with John Ingamells at King's Lynn.

After the success of the previous year's Young England v Young Czechoslovakia Test match Tilehurst was again awarded the final tie in the series. Once again it was a last-heat decider, the visitors winning the match 55-53 and the series 4-3.

Earlier in the year a Young Sweden team had ridden a series on Division Two tracks. The fourth of the five Tests was allocated to Reading. The Swedes lost the series 4-0 (they drew at Berwick), but produced the star of the series in 19-year-old Tommy Johansson. He came to Reading having scored an 18-point maximum in the previous Test at Berwick – and repeated the feat at Reading. As if that wasn't enough he also broke the track record. He equalled Mick Bell's record in the opening heat, only to see it immediately wiped from the record books as Richard May won heat 2 in a time of 71.0. Johansson responded by coming out in his next ride and lowering the record further, to 70.4. May top scored for Young England in this series.

Two other riders of interest featured in the series, but were unavailable through injury by the time of the Tilehurst Test. Both were brothers of future Racers. One was 17-year-old Tommy Jansson who rode in his first World Final only a year later. Tommy's brother Bo very briefly became a Racer in 1977. The second was Lennart Michanek, younger brother of Anders.

The older Michanek had one of his best seasons, averaging 10.98 in Division One. Only Ivan Mauger outscored him. In 1970 Mauger became the only rider ever to win three world titles in a row with victory at Wroclaw in the first-ever Polish-staged World Final. Michanek finished on 7 points, equal with Barry Briggs. At the end of the season Briggo completed one of the most remarkable feats in speedway's history. Every October fans from across the country trekked to Hyde Road, home of Belle Vue, to witness the cream of world speedway competing in the British League Riders Championship. And for six years in a row they watched Barry Briggs come out on top. Joining Briggs on the rostrum in 1970 was runner-up Anders Michanek.

However, while individual success came Michanek's way, the team he rode for – Newcastle – were not faring so well.

Team: Richard May 9.57, Mike Vernam 9.01, Bernie Leigh 6.91, Bob Young 6.12, Phil Pratt 5.36, Dene Davies 5.28, John Hammond 5.05, Cec Platt 4.20

1971 – Mixing it with the Big Boys

Unlike most other winters, the close season that preceded the 1971 season was an eventful one down Tilehurst way. In November Reg Fearman revealed that Canterbury would be the Racers first opponents in 1971. Mike Vernam and Bob Young would be staying, but First Division target Richard May had yet to decide where he wanted to ride. Rumours of new tracks gave the speedway press something to speculate about. Sunderland, one of the more solid prospects, applied to join Division Two under the Allied Presentations banner.

In the previous three seasons Newcastle had been led by Ivan Mauger, Ole Olsen and Anders Michanek. But these superstars were not enough to lure crowds through the turnstiles at Brough Park and the club struggled financially in 1970. Then at the beginning of January the *Evening Post* revealed that Reading would be the first British League Division Two team to make it to Division One. Allied Presentations would do a straight swap – Newcastle would become Reading, and Reading would become Newcastle.

Division One speedway was much more expensive and Reading attracted the size of crowds that could support the higher cost base. Pay rates for 1971 were £2.25 a point and £1.40 per start in Division One; in Division Two it was £1 a point and 75p per start. This winter also witnessed the disappearance of shillings when Britain went decimal in February.

A few weeks later Newcastle pulled out of Division Two; the stadium owners at Brough Park decided they didn't want Second Division racing! Allied Presentations made the obvious move and switched Reading's Division Two licence to Sunderland instead. In 1975 the Diamonds returned and Newcastle proceeded to dominate the National League (as Division Two had become) for the next nine years. They won the League three times, had a further four top three finishes and never finished lower than sixth.

Speculation about the make up of the Racers team began. Which of the previous season's Newcastle team would end up at Tilehurst and what would become of the riders who had worn the winged wheel in 1970? Meanwhile Bob Tabet supervised the relaying of the track – the grey granite surface was replaced with red shale and the banking increased.

The Rider Control Committee released the team allocations at the beginning of March. The new-look Racers would include four former Diamonds, Poole heat leader Geoff Mudge, John Hart (via Leicester) and Richard May. This allowed the Reading management to firm up loan arrangements for Bob Young and Bernie Leigh. Both were destined for Rayleigh. Poole-owned Mike Vernam had been fixed up at Romford. Both Long Eaton and Peterborough hoped to include Dene Davies in their line-ups.

The four Diamonds became three when New Zealander Dave Gifford decided to spend the year in California. Many years later[14] he explained: "Allied had done their asset stripping hatchet job at Newcastle and there was no way I was going to ride for Fearman at Reading." Gifford rode in the United States Championship and finished fourth behind winner Mike Bast; Scott Autrey came fifth. These were the first stirrings of a new speedway boom which would generate four American World Champions and countless other exciting world-class performers.

Gifford should have been Reading's third heat leader, but Reading took a gamble and filled the vacancy with Bernie Leigh. Another familiar face returned to the Racers fold when Mick Bell replaced John Hart in the Racers starting seven. Birmingham-born Hart moved to Cradley where he had previously ridden in 1965.

Finally Reading had a team, on paper one of the league's weaker sides:

---

14 In an interview with the excellent Speedwayplus website. Visit www.speedwayplus.com for a wealth of speedway nostalgia

- Anders Michanek – had taken over from Ove Fundin as the number one Swede and was widely expected to be the next World Champion to hail from that country.
- Geoff Mudge – experienced Aussie heat leader with eleven years in Poole colours, rode in the 1970 World Ice Speedway Championship.
- Geoff Curtis – started riding in 1966 at the Sydney Showground, where he made his Australia Test debut on 18 January 1969. After a superb 1969 season in British League Division Two for Crewe he moved on to Newcastle.
- Richard May – the one member of the 1970 Reading team certain of a place.
- Mick Bell – spent 1970 back at Oxford, highlight of his season was third place in the British Junior Championship behind Barry Thomas and Dave Jessup.
- Dag Lovaas – Norwegian, born in 1951, who struggled in his first season at Newcastle. Dag only ended up at Newcastle after the club's original target – brother Ulf – turned them down!
- Bernie Leigh – widely seen as a stop gap until a replacement for Dave Gifford was found.

Did Tony Blair follow the Racers in 1971? Unlikely, but the Tilehurst team were rechristened – 'the New Racers', over 20 years before the Labour Party turned into 'New Labour'. What happened to the 'old Racers' who wore the winged wheel in 1970?

The "New Racers" – left ro right: Richard May, Dag Lovaas, Mick Bell, Geoff Mudge (on bike), Anders Michanek, Bernie Leigh, Geoff Curtis and Dick Bailey (team manager). (Retro)

Bob Tabet and John Hammond rode for Canterbury, and later in the season were joined by Phil Pratt who started the year at Eastbourne but lost his place after one league match. Pratt went on to become well known in the sport as an engine tuner. Dene Davies also switched teams during the season, starting at Teesside before ending up at Romford where he replaced ex-Racer Mike Vernam. Tabet and Rayleigh's Bob Young were second-half regulars at Tilehurst in the earlier part of the season. Terry Chandler also appeared in second halves (and a couple of Racers fixtures as an emergency stand-in). Chandler made more impact on the other side of the fence, becoming Poole promoter in 1980.

The season opened with 5,000 spectators witnessing a Metropolitan Gold Cup clash against Hackney. Racers lost 43-35, but more seriously Geoff Mudge aggravated a knee injury that kept him out until July. Unusually both teams had a rider unbeaten – Michanek knocked up a flawless 15 points, and for Hackney reserve Barry Thomas tallied paid 12.

Racers first league outing was a low-key affair, as they fielded two guests and a junior, ending in a 45-33 defeat at Swindon. Their first home league match (and first win) came at the end of April against Leicester. Two days later a draw at Poole produced the first away point. Michanek scored maximums in both these fixtures, laying the foundations for Reading's affinity for Swedish track stars. Geoff Curtis scored 9 at Poole, one of several encouraging early season scores that earned him a Great Britain 'B' call-up for a trip to Poland. Unfortunately Curtis crashed out in the tour's first meeting and flew home early.

Two weeks later and another draw – this time at home to Belle Vue. Racers pulled back a 6-point deficit. But it was in vain as Belle Vue lodged an appeal, and a few weeks later the Speedway Control Board ruled that Dag Lovaas' s third place in heat 5 (originally awarded after Eric Broadbelt fell) should be expunged from the records.

Racers responded with a strong performance in June, chalking up two away wins – at Oxford and Cradley. At Oxford, guest Ray Wilson took a maximum with Geoff Curtis scoring 11; the key performance at Cradley came from Richard May whose paid 9 backed up Michanek's 11. In between these wins Reading dropped another point at home, to local rivals Swindon. With Josef Angermuller (temporary replacement for Mudge) making his debut a week earlier, this was the first time Reading took to the track without a guest since the opening meeting in March.

Reading speedway reached its third birthday in June as another Reading institution was born – the Reading Festival. Headliners in the first year were Arthur Brown, East of Eden and Colosseum. Genesis also performed, and a weekend ticket cost only £2.

Reading recorded their biggest win of the season against Poole at the end of July. Michanek and May both scored paid maximums in the 57-21 thrashing. Reidar Eide, Poole's number one, was particularly disappointing, failing to beat a Racer in any of his rides. Eide later atoned for this performance by coming third in the Manpower Classic, and finished the decade in Racers colours. Eight days later Reading produced their best result of the season: Leicester were fighting it out at the top of the table with Belle Vue and Coventry but slipped up on a rain-soaked track at home to a Racers team on top form. Michanek (11), Lovaas (10) and Mudge (8+2) did the damage.

August ended with a draw at home to Hackney. Unusually the score was 38-38; two races had only two finishers including a last-heat decider that went 3-2 to the Hawks. A week later Reading briefly peaked at third in the league table.

Further away success accrued to the Racers with a win at Wolverhampton and a draw at West Ham. Guest Bruce Cribb top scored against Wolves and Lovaas headed the score chart at Custom House with a full maximum, the first of his career.

Sadly lightning does sometimes strike twice, and after the season ended Racers lost the match points from their visit to Monmore Green. Due to a mistake in calculating the averages Geoff Curtis had been wrongly used at reserve and his points were removed leaving the revised result Wolves 40, Racers 34. At the time team places were determined by averages calculated over the last six matches ridden, and they had to be recalculated after every match. The error was caused by one mislaid bonus point.

The season ended with Belle Vue retaining the league title and the Division One new boys in sixth place. Had either of the two appeals failed that would have been fifth. It may have been only one place, but it meant finishing one place below Swindon instead of one above – an enormous difference given the local rivalry developing between these two teams.

But sixth place was still a remarkable first season for a team that never signed a third heat leader. The key to a successful team is to have several riders capable of improvement and five of the Racers septet upped their averages – dramatically in the case of Dag Lovaas.

Lovaas arrived at Tilehurst with an average of 3.91, a figure that could easily have seen the end of his British career. In 1971 he added a phenomenal 3.83 to that, ending the season as second heat leader. On more than one occasion during the season his love of wet tracks manifested itself. One oddity of his season – he was involved in two dead heats – in consecutive matches! First off he tied with Rick Timmo in the home match against Oxford. Then three days later on July 15 he dead heated with Ronnie Moore in the match at Wimbledon.

Both of those fixtures played a significant role in Richard May's season. Against Oxford May achieved his first maximum (paid) at senior level. This won him the right to challenge for the Golden Helmet (after winning the toss of a coin with fellow maximum man Anders Michanek). In the one-off match race challenger May beat holder Ken McKinlay from the back. At Wimbledon he had to defend it against double World Champion Ronnie Moore. Although defeated by Moore he put up a tenacious display outgating Moore, and re-passing him before Moore passed him for a second time. Shortly afterwards, May scored his first full maximum, a match-winning performance in a 40-38 win over his Dad's old team, Wembley. May's Division One career was characterised by inconsistency and this was certainly true of his 1971 season. At one stage he contemplated dropping back down to Division Two. He finished the year with a 6.13 average, well in excess of the 3.50 assessed average he started the season with.

12 July 1971 – Richard May receives the applause of a packed grandstand as he parades with the newly won Golden Helmet. (EP)

Also starting the season on a 3.50 assessed average, Bernie Leigh upped the figure to 4.75. Given that he had only been a third heat leader at second division level his performance was just as noteworthy. He even managed to start in the main body of the team for a few matches.

Geoff Curtis's 1.59 increase in average (from 5.15 to 6.74) would have attracted a lot more attention in most teams. He started the season well and performed exceptionally in the World Championship. Until 1975 Australians and New Zealanders competed in the British qualifying rounds. At the British Final he scored 6 points (the same as Jim Airey, Eric Boocock and Nigel Boocock) and progressed to the Anglo-Nordic Final as reserve.

Mick Bell upped his average by a more modest half a point. At one stage during the season *Speedway Star* reported that he experimented with an engine first used by Graham Warren in the 1940s! The pace of technical change was much slower in those times!

Anders Michanek didn't have the best of seasons, but still averaged over 10 points a match. He missed numerous matches due to international commitments and two injuries – a thumb at the beginning of the season and a knee towards the end. In the World Final on home shale he scored 11 points finishing fourth equal, his best performance so far. The rostrum positions in Gothenburg were filled by Ole Olsen, Ivan Mauger and Bengt Jansson. Making their World Final debuts that year were Tommy Jansson and Jiri Stancl.

Possibly the biggest frustration of Michanek's season came in the Swedish Championship. After tying with Gote Nordin, Anders won the run-off for the title. However, Nordin had pulled up claiming to have seen a red light. After 15 minutes of arguing the referee ordered a re-run. By this time fighting had broken out on the terraces requiring the attention of ambulances and riot police. Michanek declined to take part in the re-run so the title went to Nordin.

Racers captain Geoff Mudge, aged 36, was nearing the end of his career. Given that he missed half the season with injury an average in excess of 7 could not be regarded as a failure.

Mudge's injury was not the only disappointment. His temporary replacement Josef Angermuller became the first West German to ride in the British League, unfortunately he didn't set the league on fire scoring only 14 points in eight matches.

Reading's exit from the cup could be described as a shock – they lost at home to Cradley only five days after winning at Cradley in the league. Incidentally the cup match was due to be staged a week earlier but rain caused its postponement. In the fourth season of racing at Tilehurst this was the very first postponement.

Tilehurst played host to its first full international after the Polish travel plans required the West Ham Test to be rescheduled. On 24 May Great Britain trounced Poland 78-30. Ray Wilson completed an 18-point maximum, while Andrzej Wyglenda (11) top scored for Poland.

Reading's new prestige individual event – the Manpower Championship – was timed to be the first big meeting in Britain after the World Final. With a top line-up the chances of the new World Champion making his first appearance since winning the title were high. Ole Olsen had been booked. 9,000 spectators flooded through the turnstiles necessitating a delayed start. But there was disappointment as Olsen hadn't turned up. He was either injured or back in Denmark celebrating. His late replacement, Christer Lofqvist, did well scoring 10 points - the same as Ivan Mauger who put himself out of the running with a tape exclusion. Honours went to Barry Briggs who beat Anders Michanek in a run-off.

In October,Ray Wilson won the Peter Arnold Memorial, joining him on the rostrum were Geoff Curtis and John Louis. Two days earlier at Hackney Louis had won the Division Two Riders Championship. Two future stars scoring double figures in the Hackney meeting were 17-year-old Peter Collins and 19-year-old Phil Crump.

At the season's end, Reg Fearman announced plans to increase the capacity of the Oxford Road stadium by 2-3,000. On the rider front, Anders Michanek headed to Australia and Geoff Curtis returned to Rhodesia (Zimbabwe) where he had ridden the previous winter.

Team: Anders Michanek 10.05, Dag Lovaas 7.74, Geoff Mudge 7.23, Geoff Curtis 6.74, Richard May 6.13, Mick Bell 5.25, Bernie Leigh 4.75, (Josef Angermuller 3.30)

1972 – Could This Season Ever Be Bettered?

The hectic winter that preceded the 1971 season was in complete contrast to the quiet winter that followed it. For the only time in Racers history the starting seven saw no changes from the previous year. After letting the Racers down the previous year Dave Gifford returned to Britain, ending up at Wolverhampton. After four years in sole charge as team manager Dick Bailey decided to lighten his load and Bob Radford took over the duties away from home. Radford had previous experience as team manager, taking on the role for Newport in 1969 at the tender age of 22.

Geoff Curtis enjoyed his time in Rhodesia, finishing runner-up to Brian Collins in the Rhodesian Open Championship. Back in Curtis's homeland Anders Michanek top scored for the Swedes as they went down 5-1 in a Test series with Australia. Closer to home Wembley pulled out of the league citing lack of available dates, and Ipswich replaced West Ham. The loss of West Ham's Custom House track due to redevelopment gave cause for concern in Reading as a similar fate might be awaiting the Tilehurst track.

A change of ownership at Oxford gave birth to a new image – the Cheetahs became the Rebels. New boss Dave Lanning launched a stream of provocative press releases, many of them belittling the 'Reading Berks'.

As the speedway season got under way Reading Football Club staggered to 16th place in Division Four (currently called League Two!) – the lowest-ever position in their history. Crowds of less than 4,000 were the norm at Elm Park. In contrast the Racers sped from the starting blocks winning the Spring Gold Cup – an early season mini-league.

After slipping up in the home opener against Hackney the Racers won all seven of the fixtures that followed, finishing with a 100% away record. The final match, at King's Lynn, fell victim to the weather at the end of April and the Racers had to wait until late July to wrap up the Gold Cup title. Theoretically the Stars could have won the competition, but they needed to beat the Racers 55-23. Instead Racers powered to a 6-point win with Michanek (10) and Bell (9) heading the score charts.

The Gold Cup averages revealed an awesome solidity to the Racers line-up. Mick Bell's 6.90 only put him sixth in Reading's Gold Cup averages. Richard May started the season well registering an 8.77 average. One match (away at Ipswich) featured a brief return for 1970 Racer Bob Young who went on to have the best season of his career. He became Rayleigh's number one with a Division Two average in excess of 9 and annexed the Rayleigh track record.

Reading opened their league campaign quietly with a couple of comfortable home wins and a couple of away defeats. Then came the match of the season. In December 1971 the final stretch of the M4 was opened, making the trip down to Swindon so much easier. Many of those who made that trip continue to talk about the evening of May 6 to this very day.

After Michanek broke the tapes in heat 1, visiting fans were expecting the worst. Reserve Richard May came out and beat four times World Champion Barry Briggs. After eight heats Reading held a 6-point lead, and Swindon brought in Barry Briggs as a tactical substitute. But Richard May beat him from the gate, only for the race to be stopped and Mike Keen excluded. Although Briggs gated in the rerun it was May who took the race, passing Briggo at the end of the first lap. Lovaas beat Briggs in heat 10, but by the time Briggs gained his revenge on Lovaas two heats later the match points were already on the M4 heading back to Berkshire.

From here on Racers stepped up a gear and by the time Belle Vue arrived in town Reading had been top of the league for several weeks. The Aces were pre-season title favourites; had bookies been giving odds they would have been short. Rider control had been kind to them over the winter, the only change in the champions line-up was the replacement of Dave

Hemus with the hottest prospect in British speedway – Peter Collins. They came to Tilehurst with five wins out of six on the road – only Wimbledon had lowered their colours.

Racers stormed into a 28-14 lead. The Aces clawed back to three down giving what was described in the following week's programme as a 'record crowd' a last-heat decider. After the agony of the 1969 and 1971 clashes with Belle Vue history looked to be repeating itself when Ronnie Moore (a guest for Ivan Mauger) and Alan Wilkinson gated for a 5-1. This time the boot was on the other foot, Lovaas and then Mudge slipped inside Wilkinson on the third lap. In his attempts to stop Mudge, Wilkinson earned an exclusion for unfair riding. This led to four Belle Vue riders (Wilkinson, Pusey, Broadbelt and Collins) pulling out of the second half. While the Aces lost 40-37, it was their final defeat of the season.

With Belle Vue Aces successfully repelled, Racers went on to complete a 100% home league record for the first time. Only Ipswich came close, losing 41-36 despite a John Louis maximum. Illustrating the strength in depth of the Racers squad, Geoff Mudge rode at reserve in this match even though his 'last six' average was 7.28. Ipswich went on to emulate the Racers finishing sixth in their debut season in the top division.

By the end of the season Reading had clocked up eight wins and a draw away from home. Five of their eight away defeats were by 4 points or less. In most years this record would have been enough to land the title or at least come close. With a top four of Mauger, Soren Sjosten, Collins and Chris Pusey the 1972 Belle Vue team could only be described as exceptional. 18-year-old Collins averaged nearly 8.5 in his first year in Division One and Pusey carried an average in excess of 8 despite being a second string. Belle Vue got behind on their fixtures and it wasn't until the start of September that they deposed Reading from the top of the table. It is hard to argue with a title-winning margin of 12 points.

Racers final away victory in the league was one of the most satisfying. Three points down with three races to go Reading slammed in two 5-1s and a 4-2 to beat Oxford 42-35. A five-ride paid maximum from Geoff Curtis helped wipe the smile off Oxford boss Dave Lanning's face. But you can't keep a good self-publicist down and Lanning would reappear later in the Racers story.

Some of the year's greatest drama took place in the knock-out cup. 1972 was the last season in which ties consisted of one leg, and Racers so nearly became the first team to reach the final after three away ties.

The trail started at Wolverhampton where Ole Olsen chalked up an unstoppable 18-point maximum winning heats 10, 11, 12 and 13! But Racers clung on to win 40-38. Next up, a visit to Ipswich, and another 40-38 win. Racers came from 8 down to reach the last heat on level terms. The Witches pair gated for a match winning 4-2, but Bob Kilby (guesting for Michanek) and Richard May turned this into a 4-2 for the visitors passing Sandor Levai and Tommy Johansson.

Racers fell at the semi-final hurdle in another cliffhanger. Lovaas top scored (11+1) as Racers came from 8 down to take a 2-point lead into the final heat. This time Boulger (another guest for Michanek) and May conceded a 5-1 to Barry Thomas and Hugh Saunders.

Six days earlier Ivan Mauger had regained the world title from Ole Olsen at Wembley. Once again Michanek disappointed scoring 8 points. The World Final is remembered for Olsen's first ride fall which cost him the title, the Barry Briggs crash that caused him to retire, and the presence of six Russians and the mysterious disappearance of their bikes. Briggs subsequently returned to league speedway in 1974 and Newport heat leader Tony Clarke was later jailed for the theft of the bikes.

Mauger added the Manpower Championship to his list of honours 48 hours later. On a wet night he passed eventual runner-up Michanek in his second ride on the way to a 15-point maximum. England star Ray Wilson came third. Olsen's challenge ended when to broke the tapes, thus depriving the crowd of the Olsen v Mauger rematch.

During the summer, Britain staged an international tournament between England, Australia, New Zealand, Sweden and a combined Norway/Denmark team. It seems almost impossible to imagine now, but at the time Norway could boast far more top-class riders than Denmark. This combined team was essentially Norway plus Denmark's Ole Olsen.

Tilehurst played host to the Sweden versus Norway/Denmark fixture. Michanek crashed out of the meeting after a heat 1 clash with Olsen. Reigning World Champion Olsen dominated the competition dropping only one point in four matches. That point went to Christer Lofqvist in heat 6 of the Reading match. Although Olsen dropped a point in the Tilehurst fixture Dag Lovaas didn't. His heat 13 win completed his maximum, but it wasn't quite enough to prevent a Swedish win – by a 40-38 score.

Earlier in the season (May 15) Olsen smashed the Tilehurst track record. His 67.4 time still stood when the bulldozers moved in 18 months later.

15 May 1972 – Ole Olsen leads the Racers pair of Anders Michanek (left) and Geoff Curtis (right) in the fastest race ever seen at Tilehurst. (EP)

The following week's meeting provided one of the season's few low points. Towards the end of a World Championship qualifying round Clive Featherby and Eric Broadbelt collided, leaving Featherby with a badly broken leg that led to his retirement after a career that started with Norwich back in 1958.

No less than six of the Reading seven improved their averages, Geoff Mudge being the only exception. He still averaged over seven and the modest drop of 0.16 in his average was dwarfed by his team mates' progress.

Once again it was Dag Lovaas' average that increased most, from 7.74 to 8.78. For the second year in a row Lovaas came second in the Norwegian Championship – pipped the previous year by Reidar Eide, it was brother Ulf's turn in 1972. On the brink of stardom the threat of national service back in Norway seemed to be the greatest obstacle to Dag's climb to speedway stardom.

Mick Bell and Geoff Curtis didn't miss a single fixture between them. In the process each increased his average by a point. Curtis's continued improvement came as no surprise. He reached the British Final of the World Championship as reserve and represented Australia in the World Best Pairs semi-final. No Racer won the Golden Helmet in 1972 but Curtis came closest, challenging Glasgow's Jim McMillan in June. After a low profile year in 1971 Mick Bell's progress came as a pleasant surprise. He started the season strongly and qualified for the British semi-finals after scoring heavily in his three qualifying rounds.

A half point improvement may not sound a great deal but when that is from an average in excess of 10 to start with, it is quite impressive. That's what Anders Michanek achieved in 1972, ending the season third in the league averages behind Ivan Mauger and Ole Olsen. Once again his international commitments caused Racers to field several guests and generated a fair amount of adverse comment. One of his trips back to Sweden resulted in him gaining his first Swedish title, finishing 2 points clear of runner-up Bengt Jansson.

Bernie Leigh and Richard May both upped their averages by a quarter of a point, starting well but tailing off after injuries. May picked up a back injury in the Silver Plume at Swindon that still caused him trouble at the start of the following season; his away form was particularly disappointing. On July 28 Leigh broke his shoulder at Newport to put a dampener on Reading's biggest away win in the league (Newport 32 Reading 46).

Racers gave several outings to number eight Graeme Smith, mainly covering for Leigh. Smith, a New Zealander, rode for Sunderland in Division Two. Reading were also attempting to cultivate their own juniors with regular second-half races. Jack Walker first appeared in one of these at the beginning of July. In August he came third in a junior meeting at King's Lynn, won by Keith White (son of former Racer Vic). That meeting also featured Rob Hollingworth, a rider still active in 2006. In September Walker made his first team debut in a challenge match against Swindon.

In a fantastic season Reading clocked up 16 away wins (eight league, four Spring Gold Cup, two knock-out cup, one Metropolitan Cup, one challenge). At both Wimbledon and Ipswich, Reading won three times from three visits. This tally was never bettered not even in their championship-winning seasons. Reg Fearman had built a very solid foundation for track success, but not everything was rosy in the world of Reading speedway.

Team: Anders Michanek 10.51, Dag Lovaas 8.78, Geoff Curtis 7.73, Geoff Mudge 7.07, Richard May 6.38, Mick Bell 6.24, Bernie Leigh 5.02, Graeme Smith 3.77

1973 – One Last Stand?

Reading went into 1973 knowing it would almost certainly be the last at Tilehurst. Stadium owners, the Greyhound Racing Association Property Trust (GRA), had already been responsible for the demolition of West Ham's Custom House home in 1972. Next they set their sights on Tilehurst. Their determination to demolish the Oxford Road stadium became clear at a two-day public enquiry in October 1972 that re-examined the 1970 application.

'Save Reading Speedway' stickers appeared in cars across Reading, as supporters got petitioning and lobbying. Reading councillors took note of the strong public feeling and continued to oppose the plans. However, the GRA got their way when in January the Government Minister granted the appeal.

With a detailed planning application to follow it would have been impossible for builders to move onto the site for many months. At least Racers would take to the Tilehurst track for one more year. Having gained a sympathetic hearing from the council Allied Presentations enlisted their help in the search for a new site.

By early April a favourite had emerged from a list of 12 possible sites produced by the town's planners. They had found an 18-acre site to the south-west of the town – with the less than attractive title of 'Smallmead Tip'. Allied Presentations submitted an outline planning application in August.

It wasn't the best of atmospheres to launch a speedway campaign, but 1972 runners-up Reading prepared themselves for one last stand.

New Year's Day marked the entry of Britain into the European Union, then known as the 'Common Market'. The immediate concern in the speedway world was the impact of introducing VAT (originally at 10%) on admission charges. (Allied Presentations put the cost of adult admission up to 50p in May.) Riders were paid £1.90 a start and £2.50 a point in 1973.

In the long term, and of greater significance, was the changed status of foreign riders. Danes and Germans would no longer need work permits to ride in the British League, but Australians and New Zealanders would. The impact was not immediate, but it created the conditions that eventually allowed home-born riders to become a minority in British speedway.

The British Speedway Promoters' Association came to an agreement with SVEMO, the body overseeing Swedish speedway. It meant that Anders Michanek and other top Swedes would be riding in the UK, and hopefully missing fewer meetings. A second team worry evaporated after Norwegian authorities released Dag Lovaas from national service on health grounds[15] – after just three weeks.

Skipper Geoff Mudge announced his retirement, although Newport tempted him back onto the track mid-season and he continued riding until 1976, several months after he turned 40. Outside of Reading a more noteworthy retirement was that of twice World Champion Ronnie Moore.

Mudge's retirement triggered a search for a replacement. Inexperienced Jack Walker came into contention, but he ended up signing for Division Two Peterborough in April. A paid 7 on his debut signalled a season of progress for him. Incidentally top scorer for the Panthers in Walker's debut meeting was John Davis with a paid maximum.

Racers signed Sunderland's Jack Millen as number eight. A colourful New Zealander with a reputation for 'forceful' riding, he ran up a long list of injuries, few of which stopped the 'hard man' riding.

---

15 Presumably an allergy to uniforms!

Eventually rider control allocated Peter Murray from Wimbledon, a rider familiar to Tilehurst fans from Division Two days.

The vacant captain's position went to Mick Bell, while on the other side of the fence Bob Radford replaced Dick Bailey as team manager. Bailey became Clerk of the Course, and the announcer's box had a new occupant – David 'Diddy' Hamilton. Hamilton already well known as a Radio One DJ took over the afternoon show (one of the cornerstones of Radio One's schedule) later in 1973. A genuine speedway fan his official website states that he: "retains his childhood passion for speedway and was announcer at Wembley". Reading doesn't get a mention!

After defeats to Hackney in each of the previous two seasons' opening meetings, a change of opponent seemed like a good idea. Ipswich thought otherwise, crushing the race-rusty Racers 45-33 in front of a 6,500 crowd. Bell, May and Murray all failed to score and Curtis managed just one point. Things didn't improve the following week. After conceding 5-1s in the first two races Wimbledon took the points by a 42-36 score.

Reading finished bottom of the Spring Gold Cup with just two wins out of ten matches. Competition winners King's Lynn also took a point away from Tilehurst. In an era of mainly black leathers, Lovaas and May added some colour to the team with their bright jerseys (red for Lovaas, pale blue for May), but their form caused much concern and Peter Murray wasn't settling.

At least Racers thrashed Swindon by 14 points at Blunsdon in a challenge match, notable for a Mick Bell maximum. The form of Anders Michanek provided the other consolation. His win in the Daily Express Spring Classic at Wimbledon was the first of many big open meetings that went to the Swede.

Racers kicked off the league campaign with a 55-22 thrashing of Coatbridge, on a very wet track. Predictably Lovaas top scored with 10 paid 11. Dag's wet-weather winning habit could be traced back to his winter practice regime – on the frozen lakes of Norway.

Wins at Cradley and Wolverhampton followed. Cradley United (the 'Heath' had been dropped in an attempt at re-branding[16]) went down by a massive 18 points, while a last heat win by Michanek against Olsen was needed for the second away win.

Wolves had been unlucky not to win at Tilehurst ten days earlier. Olsen had arrived late, missed his first ride and suffered an exclusion in heat 13. Yet Wolves only lost by 4 points. That match marked the final appearance of Peter Murray. For the remainder of the season the number seven slot was filled by the two Jacks – Millen and Walker – and an assortment of Division Two guests. Murray resurfaced later in the season at former club Canterbury.

The fragility shown against Wolves manifested itself two weeks later when Sheffield kick-started their title charge with an unexpected win. The Tigers possessed enormous strength in depth, even their reserves were averaging nearly 7 points a match. The visitors' reserves (Doug Wyer and Bengt Larsson) totalled paid 19 points between them at Tilehurst.

The Sheffield fixture is also remembered for the night's off track events. Since the start of the season announcer David Hamilton had brought a stream of famous faces to Tilehurst as his guest. Many of them would no longer be recognised but that night's guest remains famous, albeit for entirely the wrong reasons. With two number one and two number two hit singles in 1973 Gary Glitter had star written all over him. His presence encouraged many teenage girls with no interest in the racing to attend the meeting and drew a backlash from hardcore supporters who regarded Glitter as a distraction. Their behaviour towards Glitter attracted stern words in the following week's programme! The *Evening Post* gave the visit front page coverage: "Fever as Glitter hits Reading", ran the front page headline. Page 4 carried further pictures of the Glitter visit next to a story giving the latest developments in the Watergate scandal.

---

16 An experience that John Postlethwaite would have done well to note.

Anders Michanek continued to be the 'Leader of the Gang' coming within inches of winning the prestigious Internationale at Wimbledon. Leading his final race until the final bend he allowed Ole Olsen to pass him and force a run-off. The Dane won the run-off. Young Swedish sensation Tommy Jansson took third after a run-off with Ivan Mauger. Twelve days later (June 9) Michanek and Jansson teamed up to win the World Pairs for Sweden, a meeting that also saw Dag Lovaas representing Norway.

Mick Bell won a World Championship round at Coatbridge and unexpectedly qualified for the British Final. He scored 4 points in a meeting won by Leicester's Ray Wilson. Wilson became the first British rider to win the British Final for a decade. New Zealanders Ivan Mauger and Barry Briggs had shared the last nine titles between them! 1973 marked the start of a golden decade for British speedway. Just five years after its birth, Division Two had become an incubator for exciting new talent. Dave Jessup, John Louis, Peter Collins were already stars, and riders like Gordon Kennett, John Davis and Chris Morton would soon follow.

In mid-June Racers boosted their credentials as title challengers with two wins from three away matches in three days. Lovaas scored 12-point maximums in both the wins at Poole and Newport.

Although Reading's league record looked encouraging the team still wasn't clicking. Michanek and Lovaas could not be faulted, their July green sheets (based on matches to June 15) were 11.73 and 10.24. May's average had fallen by over 2 points a match, while Curtis and Bell were over a point down on the previous season. Leigh was also down slightly and covering the number seven spot remained problematic.

League competition took a back seat at the beginning of July when the *Daily Mirror* sponsored International Tournament took centre stage. The biggest international competition in speedway's history it started with a seven-team league, followed by semi-finals and a grand final at Wembley. Reading were allocated the New Zealand v USSR fixture. The Kiwis needed to win to make the semi-finals.

The result on July 9: New Zealand 43 USSR 34. Ivan Mauger scored a maximum; both Moore (11) and Briggs (9) gave good support despite being semi-retired. The Soviets accrued six tape exclusions causing the meeting to run perilously close to Tilehurst's 10 p.m. curfew. The stadium was plunged into darkness as the presentation for the winners of the second-half tournament was taking place.

On the same evening Racers competed in a four-team event at Exeter. They came second; the inevitable Michanek maximum was supplemented by 9 points from guest Ulf Lovaas who out-scored brother Dag (4).

Five days later 41,000 fans flocked to Wembley for the International Tournament Final, one of the greatest occasions speedway has seen outside of a World Final. England and Sweden couldn't be split over 13 races. The two teams were never more than 4 points apart. The match finished with six drawn heats! Michanek scored 11, dropping his only point to Peter Collins in heat 9, but gaining his revenge in heat 12. Christer Lofqvist won the last heat ahead of England's top scorers Malcolm Simmons and Terry Betts (10 paid 11 each). A run-off would decide the tournament.

England team manager Len Silver nominated teenager Peter Collins; for Sweden Michanek was the obvious choice. Collins took the lead, but on the third bend drifted off the line. It was the tiniest of gaps, but Michanek couldn't resist it. As the super Swede dived under Collins, the Belle Vue youngster found himself heading towards the safety fence. As the *Speedway Star* headline asked: “Did he fall or was he pushed?” Experienced referee Arthur Humphrey felt confident in his judgement and excluded Michanek.

Racers returned to league action clocking up three away defeats in the remainder of July. In the last of these Michanek unsuccessfully challenged Eric Boocock for the Golden Helmet.

At home Jack Walker made his league debut for the second time, the first (against Exeter) had been abandoned after he had scored paid 5 from two rides. And the following week Bobby McNeil wore the number seven race jacket scoring 9 paid 12 from eight rides in a double header against Belle Vue (comfortably beaten for a change) and Newport.

In August, Racers moved to the top of the table, winning eight and drawing one of their nine league matches. Ironically they produced their least convincing performance on the night they went top (August 6). In a double header Racers beat Newport, but could only draw with King's Lynn. In both matches the three heat leaders (Michanek, Lovaas and Curtis) won at will while the rest of the team scored next to nothing. In contrast Lynn's top scorer was reserve Bob Humphreys (11+1). This performance mirrored some matches earlier in the season, but turned out to be an aberration in a strong finish to the season.

Racers scored more than 50 in five of their last seven home matches, including the 59-19 slaughter of Halifax. Four of their August wins were away, starting with an easy 50-28 thrashing of Hackney aided by a five-ride paid maximum from Richard May. The following night at Swindon, Racers gave the Robins an 8-point head start before concluding the match with four 5-1s in the last five races. The visitors adapted better to the wet track, and predictably Lovaas got a maximum. There had been a gratifying increase in Curtis's scoring. Bell and May were also considerably better than in the earlier part of the season. Leigh took a bit longer but he did eventually regain his form after a mid-season slump.

Michanek's form remained faultless despite the distractions of the world title race. He started August by winning the British/Nordic Final – a meeting best remembered for Eric Boocock's walk out in protest at the use of video replay to exclude him. Controversy overshadowed the next stage too, when the British authorities were forced to withdraw John Louis after a dispute about a previous positive test for fuel additives. Michanek won the meeting with a 15-point maximum.

The Manpower at Tilehurst was just one of a long string of individual meetings Anders Michanek won in a phenomenal 1973. Here he takes the victor's tractor ride flanked by third place Reidar Eide (left) and runner-up Ole Olsen (right). (EP)

With these wins behind him and top spot in the British League averages ahead of Ivan Mauger, it looked as if Michanek could at last take the ultimate prize. The World Final in

Chorzow (Poland) beckoned.

Ivan Mauger fell in the deciding run-off, and Jerzy Szczakiel somehow became World Champion. Although he did win his opening ride in his one and only Tilehurst appearance (in the 1971 Great Britain v Poland match) his record in domestic and international competition made Szczakiel a rank outsider. Michanek didn't just fail, he failed spectacularly, starting with a last place and picking up only 6 points in total.

Bad luck comes in threes – well it certainly did for Anders Michanek that September, more disappointment followed.

Six days later Racers were thrashed at Belle Vue, a scoreline that wasn't helped by Michanek's walkout after an engine failure in his second ride. His refusal to borrow a bike or bring his own spare drew criticism from Racers team manager Bob Radford.

To paraphrase Lady Bracknell[17]: "one walkout may be a misfortune; to have two looks like carelessness." Yes, less than a fortnight later Michanek did it again. A short odds favourite to win the Swedish Championship, he started with two wins. Then in his third ride an exclusion for unfair riding prompted him to quit the meeting. Former Tilehurst track record holder Tommy Johansson took the title in Michanek's absence.

In the other major international event of the month a Great Britain team won the World Cup from Sweden with Peter Collins scoring a maximum, and taking the only point off Sweden's top scorer Anders Michanek. Another indicator of the 'wind of change' blowing through British speedway was the omission of Ivan Mauger from the Great Britain team leaving five English riders to fly the flag. (Only two years earlier Great Britain had been represented by three New Zealanders, an Australian and lone Englishman Ray Wilson.)

The last couple of months of the season saw Curtis averaging over nine, Leigh return to form and Bell register the most productive spell of his career. He chalked up his first senior maximum in a 58-20 thrashing of Exeter – a fixture that had to be run three times after rain forced abandonment not once, but twice. When Racers went to Brandon and steamrollered Coventry 48-30 at the end of September the title was within sight.

On Monday October 1 Sheffield lost at Wimbledon thereby ruling themselves out of the title race. Only King's Lynn could draw level on match points with Reading, but race points were in Reading's favour by a wide margin. For all practical purposes the title now belonged to Reading. The *Evening Post* agreed, Tuesday's front page carried the headline "We Are the Champions". Just to be sure Racers wound up their away programme by winning at King's Lynn from six down, with the obligatory Michanek maximum.

News of Sheffield's defeat reached the Racers fans who were at Tilehurst watching Reading host Belle Vue in the Knock-Out Cup Final. After an easy passage to the final, the soon-to-be-crowned league champions were facing the team they deposed. The heat leader trio produced their usual strong showing with 31 points, principal support came from Mick Bell (7+2). Peter Collins top scored for the visitors who were disappointed by the return from guest John Louis (in for Chris Pusey) – just 3 points. The outcome, a 47-31 home win, left the tie finely balanced. Timekeeper John Homer clocked Michanek at 67.6 seconds in opening heat, the fastest-ever time by a Reading rider at Tilehurst, just one fifth of a second shy of Olsen's track record.

Rain delayed the second leg by two weeks and it finally took place on October 24[18]. Because it was so late in the season, provision had already been made for a run-off in the event of a tie. And that's just how it ended.

---

17 A creation of Oscar Wilde. Reading is often held up as the archetype of characterless towns with no history. The fact that the most significant piece of culture associated with the town is *The Ballard of Reading Gaol*, written by a man whose presence in Reading was involuntary, tends to support this.

18 Unfortunately this was a school day, and I couldn't persuade my father that my education would be better served by a trip to Manchester than a day in the classroom.

Although after nine heats they stood at 6 down on the night, the Racers were still 10 up on aggregate and looked to be in control. Then Peter Collins and Alan Wilkinson took a 5-1 off Michanek and Lovaas, and the Manchester crowd sensed a comeback. In the last-heat decider Sjosten and guest Jim McMillan sped from the tapes for the 5-1 that would give Belle Vue the cup. The drama wasn't over; on the second lap Michanek passed McMillan leaving the two sides level after 26 heats.

End of season celebrations with the League Championship trophy. Left to right: Geoff Curtis, Bobby McNeil, Mick Bell (kneeling) and Dag Lovaas. (EP)

For the run-off Michanek borrowed Bernie Leigh's bike, his only machine having packed up earlier in the meeting. Belle Vue nominee Peter Collins carried a hand injury. The race is a serious contender for the title of the greatest race ever, with the two stars passing on every bend. Michanek on the inside would dive under Collins entering the odd-numbered bends and Collins on the outside would power back round him exiting the even-numbered bends. Collins won the dash to the line and Hyde Road, already witness to so much speedway history, further enhanced its claim to be the greatest speedway venue ever seen in Britain.

Three days later rain caused the postponement of the British League Riders Championship until November 3. A tape exclusion cost Michanek a shot at the title, and he finished third after a four-man run-off for second. Reading riders have an abysmal record in the BLRC and Michanek's third place remained the best performance by a Racer in the event until 1992 when Per Jonsson finished second. Ivan Mauger picked up the title, after a season in which he had been largely overshadowed by Michanek and haunted by his fall in the World Final run-off.

Michanek just dominated 1973, topping the league averages on 11.55. He won a string of open meetings against the toughest of opposition. The Spring Classic (Wimbledon), Manpower (Reading), Pride of the East (King's Lynn), Blue Riband (Poole), Golden Gauntlets (Leicester), Brandonapolis (Coventry), Superama (Hackney), Champion of Champions (Wolverhampton), Prince of Wales Trophy (Newport), Autumn Classic (Halifax), Brew XI Trophy (Wolverhampton) all ended up in Michanek's trophy cabinet. Most remarkable of all – his record in league racing at Tilehurst: 64 starts, 63 wins, a second place to Geoff Curtis, and a perfect 12.00 home average.

Lovaas ended sixth in the league averages and finally became Norwegian Champion. Add in Geoff Curtis and Racers had an overpowering heat leader trio. Bell, May and Leigh all saw slight falls in their averages and it is tempting to conclude that the team of 1972 was a better one than the 1973 champions. It was certainly a better balanced one.

The final season at Tilehurst saw Racers exit in a blaze of glory. Despite five rain-offs attendances were high, 'regularly exceeding 5,000 and rising to 7-8,000 for big meetings' according to David Hamilton in one of his programme columns.

The home season ended on October 8 with a challenge against Ole Olsen's United Seven. Racers won by 12 points, Michanek scored a maximum; Olsen dropped his only points to Michanek and Curtis. Olsen received most of his support from future Racers Reidar Eide and Dave Jessup. Due to all those rain-offs the Peter Arnold Memorial Trophy had been squeezed out of the fixture list. Instead it rounded off the Tilehurst era for the Racers as the second half of the farewell meeting. The trophy final was the last-ever race at Tilehurst. It was won by the man whose dominance in 1973 has never been emulated – the mighty Michanek.

The programme for that meeting signed off:

> ***"The Management, Officials and Riders of Reading Speedway offer sincere thanks for your support over the last six seasons and hope we shall meet again at Smallmead next Spring."***

Team: Anders Michanek 11.36, Dag Lovaas 10.06, Geoff Curtis 8.23, Richard May 6.05, Mick Bell 5.84, (Bobby McNeil 5.28), Bernie Leigh 4.46, Jack Millen 3.20

Soon after the last greyhound meeting at Tilehurst on 10 November 1973 the demolition crew moved in. (EP)

1974 – Hibernation

Racers fans entered the winter sustained by the warm glow of 1973's success. What already promised to be a fraught winter very quickly became a lot gloomier. The news from Down Under couldn't have been more devastating. Geoff Curtis had been killed on track, racing at the Sydney Showground on December 15.

Riding in the New South Wales Championship in a field that included top Aussies Bob Valentine and Jim Airey, Curtis started with two second places. He looked destined for his first win of the night when he led from the gate in heat 11, but he hit the fence and died from head injuries hours later[19].

The Sydney Showground closed as a speedway venue in 1996; a plaque commemorating Geoff and others who died there can be seen adjacent to the former site of the starting gate. When Smallmead stadium finally opened the naming of the Geoff Curtis Bar ensured that this quiet but popular Racer would not be forgotten in Reading.

The last greyhound meeting took place at Tilehurst on November 10 1973. The GRA had obtained permission for the development of a commercial estate. The wrecking crews moved in quickly and soon the fabric of the stadium was ripped to shreds.

Just a few days before Curtis's tragic accident Reading Council had granted approval for outline planning permission. It should have been clear then that a new stadium could not possibly be ready for 1974, but the public fiction that Reading would be participating in the 1974 British League was maintained until the end of February. Reading were even included in the 1974 Knock-Out Cup draw, being matched against Exeter.

At the Supporters' Club AGM in December 1973 Reading director Len Silver told the audience that Smallmead would not be open before mid-season. As late as mid February 1974 the *Evening Post* reported that: "it is widely expected in the speedway world that the licence will be transferred temporarily to a nearby track – such as Aldershot – with the team based there still keeping the Reading Racers tag."

The winter of 1973/74 was a long dark one, and it felt as if the new stadium would never materialize. The quadrupling of oil prices following the Middle East War triggered a global economic crisis. Industrial action by the miners led to a three-day week and regular power cuts, culminating in the inconclusive election of February 1974.

Detailed plans for Smallmead were drawn up, submitted, and finally approved in July. The council (as owners of the land) granted a lease to Allied Presentations and now it was all systems go. The 99 year lease provided for payment of £6,000 per annum in rent and required Allied Presentations to foot the cost of the access to the stadium. At this stage the cost of the project was estimated at £200,000. It would have a capacity of 10-12,000, including seating for 2,000 and parking for 2,000 cars. In August the builders swung into action. Mick Bell and Richard May posed with a bulldozer and the 1973 League Championship Trophy on site to mark the 'lifting of the first sod'.

One other noteworthy development during the battle for a new stadium was the break-up of Allied Presentations. Crewe, Peterborough, Teesside (Middlesbrough) and Rye House became stand-alone promotions. Reg Fearman kept the Allied name at Reading, where the shareholders were now Fearman, Len Silver, Frank Higley and Bill Dore.

Dore and Higley were brought in by Fearman to contribute their expertise. Higley and

---

19 Accounts of that fateful night vary. At the time international phone calls had a luxury status and news from Australia often took a couple of weeks to arrive. The *Evening Post* reported the events based on accounts passed on by distraught friends who received the news via brief but extremely distressing calls straight after the event. I have relied on the version produced by Australian speedway historian Ross Garrigan. See http://www.ausm.info/aus_history/past_era/g_curtis.htm

Dore both had backgrounds in construction. Higley was a long-standing friend of Fearman with an interest in motorcycling while Dore owned a string of greyhounds. Both, but particularly Dore, would eventually take a much more central role.

In March Princess Anne was the victim of a kidnap attempt and a passing member of the public ended up with the Queen's Gallantry Medal. He later became well-known in speedway circles – Ronnie Russell, promoter at Arena Essex until 2006. The three-day week caused huge problems. Soaring petrol costs and a floodlight ban made for an unpromising backdrop. The fixture list didn't appear until April with the season already under way. The Reading team of 1973 was dispersed and the season swung into action without the Racers.

A ban on commuting Swedes ensured that no team in Britain would benefit from Michanek's brilliance. It also deprived Hackney of their number one, Bengt Jansson. Dag Lovaas was allocated to the Hawks to fill the gap. Richard May went to Poole, Mick Bell to Leicester and Bernie Leigh to Swindon. Both May and Lovaas had hinted that they would like a new team even before Reading pulled out of the League. Team manager Bob Radford had also moved on, handing his notice in very soon after the previous season ended. He became general manager at Oxford. Therefore it was probably not a coincidence when Oxford advertised heavily in the Reading *Evening Post* with the aim of enticing Racers fans to Cowley for their speedway fix.

Bobby McNeil and Jack Millen both had high-scoring seasons finishing high in the Division Two averages. One other Racer from the Tilehurst era re-emerged in 1974 – Josef Angermuller. He signed for Division One newcomers Hull. Despite conflicts between his continental bookings and British League commitments, a 5.11 league average could be considered a respectable performance. Sadly he didn't ride in Britain again. A crash in a World Championship Qualifying Round cost him his life in April 1977.

For all Racers supporters the highlight of the year (apart from those vital planning consents) occurred in Gothenburg at the start of September. After so many disappointments Anders Michanek did what he had threatened to do for several years. He became World Champion, and he did it in a manner so convincing that it remains the benchmark against which other one-horse races are judged.

Not only did Anders win all five of his races, he set a new track record in three of them. He was over a second faster than any other rider that night, and ended 4 points clear of the runner-up. That position was filled by Ivan Mauger after he defeated Swedish veteran Soren Sjosten in a run-off.

With no British commitments Michanek had a fairly quiet year. Predictably he topped the Swedish averages, but lost out to 'young pretender' Tommy Jansson in the Swedish Championship. There were efforts made by injury-hit Coventry to sign him mid-season, but his UK appearances were restricted to a handful of open meetings and the World Pairs Final. Belle Vue hosted the event in July. Michanek, partnered by Sjosten (a Belle Vue rider since 1962), retained the title with Australia (Phil Crump and John Boulger) second.

Dag Lovaas also made it to Gothenburg, scoring 6 in his one and only World Final appearance. Dag had a good season, finishing seventh in the final league averages, retaining his Norwegian title and challenging John Louis for the Golden Helmet. (In 1974 the Golden Helmet reverted to a monthly contest as the best of three legs.)

The international balance in the speedway world was changing. For Sweden, Michanek's triumph represented the last stand of a golden generation. Only Tommy Jansson looked set to emulate his predecessors. Although the Swedish Under-21 Championship produced an interesting new name in winner Jan Andersson. For the next decade, Sweden were in decline. Still Swedes were conquering the world in other spheres. This was the year Abba sang 'Waterloo' at the Eurovision Song Contest, launching them on the path to worldwide fame. Such is their legacy, an Abba museum is now under construction in Stockholm!

The nations that were to become the speedway superpowers of the 1980s were just beginning to step up to the plate. In 1973 American Scott Autrey arrived at Exeter. The following year he became a top-line star, a vital factor in Exeter's British League title victory. Back in California a 17-year-old youngster won the handicap main at Costa Mesa's season opener. The name to keep an eye on was Bruce Penhall. The Danish rise was also under way. Finn Thomsen followed Ole Olsen to Wolverhampton and became the first of many to successfully follow Olsen's path to stardom.

With the Poles faltering, the opportunity for Britain to become the major speedway power presented itself. Britain was well equipped for the task, of the 21 riders averaging over 9 in the 1974 British League 10 were English, and an 11th was Scot Jim McMillan.

Division Two had produced a stream of fresh talent, but change was in the air. Division Two had grown up, promoters wanted to be more than feeder tracks servicing their big brothers in the top league. Riders, such as John Jackson, were discovering that a career as a Division Two 'big fish' could be an attractive alternative to becoming a Division One journeyman. After 1974 Division Two ceased to be, as the lower league underwent a re-branding, becoming the New National League in 1975.

With Britain winning the World Team Cup again speedway had a high profile. Barry Briggs even appeared on 'This is your Life'.

1974 marked the first occasion a rider received a testimonial. Halifax's experienced Eric Boocock became the first recipient. At the other end of the scale a youngster who went on to become one of Reading's most prolific point scorers first emerged in second-half racing. Controversy surrounded the diminutive Mitch Shirra, his season ending prematurely because he was found to be only 14. The following year he rode in the New National League for Coatbridge despite still being too young. Interestingly the 1976 'Who's Who of Speedway lists his date of birth as 27.9.58 , later publications give 27.9.**59** as his birth date.

During the summer Reading Football Club acquired a new nickname. 'The Biscuitmen' no longer seemed appropriate; the decision by Huntley & Palmers to cease production in Reading had been made public in November 1972. A competition in the *Reading Chronicle* came up with 'The Royals'. So the year ended with a new name for the football team, and the foundations of a new stadium for the Racers emerging from the rubbish at Smallmead.

1975 – Roaring Back

The previous autumn's rumours of speedway opening at Slough or Aldershot evaporated and the focus switched to the race to complete Smallmead. Before Christmas, Reading had been confirmed as starters for 1975. Wet weather slowed construction at Smallmead and the original target for the 'Grand Opening' against Ipswich drifted back from March 31.

The biggest hurdle came in the shape of building regulations. Normally planning consent is granted with the caveat that building regulations have to be approved prior to construction. It would appear that little attention was paid to building regulations and come March the Council was threatening enforcement action that could have jeopardised the opening. Thankfully compromises were reached and on the morning of April 28 council officials made their final inspection and gave Fearman the thumbs up.

Five of the Racers team (plus Allied Presentations director Len Silver) took to the new track for a practice the week before.

The drive to the new stadium from the centre of town was fairly unexceptional. It took you past the parade of shops on Whitley Street where the 'Wilkins Family' lived, and reality TV was born. (The fly-on-the-wall documentary called 'The Family', produced by Paul Watson, first aired in 1974). On the other side of Whitley Street is Milman Road, where Marianne Faithfull grew up. Then down the hill and onto the Basingstoke Road, past the Gillette's factory and on up to the junction with Bennet Road. Situated by that junction were a couple of buildings occupied by Racal, then a fairly low-profile electronics company; subsequently it spawned Vodaphone now one of the ten largest companies in the UK. A few hundred yards down Bennet Road on the left the household refuse tip still operated, then over a small bridge and into the vast expanse of the new stadium's car park[20].

On the first night huge queues of traffic built up along the Basingstoke Road as 8-10,000 spectators (estimates vary) headed towards their new home. A 45 minute delay in the start allowed them to get in. On walking through the turnstiles the first thing that you really noticed was the centre 'green' an uneven expanse of mud. Round it ran the new track, slightly shorter than Tilehurst (307 metres against 329 metres). Because Smallmead had been built from scratch whereas the Tilehurst track had to be accommodated within an existing stadium the shape was better, the bends more rounded. Maintenance would be the responsibility of Eddie Lack (who as a rider had partnered World Champion Jack Young in the 1951 Edinburgh team). He carried out the task for three years until succeeded by Dougie Harris.

Looking beyond the track, neat terracing made of pinned wooden planks built up with soil provided viewing from the four bends. In front of the Geoff Curtis and Long bars on the home straight the seating area lacked seats! Seating finally arrived in July.

The cost, previously quoted at £200,000, exceeded £250,000. For Reading fans though, that evening was priceless.

The late start to the season meant no warm-up challenges, it was straight into league action with Hull the first visitors. Jim McMillan won the first race at Smallmead, thus becoming the track record holder for seven days. Second-placed Anders Michanek carrying an injury from grasstracking the previous day pulled out of the meeting. Fortunately reserve Bob Humphreys provided excellent cover. His paid 15 maximum ensured that Racers ran out comfortable winners by 48 points to 30.

---

20 The bridge over Foundry Brook was not ready for opening night, and Commercial Road provided an alternative access route. Building a stadium on a refuse tip is asking for trouble. There was some settling in the car park, which resulted in a call for the driver of a 'speedway special' Reading Corporation Bus to rescue it from the car park where it was sinking. My recollection is that this occurred at the second meeting, but I wouldn't swear to it. Larger crowds and lower car ownership meant that there was plenty of demand for the 'speedway specials'.

A packed stadium awaits the start of a new era on Smallmead's opening night. Left to right: Bengt Jansson, Mick Bell and Anders Michanek lead off the parade. (EP)

Reading tracked four of the team that last rode together in 1973. The three newcomers were Bob Humphreys, John Davis and Bengt Jansson. However, the formation of the new team could not be described as straightforward. The tortuous path to the final line-up had many twists and turns, including a court injunction!

Lovaas and May had indicated they wanted transfers, Mick Bell wanted a Saturday track, Bernie Leigh was happy at Swindon and Anders Michanek was caught up in the ban on commuting Swedes. Positive news that the Swedes would be back was tempered by the indications that Michanek would not be among them. Original rider control allocations gave Reading Bengt Jansson and Tommy Pettersson, augmented by returning Lovaas, May, Bell and Leigh. Pettersson, the 1972 Swedish Junior Champion, finally made it to Britain in 1977, but he averaged less than 4 in a handful of matches for Leicester and Bristol.

When Anders Michanek had a change of heart, Jansson and Pettersson dropped out of the Reading line-up. In February Aussie Bob Humphreys became the next addition to the team sheet. After four years at King's Lynn a poor 1974 had convinced him to ask for a move.

With one slot to fill, chaos became the order of the day when on March 21 a Speedway Control Board inquiry ruled that Ole Olsen could stay at Wolverhampton, overturning his allocation to Oxford. This necessitated some last-minute changes. Dag Lovaas would fill the number one gap at Oxford, and in return Reading would receive John Davis. The Rider Control Committee decreed that with Olsen back at Monmore Green, Wolves no longer needed Bengt Jansson, who reverted to Reading.

To complicate matters, Jansson and Davis made their season debuts for Wolves and Oxford on the same day as the inquiry verdict. To make matters even more bizarre, John Davis guested for himself the following night when Oxford rode at Coventry!

As Reading prepared for their first match in 18 months, Wolverhampton promoter Mike Parker considered his options. With Olsen reluctant to return to Monmore Green he was unwilling to relinquish his claim on Jansson. On the eve of Reading's return fixture, a Spring Gold Cup match at Hackney, Jansson rode at Wimbledon in the Daily Express Spring Classic. During the meeting he was served with an injunction preventing him from riding. The injunction also prevented Reg Fearman "advertising Bengt Jansson as a member of the Reading team".

Within a week matters had been sorted. Olsen returned to Wolverhampton with the promise of a transfer at the end of the season and Bengt 'Banga' Jansson made his debut for the Racers at King's Lynn. He scored 9 as Racers drew. Bob Humphreys (10+1) enjoyed the return to his former club.

After April's excitement the rest of the season seemed a bit of a let down. For everyone involved the sheer exhilaration of seeing Reading back on track made the year a great one, but results were acceptable rather than exceptional.

Racers didn't record an away win in any competition until the second week of July with their first visit to Hull. The inevitable Michanek maximum was supplemented by 12 from Mick Bell and paid 11 from Jansson as Racers ran out winners 42-36.

Despite failing to win away, Reading qualified for the Spring Gold Cup Final where they were soundly thrashed by Newport. The Wasps also knocked Racers out of the cup, winning both legs. 1975 became the high point in the Welsh club's speedway existence. Led by Phil Crump (bought from King's Lynn the year before for £1,750[21]) and benefiting from the presence of Neil Street they came very close to winning the league. Key to their success was the Street four-valve engine which soon revolutionised speedway.

Crump's victories in 1975 included the Manpower Trophy. A crowd of 10,000 watched him drop his only point when passed by Ole Olsen. The World Champion chalked up four wins (including one over Michanek from the back), but shed a chain while leading his other ride.

Reading finished the season in sixth place. Although unfamiliar with their new surroundings Racers only lost one league match at home – to eventual champions Ipswich. That came in August when only Bernie Leigh (10+2) provided much support to Michanek.

After the win at Hull, Reading picked up a second away win (also in July) at Cradley. A belated burst saw them gain three more away victories in late September and early October. These came from trips to Coventry, Hackney and Poole. John Davis scored heavily in all three matches. Richard May, in an otherwise undistinguished season scored 11 at Poole. Right from the practice where he had been the only rider to express dissatisfaction with the new track it appeared that he hankered for a return to Poole, his 1974 team.

Three Reading riders improved on their starting averages. Humphreys scored solidly in the first few weeks of the season, while Leigh's run of form came later in the campaign. Most significant though was the progress made by John Davis. He only added half a point to his average (7.37), but gained international recognition. Still only 20, Davis represented his country in Poland, Sweden and Australia, winning 15 caps. In October the first staging of the Geoff Curtis Memorial Trophy went to a run-off with Davis, Dag Lovaas and Tommy Jansson tied on 14 points. Davis won the run-off. Just four days after Reading commemorated Curtis, another Anzac rider lost his life on track. Wolverhampton's Gary Peterson (a participant in Tilehurst's inaugural meeting) lost control while challenging for second place, hit a floodlight pylon, and died on the way to hospital.

Skipper Mick Bell had a quiet year. Injury at Ipswich meant he missed a Racers fixture for the first time since he rejoined Reading at the start of 1971. This ended a club record sequence that still stands in 2008 of 148 official fixtures without missing a single one.

Richard May's form in the early part of the season gave cause for concern; in June his official average fell to 3.50. He fell from number four in Reading's starting averages to number seven by the end of 1975. May's average was down by over a point, but even worse Bengt Jansson's fell by nearly 2

---

21 What a bargain!

Reading's first ever 5-1 at Smallmead. Bernie Leigh (left) and Bob Humphreys (right) lead Hull's Robin Amundsen in heat 2 of the opening night match. (EP)

Already 32 years old, Jansson's days as a world class rider were drawing to a close. With four World Final appearances, all ending in top five finishes, and seven World Team Cup Final appearances for Sweden he had a record to be proud of. Seven years before only a run-off with Ivan Mauger stood between him and the world crown. Apart from a maximum against league leaders Belle Vue at the end of June which was the first of five consecutive paid double-figure scores in ten days there was little to shout about. He did manage to be ever present – a rare feat for a Swede[22].

Although Michanek's average had fallen, it still exceeded eleven in league matches. Only by comparing with the magnificent feats of 1973 could 1975 be described as a failure. He didn't retain his world title, finishing second in the Wembley final to Ole Olsen. Michanek and Olsen met in heat 4; Anders came third, the only points he dropped all night. John Louis joined them on the rostrum, becoming the first Englishman to do so since Peter Craven in 1962. Making his third World Final appearance that evening was experienced Pole Henryk Glucklich.

Michanek did establish one impressive record in 1975. With the aid of Tommy Jansson he notched up his third World Pairs title in a row. The next time Sweden won gold in any of the three world championships (individual, team and pairs) would be 15 years away. As well as top scoring for Sweden in the World Team Cup Final, Anders also appeared in the World Longtrack Final. He finished sixth, two places down on the previous year, but one ahead of a young German called Hans Wassermann.

This year the Swedish Championship did go to the nation's top rider, Michanek winning his second national title. One prestigious title that eluded Michanek in 1975 was the Golden Helmet. Nominated to challenge Phil Crump, the first leg went to the holder. In the return at Reading a 2-1 Michanek victory ensured the battle would go to a deciding leg. Incidentally the Smallmead track record was lowered in all three second leg races. At the end of May the two protagonists arrived at Poole for the showdown. In the first race the two riders fell, with Crump being adjudged the cause of the stoppage. The referee awarded the race to Michanek.

22 If only Anders Michanek could have managed that.

The Swede could not take place in the remaining heats due to injury and the tie went to Crump.

With four ever-presents, and only Michanek missing more than three matches there were few opportunities for juniors. Bracknell-based Colin Richardson took those that were available. As an inexperienced 16-year-old with just a handful of matches for Eastbourne under his belt he graduated from second halves at Smallmead to a place in the team. He scored paid 7 on his debut and went on to make two further league appearances in 1975. He switched to Wimbledon the following year and went on to have a respectable career, which included winning the National League Riders Championship in 1977. He retired in 1986 after making over 300 British League appearances and nearly 200 in the National League.

Another 16-year-old made an even bigger impact on British speedway in 1975. Michael Lee finished his first season with a Division One team with an average of nearly 7.5 points. By October a first full maximum had been credited to his name. He scored it against Reading.

Few people anticipated another new arrival to the British League, that of Zenon Plech. In September Hackney did a deal with the Polish authorities to allow the charismatic star to ride in Britain. He made a quiet debut (in the Southern Riders qualifier at Reading), but a week later top scored for Hackney as they were thrashed 53-25 at Smallmead. Plech's presence opened the way for more Poles to travel across the English Channel. Reading fielded three over the next three years[23].

Allied Presentations director Frank Higley took over as Racers team manager in 1975. Dave Lanning made his first appearance in the Reading set up – as announcer. His predecessor David Hamilton acquired the title 'Master of Ceremonies'.

With a new track settling in, there were plenty of track record holders. Jim McMillan's place was quickly taken by Michanek, who lost it to Phil Crump before regaining it and then losing it to Crump again. Bengt Jansson got a share of Crump's record, but two races later Michanek regained his place in the record books. And it was still only June.

In July Smallmead hosted the World Team Cup qualifying round, comfortably won by England. Peter Collins, Dave Jessup and John Louis all scored double figures. Of their opponents, only Ivan Mauger made it into double figures. Mauger also ensured his name was in the programme every week by equalling Michanek's 61.8 track record. Nobody else managed to match or beat that time for the remainder of the season.

Team: Anders Michanek 10.91, John Davis 7.37, Bengt Jansson 7.06, Bernie Leigh 5.59, Bob Humphreys 5.56, Mick Bell 5.21, Richard May 4.99

---

23 Another event that has helped shape British speedway in the decades to come occurred in June when the UK voted 'yes' in a referendum on membership of the European Community. Newly elected Conservative leader Margaret Thatcher actively campaigned for the yes vote.

The scores were tied at 30-all. Racers had gone top of the league four days earlier and another away win was within their grasp. Reading's Dave Jessup lined up against home hero Dave (brother of Chris) Morton. Both riders were averaging nearly 11 points a match. Morton sped into the lead, but on the third lap Jessup made his move. As Jessup went inside him down went Morton. On went the white[24] exclusion light. With Jessup out Reading's hopes looked precarious. Very soon they plummeted to zero as no Reading rider appeared for the re-run, or the final two heats. Angered over the decision Reading had staged a walk out.

Their actions cost £500 in fines and compensation, but had a much more damaging effect. The momentum of Reading's challenge for the league title stopped dead. They arrived at Hackney on August 6 with four wins and a draw from nine away matches plus a 100% home record. After three consecutive away wins and a 40-38 home win over title rivals Belle Vue there could be no doubting that Reading were serious contenders.

After the Hackney histrionics Racers didn't win away again until mid-October. Worse still they dropped 6 points at home. Draws against White City and Newport were followed by defeats at the hands of Ipswich and Hackney.

The great irony of the events at Waterden Road is that in the previous Monday's programme Reg Fearman wrote a strongly worded editorial defending referees. In October a grudging (and slightly tongue in cheek) apology appeared in the Smallmead programme:

> *"The Reading management express sincere regret that the Hackney and Reading public were robbed of the opportunity of watching one of the best club sides in the world after heat 10 on 6th August."*

It was probably not a coincidence that within a month of the walkout Hackney boss Len Silver had severed his links with Allied Presentations, selling his stake to Higley, Dore and Fearman.

Two other events prior to the Hackney horror affected Racers title hopes – one detrimentally, and one for the better. Denis Healey and Marks and Spencers were at the centre of these two events.

Ever since the 'oil crisis' of 1973/74 inflation had been running at double digit rates, peaking at 26.9% in August 1975. During the summer of 1976 Healey went cap in hand to the International Monetary Fund and negotiated a £2.3 billion loan. Economic uncertainty caused the value of the pound to slump. At the beginning of the year a pound bought 8.9 Swedish kroner, in the second week of June it had fallen to 7.9. For commuting Swedes like Bengt Jansson and Bernt Persson that represented a cut in their earnings of over 10%. Both decided to pack their bags and returned home in early July. Jansson had started the season well but immediately prior to his departure mechanical problems had depressed his average.

Although Racers response to Jansson's departure consisted of three away wins in quick succession, in the longer term guests didn't match Jansson's scoring power. An August Bank Holiday morning defeat at Exeter started an away sequence that went: lost 40-38, lost 40-38, lost 41-37, lost 40-38. Mick Bell's alarm clock probably cost Reading a win at Exeter. It failed to go off, and caused Mick Bell to miss his fourth fixture in six years as a Racer.

The last of the three events, but the first chronologically happened at Marks and Spencers in Broad Street. During the winter BSPA chairman Reg Fearman had persuaded the Polish authorities to allow four of their riders to spend the season in Britain. Of the four only 21-

24 The ultimately pointless change from white to green helmet colour would be many years in the future. From the 1940s to the 1990s the visiting team helmet colours were white and yellow/black quarters.

year-old Eugeniusz Blaszak had any form, having come third in the previous year's Polish Junior Championship. Blaszak ended up at Reading, replacing Poole bound Richard May. It soon became apparent that he was the only one of the four that could compete in the British League.

He quickly became popular, scoring enough points to justify persevering with him. The fall of the Berlin Wall was still 13 years in the future, and the availability and variety of consumer goods would have seemed miraculous to a person who had grown up in a Communist state. Temptation got the better of 'Yoogy' and a store detective apprehended him. His haul consisted of one pair of socks, one pair of pants, a pair of swimming trunks and a casual shirt, total value £7 (about £40 at today's prices). At the time of his arrest he claimed to be testing the store's security system! On April 26 he was convicted of shoplifting and given a conditional discharge. The Polish speedway authorities took a dim view of events. After a month of efforts to keep him at Smallmead (during which he continued to ride) Blaszak found himself recalled to Poland.

Marks & Spencer's favourite customer – Eugeniusz Blaszak. (DA)

Blaszak disappeared for two years, finally resurfacing in 1979 when he made the first of four Polish Championship Final appearances. In 1980 he took runner-up spot in the Polish Golden Helmet, and continued riding until 1988.

The Polish authorities provided a replacement for Blaszak. They were probably embarrassed by the poor showing of the original quartet, and sent a much stronger performer to fill the vacant team berth at Reading. Boleslaw Proch's trophy cabinet already contained the Polish Junior Championship and Polish Silver Helmet, both of which he won in 1975. After just ten matches his average broke through the 6-point barrier. Both his scores and riding were erratic. His best performance came at Cradley where he top scored with 9 as Racers went down 40-38. The home team's top scorer, John Boulger, bagged an incredible 21-point maximum. (Cradley used rider replacement for devaluation blighted Bernt Persson.) Proch also recorded a victory over Peter Collins in a late season challenge match, ensuring him a place near the top of Reg Fearman's shopping list for the following year's team.

The year had started very quietly. Once again Anders Michanek announced his retirement from British speedway. Although it turned out not to be permanent, it did lead to Reg Fearman seeking a replacement. England star Dave Jessup (23 in March) wanted away from Leicester. In January a transfer fee of £4,500 secured his services for Reading. With rider control allocations announced in January, Reading were set to field Jessup and a new Pole instead of Michanek and May. Davis, Bell, Leigh and Humphreys all returned, along with Bengt Jansson (the exchange rate had improved).

Jessup was appointed captain, and Davis signed a new three-year contract with the infamous (but almost certainly unenforceable) 'no marriage clause'. Racers fans acquired a new source for their latest news with the launch of Radio 210 Thames Valley in March.

Facing the threat of redevelopment, neighbours Oxford moved to White City. Oxford re-emerged in the National League where they spent the next seven years. The British League grew from 18 to 19 teams with the elevation of National League champions Birmingham. The Brummies faced a tough baptism, suffering defeat in each of their first four home league matches. Low point for the Brummies was a 51-27 thrashing at the hands of Reading. Jessup, Davis and Leigh remained unbeaten as Racers chalked up a club record away win. Silencers were introduced to the British League.

On March 15, the first official day of the season, 6,000 fans paid £1 (children 50p) to see Dave Jessup score a maximum on his debut. For the first time since 1969 Reading won their opening fixture, beating Hackney 44-34.

Being a speedway supporter was much easier 30 years ago. Reading went on to stage 34 meetings, racing every Monday until the final meeting fell victim to the weather on October 25. The re-staging on November 1 was the last on the British calendar making Reading first to open and last to close. Motor sport continued at Smallmead in November and December with the introduction of stock cars. These were promoted by former speedway rider Trevor Redmond.

A massive crowd turned out on a hot Sunday afternoon for the 1976 Southern Riders Championship. Heat 1 shown here featured: Terry Betts (1), Michael Lee (2), Kevin Holden (3) and Boley Proch (4). (DA)

In addition to all those Mondays, Reading staged one Sunday meeting: the Southern Riders Championship (1-2-3: Louis, Simmons, Davis) in June. A crowd of 12,000 streamed through the turnstiles for this meeting. A similar sized crowd witnessed the Manpower in September. Peter Collins stormed to victory with a 15-point maximum in meeting tinged with nostalgia owing to the appearance of Anders Michanek. Fresh from the previous day's World Team Cup Final at White City, Michanek finished runner-up to newly crowned World Champion Collins.

13 days earlier Collins followed in the tyre tracks of Belle Vue's other PC – Peter Craven.

His title triumph gave England its first World Champion since Craven's 1962 victory. Malcolm Simmons and Phil Crump joined him on the rostrum in a final notable for the lack of Scandanavian representation. 1976 is remembered for its long hot summer, June 26 turned out to be the hottest day of them all. On that day a hot and sweaty Wembley witnessed the Inter-Continental Final, won by Collins. The competition proved too hot for Olsen and Michanek, both were eliminated. Michanek actually led the field after winning his first two races!

An even bigger shock took place in the World Team Cup. England failed to qualify. Australia beat them at Ipswich in May. Jessup scored 8 for England; Bob Humphreys filled the reserve berth for the victorious Aussies but didn't get a ride. In one of the closest finals ever, Australia ended on top. Garry Middleton replaced Humphreys at reserve for Australia, but there was Racer interest elsewhere with Boley Proch at reserve for runners-up Poland and Sweden fielding Michanek (11) and Bengt Jansson (1).

For Sweden the season consisted of one low point followed by another. The lowest of them came in May during a Swedish World Championship round when an accident brought a premature end to Tommy Jansson's life. A world finalist at eighteen in 1971, many people considered Jansson to be a World Champion in the making. Just a week before his death he retained the Golden Helmet winning both legs 2-1. His opponent, averaging over 11 at the time, was Reading's Dave Jessup.

Jessup started the season with four consecutive maximums and finished sixth in the league averages. He more than adequately filled Michanek's shoes, and as an added bonus he never missed a single league or cup fixture. Jessup won the Daily Express Spring Classic and the Geoff Curtis Memorial Trophy.

Runner-up in the Curtis Memorial was John Davis. He formed a formidable spearhead with Jessup, lifting his average in official fixtures from 7.37 to 9.33. Only Belle Vue (Collins and Morton) and Ipswich (Louis and Sanders) had stronger top twos. The 4-valve became ubiquitous in 1976, but Davis stayed with the 2-valve. His season ended with a hospital trip in the home match against Hackney, one that probably cost Racers the points.

In 1976 the Soviet Union toured Britain. This shot of first-bend action at Smallmead features (left to right) Bob Humphreys, Grigori Khlinovsky, Nikolai Kornev and Mick Bell. (EP)

Bernie Leigh also upped his average by over a point, overtaking Bengt Jansson for the third heat leader spot. His best score of the season came when guesting for Hackney at Hull – 15+1. Sadly he got a duck when he returned to Hull in Racers colours. He did score 12+3 for Racers at Newport – from eight rides. Speedway is littered with bizarre rules, and 1976's rider replacement rule comes into that category. When operating rider replacement the rider immediately above in the averages could take one ride, and any rider with an average below the others. This meant Leigh could have three of Jansson's rider replacement rides, as well as a tactical substitution. He rode in heats: 2, 3, 5, 6, 8, 9, 10 and 12.

Bob Humphreys had good reason to be satisfied with his season, increasing his average by almost a point. He rode in every Racers match. He certainly had no excuse for missing home meetings, he lived in a caravan in the Smallmead car park. Highlights of Bob's season included a 9-point haul in the Manpower and a maximum against Halifax.

Also scoring a maximum against Halifax was Mick Bell. Retirement beckoned for Bell, although he later re-emerged in Coventry's colours. Bell did three years for the Bees before returning to Reading as team manager in 1980.

Reading's second-half programme produced Ian Gledhill from Leamington Spa. He made seven league appearances, scoring 5 against Sheffield. At the end of July he joined Eastbourne on loan, achieving paid 7 on his debut. Also making their National League debuts in Eastbourne colours that year were Roger Abel and Colin Ackroyd.

Reg Fearman was quick off the mark, staging the 'Jubilee Trophy' to commemorate the Queen's Silver Jubilee – a year early! Winner Ole Olsen picked up the Smallmead track record to add to his Tilehurst one. *Speedway Star* reported an attendance of 9,000. With each race sponsored Olsen came away with: a pair of silver goblets, car first-aid kit and fire extinguisher, crash helmet, car radio, and a bottle of champagne.

Speedway at Smallmead looked to be here for the long haul. The accounts showed a healthy turnover of £318,000, although an interesting note revealed that the company's bookkeeper had defrauded Allied Presentations of £25,749.65. This resulted in a three-year prison sentence for the bookkeeper. As if that wasn't enough the uninsured loss of the safe and its contents cost the company another £2,500.

Back in the town though, the era of 'beer, bulbs and biscuits' was coming to an end. Huntley & Palmers baked their last biscuit at their Kings Road factory and Suttons Seeds decamped to Devon. Instead the national offices of large companies were migrating to Reading. Most visible of these was the Metal Box HQ near the station opened in 1975. Thankfully for the inhabitants of the Smallmead bars the beer stayed put!

Team: Dave Jessup 10.35, John Davis 9.33, Bernie Leigh 6.75, Bob Humphreys 6.42, Bengt Jansson 6.36, Boley Proch 5.37, Mick Bell 5.16, (Eugeniusz Blaszak 3.67), (Ian Gledhill 2.32)

1977 – The First Victims of the Points Limit

Only in speedway would an event called the Spring Gold Cup be staged at the end of October. One meeting (a league match against Wolves) had already been fogged off in October before Reading beat Poole 48-30 in the second leg of the final on October 31. At last Racers had some silverware to show for a season that promised so much but ultimately delivered so little.

The 1977 league title is the one that got away. Reading fans left the stadium at the end of the season believing that 'we wus robbed'. Not until 2006 would that feeling be so intense again.

John Davis celebrated the new year in Australia with his British Lions team mates. Another Racer made an impression Down Under that winter – Boley Proch. Meanwhile at the BSPA conference in Malta promoters were declaring the death of rider control. They unveiled a totally new concept: 'the points limit'.

A combination of Boley Proch and the points limit created mid-year turmoil for Reading, cruelly dashing their championship aspirations.

Reg Fearman came away from the conference looking for replacements for Bengt Jansson and Mick Bell and with Proch's availability dependent on the Polish authorities. Reading's unofficial motto (and one that has generally served them well) is 'when in need sign a Swede'. Fearman tried to sign Lars Ake Andersson, an unexpected pick for Sweden's World Team Cup squad at White City the previous September. Top scorer for Swedish champions Njudungarna (Vetlanda), he surprised pundits with a useful 5-point tally that day. Andersson never rode in the British League. Fearman produced a surprise of his own – he re-signed 'Banga' Jansson, despite a further fall in the sterling/kroner exchange rate. Proch then dropped out of consideration after breaking his ankle in Australia.

Reading's search for new reserves continued; an approach to Weymouth number one Martin Yeates established that he wished to remain in the National League. The hunt moved abroad and three foreigners came into contention. Glyn Taylor already had one British season under his belt. He spent 1973 as a second string for Division Two Crewe. His father Chum won the 1966 Australian Championship and reached the 1960 World Final. Bo Jansson was also the son of a world finalist (Joel in 1958), and the brother of much-missed Tommy. The third signing, Hans Wassermann, came from West Germany. In 1976 he reached the Continental Final of the World Championship and scored heavily in the German League.

These three were supplemented by number eight Ian Gledhill, and Racers went into the season with four riders competing for the reserve berths.

Bo Jansson's Reading career couldn't have been much shorter. In the opening league fixture at home to Birmingham, aware of the need to make an impression, he sped out of the gate and straight into the first-bend fence. He left the track by ambulance, and although fit enough to compete in the following week's second half he was soon released. Jansson's absence for the rest of the Birmingham match gave fellow reserve Ian Gledhill the chance to shine. With 8 points and two wins, including one over Brummie heat leader Alan Grahame, he did just that.

Racers won 52-26, and 48 hours later completed the double with an unconvincing 41-37 win at Perry Barr. Birmingham's Midland neighbours Cradley were the next visitors. After years as speedway also-rans things were changing. New owner Dan McCormack made an immediate impact. After four years as Cradley United the name reverted back to Cradley Heath, much to the delight of the Dudley Wood faithful. McCormack had been general manager at Newcastle in 1970 where Anders Michanek was the number one. This probably helped him pull off the dramatic signature of Michanek. The prospect of seeing Anders again had the Smallmead terraces buzzing with anticipation.

There was to be no let down. In a meeting that ranks as one of the best-ever seen at Smallmead Michanek came, saw and conquered. When he completed his full maximum by winning heat 12 Heathens scented victory. Only a 5-1 in the final heat could give Reading a win. With Bernt Persson (the only rider faster than Michanek) lining up for Cradley it was going to be a tough task. Racers hopes rested on John Davis and Bernie Leigh. The duo showed in front, but found Persson snapping at their heels for the entire race. After 64.6 heart-stopping seconds victory belonged to Reading.

Two days later Davis and Leigh had an easier time in heat 12 at White City. Kai Niemi and Gordon Kennett both fell giving the Reading a pair a 5-0 that put Racers ahead for the first time in a match where they had trailed by 8 points. A Jessup/Jansson 4-2 in the final heat sealed the match – White City 36 Reading 41.

At the end of April, a crowd of 20,000 squeezed into Eastville to witness the return of speedway to Bristol. The squarish track round a football pitch and shared with greyhounds proved difficult to master. Dave Jessup and Swindon's Martin Ashby both pulled out after one ride. John Davis picked up a very nasty shoulder injury that kept him out of the saddle for three weeks.

Despite Davis's absence Racers went to Ipswich the following week for a Spring Gold Cup match, and won. Reigning league champions Ipswich came into this fixture with 58 consecutive home wins! In a 42-36 win Jessup scored 17, guest David Gagen 12+1 and Hans Wassermann 7+3 – his best yet.

Reading went seven weeks between league matches at Smallmead. With a shortage of opportunities they plummeted to 15th in the league table. Wassermann's scoring guaranteed him one of the reserve berths, but Glyn Taylor found it hard going. Ian Gledhill joined Stoke on loan at the beginning of May. Boley Proch's ankle had healed and he wanted to return to Reading.

On June 6 Proch returned and Taylor packed his bags for the return trip to Australia. A month later on July 6 with consecutive away wins at Leicester, Wolverhampton, Hackney and Hull Racers had made a dramatic climb to second in the league table.

The match at Leicester coincided with the Queen's Silver Jubilee. The match-winning contribution came from Wassermann with paid nine. The following month Reading commemorated the Silver Jubilee (for the second time!) with a star-studded individual meeting. Appropriately Englishmen filled the top three places: 1st Michael Lee, 2nd Peter Collins, 3rd Dave Jessup.

An exhilarating performance on track gave Racers a 45-33 win at Hackney on July 1. Bengt Jansson riding at the track where he spent six seasons at the height of his career turned back time and produced a superlative performance. He passed both Hackney riders in his first two rides and came from the back again in his final ride to complete a magnificent maximum. But events off-track were taking a disquieting turn.

Considerable animus existed between Reading and Hackney following the previous year's walk-out. It flared up again in May when Dave Jessup team rode Bernie Leigh home in a World Championship qualifier at Hackney. It resulted in Leigh going through at the expense of home rider Keith White, and Len Silver was furious. When Reading turned up at Waterden Road for the league match Silver made a protest about the Reading line-up, arguing that if Proch rode it should mean the dropping of Wassermann.

Within a week the BSPA management committee had allowed Reading to carry on including both riders in their team. This over-ruled the Rider Control Sub-committee's recommendation and prompted all three members to resign. Martin Rogers, Len Silver(!) and John Berry's actions in resigning prompted the Management Committee to reconvene, and on July 15 they reversed the original decision forcing Reading to release a rider. Reg Fearman appealed and Racers operated a rotation system while waiting for the appeal to be heard. On

August 4 Reading lost their appeal. The following week a rider swap sent Proch to Leicester and Dougie Underwood in the other direction.

Reading had good cause to feel aggrieved. Now, after 30 years, most speedway fans are familiar with the operation of a points limit; then it was a novelty. The rules were fairly rudimentary and much of the debate over its operation confused.

Years before Jeremy Doncaster joined Reading, Hans Wassermann is introduced to a very different donkey. (EP)

Many of the arguments put forward seemed to miss the matter that it was an average-based system. In practice Reading started the season with Glyn Taylor (assessed 6-point average) and replaced him with Boley Proch (average 5.58). The basic rule prevented teams from bringing in new riders if the team average exceeded 48, but only requiring them to de-strengthen them if the average rose above 52. Work permits were introduced into the argument, a complete red herring. Reg Fearman pointed out that West Germany belonged to the EEC so Hans Wassermann shouldn't need a work permit.

Bristol had already been allowed to breach the limit; Wolverhampton were permanently fielding guests for a non-existent rider; White City used rider replacement throughout the season for a rider who had retired before the season started (Dag Lovaas); And Hull used permanent rider replacement for a rider who had no intention of appearing in England (Egon Muller). All Reading were doing was re-introducing one of their existing riders into the team. It seemed everyone had a special dispensation!

Had Proch not been injured at the start of the year it is probable he would have been in the starting line-up. The core of Fearman's case was that Reading were not really introducing a new rider. In the context of the flexibility that seemed to be inherent in what was then a new system they were hard done by.

Proch's performances didn't quite match his 1976 form. Only a 10-point haul against King's Lynn in the Spring Gold Cup showed him at his best. The 50-28 win over King's Lynn made Reading the group winners, earning them a head to head with Poole in the final. His form at Leicester picked up a little, but it turned out to be his last experience of the British League.

Boley went on to have a successful domestic career back in Poland. He was a model of consistency finishing between 7th and 12th in the Polish league averages nine times in ten years (from 1977 to 1986). He rode in the final of the Polish Championship eight times, twice finishing second. In 1978 he came runner-up in the Polish Golden Helmet; three years later he went one place better and won it.

Dougie Underwood, a 28-year-old Australian, had ridden for Hull, Scunthorpe and Teesside in Division Two before moving to Leicester full time in 1976. He played a part in an odd incident that year when he rode for Leicester at Swindon; he was the only real Lion in the team that included six guests! He arrived at Reading with a 4.04 average from 27 official fixtures in 1977.

Underwood made his debut on August 15 as Reading dropped their first home point of the season in a draw with Poole. 18-6 down after four races, two 5-1s from Malcolm Simmons and ex-Racer Richard May brought the Pirates back into contention. John Davis's last heat engine failure allowed the Pirates to complete their comeback.

Two weeks later another point went west as Exeter shared the spoils. It could have been worse; the visitors opened up an 8-point lead after just two races and still held it with five heats to go. Reading were still reeling from the morning's drubbing at Exeter. After losing 59-19 (a Division One record defeat) in the now traditional Bank Holiday morning encounter, a draw at home seemed like a good result at the time.

Including the Exeter nightmare Racers lost their first four away league matches after Proch's departure. By the time they rediscovered their form White City had put together a 15-match winning sequence to open up an 8-point gap at the top of the table.

It equalled the longest winning run since the formation of the British League in 1965. White City's chance to set a new record came on September 26. They failed going down to the Racers by 8 points.

The previous day a rare Sunday meeting ended in farce. Neil Middleditch, booked as a guest for Hans Wassermann, stood there perplexed by events. Wassermann missed his flight and turned up at Smallmead prompting visitors Belle Vue to object to the use of Middleditch. Reading protested that Hans couldn't ride without receiving a ban from the German authorities. After 40 minutes the match finally got under way without Middleditch (who had already left the stadium, justifiably exasperated). One heat later the meeting was 'put out of its misery' by a heavy rain storm.

Rain-offs, cup runs and a varied fixture list meant a busy October for Reading. They rode 14 matches, including three double headers, in October. They rounded off their league programme with a flourish, winning three and drawing the fourth of their remaining away encounters.

A particularly satisfying win at Swindon kicked off the month, Racers winning 46-32 despite mechanical problems for Dave Jessup. By the time Racers drew at Belle Vue, the league title had been sewn up by the Rebels. The final table showed White City on 55 points, two ahead of Exeter and third placed Reading. There is no doubt that the use of rider replacement for the entire season for a rider who had retired before it even started sat uneasily against the BSPA management committee's treatment of Proch. Lovaas commenting on his role said[25]: “At least my name was in the programmes, but I suppose they won't be sending me a replica trophy to go with the one from Reading in 1973”.

The Knock-Out Cup still presented Racers with a chance for glory. It had been a long hard road to the final. Racers drew Poole in the first round and took an 8-point lead down to Wimborne Road for the second leg. With the scores tied at 12-all Kevin Holden fell attempting to go round Bob Humphreys. It appeared to be an innocuous crash, but from the frantic activity of the medical staff it quickly became clear that it was serious. Holden died on the track and the meeting was abandoned. A month later a six-ride Jessup maximum ensured that Reading went through.

Halifax provided little opposition in the second round. A 15-point maximum in the away leg from John Davis helped secure victory at Halifax. Tougher opponents presented themselves in the next two rounds. Belle Vue fell to a Doug Underwood paid maximum that contributed to a 51-27 first leg triumph.

---

25 *Speedway Star*, 8 January 1978

A semi-final tie against Bristol left most Racers fans apprehensive. Reading's first visit to Bristol (and Proch's last appearance in the winged wheel) back in August created controversy. After four heats the Racers threatened to walkout claiming the track was too dangerous. After a half-hour delay the match resumed. However, most of the Reading team were only going through the motions and in the remaining nine heats only Bernie Leigh defeated a Bristol rider (which he did twice).

A 16-point lead from the home leg didn't look like enough, particularly after Bernie Leigh picked up an arm injury at Wimbledon the night before the return leg. A good team performance ensured that those worries evaporated, Reading winning 83-73 on aggregate.

Ten days later King's Lynn visited Smallmead for the first leg of the final along with 7,000 fans. Michael Lee (15-point maximum) and Terry Betts (12 from 5) kept the Stars in contention. However, the crucial psychological blow was struck in heat 12 when Ian Turner passed Dave Jessup to join Lee in a 5-1. Jessup's 8-point tally was his lowest home score of the season. Had Wassermann not scored paid 10 (losing only to Lee) King's Lynn could have easily won.

10,000 people turned up at King's Lynn on October 26, most of them hoping to see the Stars pick up their first major trophy. Jessup made amends for his first leg performance with a 15-point maximum. When he lined up in the final heat with tactical substitute John Davis only a 5-1 could stop a King's Lynn victory. For three and seven eighths laps the 5-1 was on, but Lee roared under Davis. Only 1973's cup final had been closer, and Reading had come out second best in that one too. Bernie Leigh's injury probably swung the tie against Reading; Ian Gledhill replaced him in both legs scoring only 2 points at home and none away.

The 1977 England World Team Cup squad at Smallmead (from left to right): John Berry (manager), Michael Lee, John Davis, Peter Collins, Malcolm Simmons and Dave Jessup. (EP)

In 1977 England ruled the globe. No opponent could make a match of it against the England team, so they rode against a Rest of the World team. Dave Jessup rode in all five Tests; John Davis gained a cap in the Reading staged fourth Test. Jessup would want to forget the Reading match; he failed to score as England went down by 16 points. England regained the World Team Cup, Jessup scoring 9 and reserve John Davis coming in twice winning both times.

In the World Championship both Jessup and Davis fell at the penultimate hurdle – the Inter-Continental Final. Davis's aspirations were cruelly shattered when Ivan Mauger, desperate for points, crashed into him. To the disbelief of the partisan White City crowd referee Gunter Sorber excluded Davis for unfair riding. Needing points in his final heat Jessup fell, leaving both Reading riders a point short of qualification. (The White City meeting gave British fans their first chance to see Bruce Penhall.) Davis watched the World Final from the pits having qualified as reserve. In truly foul conditions Mauger won his fifth title. Swedish hopes rested on Anders Michanek, but his 8 points didn't even make him top Swede. That honour went to 'Banga' Jansson (9).

Dave Jessup ended the year with his name on the Smallmead track record; the timekeeper clocked him at 60.8 in a pairs meeting in May. His 498 points in official fixtures set a new club record for points in a single season. Both Jessup and Davis finished in the top ten in the league averages.

Hans Wassermann improved visibly as he adapted to the British League. His heavy continental schedule did cause a few headaches though. Highlight of his season came at Belle Vue where, together with Egon Muller, he gained the bronze medal position in the World Pairs Final. England were easy winners and Sweden relying entirely on Anders Michanek (16) second. Wassermann must have been disappointed with his poor display in the World Longtrack Final, surprisingly won by Michanek.

Economically the mid-1970s had been a difficult time, but the strength of the British speedway boom had insulated most tracks from these problems. 1977 saw the first indications that this was no longer the case. Falling attendances (Reading reported a slight fall), rising costs accelerated by the spread of four valves and a lack of riders left British speedway slightly bruised despite its global dominance.

A rapidly emerging challenge was coming from Denmark. Finn Thomsen qualified for his first World Final; he also won Reading's Manpower Trophy. Wolverhampton gave Hans Nielsen his first British outings. Dane Alf Busk won the first European (now World) Under-21 Championship. Tied in fourth were Nielsen and Zajtun Gafurov (father of Renat).

With Reading FC once more relegated to Division Four of the Football League, Reading's speedway fraternity were confident that theirs was the number one sporting team in Reading. That would change to an unimaginable degree over the next three decades. But who could have realised that when the first issue of *Thames Valley Trader* appeared on the newsagents' shelves in 1977 - probably not even proprietor John Madejski.

Team: Dave Jessup 10.32, John Davis 9.80. Bengt Jansson 6.80, Bob Humphreys 6.05, Bernie Leigh 5.88, Hans Wassermann 5.58, Boley Proch 4.85, Doug Underwood 4.37, Ian Gledhill 3.27, (Glyn Taylor 2.53)

1978 – Backsliding

It is hard to find anything positive to say about 1978. Racers spent much of the season one place off the bottom of the league; crowds were down; there was off-track unrest and there were two career-ending injuries.

On paper the team looked reasonable. Jessup, Davis, Leigh, Humphreys, Underwood and Wassermann all returned. Experienced Pole Henryk Glucklich replaced departing Bengt Jansson.

Glucklich arrived at Smallmead with three World Final appearances under his belt and a gold medal from the 1969 World Team Cup. Although at the veteran stage at 33 he was still two years younger than Jansson. He topped the Polish averages in 1971 and remained in the top ten until dropping to 13th in 1977. He scored paid 7 in his league debut against Birmingham, but apart from top scoring with 7 in a Bank Holiday thrashing at Exeter (25-53) he was an unmitigated disaster. In 25 league, cup and Spring Gold Cup appearances he averaged just 2.68. The most memorable event of his season was probably a bout of fisticuffs with Ipswich's Billy Sanders in September.

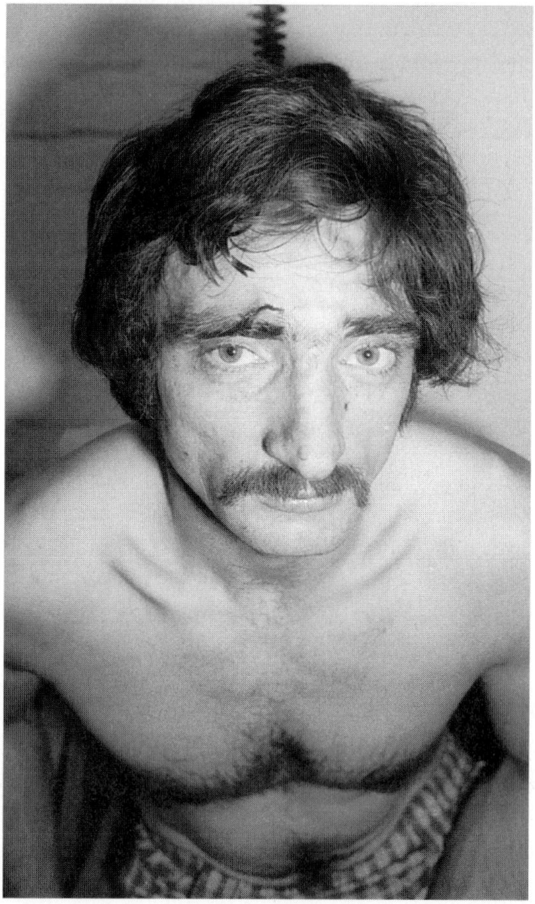

Although a former World Finalist, Henryk Glucklich did little of note at Reading. The most memorable event of his season was an off-track disagreement with Billy Sanders. Here he shows off the scars from the encounter. (EP)

Bob Humphreys also failed to meet expectations. After averaging over 6 in the previous two seasons his form dipped alarmingly. Two months into the season, carrying an average below 3, Humphreys announced that he was quitting. The next day he changed his mind, but shortly after he was dropped. A few weeks later he went on loan to Milton Keynes. Scoring a 15-point maximum on his debut, he quickly regained his form and turned Milton Keynes's season round. His 10.59 league average put him second in the National League rankings to Newcastle's Tom Owen. He remained in the Racers back-up squad, going out on a high note with paid 11 against Cradley.

With Humphreys and Glucklich dropping out of the team, Reading needed new blood and looked to the National League. No less than six riders filled the vacant berths. Five of the six met with a degree of success. The exception, Boston's Steve Clarke, met with a career-ending injury in his third match in Reading's colours. In a cup match at Cradley he clipped the machine of fallen Bruce Penhall and careered into the starting gate, snapping his bike clean in two. Clarke suffered multiple fractures.

Racers still won the match (but went out 79-77 on aggregate), largely thanks to a paid 12 contribution from guest Phil Collins. A month later Cradley signed Collins from Ellesmere Port for a reported fee of £15,000. Phil had recently become the third Collins brother to win the British Under-21 title, 5 points clear of runner-up Ian Gledhill. Still riding for Stoke in the National League, Gledhill averaged over 4 in his appearances for Reading. New Zealander Roger Abel made his debut for Reading in the match at Cradley, and 48 hours later Mel Taylor's first appearance yielded paid 6.

Taylor and Abel became the preferred choices for the reserve berths, Taylor averaging 4.53 and Abel 4.00.

The remaining two squad members came from Rye House. Ashley Pullen did enough to warrant retention the following season, eventually graduating to a full-time team berth in 1981. Least experienced was Kevin Bowen. Dropped from the Rye House junior team that rode in the Anglia Junior League, he scored 5 points on his league debut for Reading beating Keith White (an Inter-Continental Finalist just 12 months earlier).

The season started on a low note with Swindon walking out of the opening meeting at Smallmead. An impromptu pairs contest between the remaining eight riders gave the 4,000 crowd a whiff of methanol and a taste of action after the close season. Racers started the season without Dave Jessup who broke an ankle during winter training. He missed the first half-a-dozen fixtures including a humiliating 48-30 defeat at home to Ipswich in the Spring Gold Cup.

Jessup returned in a 56-22 defeat at Wimbledon, quickly followed by a 38-point thrashing at Halifax and home defeats to White City and Poole. Health problems restricted Frank Higley's ability to carry out his duties as team manager and he resigned. His replacement, former Coventry team manager, Mick Blackburn's tenure started with a run of seven losses in a row. There was further sadness at Smallmead when news of former number eight Jack Millen reached Reading. The Berwick rider had died in a road accident returning from a rained-off meeting at Edinburgh.

July turned out to be the pivotal month in Reading's season. Firstly on July 6 Racers travelled to Foxhall Heath and put up one of their best displays of the year. Only a mix-up over racing lines between John Davis and Mel Taylor in the re-run of heat 12 prevented Racers taking a league point. But in addition to losing 39-38 Reading also lost Hans Wassermann, falling in a crash with Ted Howgego in the original staging of heat 12. Wassermann had cracked vertebrae. The initial prognosis was not good, but fears that he might not walk again abated. By the end of the year Hans had started talking about riding again, but this turned out to be a false hope.

Five days before this incident Wassermann had reached a new pinnacle in his speedway career. He won the Continental Final, held in Prague, and with it a ticket to the World Final. Oddly he achieved victory by the drawing of lots after he had tied on 14 points with future Racer Jiri Stancl.

His scoring had increased slightly on the previous year, paid 11 at Birmingham being his best effort. Fortunately rider replacement allowed extra rides for Jessup, Davis and Leigh; so Racers were able to cover for him until Bernie Leigh's average exceeded Wassermann's in October. (In 1978 rider replacement only covered absent heat leaders, and allowed any rider to have one extra ride.)

Within a week of Wassermann's injury Racers fans were hit by another bombshell – Reg Fearman had resigned. Considerable disagreement behind the scenes had resulted in a parting of the ways. Fearman's colleagues felt that he had been spending too much time on his many other speedway interests. These included membership of the BSPA management committee, his continued involvement at Halifax and Leicester, and a new project – the introduction of speedway to the Middle East. His partner in the latter venture was former Tilehurst junior

Terry Chandler.

Fearman's co-directors wanted a promoter more focused on happenings at Smallmead. Higley's health problems prevented him from taking over and Bill Dore had no inclination to do so. They filled the gap by getting stadium manager Brian Constable to take on the role. Constable had also been a sponsor of Swindon's Jan Andersson.

17 July 1978 – Reg Fearman's last meeting in charge, just a few days after the shock news of his departure broke. (EP)

Despite these events, results started to pick up. A 53-24 thrashing of Hackney at the start of the month hinted at the team's potential. Bernie Leigh scored his first league maximum since 1970 (and that had been in a Division Two match), and Wassermann paid 9 in his final home appearance.

Nevertheless, at the end of July Reading's home record comprised four wins, a draw and four defeats. Away from home the tally stood at 12 losses out of 12. But from the start of August they won seven home matches in a row and took 5 points from the last six matches away from home. The away wins came at Hackney and Wolverhampton. The most exciting finish came in the draw at King's Lynn where Racers came from 8 points down after Dave Jessup won heats 11, 12 and 13. Improved form from John Davis and Bernie Leigh and the contributions from Mel Taylor and the other loanees, helped Reading to a more upbeat finish. Stability behind the scenes following resolution of the Fearman situation must have helped.

The late revival took Reading up to 14th in the final league table. After six consecutive top six finishes, 1978 could only be regarded as a dismal failure. Between 1971 and 1996 Reading raced 25 years in the top league. In 24 of them Reading fielded at least one Swede on a regular basis. 1978 was the exception – no wonder results were so poor! But if it wasn't for one trifling little component then all the poor league results might have been forgotten.

On September 2 a crowd in the region of 85,000 packed in to Wembley for the World Final. Dave Jessup lined up for heat 3, on paper his easiest of the night. A smart first bend gave him the lead over Jerzy Rembas, Jan Verner and Jan Andersson. Disaster struck on the third lap as Jessup's bike ground to a halt. A cracked push rod cap cost Jessup 3 points. But as the meeting progressed it became apparent that Jessup had lost a lot more than 3 points. Three wins, including one over Ole Olsen, left him tied on nine with Gordon Kennett, Scott Autrey and Michael Lee. One point ahead was Olsen, whose heat 17 win gave him the title. Kennett, Jessup and Lee met in heat 19, with Kennett beating Jessup to take the silver medal.

Jessup's tally of 11 could so easily have been 14, and with that would have come the world crown. Autrey went on to beat Jessup and Rembas in a run-off for third place. In the post-match coverage much was made of Jessup's decision to play golf instead of attending the practice.

Wembley marked Anders Michanek's tenth and final appearance. He only scored 7, but did beat Olsen. Making his World Final debut, Andersson had a quiet night – just 3 points.

To qualify for the World Final Jessup had finished second to Lee in the British Final. John Davis suffered elimination in that meeting, but more controversially so to did Peter Collins. After a series of machine failures on the night and in a meeting at Sheffield the day after Collins had his fuel analysed, and discovered that it contained sugar. The British Final generated yet more column inches because its re-staging date clashed with the fourth match in the Durex sponsored England v Australasia Test series. With 16 of the top English riders committed to riding at Coventry in the British Final, the under-strength England side that lined up at Hull endured a 70-36 pasting.

Jessup recovered from his late start to the season to have another excellent year. He moved up two places in the league averages to seventh and rode in England's World Cup team. (The first round of the World Cup, staged in May, was Smallmead's first televised meeting.) In October Jessup challenged Peter Collins for the Golden Helmet, losing 2-0 at Belle Vue and 2-1 at Reading. Later in October Jessup returned to Belle Vue for the British League Riders Championship, but withdrew from the meeting after a first-ride engine failure.

Peter Collins held the Golden Helmet for the whole of 1978. Nobody came closer to relieving him of it than John Davis. Here Davis is seen leading Collins in the Smallmead leg of their encounter. (EP)

John Davis's disappointment at British Final elimination was balanced out by success elsewhere. Ole Olsen pioneered a grand prix style competition called 'The Master of Speedway'. Shunned by British promoters it ran over four rounds in Sweden, Denmark and

West Germany. Peter Collins won the first two rounds, but round three (on May 23) at Ullevi went to Davis. In the final standings he finished fourth behind Collins, Olsen and Lee.

The following week he came close to winning the most prestigious individual meeting of the British domestic season – the Internationale. Leading the field on 11 points, Davis met Peter Collins in heat 19. The clash produced four entertaining laps with Davis just edging it as they raced out of the fourth bend for a final time. With the finish line in sight a puncture robbed Davis of victory. Collins went on to win a three-man run-off for the title with Malcolm Simmons second and Davis third.

Only a month earlier Davis had another confrontation with Collins, in the Golden Helmet. This one went to a deciding leg at Leicester on April 18. After Davis won the opening race Collins took the next two to retain the Helmet. Throughout the season Collins made seven successful defences, though none were as close as the showdown with Davis.

Davis gained individual glory at Smallmead, winning both the Manpower and the Geoff Curtis Memorial Trophy. In the Manpower meeting third-placed Peter Collins lowered the track record to exactly 60 seconds.

With all this individual success it comes as a bit of a surprise to discover that his Reading average fell by nearly a point. A consequence of this was that Davis received fewer England call-ups than his individual form warranted. This resulted in some flak from Smallmead being directed at England Team manager John Berry.

All this happened in British speedway's golden jubilee year. Fifty years after High Beech in the heart of Epping Forest hosted the first meeting, Hackney staged a special meeting. Held in the middle of February it is hard to imagine a colder day. Later in the season Reading staged yet another Jubilee Trophy. Both meetings were won by Michael Lee.

How healthy was the sport in its jubilee year? The assessment is mixed. There were 39 tracks in the British and National League – an all-time high, never since bettered. Sponsors were plentiful: Gulf Oil sponsored the British League, and meetings at Reading promoted Golden Wonder, VW, Leyland Cars, Strongbow and the *Daily Mirror*. It's hard to imagine so many household names like these investing in speedway now.

However, crowds were down at most tracks. Poor results exacerbated the trend at Smallmead. There were other attractions at Smallmead, the first show-jumping event took place in September. Back in the town centre the Hexagon Theatre provided a new attraction. The Hexagon opened the previous November with a grand charity concert featuring Bobby Crush and Ted O'Connor. During its first year events included Whitesnake, Godspell, Kenneth McKellar and wrestling.

The British League struggled to find riders, more and more second strings chose to ride in the National League. British League promoters plugged the holes with more and more foreigners, many of them not up to the job. Promoters also faced a squeeze on costs; fuelled by the proliferation of 4-valves, riders pay demands multiplied. Officially the 1978 pay rates were £2.50 a start and £4 per point, but most riders received considerably more than the published rates.

With Denmark's first-ever win in the World Team Cup, it looked as if England's domination wouldn't last much longer. With more and more experienced journeymen in the National League where were the next generation of English stars? Hottest prospect of 1978 was undoubtedly Kenny Carter at Newcastle. Back at Smallmead a young grasstracker made his second-half debut – Simon Wigg. He won his debut race on September 11 after race leader Mel Taylor had an engine failure.

An even more obscure debut occurred in the pages of *Speedway Star*. The December 2 issue carried a photo of the Kent Youth Grass Track annual presentations. Lurking in the front row is a 13-year-old Dave Mullett – who would on to gain the record for most appearances in Reading colours.

Team: Dave Jessup 10.20, John Davis 8.93, Hans Wassermann 5.91, Bernie Leigh 5.90, Doug Underwood 4.71, Melvyn Taylor 4.53, Roger Abel 4.00, Bob Humphreys 3.69, Henryk Glucklich 2.94, Kevin Bowen 2.56

Racers 1979 squad, notable for the inclusion of novice Simon Wigg. He never rode for Reading but went on to become one of the leading British riders of the 1980s. Full line-up left to right, back row: Terry Betts, Jan Andersson, Bernie Leigh, Mick Blackburn (Team Manager), Doug Underwood, Sigvart Pedersen, Bob Humphreys, Simon Wigg. Front row: Ashley Pullen, John Davis (on bike) and Kevin Bowen. (EP)

1979 – Spending Spree

Transfer stories dominated the close season. Speculation that Jessup and Davis both wanted to be number one crystallised with the news that Jessup was for sale. Promoter Brian Constable felt his financial demands were unreasonable and put a £30,000 price tag on his head. At the beginning of February King's Lynn secured Jessup's services for £20,000[26].

Although Jessup went on to finish second in the 1980 World Final he was over-shadowed by his team mate (and 1980 World Champion) Michael Lee. In addition the loss of Sunday continental bookings due to the switch to a Saturday track (as King's Lynn then was) resulted in Jessup subsequently describing the decision to leave Reading as the worst one of his career (*Five-One*, April 1998).

This left Davis as Racers number one, and Constable with the financial muscle to fill the remaining heat leader spots. He quickly signed Jan Andersson from Swindon. This allowed Phil Crump to move from Bristol (closed by an injunction from local residents) to Swindon, ending Reading's interest in him. Plans to acquire Jiri Stancl got bogged down in red tape with the Czech authorities, and on the eve of the season Constable snapped up veterans Terry Betts (35) and Reidar Eide (38).

Betts had spent the last 13 years with King's Lynn, in contrast Eide had represented eight clubs in the same period. Both had averaged over 9 points a match for most of this period, and they each had a World Final appearance to their credit. Their 1978 averages (Betts 8.10, Eide 8.44) suggested they could still make a useful contribution.

The other new signing received less attention. Sigvart Pedersen, an unknown Norwegian, arrived with little pedigree. He had ridden in Norway's World Cup team the previous year, but only scored a point.

With promoters agreeing to retain the 50-point limit the number seven position went to a junior with a 3-point average. Initially Kevin Bowen filled this spot. Andy Campbell later took his place (although he never rode in an official fixture).

The remaining spot belonged to the new captain, Bernie Leigh. Ten years after he started his career at Tilehurst, Bernie became the first Reading rider to receive a testimonial. Leigh didn't miss a match all season, and upped his average to 6.31 (only in 1976 did he exceed that figure in the top league). He also competed in the World Longtrack Championship, reaching the semi-final. His testimonial year was packed with events, including a dance at the Top Rank Suite on Station Hill (tickets £1.25). The testimonial meeting on August 12 consisted of a four-team tournament won by Bernie's Select. One of the other teams participating was Krumbach, Hans Wassermann's team. They must have been expensive to bring over from West Germany, and did not add a great deal to the meeting. At the end of the season Bernie's testimonial proceeds were considerably lower than expected, probably between two and three thousand pounds. There was an exotic finish to Bernie's year when he travelled to the Middle East, riding in Cairo and Abu Dhabi.

Unlike his team mates, Leigh avoided injuries. On May 7 Siggy Pedersen broke a leg in the second half at Exeter. He did not reappear until the start of 1980, when after three early-season challenge appearances for Reading he drifted on to Eastbourne and then Wimbledon. Pedersen's 1979 Racers form was ambiguous, just a point from six away matches, but a healthy 6.09 average from his seven home fixtures. (Most of these were Spring Gold Cup appearances.)

---

26 Most press reports of the time quoted the figure as £20,000, but Martin Rogers states the figure was £18,000 in his book on King's Lynn speedway. (As the general manager at King's Lynn who made the purchase he should know!) A gross fee of £20,000 with Jessup receiving a 10% cut leaving £18,000 heading towards King's Lynn's coffers would explain this discrepancy.

With Pedersen injured, Mel Taylor became an almost permanent presence in the Reading team. Taylor ended the season with a National League champions medal for his exploits at Mildenhall, and third place to Kenny Carter in the British Under-21 Championship. His late season form had Reading fans hoping that Brian Constable would once again get out his cheque book.

A second broken leg followed a month after Pedersen's. His compatriot Reidar Eide missed the British League Four Team Tournament Finals at Sheffield in June to ride in a French grasstrack meeting. Eide did recover from the injuries sustained in France, reappearing in the Racers colours at the start of October. How fit he was on his return is open to question; he only scored 7 points in six league matches. However, even before his injury his scoring had fallen short, as evidenced by a 2-point drop in his average.

Until Eide returned, Bob Humphreys rode in most of Reading's matches scoring considerably better than in 1978. Ten points against former club King's Lynn must have been particularly pleasing for him.

Constable continued in his efforts to fill the holes in the Reading team. In May, Boley Proch arrived in Britain with a touring Polish under-23 team and scored maximums at Stoke and Nottingham (Long Eaton). Efforts to persuade him to don the winged wheel once more failed. Further attempts to sign Stancl floundered as Coventry sought to entice him back to replace long-term injury victim Alan Molyneux.

Eventually a concrete signing emerged. Reading's new rider had already qualified for the World Final, and later in the season went on to win the World Longtrack Final (Michanek came second, and Stancl fourth). Unfortunately he made no impact at all at Smallmead. His first appearance came in Reading's worst home league defeat ever over 13 heats – 32-46 against Cradley (August 6). Alois Wiesbock's contribution in a match that was lost when John Davis crashed out in heat 1, consisted of a single point from a three- rider race. The following week he failed to score from three rides in a challenge against Swindon. He never rode a third match.

In August Stancl finally received clearance to ride for Reading. Although below his best, it was a relief to have another regular team member. After Stancl's arrival the frequency of Ashley Pullen's appearances reduced. Pullen had one magic evening when he completed a five-ride paid maximum (against Eastbourne in the cup), but generally struggled. In the National League he rode for the powerful Rye House team where his 7.34 average still made him a reserve!

What had looked like a strong team ended up in mid-table mediocrity. Reading's injuries left them short of the strength required to chalk up away wins, but with just enough potential to keep winning at home.

Away from home Reading went down in last-heat deciders at Cradley, Exeter, Sheffield and Leicester. At Sheffield a Terry Betts engine failure while leading heat 12 cost Racers a point, while Mike Farrell's heat 13 pass of Andersson did likewise at Leicester. Eventually at the end of August Racers picked up away points with wins on consecutive days at Ipswich and Eastbourne. Both matches were won with solid scoring, Bob Humphreys providing the crucial contributions. The Racers travelled hopefully to the final away fixture at Poole. As usual Racers won at Wimborne Road. A convincing 45-33 victory with a full maximum from Jan Andersson finished the season on a high.

Those three away wins cancelled out three home defeats. First came Belle Vue in July. Reading came from 26-16 down to enter the last heat level. Les Collins passed both Reading riders (Betts and Leigh) to join brother Peter for a match winning 5-1. Then after being pasted by Cradley, prospective champions Coventry beat a Davis-less Reading in September.

In addition to these defeats there were some close scrapes. In June Wimbledon ran the Racers close losing by four after a last-heat decider. In July, King's Lynn were only six down when tactical substitute Michael Lee walked out after a tape exclusion. Two further matches were narrowly won in October after the visitors' top rider walked out. Ipswich were handicapped by John Louis's departure after a first-ride engine failure, and Swindon missed Phil Crump who didn't reappear after being excluded on the first bend of heat 3.

Of all the close matches, the most important in retrospect took place against Hull in July. The Vikings went on to finish two points behind Coventry in the final league table. The two teams met in a title decider at Brandon in October in front of nearly 20,000 spectators. Hull lost 42-36 at Coventry; a draw would have given them the title. Had they won at Smallmead the title would already have been theirs. Hull lost that match by seven despite Ivan Mauger arriving late and missing his first ride, and the Vikings conceding a 5-0 in heat 12.

In a classic example of promoters tinkering to no good purpose the Knock-Out Cup rules prevented guests or rider replacement being used. An easy win over Eastbourne sent Reading in the direction of Halifax. Tracking Weymouth riders Malcolm Shakespeare and Bryan Woodward at reserve, expectations took a dive when John Davis broke down and Reading had to borrow local junior Ian Westwell. The night is hard to forget, wild applause from the travelling Racers faithful greeted Bernie Leigh's win in heat 11. In an 18-heat match it was the only time a Racer won a race, as the Dukes crushed the Racers 79-29. Never before or since have Reading lost by a 50-point margin. To rub salt into the wounds Halifax even won the second leg at Reading, a track where they had previously performed very poorly. The cup match filled the second slot in a double header; with 31 heats to run the final race ended just after quarter past eleven!

The following winter the promoters realised that matches without recourse to guests or rider replacement do not make good speedway and wrote off the 1979 Knock-Out Cup as a failed experiment.

In the Spring Gold Cup, Racers just missed out on a final place. They rode their last match away at Ipswich needing a draw to top their group. They lost by 6 and the Witches reached the final where they lost to Wimbledon.

Before the season started Allied Presentations acquired Weymouth speedway. Intended to be a nursery for Reading, it proved to be a drain on resources. Finishing bottom but one in the National League, losses of £20,000 (£70,000 in 2008 prices) were reported. Weymouth tracked 1978 Racers Doug Underwood and Kevin Bowen. Both made a handful of appearances for Reading in 1979. Underwood retired from British speedway at the end of the season while Kevin Bowen moved on to Poole, ending up at Rye House where his son Luke now rides.

Another member of the previous season's back-up squad Ian Gledhill severed his links with Reading and became a Stoke asset. He headed his team's averages and qualified for the National League Riders Championship as reserve. When favourite Tom Owen withdrew through injury, Gledhill was promoted into the meeting. In possibly the biggest surprise in the event's 40-year history, his sharp gating won him the title.

Reading entered a team in the Anglia Junior League and the Western Junior League. They finished eighth (out of twelve) and first of four respectively. The four riders who represented Reading in these three heat second-half junior matches were: Barry Allaway, Andy Campbell, Gary Monk and Mick Fletcher.

In the early part of the season Simon Wigg appeared in a few second halves at Reading and Weymouth, but concentrated on his continental activities. Although he appeared in the 1979 press-day team photograph Wigg never rode in the Reading team. Only after Weymouth had been sold, to Mervyn Stewksbury in 1980, did Wigg finally make a serious start on his speedway career.

Back to Smallmead and in one of the year's big meetings England were shock non-qualifiers in the World Team Cup Round. Once again the non-selection of Davis caused considerable debate. For most of the season he stood at number three in the British League averages, before finally slipping to fifth (one place below top Englishman Michael Lee). Davis came second in the Internationale behind Michael Lee, and third in the Grand Prix (won by Scott Autrey). When finally selected for England he top scored in two of the four Tests he rode against Australasia (again sponsored by Durex). Given the World Team Cup meeting took place on his home track his omission from the England team was in retrospect a bad mistake. The Davis publicity machine kept him in the public eye. He topped his 1978 Sun topless pin-up pose with efforts to launch a pop career. 'Speedway Rider' with its unforgettable opening line: "The green lights, on I'm ready to go" failed to trouble the charts.

The season produced a bumper crop of new foreign imports: Danes Tommy Knudsen and Erik Gundersen, and Americans Bobby Schwartz and Dennis Sigalos all started their British careers in 1979.

It was another American, Bruce Penhall who featured in the race of the season at Smallmead. September's Manpower Trophy ended in a tie between the charismatic American and English crowd favourite Peter Collins. In a thrilling run-off PC powered off the final bend to pass Penhall on the run in to the line. Penhall also came second (to Dave Jessup) in the Traders Trophy[27].

An action shot of the 1979 Manpower run-off, possibly the greatest race in Smallmead's 33 year history. Bruce Penhall leads Peter Collins, but on the last bend Collins stormed past Penhall to take the title. (EP)

Crowds were slightly down at Smallmead. There were larger falls elsewhere, but the disaster that was 1978 depressed the base from which any fall would have been measured. Attendances in the region of 6,000 were reported for both the opening and closing meetings. Speedway viewing became more expensive in June when Chancellor Geoffrey Howe increased the rate of VAT from 8 to 15%. (Margaret Thatcher came to power in May promising not to double VAT.) Another downward pressure on Smallmead attendances was the state of the stadium, the neat terracing on the bends had crumbled, though the stadium

27 The event was formerly known as the Jubilee Trophy, but changed title when management ran out of ideas for events to commemorate!

restaurant did open for business. (Sample menu: Prawn Cocktail 90p followed by Chicken Maryland £2.45.)

The speedway had a new neighbour, the Courage beer factory at Worton Grange opened in July. The following year their Bridge Street site (formerly Simmonds Brewery) was vacated, eventually paving the way for the Oracle shopping centre. This would be the precursor to substantial development adjacent to junction 11 of the M4 that would become a significant factor in Smallmead's future 20 years down the line.

The transfer market had exploded. Dave Jessup arrived at Reading as a star with a 10-point average, and three years later left with his status unchanged. However, his value had nominally quadrupled. The key to Reading's season ultimately rested on how well the Jessup transfer money was spent. It should be noted that Bill Dore and Frank Higley, holders of the purse strings were willing to allow Constable to spend more than he received. Like football transfers, fees quoted in the press should always be taken with a pinch of salt, but Andersson (£10,000), Betts (£10,000[28]), Eide (£6,000) and Stancl (up to £7,000) was quite a shopping spree.

Betts performed reliably, missing only five matches (due to a broken collarbone in June). His average dropped by less than half a point, perfectly acceptable for a veteran. But how many more seasons did he have in him? Eide's average had fallen by over 2 points a match even before he broke his leg, and his signing could not be regarded as wise or successful. Stancl's average fell by a point, and his availability could never be guaranteed, but at 29 there might still be time for him to make good the outlay.

Collectively these signings gave Reading a rather geriatric look. Bernie Leigh (35 in November) was only the third oldest member of the team. No matter how poor his other buys were, Constable should be remembered with gratitude by a generation of Racers fans for bringing Jan Andersson to Reading. He went on to top the Reading averages six times in the 1980s, and was still winning league championships for the team in the 1990s. What a bargain.

The year ended with a double bombshell. In quick succession Brian Constable resigned as promoter (or "speedway controller" as the Smallmead programme referred to him), and Mick Blackburn left to take up a speedway management role at Wolverhampton. Both remained diplomatic about the reasons for their departure while hinting at disagreements behind the scene. Quoted in *Speedway Star*, Constable said: "I ... only enjoy my work when I feel I can get satisfaction – which I do not feel I can obtain with the present structure at Reading." Constable did not pursue another role in speedway management, commenting: "The sport as a whole is spending more money than it has. Unless there are big changes I think the future of the sport is bleak."

Constable did return to sports administration many years later as the owner of Witney Town Football Club, which he wound up in 2001.

Who would be next in the Smallmead hot seat?

Team: John Davis 10.32, Jan Andersson 8.64, Terry Betts 7.75, Bernie Leigh 6.31, Melvyn Taylor 5.65, Reidar Eide 5.23, Bob Humphreys 5.17, Jiri Stancl 5.12, Ashley Pullen 3.75

---

28 As quoted in the *Evening Post*, 12 March 1979. A variety of figures appeared in the press for this deal. Betts himself later revealed in an interview with *Five-One* magazine (August 1998) that the fee paid was £12,000, half of which went to King's Lynn and half to Betts.

1980 – Dave Lanning Works His Magic

The year opened with Jan Andersson winning the Birmingham NEC indoor meeting and concluded with an Andersson maximum at December's Wembley indoor event. In between Racers fans experienced an exciting and enjoyable season and a nerve-wracking title race.

The man at the centre of it all never rode a lap. In January Dave Lanning joined Reading as 'Speedway Executive', effectively the man employed by owners Bill Dore and Frank Higley to act as promoter. Lanning's extensive experience in speedway as an administrator, journalist and broadcaster made him a high profile capture. His track record suggested that Racers fans would be in for a lively time. He had been announcer at Smallmead since 1975. After three seasons at Coventry as a reliable second string Mick Bell retired for a second time. He quickly returned to Reading as the new team manager.

The BSPA conference agreed to retain the 50-point limit, dismissing suggestions that it should be lowered to 48. Bobby Schwartz said that he wouldn't ride in Britain if discarded by Cradley to comply with the points limit. Potential target Mel Taylor signed for King's Lynn (for a fee of £15,000). Kevin Bowen signed for Poole who paid Reading £800 for him. Then at the end of February things really started to get interesting.

Lanning turned up the heat by announcing that the Reading team would be on a £40,000 win bonus if they won the British League. In addition Davis and Andersson would stand to gain £7,000 if they finished on the rostrum in the World Final. The deal, done for a premium of £1,000 through Lloyd's underwriters was basically a bet! However, it later emerged that there was more to the deal.

With six of last year's squad (Davis, Andersson, Betts, Leigh, Eide, Stancl) expected to return, the underwriters' money looked safe. March opened with a big fanfare as Tony Briggs signed on the dotted line. A target for most clubs, he turned 18 as the season started. The previous year Briggs based himself in California riding regularly against the likes of Shawn McConnell, Mike Faria, Eddie Castro and Bobby Schwartz. (All four were still riding regularly in California in 2007.) His signing included the sponsorship of Fabergé which put him in the company of Henry Cooper and Barry Sheene.

With the team complete 5,000 fans witnessed Tony Briggs's first meeting. In a challenge against Swindon he took a second place from the back in heat 4 and beat Cradley heat leader Alan Grahame (one of three guests in the Swindon team) in the final heat. Racers slumped to defeat with non-starter Terry Betts replaced by Siggy Pedersen. Betts had appeared at practice day, but couldn't agree terms with the Lanning.

Barely had the news of Betts's likely retirement sunk in than Lanning came up with another masterstroke – the signing of Bobby Schwartz. Like Briggs the competition for his signature was strong, and Reading got a bargain, paying only £7,000. Compare that with a £3,000 fee paid for Ashley Pullen in the same month. Pullen returned to Rye House on loan, making a handful of appearances for the Racers in 1980.

The first positive on track news came from Wimbledon where John Davis carried off the Daily Express Spring Classic. March ended with Martin Ashby joining Reading for a £4,000 fee.

April started with the Ashby signing falling apart when neither party was prepared to pay Ashby's cut. Ashby made his Swindon debut back in 1961, so the length of service-based fee came to quite a tidy sum. Two weeks later with the problems resolved, the deal finally went ahead.

Ashby made his debut in a Spring Gold Cup win at Hackney scoring paid 8. With eight riders competing for seven places Jiri Stancl seemed to be favourite to drop out, but Reidar Eide solved the problem by asking for a move. Eide went on to ride for Swindon, Eastbourne and Wolverhampton bringing his total number of British clubs up to 12 before retiring at the end of the season. April also saw the departure of Bob Humphreys, sold to Milton Keynes, whose averages he topped again in 1980 and 1981.

In May most Americans were transfixed by the eruption of Mount St. Helens in Washington State. For the speedway fraternity America faced England in the first-ever official Test series between the two countries. It started with a classic encounter, a 54-all draw at Wimbledon, and finished with the Yanks winning the deciding Test at Swindon. Bobby Schwartz formed a potent partnership with Penhall; John Davis appeared in four of the five matches. Davis also challenged Penhall for the Golden Helmet in this month. After going down 2-0 at home he withdrew from the second leg due to injury.

Racers league campaign started to gain momentum with comfortable away wins at Birmingham and Leicester. May ended with a setback, a 40-38 defeat in a last-heat decider at Hull without Davis or Andersson. Swedish World Championship qualifying rounds explained Andersson's absence – he duly became the first rider to qualify for the Gothenburg staged final in September.

Reading didn't have a single away league match in June. At home Tony Briggs scored a paid maximum in a challenge against Poole and Bernie Leigh won Smallmead's 'wrong way round championship'. With little league activity Racers mid-table position didn't truly reflect their potential. Stancl, Schwartz, Andersson and Briggs's scores all represented big improvements on their starting averages.

Racers stepped up to the plate in July and reeled off three away wins in quick succession. A John Davis/Bernie Leigh 5-1 in heat 13 gave Reading a 40-38 win at Poole. Wimbledon lost by 8 points in a match that saw Tony Briggs (paid 7 in the match) stretchered off in the second half and taken to hospital in the back of an estate car. With no ambulance present the riders refused to continue and the second half was abandoned.

Without Briggs and Stancl (riding for Czechoslovakia in a World Team Cup qualifier) Racers travelled to King's Lynn with trepidation. Reading came from eight down, going ahead when Jan Andersson passed Dave Jessup on the last bend of heat 12. The 40-38 away win was King's Lynn's only home defeat of the year, and just one of eight league matches the Stars lost 40-38 in 1980!

New Zealander Briggs recovered in time to ride in the following weekend's European Under-21 Championship Final. The potential packed top four at Pocking were: Tommy Knudsen 14, Briggs 12, Dennis Sigalos 11, Erik Gundersen 11.

Racers were now third with championship pacesetters Hackney in their sights. Swindon arrived at Smallmead with a run of eight away defeats, but left with two league points after a 40-38 win. Scott Autrey passed Jan Andersson in heat 13 to seal Racers fate.

This loss made the following Friday's showdown at Waterden Road even more vital. The Hawks took an 8-point lead, a Davis/Briggs 5-1 reduced the deficit to 2 points with two heats to go, but Hackney hung on with two 3-3s. Meanwhile Stancl travelled to Lonigo for the Continental Final where he qualified for Gothenburg. In his place at Hackney guest Kai Niemi failed to score. Niemi received a very rough reception from Racers fans for the rest of the season. The grievance was so deep seated that some were still booing him a decade later.

Racers gained revenge over the Robins with a commanding 45-33 win at Blunsdon on August 2, Davis scoring a maximum. The next day he qualified for the World Final in a meeting that left Ivan Mauger a spectator at the World Final after 14 consecutive appearances.

The following weekend Hackney won at Wolves on the Friday. The next night Coventry beat the Racers despite an Andersson maximum. Stancl's absence looked costly. It looked even worse when news filtered through from Halifax that Hackney, inspired by a Zenon Plech paid maximum, had come from 31-16 down to win 39-38.

Reading now stood 8 points behind Hackney with just one match in hand. Racers next competed for league points at Wolverhampton where they won 51-27, increasing the pressure on embattled Wolves manager Mick Blackburn. Back to Smallmead on the Monday and the opening race came to a sudden halt when Kenny Carter knocked John Davis off. Martin Ashby couldn't avoid Davis and ended up with a broken collarbone and two months on the sidelines. Racers still won easily with all three heat leaders unbeaten.

Earlier in the month Reading had slipped up at home to Cradley in the Knock-Out Cup, so the second leg at Dudley Wood on August 21 seemed like a formality. It turned out to be a classic encounter. A Davis/Pullen 5-1 over Erik Gundersen in heat 13 put Reading 2 up on the night. After Schwartz won heat 17 to complete a seven-ride 21-point full maximum, the only one in club history[29], the aggregate scores were 105-105 with one heat to go. Stancl led the deciding heat for three and three-quarter laps before Bruce Penhall stormed round the outside for a draw on the night and a 2-point win overall for the Heathens.

On Sunday (August 24) the Racers recorded a routine win over King's Lynn on a very heavy track. Hackney arrived the following evening with a run of 12 wins in a row. Once again the visitors expressed disquiet at the track conditions, and Reading went on to win comfortably with Schwartz scoring his fifth maximum in a row.

Next a paid 11 from guest Kelly Moran (in for Stancl) and paid 6 from new boy Dave Trownson helped Reading to a draw at Halifax.

All eyes briefly turned from the title race to the World Final at the Ullevi Stadium Gothenburg. Andersson finished fourth with 11 points, just missing out on the £7,000 bonus Lanning had arranged for a top-three finish. Davis scored 9 and Stancl 5. Ex-Racer Dave Jessup finished runner-up to his King's Lynn team mate Michael Lee.

A comfortable win at home to Poole on September 8 put Reading on top of the table. On September 11 Reading (at Ipswich) and Hackney (Sheffield) both won away. A day later a home win put the Hawks back in pole position.

The traditional post World Final staging of the Manpower produced another English one-two, Chris Morton and Michael Lee occupying the top two spots. Schwartz came third but the story of the night centred around John Davis and heat 19. Needing a win to keep his title chances alive the home star led Nielsen, Lee and Morton. Had it stayed that way the title would have gone to Davis. On the second lap Morton passed Lee and a Davis/Morton run-off appeared to be the likely outcome. Then on the final lap Nielsen challenged Davis who fell. Lee and Morton swept past and Nielsen limped in for third.

Most of the 8,000 crowd were shocked that Nielsen had avoided exclusion and Davis had gone from champion elect to also-ran in that split second. A petulant display by Davis who stormed out to break the tapes delaying the start of heat 20 and boisterous jeering from the crowd during the presentation left a sour taste. Lanning would be particularly critical of the Smallmead spectators.

Without Jan Andersson, Reading lost 43-35 at Belle Vue (Sept 17), the first time all season they had lost by more than 6 points in any match. John Davis didn't get a ride in Wroclaw as England completed the triple crown (individual, pairs and team) by winning the World Team Cup. Schwartz and Stancl represented their respective countries in the final too.

October opened with Poole boss Terry Chandler sacking number one Malcolm Simmons for not trying in the final race of a pairs meeting. This quickly led to speculation that John Davis could be the ideal replacement. Dave Lanning responded with typical bravado, putting a £100,000 price tag on his head.

The title race took a turn in Reading's favour when Hackney surrendered their 100% home record to Cradley. The top of the table now read: Hackney 42 points (28 matches), Belle Vue

---

29 Phil Morris (in 2004) and guest Simon Stead (2005) both achieved 21-point maximums from six rides including a 6-point tactical ride. Matej Zagar did likewise in 2005 with a paid maximum.

42 (30), Reading 41 (27).

A sixth home rain-off on October 6 postponed Reading's return to the top until the following Sunday. Reading didn't just take 2 points from their visit to Eastbourne, they completely overwhelmed the Eagles registering nine heat advantages in a 52-26 slaughter. 27 years on this result still stands as Reading's record away win.

When an under-par Hackney tumbled to defeat at Coventry, Reading knew that all they needed to do was win their last two home matches. But the first of these presented a tough challenge. Cradley, victors at Hackney, had already defeated Reading at Smallmead in the cup. Martin Ashby returned to action, scoring paid 7, but it still required a dramatic last-heat overtake to take a last-gasp 40-38 win. Needing a 5-1 to win in the final heat Bruce Penhall and Illa Teromaa gated only for Andersson and Schwartz to speed past Teromaa, one either side.

It all came down to the last Sunday in October, the opponents were Wolverhampton. A comfortable 20-point victory was assured when Leigh and Schwartz took a 5-1 in heat 9. Tony Briggs showed well, his paid 9 included the scalps of Jim McMillan and Hans Nielsen. The championship and the £40,000 win bonus belonged to Reading.

The league champions receive their presentation cheque. Riders left to right back row: Dave Trownson, Jiri Stancl, Ashley Pullen, Bernie Leigh, Martin Ashby. Front: Bobby Schwartz, Jan Andersson, John Davis and Tony Briggs. Conspicuous by his absence is Dave Lanning who subsequently sued for a share of the win bonus. (EP)

Throughout the season Hackney provided stiff opposition. Even Hawks fans were surprised. Their team finished bottom in 1978 and 1979, and started 1980 with four home losses including a 57-20 home defeat in the Spring Gold Cup to King's Lynn. A key element of Hackney's success came from Poland, Zenon Plech had a fine year and new boy Roman Jankowski impressed.

The presence in the British League of half a dozen Poles and half a dozen Czechs seemed anomalous as the Cold War reached an intensity not seen since the early 1960s. The Soviet Union had invaded Afghanistan causing the United States to boycott the Moscow Olympics in the summer of 1980. Yet the seeds of communism's downfall were germinating. After five weeks of unrest in Gdansk's Lenin shipyards, the birth of the Solidarity trade union signalled that the Iron Curtain was more fragile than it looked. In his youth Solidarity leader Lech Walesa had cheered on the Gdansk speedway team from its steeply banked terraces.

Reading rounded off the season with home and away victories over Swindon in the Duplex Litho Trophy. 8,000 crowded into Smallmead for the end-of-season celebrations. The £1,000 Manpower Golden Snowball went to Jan Andersson from Davis and Stancl. The mechanics race was won by Denny Pyeatt. In the return at Swindon Martin Ashby, in his last-ever speedway match, scored 6 points against the team he had served so loyally and with distinction for two decades. At the start of 2008 he still held the record for appearances and points scored for Swindon.

Duplex Litho printed Reading's 1980 programme, one of the best in the club's history. Among the items included was 'Hudson's Humdinger' – a fiendishly difficult quiz on the history of Reading Racers. Third prize went to Arnie Gibbons, second to Tim Sugar. These two experts were pipped to the title by Peter Butler. Incidentally he designed the 1991 Reading programme cover and is still a Reading regular.

Racers owed their success to a powerful heat leader trio (Andersson, Schwartz and Davis all finished in the top 12 in the league averages), a plentiful supply of points from Stancl and a settled team. When Ashby's collarbone prevented him riding, Dave Trownson and Steve McDermott both filled in with distinction. Another rider who turned down the opportunity of filling in for Ashby was Mick Bates, now a leading referee.

Regular team members Davis, Andersson, Schwartz, Leigh and Briggs received £5,000 each. Stancl (£4,500) and Ashby (£3,500) received slightly less. The back-up squad also shared in the windfall: Trownson (£1,000), Pullen (£1,000), McDermott (£500), Leslie (£300) and Campbell (£300). Leslie and Campbell received a share even though they didn't ride in any league matches! The balance went to Mick Bell and guest riders used during the season.

Mark Leslie and Andy Campbell made regular second-half appearances. At the start of the following season Campbell was sold to Exeter for £500. Four years later Belle Vue paid £15,000 for him!

Above all, though, the presence of Dave Lanning turned Reading into champions. Would Schwartz and Briggs have come to Smallmead without Lanning's presence? The motivation provided by the £40,000 win bonus enhanced an already high team spirit. As well as publicity, Lanning's professional approach ensured that riders were available – even if it did mean a lot of fixture changes. However, this came at a financial cost (which included Lanning's salary) and despite increased attendances the club barely broke even.

As a post script, Dave Lanning subsequently sued Allied Presentations for what he claimed was his share of the £50,000 win bonus. Note that the insurance pay-out included £10,000 never intended for the riders. After a court hearing in April 1983 at which Davis, Briggs, Andersson and Leigh all testified, the parties settled out of court. *Speedway Star* reported (11 June 1983) that Lanning received £3,000.

What Lanning did lack was a rapport with the terraces. However, when news of the failure to agree terms for a 1981 contract with Bill Dore and Frank Higley broke in November most supporters knew that he would be missed.

Team: Jan Andersson 10.04, Bobby Schwartz 10.00, John Davis 9.59, Jiri Stancl 7.38, (Dave Trownson 7.29), Bernie Leigh 5.87, Martin Ashby 5.30, Tony Briggs 4.98

1981 – Bill Dore Takes Charge

In their programme editorial on June 29 co-promoters Bill Dore and Frank Higley stated: "We've virtually reached the half-way stage of the season – and we can confidently say the best is yet to come." They couldn't have been more wrong. That night John Davis's desire for a transfer became public, and unrest in the team clearly spread further. Racers went from mid-June to late August without a single league win. In that period Davis bowed out and a serious injury exacerbated Reading's troubles. After a promising start Racers season went into free fall.

With one year of a three-year contract still to run, Racers captain Davis re-signed reluctantly at the start of the season. His League Cup average was more than a point down on his 1980 form, and with the Lanning publicity machine gone, Davis missed the spotlight. Meanwhile at Poole a knee injury had ruled heat leader Ron Preston out for the season, increasing the urgency of the Pirates long standing interest in Davis. Reading's management quickly concluded that they should bow to the inevitable and let Davis have his wish.

The response was immediate – Leigh replaced Davis as captain and Schwartz moved up the order to take over the number one berth. A £30,000 price was put on Davis's head and the search for a replacement commenced. To compound Reading's problems the dissatisfaction spread beyond Davis; Pullen hankered after a return to the National League and Schwartz seemed less than content. *Speedway Star*'s headlines ran "Crisis at Reading" and "Vultures at Smallmead", and the *Evening Post* columns overflowed with correspondence, much of which was highly critical of the management. The Racers publicity man (a journalist himself) rebuked the press for "ill-considered and unconstructive criticism."

Management said that Davis could not go until a replacement had been sorted out. After four weeks Reading and Poole agreed Davis's transfer for a fee of £20,000. Davis would make his final appearance at home to Coventry the following week (August 3), and his Poole debut 48 hours later. Reading and John Davis were getting divorced just as Prince Charles and Lady Diana Spencer were getting married.

No replacement had yet been found and the programme for the August 10 meeting contained a blank space. The Czech authorities put too many barriers in the way of first-choice replacement Jiri Stancl. Other names in the frame included Martin Ashby, Terry Betts, Anders Michanek, Peter Collins, Bob Kilby, Lance King and Dave DeTemple. The last-named rider competed against the best in America despite missing a leg. In that year's American Final he scored 6, just one less than Bobby Schwartz and Steve Gresham.

Davis had received some hostile responses on the terraces and in the letters columns, but most supporters regarded his departure as a sad occasion and a large crowd turned up for his final appearance on August 3. Racers entered the second leg of the Coventry cup tie only 4 points down.

After five heats Coventry had extended their lead to 14 points, leading 20-10 on the night. A paid 9 from Ian Gledhill helped Reading get back into contention and they entered the final heat 2-down on aggregate. A 5-1 still looked a tough proposition as Coventry fielded Ole Olsen and Mitch Shirra. For Reading Jan Andersson joined Davis for his farewell race. The Racers pair stormed to the front and in four of Smallmead's most nail-biting laps clung on to their match-winning position.

On July 11 the first leg of the Coventry cup tie contained the other pivotal event of Reading's season. With John Davis (headaches) and Bobby Schwartz (riding in America) missing, Reading had done well to stay in contention. Jan Andersson led heat 14, but behind him Tony Briggs fell off on the second bend in the latter stages of the race. It looked to be a simple fall. Only five days earlier he had experienced a far nastier fall at Smallmead, flying through the air, but got up and walked away. This time the prognosis was not so good. He hit a gate post and required extensive medical treatment. The outcome – a broken bone in his neck.

Briggs did make a full recovery but never rode in the British League again. In later years he made appearances on and off in California, and had a rather surprising spell with Wybrzeze Gdansk in 1991 in the Polish Second Division. His 1981 form disappointed, but his age, pedigree and debut season still suggested considerable potential. Unfortunately it was never realised, and with that accident all hope of a successful follow-up to Reading's 1980 championship winning season evaporated.

The season had begun promisingly. Bill Dore and Frank Higley, directors of Allied Presentations since 1975, had taken over as co-promoters. Dore's background in greyhounds and construction left many wondering what qualified him to run a speedway team. Higley who had been team manager from 1975 to 1978 came to that role with two decades as a speedway supporter. Also involved in the running of speedway at Reading would be Bill's daughter Pat Bliss, described in the programme as 'meeting secretary'.

Improvements to the stadium were promised, leading to the part-completion of the back straight bar. For years it remained a skeleton, a reminder of oft-promised but never-delivered improvements. Management set adult admission at £1.80. The BSPA set the minimum pay rate at £4 a point, but most riders were on negotiated deals, up to £20 a point for number ones. To cut tyre costs, riders would only be allowed one edge per meeting. Increased cost had led to Wolverhampton dropping down to the National League (as Exeter had the previous season) resulting in a smaller British League for the third year running.

The BSPA also promised a tightening of the guest rider rules. As a result fewer guests were used in league matches than in any year since 1967, only 50 in total, an average of three per team for the league programme.

Racers team building seemed fairly straightforward. Ashby had retired and Stancl made way (saving a fortune on air fares) to keep Reading below the 50-point limit. In February the first replacement signed on – a young American called Denny Pyeatt. During the winter an American team participated in a tri-nations Test series with England and hosts Australia. Pyeatt had scored well enough without pulling up any trees to suggest he could be a solid signing.

The final spot wasn't filled until the eve of the season. It went to Ashley Pullen.

The season opened with a new competition – the League Cup. The 16 teams were split into two groups of eight with the winners meeting in the final. Reading won all their home matches comfortably, and with wins at Wimbledon, Eastbourne and Ipswich and a 4-point defeat at King’s Lynn prospects of a final place were good. A win in one of their last two away matches would have seen Racers in the final. Luck deserted the team at Hackney where a single-point defeat caused by two Davis engine failures and a 5-0 conceded in heat 14 deprived them of a win. Then after losing 50-46 at Swindon the place in the final went to King’s Lynn who topped the group by a single point.

The home League Cup encounter with King’s Lynn, on a wet night, turned out to be a dramatic event. Rookie referee Frank Ebdon made his first Smallmead appearance. As well as awarding a dead-heat (Bernie Leigh and Lynn's Pierre Brannefors) he dished out numerous fines including three to Michael Lee alone. Soon there were calls for him to be banned – but over 25 years later he's still going strong! That meeting also gave a hint of things to come as Michael Lee suffered a troubled season culminating in his first drugs conviction. Lee's troubles were the primary cause of King’s Lynn's disintegration, and the Stars finished below Reading in the league and went down heavily to Coventry in the League Cup Final.

Jan Andersson topped the League Cup Southern section averages. From the Northern section only Bruce Penhall out-performed Andersson. Pullen exceeded expectations averaging over five and a half in the League Cup. It looked like the Racers team could mount a serious title challenge.

On the international front England beat Denmark in a Test series. Smallmead staged the second Test, England winning 58-50, despite being four down at the halfway stage. Kenny Carter (14) and Erik Gundersen (15) top scored in the match. The other early season international event at Smallmead was the World Team Cup qualifier. England won easily, and John Davis although named at reserve didn't get a ride. New Zealand could only manage 8 points, 4 of these coming from Tony Briggs. Bobby Schwartz scored 8 for runners-up America. Attendances for these two meetings were reported in the *Evening Post* as 5,000 and 7.000 respectively.

Bobby Schwartz – a lively presence in the Reading team. (DA)

In June Schwartz partnered Bruce Penhall to victory in the World Pairs Championship at Katowice, Poland – a first world title for both of them.

By June the league campaign was well under way. Early results were promising. Two wins (Halifax and Sheffield) and a draw (Poole) from the first six road trips suggested that Reading would be challenging for the title along with Coventry and Swindon. The win at Halifax was a bizarre affair – 11 of the 13 heats were 3-3s, only heats 9 and 11 which produced 4-2s to Reading bucked the trend.

Then came the June 29 bombshell. That night Racers lost at home to Cradley with Davis only scoring 5 paid 7. With the benefit of hindsight that result doesn't look so bad. It was the third of 20 consecutive wins Cradley clocked up on the way to a convincing first-ever league championship.

However, the rot had set in. Between June 15 and August 24, Reading rode 12 league matches without a single victory. In this case the margin between success and failure was a slim one; five matches were drawn (including a remarkable four in a row), and five more lost by 5 points or less. In consecutive matches Reading surrendered leads of 8, 10 and 10 points to only scramble a draw. By the end of July Andersson and Schwartz were scoring less freely in the League than in the League Cup, and Denny Pyeatt had moved up to fourth in the Racers league averages – with a modest 4.62 average.

Later in the season Reading picked up two more draws (Hackney at home and Birmingham away) to end the season with seven draws. This broke the previous record, six by Milton Keynes in 1978. Oxford also drew six times in their 1988 British League campaign, but no team in the 78-year history of league speedway has matched Reading's tally.

Reading's first match post-Davis was one of the draws. Remarkably the opponents were Poole, so Davis made a quick return top-scoring with ten. In his place Racers gave a debut to emergency loan signing Andrzej Huszcza. As late as the previous Friday no signing had been announced, and team manager Mick Bell indicated that he could have to come out of retirement! Huszcza's 5 paid 8 tally turned out to be more than he scored in his other four appearances. His Reading stint may have been brief, but his career is one of the longest in the sport's history. He made 16 appearances in the Polish Championship Final (plus two as reserve), including a win in 1982. In March 2007 he celebrated his 50th birthday, and spent the season riding for Poznan (in Polish League Division One) and Plzen (in the Czech Extra League). At Plzen Huszcza lined-up with team mate Zdenek Simota.

Once Huszcza had finished his stint a more familiar name filled the blank space in the programme for Reading v Swindon on August 31. For 62.1 glorious seconds the clocks were turned back as Anders Michanek, making his first appearance for the Racers since 1975, sped to victory over Phil Crump in his opening ride. Michanek's return had been announced in the previous Thursday's *Evening Post* and a work permit approved in double-quick time on the Friday. Unfortunately for most of the 6,000 crowd (an indication of Anders' pulling power) Swindon went on to win easily with Crump unbeaten for the rest of the match.

Although now 38 Anders still had his moments. A maximum against Hackney and third place in the World Longtrack Championship being the highlights of his 1981 stay. He also scored an 18-point maximum for Sweden in a Test match against an American team featuring Penhall, Schwartz, Shawn and Kelly Moran, and Denny Pyeatt. The few appearances he made were his last in the British League[30]. He continued riding in Sweden until 1985. By the time he retired he had replaced Olle Nygren as the all-time record points scorer in the Swedish League. As Michanek bowed out in England a new name emerged back in Sweden. The 1981 80cc Under-16 Swedish Championship went to a young lad by the name of Per Jonsson.

The gap left by Tony Briggs's injury gave opportunities to Steve McDermott, Ian Gledhill (who returned to the Racers fold after top scoring for Hackney in an early season Smallmead fixture) and Colin Ackroyd. They were joined by two Germans – Peter Wurterle and Max Schollhorn. Wurterle averaged less than two and Schollhorn was worse. Schollhorn lost his life grasstracking in France three years later. One rider who nearly ended up in the Racers back-up squad was Simon Wigg. But the promoters baulked at paying for his travel back from the continent – after all he was only a National League rider! These riders had further opportunities in the final month of the season when Ashley Pullen returned to the National League, finding a berth in his home town, Oxford.

The against-the-odds cup victory over Coventry did give Racers fans something to keep the season alive. The semi-final draw, against a modest Birmingham team, gave Reading a real chance of a cup final appearance to lighten the gloom. In the first leg Racers started badly, but fought back to 38-34 down. Brummies closed the meeting with four 4-2s in a row to take a solid 12-point lead down to Smallmead.

As Reading hadn't won a match by that margin since the Davis transfer bombshell the return leg looked a tough proposition for Reading. Although Racers eventually won the second leg 49-47 they were behind for much of the night making Brummies qualification a near certainty from early in the match. As well as a place in the cup final (where they lost to Ipswich) the Brummies also left Smallmead with the track record. Hans Nielsen became the

---

30 Michanek made two further appearances on the Smallmead track: in 1983 for Getingarna, and in 1988 at the Jan Andersson Testimonial.

first man to go under 60 seconds at Smallmead when he clocked 59.7 in the opening heat.

Although his league form had been poor, Bernie Leigh did manage to pick up a silver medal in the European Grasstrack Championship in September. The Manpower fell victim to the weather and didn't get restaged. Reading's season petered out. After a very wet September and October the British speedway season finally ended on November 7 at Canterbury.

Relatively unaffected by the season's turmoil Jan Andersson continued to perform at the highest level. In Sweden he scored 50 points in a three-match Test series against the USA (top scorer Bruce Penhall 43), and won his third Swedish title in a row. In official fixtures Jan gained 594 points (plus 9 bonus points) for the Racers, a new club record that stood for a decade until another Swede had an even more productive season.

But for a rider of Andersson's class there is one meeting above all that matters – the World Final. In one of the sport's most dramatic meetings Kenny Carter, Erik Gundersen and Dave Jessup (twice) all fell by the wayside with engine failures. Andersson didn't rise to the challenge and finished with 9 points and sixth place. With reigning champion Michael Lee, Hans Nielsen and Jiri Stancl in the bottom half of the field that left three riders fighting it out for the rostrum positions.

Bookies favourite Bruce Penhall triumphed over Danes Ole Olsen and Tommy Knudsen after two of the greatest races Wembley has ever seen. In heat 7 he passed Olsen on the final lap and in an even closer finish did the same to Knudsen seven heats later. Fifteen months later the news that speedway would never return to Wembley broke. For its final show Wembley had produced an enthralling meeting and a popular new champion.

Team: Jan Andersson 10.26, Bobby Schwartz 9.32, John Davis 8.86, (Anders Michanek 6.73), Bernie Leigh 5.30, Tony Briggs 5.00, Denny Pyeatt 4.86, Ashley Pullen 4.55, (Ian Gledhill 3.82), (Peter Wurterle 1.52)

1982 – Hackney, July 16

John Grahame (far left) wipes a tear from his eye during the minute's silence for Denny Pyeatt. Also pictured, before the start of Reading's match with Swindon just two days after Denny's death, are guest Shawn Moran and Tim Hunt. (EP)

A single red rose in the empty pits space allocated to Denny Pyeatt symbolised the heartbreak felt by everyone at Smallmead. Riders were moving round like automatons and the spectators seemed eerily silent. Although Racers came from six down to beat local rivals Swindon that night, celebrations were muted as minds were still on the events of the previous Friday.

Seven days earlier, on Monday July 12, Denny Pyeatt and Jan Andersson teamed up three times. Each time they rode together Reading recorded a 5-1, the last one against Hans Nielsen. As Reading only won by 6 points, Pyeatt's performance warranted the description – match-winning. Three days later he top scored at Wimbledon winning three races. Although Reading narrowly lost they returned to London the following night for a clash with Hackney.

Friday July 16 was shaping up to be the night Racers recorded their first away win (in the league) for over a year. After eight heats Reading held a 27-21 lead largely down to Pyeatt's two race wins. Team manager John Smith put Pyeatt into heat 9 in place of John Grahame.

Riding against Bo Petersen (Hackney's top rider) and 18-year-old debutant Marvyn Cox, the Racers young American entered the third bend just ahead of Cox. The Hackney youngster (and future Racer) clipped Pyeatt's back wheel sending him catapulting towards the fence. Denny was unlucky, firstly his trajectory took him over the safety fence, and secondly there was a lamp standard in his path.

From the moment of impact everyone could see the situation was serious. Riders rushed up to be close at hand, but were signalled away. The crowd waited in near silence. Only three years earlier Vic Harding had lost his life at Waterden Road, and earlier that season Brett Alderton suffered fatal injuries at King's Lynn.

The ambulance rushed Denny to Hackney Hospital (a former Victorian workhouse less than a mile from the stadium) and after half an hour a clearly distressed Len Silver announced the abandonment of the meeting. The Reading team gathered at the hospital, with John Smith and Denny's girlfriend Hazel Sillence. These two stayed the night with Denny in a coma and on a life-support machine.

At 8.45am on the Saturday morning Denny passed away.

Denny's body was flown back to the States and on July 29 a memorial service took place at Christchurch on Christchurch Road in Reading. The packed congregation included many familiar names. John Davis, Hackney's Finn Thomsen, Scott Autrey, Brad Oxley, Gary Guglielmi, Tim Hunt, John Grahame, Tony Briggs, Bernie Leigh, Bill Dore, Frank Higley, Mick Bell and World Champion Bruce Penhall all took the time to pay tribute to the man who died wearing the winged wheel.

The following Monday a 29-heat memorial event took place with a 4,000 attendance. The Smallmead crowd witnessed two 13-heat challenges involving 28 riders plus a three heat individual tournament for the Denny Pyeatt Memorial Trophy. After scoring a maximum in his team match it caused no surprise when Shawn Moran won the event. In the team matches Jan Andersson's Seven beat John Davis's Seven 47-30 and Bruce Penhall's Seven beat Bobby Schwartz's Seven 43-35. Bernie Leigh made an unexpected return to the track in Schwartz's team, but failed to score.

Over in Denny's native California a memorial meeting at San Bernadino went to Alan Christian, with Mike Faria and Mike Curoso runners-up. The *Speedway Mail* reported that second place in the handicap final went to an unknown 21-year-old – Guy Ermolenko.

The inquest, held in September, returned a verdict of accidental death. Marvin Cox (who broke a wrist in the collision), John Smith, referee Barry Bowles and Len Silver all gave evidence. The track complied with ACU safety requirements, but Silver conceded that with hindsight perhaps more could have been done.

Long before the inquest, the Hackney accident had sparked considerable debate about rider safety. Slicker tracks and faster machines, specifically the introduction of the 4-valve, were put forward as possible causes.

However, for all the talk it took another fatality in similar circumstances before the Speedway Control Board insisted on the removal of lampposts. In September 1983 Craig Featherby of Milton Keynes lost control in wet conditions at Peterborough and flew through the air until a lamppost ended his journey.

Just a month after Denny's accident the United States appeared in their second World Team Cup Final. England had a perverse knack of failing to qualify for finals held at White City. 1982 was the third (and final) time the venue had been used, and without England the Danes provided the main opposition. Psyched-up by pre-match talk that they were going to 'win this one for Denny' the Yanks stormed to a 13-point victory. Bobby Schwartz won his first three rides before standing down to allow reserve Scott Autrey to take to the track. On an emotional victory parade the five Americans (Sigalos and the Moran brothers completed the team) clutched a large portrait of Denny.

Two weeks later America staged its first, and to date only, World Final. The Los Angeles Colosseum programme contained a statement signed by ten of the American riders racing in the UK at the time. It concluded:

> *"Denny loved speedway racing. He loved the challenge. Denny wasn't as outspoken as some of us but he carried our flag proudly and as high as anyone. Denny was not just a friend. Sometimes he was a teacher, sometimes a student. Sometimes he was like a father, sometimes like a son but most of all Denny was our brother."*

There was something unique about the American riders of the 1980s. Thousands of miles from home, the camaraderie and patriotism of this close knit group brought something special to British speedway in this decade.

Denny's contribution at Reading will never be forgotten. He was slowly improving, and in his final outings for Reading fans glimpsed a potential that sadly could never be fulfilled. In the time he wore the winged wheel Denny didn't miss a single match. Including challenges, he rode a total of 85 consecutive fixtures. When fate brought the run to an end his 6.25 league average left him third in the Racers averages, only outscored by Andersson and Schwartz.

As 1982 dawned the country faced a severe economic recession. In January unemployment figures broke the 3 million barrier, in February Laker Airways (the first low cost airline) went bust. The speedway community felt the impact too. Wolverhampton and Workington both went out of business as did Duplex-Litho printers of speedway programmes for 22 tracks including Reading. Sponsorship budgets are often the first to be cut in times of hardship. Reading lost Manpower's backing (worth £8,000) and Bobby Schwartz no longer had the support of Norman Reeves motors.

The Millers Arms in Caversham hosted the Reading Supporters Club annual general meeting on January 27. Those present listened in shock as a statement signed by co-promoter Frank Higley was read out by John Spindler (a long-established sponsor of Bernie Leigh). It announced the closure of the Supporters Club.

The previous year there had been wholesale changes to the membership of the committee, and the newly elected committee found it hard to establish a constructive relationship with the management. The Davis transfer affair provoked further tension and the scheduling of the Birmingham cup semi-final away leg on the same night as the annual dance heightened the disaffection between the parties. The annual dance (at the Top Rank Suite) lost £258.02.

A management run "social club" without democratically elected officers started the season running coaches to away matches, but faced opposition from former secretary Frank Nunn. The battle was brief. Reading fans voted with their feet and soon the 'official' Dore-backed venture stopped organising coaches. The dedicated followers backed the breakaway group. This rift lasted for a long time and guaranteed that Reading fans would always regard Bill Dore with suspicion.

The following year, the role of organising away coach trips (under the Berkshire Speedway Club banner) fell to 1982 team manager John Smith.[31] John, a Racers fan who went on to organise trips to the continent under the 'JMS Allstars' banner and became manager of the American team, took over the team manager's role from Mick Bell. The Racers former captain went on to act as team manager for Coventry from 1983 to 1991 (winning league championships with them in 1987 and 1988) before moving on to Swindon and more recently Somerset. He announced his retirement at the end of 2006.

When Mick Bell first rode for Reading in 1969 his team mates included a novice by the name of Bernie Leigh. After 13 seasons, 12 of them in the winged wheel the time had come for Bernie to bow out gracefully. Shortly before the season started he confirmed the rumours circulating that he had ridden his last.

A likeable and unassuming presence, he remains one of the most popular riders ever to wear the Racers colours. He donned the winged wheel on 431 occasions in official fixtures. He was an ever-present in 1970, 1971, 1973, 1975, 1978, 1979 and 1980. Only Jan Andersson, Dave Mullett and Phil Morris have since overtaken Leigh's appearance tally.

With Davis, Briggs and Pullen all needing replacement from the previous year Reading

31 Reliability was never a strong point of coaches hired by John Smith, and actually arriving at the visiting track before the advertised starting time became an achievement.

required four new riders. In February, Reading announced that Jiri Stancl would be rejoining the team. Alan Grahame and Kevin Jolly were the leading candidates for the heat leader vacancy, but at the beginning of March Steve Gresham came on board for a reported fee of £8,000. With a week before the season's start the final pieces of the jigsaw emerged. Ipswich sold Tim Hunt to Reading – for a fee in the region of £8,000. Peter Wurterle was to be given another run and Dave Trownson would return as number eight.

Although named in the opening night's programme Wurterle didn't join the team. (He did make one second-half appearance in July.) Instead John Grahame, having failed to retain his place with National League Oxford, was given a reserve berth in the British League.

The 1982 Team left to right: Bobby Schwartz, Denny Pyeatt, Jiri Stancl, Jan Andersson (on bike), John Smith (team manager), Steve Gresham, Tim Hunt and John Grahame. (Retro)

The campaign opened with the League Cup. Racers won their final away match in the competition, 40-38 at Wimbledon where Jan Andersson equalled the track record. However, they had already dropped 4 points at home with Ipswich and Eastbourne victorious at Smallmead. Bobby Schwartz missed several matches due to injuries sustained while riding in Germany. Although riding for the Racers, he still hadn't agreed terms with the Smallmead management and persistent rumours of a swap with Mitch Shirra (in dispute with the Coventry management) had an unsettling affect. These continued even after Shirra re-signed with Coventry in late May, due to an incident at Smallmead in June when Shirra expressed displeasure after being taken out of a race.

The only positive from the League Cup campaign came from an unexpected quarter. Expected by most to sink without trace, John Grahame averaged over five in his first seven matches. But a poor start from Tim Hunt meant Grahame quickly found himself in the top five and there he found life much harder. He did last the full season and emerged from the year with credit.

Before the league campaign got under way seriously, Racers experienced cup action with a tough tie against Belle Vue. The first leg is not remembered with any fondness by Reading fans. On a very wet track, with rain continuing to fall and lightning nearby, the referee and home team were determined to complete the match. The tension heightened after a clash between Belle Vue team manager Ian Thomas and Steve Gresham. After a racing incident Thomas approached Gresham on track and received a kick in the testicles! A few races later there was a confrontation between Gresham and his team mate Bobby Schwartz. After ten heats Racers trailed 42-18 and race times were seven seconds outside the track record. John Smith pulled the team out and the Aces rounded off the meeting with three unopposed 5-nils.

With cup interest ended the league campaign started in earnest. Away wins are crucial to a high placing. Reading didn't manage one until their penultimate away fixture. Schwartz and Dave Trownson took a 4-2 in the last heat to seal a 40-38 win over Poole. Schwartz with a maximum and Trownson (paid 9) had been the men primarily responsible for the win. Poole only won three matches in their 1982 league campaign so Racers victory was not entirely unexpected.

Reading also drew at Swindon and Ipswich, but three defeats at home more than cancelled out the few away successes. In June Cradley steamrollered the Racers with a 46-32 win at Smallmead, equalling Racers record home defeat over 13 heats (also against Cradley in 1979). In July, shortly after Denny's death, Ipswich took the points. Schwartz (15-point maximum) and Andersson (14) fought a two-man rearguard action. Witches had a trump card in rookie reserve Jeremy Doncaster (paid 9).

Belle Vue became the third team to win at Smallmead in the league with a victory in October that virtually sewed up the league title. They did so despite Peter Collins finishing bottom of their score chart. As happened on countless occasions that year, Andersson and Schwartz did the bulk of Reading's scoring.

Two days earlier Reading Football Club drew a crowd of under 2,000 for a league match at home to Preston, as they fought to avoid relegation back to the bottom division of the Football League. The club went up for sale valued at half a million pounds. Bill Dore proposed relocating Reading FC to Smallmead. The proposal seems ludicrous 25 years later, but even then football fans didn't fancy co-locating at the decaying greyhound and speedway stadium. The entry "director of Swindon Town FC" on Bill Dore's CV can't have endeared him to the Elm Park faithful either. Attention quickly moved to two prospective bidders: Berkshire-based Deep Purple vocalist Ian Gillan and local businessman Roger Smee.

Six months later Reading FC very nearly disappeared as Oxford United owner Robert Maxwell proposed merging the two clubs under the banner Thames Valley Royals! Suggestions that Swindon Town FC should also participate in the merger were firmly rebuffed by their director Bill Dore. Smee subsequently steered the Royals back to more stable waters.

The cheapest Reading FC season ticket cost £33 in 1982/83. In 2007/08 the equivalent figure was £545. Of course in those days that would get you a spot standing on the terraces at Elm Park watching the likes of Rochdale whereas last season Manchester United graced the visitors' dressing room at the all-seater Madejski stadium. A similar rate of inflation applied to Smallmead admission prices would have uplifted the £2.50 adult admission charge of 1983 to £41!

Racers finished ninth out of 15, though one more win would have moved them up to sixth. As the season progressed it became obvious that Reading's attendances were in decline – a combination of poor results and the economic downturn. The added competition of football's World Cup caused just 1,500 people to turn out for the league clash with Poole that coincided with England's elimination at the hands of Spain (July 5).

It would be easy to attribute Reading's poor season to July's tragedy, but results in the League Cup and early British League matches clearly suggest that the team hadn't gelled. There were three main causes for Reading under-performing.

Firstly Jiri Stancl managed to ride in only 13 of Reading's 28 league matches. Continental commitments and a spat with the Czech authorities, not injuries, were the cause. When he did make it his returns were disappointing, roughly 2 points per match down on his 1980 scoring.

Although he reached the World Final and won the Czech Golden Helmet (a meeting that Andersson and Hunt also rode in), the big disappointment of Stancl's season was the loss of the Czechoslovakian Championship to Ales Dryml Snr. This ended Stancl's run of ten national titles in a row. He did regain the title in 1983 for his 12th and final national crown. His 1982 World Final score of 7 points was the best of his nine appearances on the big night. He made his last World Final appearance in 1984 aged 34.

While Stancl's career progressed towards the veteran stage, a new kid on the block excited plenty of comment – Toni Kasper jnr. His father had ridden for Coventry, won the Czech Golden Helmet and qualified at reserve for the World Final. The son went on to exceed these achievements, starting with a win in the 1982 European Junior Championship. But his season ended early after a fall while guesting for Reading in September. He suffered a fractured pelvis and dislocated hip after he clipped the back straight fence while leading in his first ride. The Reading track has a good safety record and serious injuries have been few, but this was one of those exceptions.

Stancl wasn't the only rider who failed to live up to expectations, Steve Gresham arrived with a 7.5-point average. He scored double figures twice in the opening four League Cup matches, but failed to do so again in an official fixture. His average dropped to 5.5, a dire figure for a heat leader.

Gresham had been an unpopular visitor in Swindon colours, notably after a run-in with Tony Briggs and his father Barry. His form and his relationship with Schwartz meant he continued to be regarded as an outsider. On September 20 referee John Homer (the Smallmead timekeeper until 1981) banned him from a second-half final after an incident with Kevin Smith and Poole team manager Pete Jarman. By the end of the season the fans on the terraces and management were for once in harmony, both expressing doubts about Gresham[32] and Stancl returning.

The third rider to disappoint, Tim Hunt shed a point from his average. A modest and likeable character off track, his on-track riding style made him an unpopular opponent. (In later seasons this resulted in him becoming an unpopular team mate too!) His best performance of the season came at his former track with paid 10 in the League Cup encounter at Ipswich. In 1982 he gained the only international cap of his career representing England in the Reading leg of the international fours, a low-key contest against the USA (the winners), Denmark and Australasia.

In a recent interview (*Backtrack*, March-April 2007) John Grahame reflected on riding with Hunt and Gresham: "It was a team that wasn't really knitting together at the time...every race was like an individual – it was a fight for survival."

The gaps left by Stancl's absences and Denny's death were largely filled by National League riders taking a number eight role. Trownson proved reliable riding in half of Racers league matches. Oxford youngster Colin Ackroyd rode for Reading a few times the previous year, and continued to show promise in 1982.

Bernie Leigh and Tony Briggs both featured in speculation about permanent replacements for Pyeatt. Despite Sweden's eclipse as a speedway superpower, Reading once again stuck to the mantra 'when in need sign a Swede'. Eastbourne beat them to Lillebror Johansson, the first name in the frame, but Reading's management secured the signature of another Swede – Uno Johansson. His sixth place in the previous year's Swedish League averages suggested potential, but his poor record in the Swedish Championship and age (25) gave reason to be cautious. He made the briefest of appearances in England in 1978, riding for Belle Vue in the Knock-Out Cup Final. Apart from paid 8 in his second match he failed to justify his place in

---

32 I disliked Gresham so much that I very pointedly cheered for the opposition when Gresham was on track.

the Racers team.

It was left to Andersson and Schwartz to make up for these deficiencies. Andersson finished third in the League Cup averages behind Bruce Penhall and Kenny Carter. Although not quite as dominant as the two previous years he still ended the season with an average of 9.96 in official fixtures, just enough to keep top spot in the Reading rankings. He lost his Swedish title to Anders Michanek, and had a quiet World Final scoring 8.

In league matches alone Schwartz outscored Andersson, finishing sixth in the league averages. In the seven matches immediately after Denny died Schwartz scored 90 points (averaging 11.25). After the British season ended Schwartz won his second World Pairs title, racing to six 5-1s with partner Dennis Sigalos. The unusual staging date arose from the choice of venue for the final – Liverpool, Australia.

One American who could give Schwartz a run for his money at Smallmead was Shawn Moran. Not since Graham Plant in 1968 had a visitor been so dominant. In six matches (three of them as a Reading guest) he recorded five maximums and in the sixth match posted three wins and an engine failure. His first appearance of the season on June 14 (the date of the Argentinian surrender at Port Stanley in the Falklands) saw him break the track record.

Another American took the lion's share of the headlines in 1982, World Champion Bruce Penhall. Having ended 1981 as a popular World Champion, he finished the following season as one of the least popular. His downfall and rivalry with Kenny Carter were the central stories of 1982. On July 4 he decided to coast round at the back in heat 19 of the Overseas Final at White City. This enhanced his compatriots' qualification chances but turned a large slice of public opinion against him.

Then just before the World Final he withdrew from the British League. Cradley Heath had looked a certainty to retain their title, but Penhall's departure allowed Belle Vue to overtake them. Cradley did beat Belle Vue in the Knock-Out Cup final, despite the Aces using their new 16-year-old wunderkid Andy Smith.

The Los Angeles clash between Penhall and Carter remains one of the most talked about in speedway history. The record books show Penhall victorious and Les Collins the surprise runner-up, but the debate over the rights and wrongs of that Penhall/Carter clash will continue. The announcement of Penhall's retirement came just two weeks after his final Smallmead appearance – in the Denny's memorial meeting.

Team: Jan Andersson 9.96, Bobby Schwartz 9.83, Steve Gresham 5.57, Denny Pyeatt 5.28, Jiri Stancl 5.23, Tim Hunt 5.08, Dave Trownson 4.66, (Colin Ackroyd 4.00), John Grahame 3.87, (Uno Johansson 2.78)

1983 – The Tail That Didn't Wag

Throughout the 1980s, Reading team building tended to be based on a strategy of finding three strong heat leaders and hoping the tail would look after itself. The story of 1983 epitomised this approach.

In February, Reading, Swindon and Coventry completed a complicated triangular deal that saw Racers acquire Mitch Shirra while Steve Gresham returned to Swindon and Steve Bastable moved from Swindon to Coventry to replace Shirra. The deal, which also transferred Alf Busk from Coventry to Swindon, valued Shirra at £15,000. Reading definitely got the best deal; Shirra went on to have a superb first season at Smallmead while the other three riders all dropped their averages. Gresham's British career ended in July when Swindon sacked him.

With Andersson and Schwartz returning, Bill Dore needed to fill the four remaining team spots. In January, Glyn Taylor had come second in the Australian Final of the World Championship, qualifying for the Overseas Final with Billy Sanders at the expense of Phil Crump. Taylor decided that he needed a British team spot, and Dore gambled on him being able to improve substantially on his sub-3-point form of 1977.

Unable to get satisfactory assurances as to Stancl's availability, Dore accepted a young unknown (and hopefully more available) Czech: Stanislav Urban. He had finished 15th in the previous year's Czechoslovakian Championship, but apart from a sixth place finish in the 1979 European Junior Championship little else was known about him. He started the season late, finally making his debut at Eastbourne in mid May but then missing the next four matches. Number eight Dave Trownson replaced him in the early fixtures.

Tim Hunt and John Grahame returned to complete the team. None of the four riders who filled the second string and reserve berths on the opening night (a resounding 33-45 defeat at the hands of Wimbledon) kept their places for the whole season.

The riders found a new team manager looking after them; Bob Radford, who steered the Racers to success in 1973, replaced John Smith. His appointment was confirmed just a week before racing got under way. Radford's unusually blunt programme notes soon made clear his frustrations with the Racers tail, and he quickly set about reshaping it.

His first move took everyone by surprise. Pierre Brannefors, son of 1966 World Final reserve Bengt, had tried to make his name in Britain at King's Lynn two years before. He averaged barely 3 points a match and did little in 1982 to suggest that he warranted a second chance.

Any doubts about the wisdom of his signing evaporated when he made his debut on April 11. After paid 13 against Hackney in his first match, he went on to register his first maximum within a month. His previous team King's Lynn provided the opposition on that occasion. His popularity was assured by a series of robust performances throughout the season, which he ended with an average of over 7. He capped his year by reaching the Inter-Continental Final (the penultimate stage of the World Championship) and representing Sweden in the World Pairs Final. Naturally, Jan Andersson was his partner.

Brannefors replaced Taylor. By the end of April he had been joined by another new name. At the time there were so many Danes riding in Britain that a qualifying round of the 1983 Danish National Championship was held at Hackney that year. But Danes have been fairly thin on the ground at Smallmead, Peter Glanz becoming the first in 1983. In March, Danish club side Fredriksborg toured National League tracks, and Glanz top scored at Stoke. Shortly after, he signed for Reading. The highlight of a quiet first season came at Hackney where he scored 10 paid 11. In late September he suffered a run of four scoreless matches that took his average below 4, making his signing a questionable success. Initially he filled the gap left by Urban's late arrival, but once Urban turned up John Grahame became surplus to requirements.

Grahame and Taylor both found National League berths. Taylor settled in well at Edinburgh, but Grahame found himself dropped again after six matches at Stoke. Tim Hunt fared little better. In his first eleven League Cup matches his best score was 3 paid 4. Although his scoring picked up a little when the league matches started, he failed to keep his team place, ending the season at Swindon. Hunt's riding style drew criticism from Bob Radford, and he also had a run in with the authorities over the use of an oversize carburettor at Ipswich in April.

Initially Hunt's place went to Finn Jensen. The inconsistent Dane arrived from Leicester with five consecutive zeros in his final five Lions matches[33]. At Reading he managed to extend that sequence with two more zeros. Yet in between his two appearances in Racers colours he came fifth in the World Longtrack Final. Also in that final were Jiri Stancl (second), Alois Wiesbock (fourth) and Bobby Schwartz (13th). Jensen's departure gave John Grahame another chance to stake a place in the team.

When Jensen replaced Hunt, Reading were in the position of fielding a team without a single British rider. Although a regular occurrence nowadays, this was still a novelty in 1982. However, Exeter had regularly turned out without a home-grown rider as far back as 1977.

Brannefors made the 1983 season. A bargain at £1,500, he turned a mightily powerful heat leader trio into an awesome top four. On the terraces his forceful style made him into a folk hero, earning the nickname 'Mr. Rockhard' (from a character in a TV ad for mints). But with scant backing from the lower-order riders a title challenge was never realistic.

Pierre Brannefors – a Reading legend. (Retro)

Reading finished fourth in the league, with just one home defeat more than compensated for by four away wins. Predictably the home loss came when league champions elect Cradley came visiting. Nearly 4,000 people turned up to see the Heathens team, rated as one of the greatest in history. They arrived in September with only one defeat, and that by just 2 points at

---

33 As a resident of Leicester at the time I saw most of these and the relief that he was leaving Leicester was outweighed by the dismay at his signing for Reading.

Coventry. That last sentence is slightly misleading, because come 7.30 p.m. only four Heathens were present.

Just over 24 hours beforehand Egon Muller romped to victory on German shale in the World Final. Mitch Shirra and four Heathens took part in the Norden final. Only Phil Collins managed to arrive before tapes up; Erik Gundersen and Peter Ravn arrived at 8 p.m., leaving Shirra and Lance King as non-arrivals. Despite being under-strength the Heathens won comfortably with number eight Simon Cross paid for double figures. Reading protested that referee Frank Ebdon refused to allow Phil Crump (who had been on stand-by) to guest for Shirra and attempted to claim the match points on the grounds that Cradley fielded an under-strength(!) team. To be fair to Shirra it was the only Racers match he missed all year. But as Bob Radford pointed out, if he could be back home by 1 p.m. why couldn't the riders get back for 7.30 p.m.?

Just two weeks later non-arrivals again caused controversy when Ipswich turned up minus their top two – Dennis Sigalos and Billy Sanders. Both had been competing in the Czech Golden Helmet. Sigalos had been victorious; former Racer Jiri Stancl came second. Unfortunately problems with the flight back to England left the Ipswich pair stranded in Prague. Former Racers team manager John Smith had been responsible for organising their travel arrangements, but no blame was apportioned to him. As a consequence Ipswich lost the opportunity to become the second team to take the league points away from Smallmead. Under the circumstances a 45-33 defeat was a good showing. Five days later Cradley beat Ipswich to secure victory in the league championship race, leaving the Witches in second place.

Action from a 1983 Reading v Swindon clash (from left to right): Mitch Shirra, Malcolm Holloway, Peter Glanz and Steve Gresham. (EP)

Reading's four away wins came at the four sides that finished in the bottom four positions in the league table. After wins at Poole and Leicester in June, Racers moved up to third in the league table. They spent most of the summer in fifth, briefly returning to third after a 10-point win at Swindon in August. The final away victory – an easy one, by 14 points – came in the final match, at Eastbourne.

Visits to Poole, Eastbourne and Swindon at the start of the season also provided League Cup victories. Reading finished third in their group and just missed out on a semi-final berth. Three 40-38 defeats in a row at Ipswich, Wimbledon and Hackney were frustrating, but home defeats to Wimbledon and Ipswich didn't help.

Reading saved their best performance of the season for the Knock-Out Cup. After scraping past Birmingham 79-77 on aggregate the Racers faced Ipswich. The Witches had only beaten Reading by two in the League Cup, and later in the season would only manage a 4-point win in the league encounter.

In the cup match at Foxhall Heath, Racers led for most of the meeting. It took tactical substitute rides from Sigalos and Sanders to bring the Witches back into contention. A last-heat decider looked to be going Reading's way until Preben Eriksen passed Schwartz and Sigalos forced his way past Shirra leaving the match tied.

Ipswich generally rode well at Smallmead and the second leg couldn't be taken for granted. Sigalos won heats 11, 12 and 13 in the return. The second leg was heading for another draw until Mitch Shirra passed Eriksen on the final bend of the final lap of the final race. So once again Reading progressed to the next round with a 79-77 aggregate win.

Unfortunately their next opponents were Cradley who won both legs with ease. Reading lost by 14 at home and 16 away. In both legs they carried three riders who failed to beat an opponent, exposing the weakness of Reading's tail.

Steve McDermott performed well on the few occasions he helped the Racers out. On the same evening as the away leg of the Cradley tie he triumphed in the National League Riders Championship. He wore the colours of Berwick who gave him a testimonial in 1988 after a decade of uninterrupted service to the Bandits.

On Friday September 9 Reading beat Poole 45-33 in a challenge match at Smallmead. Unusually the two teams were on three wheels. Sidecars had made appearances in second halves before, but this time they topped the bill.

The season's concluding matches included a two-wheeled challenge at Poole. Reading drew with their heat leaders scoring 36 of their 39 points. What made this meeting noteworthy was the British debut of Sam (Guy) Ermolenko, the latest in the 1980s conveyor belt of Stateside talent. There were still more to come: in February of that year *Speedway Star* columnist Dave Lanning highlighted the potential of 12-year-old infant prodigy Greg Hancock!

Ermolenko guested for Reading in their penultimate home meeting, a benefit for Marcus Williams. Signed as a junior and loaned out to Exeter, Williams suffered serious injuries in an accident on his National League debut.

Further afield, October marked Ole Olsen's retirement from British speedway. He bowed out with 12 points and third place in the Brandonapolis. A Coventry crowd of 20,000 witnessed Kenny Carter beat Erik Gundersen in a run-off, with Mitch Shirra scoring 11.

As the sport entered one of its most turbulent close seasons Eastbourne expressed an interest in Bobby Schwartz. Schwartz made half-a-dozen guest appearances for Eastbourne, during another busy season.

In April, Customs officials at Heathrow found cannabis on Schwartz and Kelly Moran. They were fined for possession, and Schwartz lost sponsors after this incident. Despite this he rode at the top of his form in the England v USA Test series racking up 61 points in the five Test series. With the series level at two-all and the final Test tied at 48-all, England raced to two 5-1s to seal the series in a dramatic climax at Sheffield.

Controversy caught up with Schwartz again in July. Staged on the eve of the first anniversary of Denny Pyeatt's accident, the Hackney v Reading clash was bound to be an emotional occasion. A poor track caused complaints from Finn Thomsen, and injuries to Jens Rasmussen (Hackney) and Jan Andersson. Schwartz, also a faller in his first ride, decided to show his displeasure with the Hackney circuit by storming onto the track and attempting to tear down the safety fence before walking out of the meeting.

Mitch Shirra's first season at Smallmead proved to be a tremendous success. Here he is shown receiving a rider of the month award. (EP)

Mitch Shirra kept the Racers flag flying at Hackney with a 15-point maximum. Jan Andersson finished top of Racers averages six times in the seven years from 1980 to 1986. The exception came in 1983 when Mitch Shirra arrived at Smallmead with a bang. His career had stalled at Coventry. In each of his last four years at Brandon his average had fallen, but switching to Reading boosted it from 7.38 to 10.02. There is little doubt it was the best year of a long and colourful career.

Team: Mitch Shirra 10.02, Jan Andersson 9.47, Bobby Schwartz 9.02, Pierre Brannefors 7.28, Tim Hunt 4.31, Peter Glanz 3.85, Stanislav Urban 3.24, John Grahame 2.74

1984 – British Speedway in Crisis

1984 brought Reading fans a new idol to worship. However, his arrival was not without its complications.

In early 1983 Racers narrowly beat a touring Getingarna team. Anders Michanek top scored with 8 points from three rides. Riding at number two was a youngster called Per Jonsson who scored 4 paid 6. He had already caused a stir in Sweden by finishing fifth in the 1982 Swedish Championship, still aged only 16. Reading, whose appetite for Swedes could never be sated, noted his name down as one to watch.

A productive domestic season in Sweden, where he finished sixth in the averages, further enhanced his reputation in 1983. A protégé of three-times world finalist Torbjorn Harrysson, his form prompted Jan Andersson to say that he wanted to see Per riding for Reading in 1984. By Christmas the deal was done.

In 1984 no less than 20 Danes raced regularly in the British League. As European Community members, Danish riders didn't need work permits. The growing feeling that the British League was being overwhelmed by foreigners resulted in those riders who did need work permits being subject to more scrutiny. Sweden's entry to the European Union was still over a decade away, so Per required a work permit.

28 March 1983 – Just turned 17, Per Jonsson tours Britain with Getingarna. This shot captures Per's first visit to Smallmead. (Retro)

Given his pedigree no problems were expected. Just days before the season started Racers team plans were thrown into confusion when the Department of Employment turned the permit application down. Despite support from the BSPA and the Speedway Riders Association (the riders' trade union), it emerged that opposition from the Speedway Control Board had been instrumental in determining the outcome.

Time after time in 1984 the SCB demonstrated a staggering degree of incompetence. On the Jonsson permit refusal SCB manager Dick Bracher said: "We've heard it all before, a lot of riders come over here with big reputations but fail to live up to them. The criteria for overseas riders is a 6-point average and one has to doubt if a rider barely 18 is capable of achieving that in their first season in the British League".[34]

On 26 March, five days after Per's 18th birthday, Reading's appeal took place in London. Pat Bliss, armed with plenty of facts and testimonials argued the case. Per's strongest advocate Bob Radford had threatened to resign if the appeal failed. The successful outcome meant he remained as team manager.

On April 1 Per made his debut at Poole scoring 7 points. The following day, watched by a dozen or more family members and Anders Michanek, he scored 8. Among the riders he headed on his Smallmead debut – Michael Lee and Sam Ermolenko.

There is no record of how red Dick Bracher's face was at this moment.

With Jonsson safely on board, Reading looked set for a fine season. Captain Jan Andersson and Pierre Brannefors returned to Smallmead along with Mitch Shirra to make a solid-looking spearhead. Peter Glanz's return was touch and go, but he was given a second chance along with Tim Hunt who returned from his loan spell at Swindon. The final spot went to Malcolm Holloway, bought from Swindon for a fee reported to be over £7,000.

Although in 1984 Racers tracked a settled team and generally fared well, British speedway endured a painful 18 months that saw eight teams quit the British League, serious injuries, rider bans and a scandal that gravely damaged the sport.

The previous autumn, speedway's equivalent of the grim reaper – property developers – brought an end to speedway at Leicester, Birmingham and White City. With Wembley unavailable and White City removed from the equation the search for an alternative World Final venue grew more frantic. Bradford eventually emerged as the choice, but the delay had led to a postponement from 1984 to 1985 of Britain's next World Final. With several British tracks falling on hard times, the profit share from the British staging of the World Final provided a lifeline. A delay of 12 months and the likelihood of a lower payout alarmed many promoters.

These fears were exacerbated by the allocation of the 1987 World Final to Amsterdam. The Netherlands had never managed to provide so much as a single World Final qualifier. It underlined the increasing marginalisation of Britain within the speedway's world governing body, the FIM.

Len Silver pulled out of Hackney, Eastbourne reported huge losses leaving their future uncertain and on the eve of the new season Sheffield threatened to drop down to the National League. Mildenhall's attempts to go in the opposite direction were rebuffed. Four tracks did join the British League – Oxford, Exeter, National League champions Newcastle and newly re-opened Wolverhampton. These changes gave rise to a very active transfer market. Oxford signed Hans Nielsen for £30,000, Wolves promoter Peter Adams acquired the services of Dennis Sigalos and Preben Eriksen from Ipswich, and Simon Wigg moved from Cradley to Oxford for £25,000. All these deals were done before Christmas; Reading's sale of Bobby Schwartz took a little longer. Eastbourne (despite pleading poverty) beat Exeter to his signature for a fee of £25,000.

One piece of good news came from Essex, where Arena Essex (now Lakeside) opened for the first time. A major talking point was the lack of a safety fence. The Arena management tempted ex-Racer Bob Humphreys out of retirement. Scunthorpe, Berwick and Glasgow had all relocated existing promotions to new tracks in the last five years, but not since 1978 had a track been opened afresh. That track had been Milton Keynes, and like Arena the number one in their debut season was Bob Humphreys.

For the first time in three years the British League and National League management committees met formally, an indication of how divided speedway had become.

Two other close-season developments are worth noting. The BSPA approved a new rule

---

34 *Speedway Star* 24 March 1984

governing starts. Riders could be excluded for just touching the tapes, no longer did they have to break them before the red light came on. Originally the new rule contained provision for excluded riders to be re-instated with a 20-yard handicap, but that part of the proposal didn't make it to the rulebook until 1999. The use of the word 'may' in the new ruling gave referees too much discretion and the inconsistent application of the new rule caused a lot of discontent throughout the season. A notable victim of the new rule was Erik Gundersen whose average dropped significantly as he picked up exclusion after exclusion under the new rules. Erik's most notable exclusion came in the run-off for the British League Riders Championship, leaving Chris Morton to beat Hans Nielsen.

Eventually the rulebook was made clearer and riders adapted to the new starting procedures. Ultimately this proved to be one of the few rule changes that made a tangible difference to the quality of racing.

The concerns about the British League becoming dominated by overseas riders resulted in proposals for a junior league to foster British talent. The British Youth League would involve six-man teams competing over a full 13 heats. Seven tracks, including Reading signed up to this new project. The BSPA vetoed the proposals by refusing to waive rule 109: "No promoter shall hold more than one meeting a week ..." A decade later British League Division Three (the Conference League) finally came into being. Instead, a league comprising of seven heat matches staged as part of the second half was established.

Reading entered and finished eighth out of nine, winning four out of fourteen matches. Michael Warren topped the Rivets averages, while Andy Passey scored most points. Warren re-emerged at the end of the decade and spent a couple of seasons riding for Hackney in the National League, but a review of the Junior League averages reveals very few riders who went on to future success. The two most noteworthy exceptions were Paul Fry (Cradley) and future Racer Ray Morton (King's Lynn).

Once the season finally got under way it didn't get any better. On March 31 in a meeting at King's Lynn, referee John Eglese excluded Michael Lee and subsequently (after Lee had visited the referee's box) excluded him from the meeting and fined him £100. The *Speedway Star* inaccurately reported that Lee "rode along the track in the wrong direction causing three other riders to take evasive action." Two months later the SCB banned him for five years, effectively ending the career of England's most recent World Champion.

In June an appeal hearing cleared Lee of "endangering the lives of other people". Given that the other lesser offences had already been dealt with at the meeting by the referee, and that Lee had already sat out five weeks of the season waiting for the appeal, everyone expected that to be the end of it. But the SCB in their wisdom gave Lee a 12-month ban.

British speedway suffered a further blow when the rider most likely to follow in Lee's tyre tracks – Kenny Carter – broke a leg at Cradley in April.

Meanwhile back at Smallmead the League Cup campaign finally got under way with a defeat at home to new boys Oxford. Wigg (full) and Nielsen (paid) both scored maximums. While Oxford quickly showed their potential, fellow newcomers Exeter had an entirely different experience. They failed to win a single one of their 16 League Cup fixtures. When Reading travelled to the County Ground at the end of April the Falcons took a 10-2 lead but still lost 47-30.

Foxhall Heath was the next stop on Reading's itinerary. Matches between Ipswich and Reading produced a remarkable string of close results on both tracks. In Reading's previous 12 visits to Ipswich the Racers had outscored the Witches, never losing by more than 6 points. Yet in the same period Ipswich came away from Smallmead with the points on no less than five occasions.

An injury picked up the previous Monday ruled Jan Andersson out of the confrontation. Bill Dore drafted in old boy Bobby Schwartz in his place and the Racers rolled up at Foxhall

Heath ready to race. John Berry lodged a protest and the referee ruled that Schwartz couldn't ride. Using rider replacement instead Racers lost 40-38 and immediately lodged their own protest.

Rule B13(c) of the 1984 rulebook caused all the furore. It stated that: "no rider who has or will appear on the track on which the fixture is being held *in a team event, other than a challenge match,* within eight days either side of the fixture shall ride as a guest rider in that fixture."

The problem arose because Schwartz was due to ride at Foxhall Heath four days later in the England v USA Test series. Did the Test fixture constitute a challenge match for the purposes of interpreting this regulation? As regulation 22A clearly defined a challenge match without excluding Test matches the answer has to be yes. Furthermore Schwartz (at Poole the night before) and Chris Morton (at Sheffield) both guested in similar circumstances during the 1984 Test series.

The BSPA determined that Schwartz should have been allowed to ride, but perversely refused to award the match or order a re-run!

In advance of the Racers visit the Ipswich programme billed Tim Hunt as 'infamous'. The week after it said that he: "normally shows the same degree of elegance and charm as a miner's picket line" before complimenting him on his performance in the disputed fixture. (The miners' strike had started in March and lasted a whole year.) Other reviews Hunt received included: "one man demolition squad" (Neil Middleditch in the Poole programme) and a request from Jan Andersson to be partnered with someone else after an incident in the home fixture against Wimbledon.

Due to ill health team manager Bob Radford also missed the fixture at Ipswich, and shortly after he resigned his position. Bill Dore took over team management duties much to the consternation of many on the terraces who soon realised that Dore lacked an understanding of some of the tactical nuances that a good team manager possesses. As the signings of Brannefors, Glanz and Jonsson illustrated, Radford had been more heavily involved in the running of the team than most team managers.

In the ensuing upheaval Pat Bliss took on greater responsibility and a higher public profile as part of the promotion team, in particular taking on most of Radford's press role. In 1983 Pat Bliss's profile increased, with quotes being attributed to her in *Speedway Star*, but it was only after Radford's departure that she was regularly described as co-promoter. Frank Higley had stepped down during the winter, leaving Dore as sole promoter according to the Reading programme. Although now clearly acting in a co-promoter role it wasn't until 1986 that Bliss received a 'co-promoter' credit in Reading's programme.

Ipswich completed the double against Reading on May 21 with a 41-37 win at Smallmead after a Billy Sanders/John Cook 5-1 in the final heat. This left Reading sixth out of nine, and needing to win at least three but probably all four of their remaining away fixtures.

By the end of May this feat had begun to look plausible after wins at Poole and Swindon. The win at Blunsdon provided a bumper pay night for reserves Glanz (8+1) and Holloway (7+1) in a 49-29 thrashing of the Robins.

The League Cup dragged on and at the end of June the remaining away fixtures (and the home match versus Swindon) still hadn't been raced. Attention largely focused on the international arena. First up, an England v Denmark Test series kicked off at Reading with one of Smallmead's most compelling meetings ever. A crowd of 'a little over' 2,000 (compare that with the 8-10,000 for big meetings in Smallmead's early years, and 5,000 for the same fixture just three years earlier) witnessed a nail-biting draw.

In the early heats Denmark's big three dominated the meeting. After 11 races the Danes led 37-29 with Erik Gundersen and Bo Petersen unbeaten. England only had one heat winner on the score chart – veteran John Louis's victory over Hans Nielsen in heat 2. Reserve John Davis won heat 12 and then Louis and Chris Morton raced to a 5-1 over Gundersen. With just 2 points separating the teams Reading's old boys, Davis and Dave Jessup, teamed up for a 5-1 that put England ahead. Jessup delivered the goods again in heat 17 beating Hans Nielsen to ensure England went into the last-heat decider 2 points up.

The final heat required a re-run after Louis fell bringing down Morton. England's northern Ace faced the Danes on his own and although he headed Petersen, Danish reserve Peter Ravn won the race leaving the teams level.

Denmark and England met again in the World Pairs Final at Lonigo in Italy. The Belle Vue pair of Morton and Peter Collins raced to victory over Denmark's Nielsen and Gundersen pairing. Reading's Mitch Shirra (15 points) partnered Ivan Mauger (10) to third place. As the hosts, Italy were seeded to the final and tracked a rising young star – Armando Castagna.

Qualification for the individual championship final reached the British Final stage in June. Malcolm Simmons pulled out, allowing reserve Simon Wigg a second chance. Wigg rode in the previous round with a broken collarbone and had struggled. In the British Final, held at Coventry on a Wednesday as usual, Wigg once again faced elimination. This time he scraped through by winning his final ride. The repercussions of this sequence of events would prove to be calamitous for speedway in Britain.

And on to July when Racers finally wound up their League Cup campaign. Despite only four heat winners (Andersson three, Jonsson one) Racers won at Eastbourne on the first. Three days later the team travelled to Oxford and came away with the points. A solid display, with Shirra (9) and Jonsson (8+1) heading the scorers, put Reading on the brink of qualification for the semi-finals. The following Sunday Swindon were dispatched 47-31 and Reading had completed an unexpected late run to head the Southern qualification group. Jonsson averaged over 7, and Tim Hunt contributed substantially more points than he had previously. Giving cause for concern, Pierre Brannefors's poor form resulted in him dropping to reserve at the start of July.

Racers League Cup campaign had seen a settled side with Hunt and Holloway ever-present. In the league campaign no less than five riders rode in every single match. In addition to Hunt and Holloway, Jonsson, Brannefors and Glanz all had 100% attendance records. Shirra (international duty) and Andersson (Swedish Championship round) both missed just a single match making the 1984 team the most stable in Reading's history.

A stable team is generally a successful one, and although Racers proved to be no match for the powerhouse outfits of Belle Vue, Cradley and Ipswich they always looked likely to be close to the top. Four easy home wins and two away triumphs gave substance to those aspirations. It has to be admitted that in the first of the two away wins Reading benefited from all the luck going. Sheffield's Shawn Moran failed to finish a single one of his four races. Moran never scored less than 9 in any other league fixture that season, so when the match concluded with a 40-38 defeat for the home side Tigers fans were naturally disappointed. Brannefors turned in his best performance of the season with paid 11 in this match.

More good news came from Vojens where Andersson and Shirra both qualified for the World Final. The main talking point of the meeting centred around Kenny Carter. Since breaking his leg he had only ridden in the British and Overseas Finals. Despite the pain he surmounted these hurdles, but the Inter-Continental Final proved to be one step too far for Carter who exited in agony.

The month ended with more drama for the Racers and tragedy for the sport. What should have been a prestigious evening, when King's Lynn staged the European Under-21 Final, ended on a sombre note. Future Racer Marvyn Cox won the meeting, making him the first British winner. It was another Racer-in-waiting, Andy Smith, who featured in the night's low spot. Leading heat 13, promising Sweden and Exeter star Leif Wahlmann's engine seized. Chasing him and screwing it on for one of his trademark outside blasts poor Smithy couldn't avoid Wahlmann as he coasted to a halt. Wahlmann passed away the following day.

Among the unfamiliar names in the under-21 meeting, one rider who caught the eye with his 8-point score was Armando Castagna. Five years later when Castagna joined Reading, the deal involved three riders. Accompanying him would be Carl Blackbird and Jeremy Doncaster.

Blackbird and Doncaster were at Reading 48 hours after the King's Lynn meeting for another confrontation between Reading and Ipswich. Fresh from their second away league win (at Eastbourne) the Racers faced a tough task as Ipswich headed the league with five away wins from six away matches.

Reading's management objected to the use of Carl Blackbird. Unable to prove his eligibility in the time available, Witches took to the track a man short. When Kai Niemi injured his shoulder after an encounter with Jan Andersson the Witches hopes were fading. They battled hard and were still in with a chance when rain caused the referee to abandon the match with Racers leading 32-28.

Ipswich management believed that the Blackbird objection was motivated by revenge for the Ipswich objection to Schwartz's inclusion in the League Cup fixture at Foxhall in May. The following week's Ipswich programme brimmed full with vitriol directed at Reading. Witches promoter John Berry wrote of Bill Dore and Pat Bliss: "... childish and petulant ... not fit to hold promoters' licences". And those were among the more measured comments!

By the time the match was re-run in late October it had become the league-title decider.

Reading's interest in the League Cup ended when Cradley comfortably took the semi-final, after a poor away leg in which only Peter Glanz won a race for Reading. Racers picked up two more away points with draws at Exeter (a much improved team since the League Cup encounter) and Wolverhampton. A Shirra/Brannefors 5-1 in the final heat clinched the draw at Exeter where former Reading junior Andy Campbell weighed in with paid 16 for the Falcons. Malcolm Holloway registered his best away score of the year at Wolverhampton, but at the end of the season the result was changed on appeal to 39-37 in favour of Wolves. Home promoter Peter Adams protested about Racers use of Bruce Cribb, and his 2 points were expunged from the records.

Jan Andersson had a good year finishing the second highest scorer in league matches to Phil Crump (as he had also done in 1981). This was the seventh and final time Crump was the league's top scorer. In August Jan took centre stage. As well as topping the league averages as the month began, he challenged Hans Nielsen for the Golden Helmet. He lost both legs 2-1 but did have the consolation of winning the Hartford Motors Trophy at Cowley straight after the second leg. (Hans Nielsen came third after a tape exclusion spoiled his maximum hopes.)

A week later both riders were in action at Ullevi for the World Final. Erik Gundersen won the first of his three titles dropping his only point to Mitch Shirra. Despite his familiarity with the circuit Jan could only manage 6 points. Shirra fared better with 10.

Andersson rode regularly at Ullevi for his Swedish team Kaparna. He was literally unbeatable scoring 176 points, and a bonus point, from 59 rides for a perfect 12.00 average. Second and third in the Swedish averages were brother Bjorn (11.17) and Pierre Brannefors (11.15). As all three rode for Kaparna it is no surprise that they won the Swedish League. A week after the World Final, Andersson (along with Jonsson and Brannefors) travelled to Karlstad for the Swedish Championship.

While Andersson was regaining his Swedish national title the *Sunday People* rolled off the press. The main headline splashed across the front page revealed: "Di and Charles' Marriage Secrets", but of more interest to the speedway fraternity the second lead across the bottom of the page shouted: "Race Ace Bribery Shock". Turning to page eight the headlines read: "Sham of the racing daredevils in the sport that's rotten to the core. Speedway Bribes Sensation – British ace cheated his way to the World Final."

The allegations centred around Simon Wigg's efforts to qualify for the World Final. Firstly that he paid Malcolm Simmons to drop out of the British Final and secondly that once in the meeting he bought off his opponents in his final race to ensure qualification. The SCB appeared to be in denial and six months later a hearing found Wigg and Simmons not guilty of bribery, but found them guilty (along with Mark Courtney) of 'bringing the sport into disrepute'[35].

Such allegations were not unique to Britain. The Polish League season ended in chaos when Stal Rzesow met Unia Leszno on the final day of the season (October 7). Both needed a draw: Leszno to win the title and Rzesow to stay up. When Leszno collapsed from 41-25 up to draw 45-all, suspicions were aroused. The Polish authorities awarded the match 41-25 to Leszno and then stripped them of the title!

Racers had a low-key September with three home wins and two away defeats. The match at King’s Lynn could perhaps have been won if Shirra hadn't walked out after one ride. Highlight of the month came from an unlikely quarter – Tim Hunt. Despite having a strong spearhead in the shape of Dave Jessup and John Davis in the late 1970s Reading had failed to make an impression in the British League Pairs Championship. Its revival in 1984 once again offered Reading a good opportunity with Andersson and Shirra first and seventh in the league averages wearing the winged wheel. Rain caused the event's postponement for 48 hours, clashing with a Swedish League match. Hunt stepped into the vacancy and everyone marked the revised Reading pairing as also-rans. Reading finished second to Belle Vue's Chris Morton and Peter Collins. Hunt claimed the scalps of Neil Evitts, Steve Baker, Sam Ermolenko, Phil Collins, John Davis and Malcolm Simmons – all better riders than the Racers stand-in.

As the season entered October, Ipswich led the league with Belle Vue and Cradley still hoping to overhaul them. All three had a Monday evening trip to Smallmead in their diaries. Reading would have a major say in the identity of the league champions.

First to visit were Belle Vue. Reading resisted the Aces challenge (40-37), with an Andersson/Jonsson 4-2 in a last-heat decider. 18-year-old Andy Smith (paid 11) top scored for the Aces. Cradley provided an even tougher challenge and Reading had to come from 6 down to win 40-38. Again an Andersson/Jonsson 4-2 in the last heat maintained Racers 100% home record.

By the time Ipswich arrived they knew that a win at Smallmead would give them the title. A defeat for the Witches, and Belle Vue would be champions if they won their last two fixtures. A 3,000 crowd, the year's largest, watched as Ipswich stormed into a 22-8 lead on the way to a convincing 46-32 win. The score equalled Reading's record home league defeat.

Racers home programme ended with a 43-35 win over Eastbourne after an Andersson/Jonsson 5-1 in the final heat. The night ended on a nostalgic note with a 'greybeards' race. It featured (in finishing order): Bernie Leigh, Mick Bell, Vic White, Mike Vernam.

Later that week another name from the past briefly made the headlines in the wake of Prime Minister Indira Gandhi's assassination in India. Describing the disturbances that followed her shooting, the *Reading Chronicle* headline screamed: “Former Racer and Wife in Indian Riot Nightmare – Train Jump Drama to Escape Blaze Death”. The identity of the ex-Racer: Richard May.

Belle Vue won at Wolverhampton, but rain meant that their final fixture (at home to Swindon) never happened. The third attempt at staging it fell foul of the weather on November

35 In his autobiography *Simmo* (Retro Publications), Simmons said of his evidence at the Tribunal: “It was a load of bollocks but thankfully Michael Limb and the other three SCB jurors believed us.” The *Sunday People* were not alone in finding the verdict unsatisfactory. *Speedway Star* signalled their unease by reprinting the *People's* critical editorial

4. Had Ipswich not won at Reading this would have been the title decider. With so much going wrong for British speedway in 1984 to have the title undecided would have been just another painful self-inflicted wound in a year that consisted of one disaster after another.

And once the season ended, the disasters kept coming. The British League imploded. Newcastle went out of business and Exeter returned to the National League after a financially disastrous year. Three longer-standing members of the senior league fell by the wayside: Eastbourne dropped down after two years of massive losses, more shockingly Wimbledon opted for the calmer economic environment of the National League leaving London without a British League track. Then there was Poole.

Reading wound up their away league programme at Poole on a wet Sunday (October 28). The stadium had the air of despondency that often attaches itself to failing promotions, and the Pirates surrendered all too easily as Racers won 40-31 before rain washed out the final heat. Poole staged no less than seven (!) individual meetings in 1984 and Mitch Shirra won three of them including the prestigious Blue Riband. Unfortunately he wasn't paid for all his appearances at Wimborne Road and when Poole went spectacularly bust in the New Year, Shirra featured prominently on the list of creditors (which totalled £200,000). Neil Middleditch faced an even worse position; most of his testimonial proceeds were tied up in the liquidation.

Poole subsequently re-emerged in the 1985 National League under new management in place of Weymouth. Reading missed the Pirates more than most. The Racers had a fantastic record against Poole winning nine and drawing two of their 13 league encounters at Poole.

Poole were one of four teams who rode for most of the season with a permanent guest, a situation hardly designed to improve their prospects or bring spectators through the turnstiles. Halifax (injury to Carter), Wolverhampton (injury to Sigalos) and Poole (Lee's ban) used 98 guests in league matches alone. The fourth team Exeter produced a most bizarre situation, with Ivan Mauger coming out of retirement to ride in home matches only. Away from home they were allowed to use a guest. The BSPA made this decision, best described as pragmatic, after Exeter had been unable to entice any top-calibre riders to the fiercely banked County Ground with its unforgiving safety fence. Short of cash after being made to pay a five-figure sum for the 'privilege' of joining the British League, the alternative would almost certainly have resulted in the Falcons withdrawing from the league.

Reading survived the 'season of woe' relatively unscathed. Even their relationship with Ipswich appeared to be on the mend. Then at the beginning of December news arrived from New Zealand that Mitch Shirra had broken his thigh. The injury proved to be serious, and Mitch's recovery became one of the central threads of the Racers story in 1985.

Team: Jan Andersson 10.05, Mitch Shirra 9.27, Per Jonsson 6.52, Tim Hunt 5.75, Malcolm Holloway 5.43, Pierre Brannefors 5.41, Peter Glanz 4.87

1985 – Waiting for Mitch

The implosion of the British League left 11 starters in 1985 against the 16 from the previous season. With team places reduced it became clear that work permits would not be easy to obtain. This made Pierre Brannefors's return unlikely. In January, Racers announced their first new signing: 19-year-old Norwegian champion Einar Kyllingstad. It became apparent that a work permit would not be forthcoming and the Reading management looked elsewhere. There were plenty of riders available, but with one month before the season started only Belle Vue had completed their line up.

The solution turned out to be a familiar face. John Davis had shown a fine burst of form at the tail end of 1981 after moving from Reading to Poole, but since then his career had stagnated. He even managed to court controversy the previous year in a *Speedway Star* interview, when he made a flippant remark about shooting miners' leader Arthur Scargill. With his 1984 team (Wimbledon) dropping down, JD needed a new home. In late February, seemingly out of the blue, Reading announced that Davis would be returning to Smallmead.

With Davis replacing Brannefors, Reading were over the 48-point limit for team building. With only modest improvement in 1984, Peter Glanz became the man most likely to leave. When the season opened, Mark Chessell filled the number seven spot. One of three racing brothers, his sub-4-point average for Rye House in the 1984 National League did not suggest that he would make a major contribution.

After some last-minute doubts about Per Jonsson's work permit the only questions remaining about the 1985 team concerned Mitch Shirra. When would he be back? And would he return to his pre-injury best?

The year had started with the announcement that ITV intended to axe 'World of Sport' depriving speedway of its main television platform. With the taint of the 'Sunday People Affair' still hanging over the sport, opportunities for additional coverage elsewhere seemed less than encouraging.

There were two new innovations for 1985. Speedway promoters are perpetually being criticised for tinkering with the rules, but occasionally they get it right (as they had with tape touching in 1984). The big change for 1985 was the introduction of the bonus point[36] for an aggregate victory in League Cup matches. Initially the bonus point would not be awarded for league matches, but as the League Cup campaign progressed it became clear that the bonus point maintained interest in otherwise 'dead' matches. So in June nearly three weeks after the first league match of the season the bonus point was extended to league matches.

Incidentally that first league match involved Reading: a 42-35 defeat at Belle Vue featuring a fine 15-point maximum from the revitalised John Davis. If any team had cause to regret the introduction of the bonus point it was Reading. The Racers failed to gain any bonus points from their first five ties in the League Cup. Three were lost 79-77 and the other two went to run-offs!

The second significant change came in the second half, with the abolition of the traditional scratch-race format and the introduction of a full junior competition. British Junior League Cup matches were held over six heats and this became seven for the league campaign.

While not quite on the epic scale of 'Waiting for Godot' the story of the Racers League Cup campaign could easily be sub-titled 'Waiting for Mitch.'

The first eight fixtures produced three home wins and five away defeats (all by 8 points or less). These included Per Jonsson's first-ever maximum (at home to Belle Vue) and the first of

---

36 An innovation so successful that it was extended mid-season. But promoters have short memories, and I have yet to hear a credible reason for its abolition in 2008.

many Golden Helmet challenges involving Reading riders. The competition had switched back from a monthly event to a single match race after each match in which the holder rode. On April 8, at Monmore Green, holder Bobby Schwartz beat Reading's Per Jonsson.

The next Golden Helmet encounter coincided with Shirra's return. Riding against Sheffield, Mitch failed to score from four rides. Racers scraped home by 4 points on the night leaving John Davis and Shawn Moran to contest a run-off for the bonus point. The same two riders then came out for the Golden Helmet match race. Smallmead track specialist Moran won both to add to his paid maximum in the match.

In his first eight official fixtures Shirra scored only 13 points (plus one bonus point) for an average of just 1.87. Now the question was: Could Mitch survive in the team for much longer?

Mitch's return coincided with a period of dreadful weather. Three matches in a row fell victim to rain in May. Over the season Reading suffered seven home postponements and three away. A further two away matches were abandoned part way through.

The one Smallmead fixture in May that did start never reached a conclusion. On May Bank Holiday Monday Wolverhampton arrived for a morning fixture. They left after the first attempt to run heat 6 resulted in further fallers. Seven riders fell (Shirra, Davis, Chessell, Jonsson, Schwartz, Rasmussen and Eriksen). Heat 6 was re-run with the one remaining rider (Tim Hunt) and Racers clocked up a 5-nil in heat 7 before about a dozen Wolves fans crossed the greyhound track and staged a sit-in on the track. With the score at 24-14 to Reading, referee Paul Gray abandoned the match.

Bank Holiday daytime meetings at Reading have a long record of poor tracks. Heavy watering beforehand often fails to prevent dust and a blue groove appearing. Slick tracks and poor racing are a common feature of daytime meetings at Smallmead. In this case watering had certainly made the track difficult to ride. Accusations flew in all directions: poor track preparation by the Racers management, Wolverhampton's walk-out, the actions of the Wolves fans, Bobby Schwartz's role (did he incite the track invasion?), referee Paul Gray's handling of events and the Reading management's refund policy all came in for criticism. Speedway rarely made it to the front page of the *Evening Post*, but a photo of the Wolves fans on the track beside the headline "This race track is a Danger" appeared on page one of Tuesday's edition.

Before May ended, the Speedway Control Board ordered a re-run of the Wolves fixture. An appeal by Reading fizzled out and in September the BSPA confirmed that the meeting should be re-staged. With virtually no publicity (the fixture was only confirmed the previous Friday) Reading beat Wolves 46-32 on Tuesday 17 September. Peter Glanz top scored (including a win from the back over Bobby Schwartz). The young Dane had returned to the Racers line-up at the beginning of June when the averages allowed him to replace Chessell in the line-up. Chessell moved on to Milton Keynes where he replaced ex-Racer Ashley Pullen.

By the time of the September re-staging Racers had long since lost interest in the League Cup after a home defeat to Swindon on June 10, when Andersson and Jonsson were absent riding in the Nordic Final. Wolves could have qualified for the semi-finals at the expense of eventual winners Coventry had they won the September fixture at Smallmead. After the furore at the original staging about the validity of re-admission tickets Bill Dore honoured the pledge he made in May to allow spectators in for nothing[37].

Although Hunt, Holloway (who scored the only maximum of his Racers career at home to Halifax in June) and number eight Neil Middleditch all scored well they could not compensate for Shirra's problems.

The first positive signs came in pairs racing. In late May Shirra scored 14 points for New

---

37 One would think that a promoter staging a free fixture would do all he could to publicise the event and attract potential new converts to the sport. But Dore did little to conceal his displeasure at being ordered to re-stage the event and everything to avoid anyone knowing about it!

Zealand in a World Pairs qualifier. His partner, 45-year-old Ivan Mauger, scored 10. Then on the last day of June, Mitch partnered Davis to second place in the British Open Pairs. His scalps included Peter Collins and Erik Gundersen. Hans Nielsen and Simon Wigg won the event for Oxford, who in their second season back in the top division went on to complete a league and cup double.

In July Shirra dropped down to reserve and his scoring began to pick up. He seemed at his most tentative in the reserves races, saving his best performances for his races against the stars. National League Glasgow attempted to entice Shirra back to the club he started with. (Coatbridge switched to Glasgow in 1977.) The Overseas Final took place without Shirra to the evident frustration of the Racers star. Larry Ross won the New Zealand Final. The national administrators then seeded David Bargh, ignoring the claims of injured Shirra and national champion Ross.

The Overseas Final was staged at Odsal, Bradford, just a day after Live Aid at Wembley. The first meeting at the resurrected venue (a World Team Cup qualifier) had taken place on 12 May – just 24 hours after the Valley Parade fire at the home of Bradford City had killed 56 people.

Also taking place on the same day as the Overseas Final, the European Under-21 Championship produced a Swedish one-two. Per Jonsson claimed the title with a five-ride maximum from Jimmy Nilsen. The Swedes also took fourth place thanks to Kenneth Nystrom who went on to have an undistinguished spell with the Racers in 1993. Further down the finishing order Kyllingstad scored 5 points.

The reigning Swedish Junior Champion, Jimmy Nilsen had long been a Swindon target. Like Jonsson the previous year he had initially been denied a work permit. Like Per he quickly proved his critics wrong, scoring paid 11 on his Swindon debut six days after finishing runner-up to Jonsson in the European Under-21 Championship. Incidentally the rider who came second to Nilsen in that 1984 Swedish Junior Championship was Tony Olsson.

July was a good month for Swedish speedway. They also pulled off a shock win over England in the World Team Cup Continental Final. Nilsen scored 11, Jan Andersson 10 and Per Jonsson 9. England's poor result prompted demands for John Davis to receive a recall to the England team. In June, Davis had been runner-up to Kenny Carter in the British Final. This was Davis's only rostrum placing in 16 consecutive appearances (1976- 1991). Until surpassed by Andy Smith in 2001, Davis held the record for most British Final appearances. The 1985 British Final line up also included Racer Tim Hunt for the only time in his career.

Davis did ride for England in the World Team Cup Final, but failed to score as England managed a meagre 13 in total. England rode without Kenny Carter who broke his leg six days earlier in the Inter-Continental Final at Vetlanda. Denmark pipped hosts USA by 37 points to 35 to complete a hat-trick of World Team Cup wins. Andersson, Jonsson and Brannefors all rode for Sweden who finished fourth on 10 points.

Racers lost two of their first five home league matches without gaining any reward on their travels to compensate. Wolves, thirsting for revenge, soundly beat Reading in the Smallmead league encounter while Oxford won an August Bank Holiday encounter by 7 points. At the beginning of August, Racers propped up the league table and mid-table mediocrity seemed the best that Racers could aspire to.

The brightest moment in August took place at Sheffield in a Knock-Out Cup replay. After failing to score in the reserves race Mitch Shirra reeled off four classy wins. For the first time since his injury he had shown world class form in a Racers jacket. Shirra beat Shawn Moran in the final heat to draw the match. Racers progressed to the semi-final where they lost both legs narrowly to Oxford in late October. However, it was a tight tie as Racers still held the aggregate lead with three heats to go in the second leg at Smallmead.

August concluded with the World Final. In the run up Jan Andersson won the Pride of the

East at King's Lynn. This rare victory in a big opening meeting made no difference to his World Final showing. Andersson could only score 7 on the big night. A 37,000 Odsal crowd witnessed one of the greatest climaxes to a World Final. Erik Gundersen retained his world title after a three-man run-off with Hans Nielsen and debut shock merchant Sam Ermolenko. Also making his World Final debut that year was Armando Castagna, Italy's first-ever world finalist.

After seeing the Danes take individual, pairs and team world titles England carried off gold in the World Longtrack Final via Simon Wigg. Ex-Racer Jiri Stancl took runner-up spot. Ivan Mauger made his last-ever World Final appearance in this event. He staged a series of farewell meetings at the end of the season including a memorable event at Belle Vue's fondly remembered Hyde Road track.

September was an unmitigated disaster for Reading. In four consecutive meetings at the end of the month Reading lost a rider to injury. Peter Glanz was injured at Coventry (September 21), then two days later Malcolm Holloway came to grief at home to Sheffield. Both riders returned before the end of the season, but the next victim was not so lucky. Tim Hunt damaged two vertebrae at Sheffield, an injury that resulted in his retirement at the age of 25. To finish the month John Davis dislocated his shoulder against Ipswich (September 30).

To fill the gaps Reading succeeded in obtaining a work permit for Einar Kyllingstad. The Norwegian only scored 2 points in five matches. More fruitful cover came from Kent. Dave Mullett had made his Reading debut in the League Cup re-run against Wolves. With a paid 4 score he did enough to warrant further opportunities. In all he made five appearances averaging 5.07. He remained a central character in the Racers story until well into the new millennium, making more appearances for Reading than any other rider.

Earlier in the season Mullett had finished second in the British Junior Championship, sandwiched between future Reading riders Andy Smith (third) and Carl Blackbird (winner). Mullett also represented Canterbury in the National League Riders Championship, won by Reading's number eight – Neil Middleditch.

The injury crisis also gave Stuart Williams, the best of Reading's juniors, a chance to don the winged wheel.

Williams topped the Rivets averages, although David Main ran him close. The Rivets finished tenth (out of 11) in the Junior League Cup and bottom of the Junior British League.

Despite the injury crisis Reading's results didn't deteriorate. Racers gained their only away win in the league at Sheffield (September 26) where Mitch Shirra scored a fine maximum. This performance lifted Shirra into the top 20 of the league averages. There was little doubt now that 'mighty' Mitch was mighty once again. With Andersson and Davis both in the top ten, Reading should have been doing better.

October started with four draws in a row. Although an unusual sequence it reproduced a similar run in 1981. Reading took a point from Ipswich and Swindon, but could only share the points at home to Sheffield and Coventry.

Despite their fairly modest league record Reading could still finish fourth if they beat Cradley by five or more in the final home fixture of the season. For the first time Reading entered the Midland Cup. On October 21 Cradley knocked them out at the semi-final stage after Racers could only win the home leg by four. The following Monday Cradley should have returned for the League match, but instead they travelled to Monmore Green for the second leg of the Dudley/Wolves Trophy.

The Dudley/Wolves Trophy may not matter much to the speedway fraternity in Berkshire, but no rivalry in British speedway has matched it[38]. Cradley snubbed Reading and fulfilled their pre-existing commitment at Wolverhampton. It was a profitable night for Cradley they

---

38 Some of the finest speedway I have ever seen, particularly the 1989 encounters.

chalked up a 30-point away win (54-24)! The Reading management were left fuming, clearly of the view that the completion of official league fixtures should take precedence.

Bill Dore and Pat Bliss hastily arranged a pairs meeting, won by Neil Middleditch and Peter Glanz. As late as Saturday the *Evening Post* still listed Cradley as the opponents for Monday's meeting. Also on the Saturday Per Jonsson guested for Swindon and scored a maximum, prompting a transfer request. Reading put a £20,000 price on him.

The season ended with further unrest as rumours that Reading intended to join the National League circulated. After the Wolverhampton League Cup furore and the Cradley no-show, Bill Dore saw no reason to hide his disenchantment. *Evening Post* journalist Dave Wright suggested: " Pat and Bill work tirelessly for the club but they need assistance," and went on to hint that Alf Weedon would be willing and able to join the promoting team.

No major events had been awarded to Smallmead, possibly a comment on the crumbling terracing. Stadium management looked for additional attractions. The stadium staged Afghan racing and hosted the Thames Valley Chargers as American football briefly flourished in the UK.

It seems hard to imagine only having the choice of three television channels now, but until Channel 4 launched with 'Countdown' on 2 November 1982 that was the choice available to TV viewers. In its search for new programming the new channel hit upon American football. The sport flourished in the UK and in 1985 organised league competition began. The Chargers relocated to Maidenhead the following year. In the early 1990s crowds started to drop and Coca-Cola withdrew their sponsorship; the boom was over. American football can still be found near Reading; the Sonning-based Reading Renegades play in the British American Football League.

John Davis's successful return to Reading was complemented by a ground-breaking move into the German League. Riding for Diedenbergen he shared top spot in the league averages with 1983 World Champion Egon Muller. There were three former Racers in the next four places (Alois Wiesbock, Jiri Stancl and Peter Wurterle). The British speedway authorities tried to block Davis from riding in two leagues, citing concerns about conflicting commitments. It is unlikely whether any of the British promoters of the time could have conceived just how much trouble this would cause in 20 years' time. Poland and Sweden were still staging league competition without the benefit of any foreign involvement.

Jan Andersson held the Golden Helmet for ten days, losing it to Ipswich's spectacular John Cook after he had won it from Kenny Carter and defended it against Hans Nielsen. He also made no less than six (!) unsuccessful challenges (four against Nielsen and two against Shawn Moran).

For all Andersson and Davis's successes, 1985's abiding memory remains the eclipse and rebirth of Mitch Shirra.

Team: Jan Andersson 9.43, John Davis 9.01, Mitch Shirra 6.79, Per Jonsson 6.33, Tim Hunt 5.59, Peter Glanz 5.57, Malcolm Holloway 4.72, Neil Middleditch 4.67, Mark Chessell 2.05.

1986 – A Low Key Finish

In February, Halley's comet made its appearance. Last time it passed the Earth in 1910 speedway had yet to emerge from the various attempts to organise motorcycle races. After another difficult year, the ability of speedway to survive until the comet's next visit (in 2061) seemed doubtful.

The main change that came out of the promoters' winter conference was the introduction of a compulsory junior to team line ups. Ostensibly done to encourage young British riders, cost saving may well have been behind the promoters' decision. 20-year-old Stuart Williams – Reading's top junior from 1985 – was the obvious candidate to fill the role at Smallmead.

Initially it looked like the transfer-seeking Per Jonsson would be the rider to make way. When Tim Hunt announced his retirement (his back injury was still giving him trouble) Jonsson was persuaded to stay. With further improvement from Jonsson expected, Reading tracked a strong top four in a team that only showed the one change from 1985.

The one new rider, statutory junior Williams, left before the season even began. The official reason was: "irresponsible and unacceptable conduct ... (that) embarrassed Reading and his sponsor." In a 2003 *Speedway Star* interview Williams recalled the incident:

> *"The sponsor and I fell out in a significant way for which I was largely to blame if I am honest. I can't avoid that, I was young, I was a teenager, a little bit rebellious ... two weeks before the season started I lost all the sponsorship I had."*

His sponsor was Roger Jones, former Oxford team manager, and subsequently promoter at Long Eaton and Milton Keynes. Williams subsequently signed for National League Exeter, averaging 1.60 from six matches before drifting out of the sport. 16 years on, older and wiser, he returned to speedway at Somerset.

In his place Racers signed 17-year-old Gary Tagg, an Eastbourne junior born in Wokingham. Tagg struggled until Billy Pinder replaced him in June. Despite outscoring Tagg in the Junior League Cup, Pinder fared even worse than Tagg in the senior league. In 22 fixtures Pinder averaged just 1.27 and achieved a highest score of just 2. Tagg fared marginally better averaging 1.35 and even managed to win a race in a September cup match against Cradley.

The Reading pair were not the only juniors to be outclassed, but their averages were easily the lowest of the statutory juniors. Only one of the juniors introduced in 1986 went on to become a top league regular without a spell in the National League – Sheffield's Sean Wilson. Meanwhile the Rivets finished seventh in the Junior League Cup and eighth in the British Junior League with Pinder scoring 212 points (including bonus) to Tagg's 211. With one less ride Tagg pipped Pinder at the top of the Rivets averages with 8.04 to 8.00.

With a weak tail, the Racers needed the top four to produce the goods. Most of the time they delivered.

Jan Andersson topped the Racers averages for the sixth time in seven years. (Shirra outscored him in 1983.) However, most teams had stronger number ones, and he narrowly failed to qualify for the World Final. He missed only two matches and came close to a rostrum place in the British League Riders Championship after finishing third in a four-man run-off for second.

Mitch Shirra missed several matches, and rode while less than fully fit due to the after-effects of his broken thigh in December 1984. (He had an operation to remove a plate from his leg in February.) His away form suffered, and he ended the season on a low note after a premature departure from Reading's league fixture at Coventry.

Despite this Shirra reached the World Final, but he finished bottom of the field at Katowice with just one point. Shirra's world title trail had also started on a low note when he was deprived of the New Zealand Championship after a retrospective exclusion deprived him of a 15-point maximum and relegated him to third behind David Bargh and Larry Ross.

After Davis's good form in 1985 Bill Dore decided to convert the previous season's loan arrangement into a full transfer. Dore was "confident that there would be no problems in completing the deal" (*Speedway Star* 8 February 86). Resplendent in his pink leathers, Davis continued to display strong form for Reading. Despite this he was only rewarded with one more England cap. He continued to ride regularly for Diedenbergen in the West German League.

Then at the beginning of September, out of the blue, came the announcement that Reading and Wimbledon were in dispute over the transfer fee and Davis couldn't ride until it had been sorted out. With Davis contemplating basing himself in Germany both parties worried that they could lose out. Talks between the two clubs dragged on leaving Davis fuming on the sidelines and threatening to take legal action seeking compensation for loss of earnings. Pat Bliss claimed at the time that: "there has never been any paperwork on the deal. It's basically a gentleman's agreement ..." (*Evening Post* 8 September 1986)

A month later Reading lost a second of their big hitters when Sweden required Per Jonsson to do his military service. Jonsson had started the season with a full maximum in Reading's first League Cup fixture, a comfortable home win against Coventry. Although his British League form failed to live up to expectations he did capture the Swedish national crown. Jan Andersson (second) and Jimmy Nilsen (third) joined him on the rostrum. That night BBC broadcast the first episode of 'Casualty'. Although the show did once run a stock car storyline, speedway has never featured despite the frequency with which speedway riders visit A&E.

Quiet man Peter Glanz improved considerably. He upped his average to 5.89 and reached double figures in three away league matches. He scored paid 14 at King's Lynn, 10 at Wolverhampton, and 11 at Ipswich (a match Racers lost 40-38 after Richard Knight passed Shirra in the final race). At Smallmead he beat Kenny Carter in a match that fell victim to the weather after four heats. (In July a second Reading v Bradford match fell foul of the weather before heat 6 could be re-run. Because heat 6 had been started re-admission tickets were not valid, causing some discontent amongst fans who felt short changed.) On October 6 Glanz unsuccessfully challenged Swindon's Phil Crump for the Golden Helmet.

The final member of the team Malcolm Holloway had a fairly quiet year. It started with a leg injury in the Easter triangle that caused his absence for most of the League Cup campaign and ended with him contemplating a drop down to the National League where he would be guaranteed more meetings.

Against a background of anxiety following the explosion at the Chernobyl nuclear power plant in the Ukraine (April 26), the League Cup campaign took up the first half of the season. It marked Reading out as a mid-table team, with just one away win to compensate for a single home defeat. The away win came at King's Lynn in their opening away match. However, as the year progressed it became clear that everyone would win at Saddlebow Road. Later in the season the poor Stars lost all ten of their home league matches, but produced the shock of the season when they won a league match at Swindon. For most of the year ex-Racer Bobby Schwartz fought a lone battle for King's Lynn, but at Swindon Einar Kyllingstad produced a flawless 15-point maximum.

The home League Cup defeat came in the final fixture. Missing Shirra and Davis due to injury, the Racers crashed 40-31 to Sheffield before rain stopped the match a race early. Reading were slightly fortunate to get this far without dropping a home point; three of the previous nine matches had been won 40-38. Most memorable of those close scrapes was a last-heat victory against Oxford when Andersson and Shirra recorded a 5-1 over Hans Nielsen and Marvyn Cox.

At the other end of the scale Racers thrashed Belle Vue 54-24 with Davis, Andersson, Shirra and Glanz all unbeaten by an opponent. Former World Champion Peter Collins could only muster 2 points. 'PC' could still beat the best, but too many meetings like this one led him to announce his retirement. On November 1 he bowed out in a league match at Odsal, with 10 points from four rides.

One positive aspect of the League Cup campaign was the form of Dave Mullett. Due to Holloway's injury Mullett rode in more than half of Reading's League Cup matches and averaged over 6 points a match – a very healthy return for a number eight.

Malcolm Holloway – over 200 appearances for the Racers between 1984 and 1989. (DA)

The league campaign also started with an away win, but this time the Racers followed up the initial victory with further away success. After a win at Sheffield came a 20-point thrashing of King's Lynn and a 47-31 victory over Belle Vue in which Jan Andersson scored a maximum. The Hyde Road victory provided Racers with their first win in 22 visits to Manchester!

While Reading won three of their first four away matches, a new vulnerability at home emerged. The home league programme opened with a draw (against Coventry). Three wins followed, then a defeat to the Wolves (August 20) triggered a run of five home matches without a win. Midway through this sequence the Davis dispute blew up, shortly to be followed by Jonsson's enforced absence.

Within days of losing Davis's services Reading had signed, and sought a work permit for, Sweden's Tony Olsson. Earlier in the season he had bagged runner-up spot in the European Under-21 Championship; only an engine failure prevented him from claiming the title. Coupled with a recommendation from Jan Andersson this provided enough reason to sign him. Four weeks later he made his debut at Bradford scoring just a point. His home debut gave more cause to be happy – a 7-point haul against Swindon. The following Monday Olsson scored a maximum against a Czechoslovakian touring team that featured 1983 Racer Stanislav Urban and recent Ipswich signing Roman Matousek.

Racers slid down the table ending in seventh place, a disappointing finish after their promising start. In August second place looked to be a realistic aspiration. Even then the championship looked like a certainty for Oxford. In the end the Cheetahs won all 18 league matches they rode with Hans Nielsen scoring a maximum in all ten away matches. Two home league matches and the home leg of both the League Cup and Knock-Out Cup Finals (both against Cradley) remained unridden. Both cups would have gone to Oxford had the second legs been run.

While Oxford had cause to remember 1986 fondly, for most of the speedway fraternity the year went down as a nightmare year. One traumatic, shocking and visceral event dominates all other memories of the season – the tragic exit of Kenny Carter. On May 21, barely a year after Billy Sanders had taken his own life on Foxhall Heath, Carter followed suit. However, Carter killed his wife with a shotgun before using it on himself. Carter had been due to defend his British title a few days later, and in an emotional meeting his Bradford team mate Neil Evitts became the new British champion.

Further examination revealed plenty of other reasons to be gloomy. No less than three of the eleven clubs remaining in the British League nearly pulled out. At Sheffield Maurice Ducker briefly contemplated giving up in June. The following month Richard Vowles walked away from Swindon and Peter Adams left Wolverhampton with debts reported at £180,000. After a hiatus, stadium owners British Car Auctions took over at Swindon and Chris Van Straaten commenced his tenure at Wolverhampton.

Speedway's decline could be gauged by the fact that for the first time in many years even the World Final wasn't televised. There were no cameras to witness the explosive clash between Hans Nielsen and Tommy Knudsen in heat 15. Nielsen dived under Knudsen who then fell. The questionable exclusion of Knudsen may have cost him the world title which eventually went to Nielsen, with another Dane Jan O. Pedersen second.

The Danes won everything in 1986: individual, team, pairs and longtrack (via Erik Gundersen). Nielsen also won the British League Riders Championship, and Denmark beat England 4-1 in a Test series. The Danes were just too dominant, and the predictability of Danish triumph diminished the excitement of international competition. (England's football team didn't fare any better, succumbing to Maradona's 'hand of God' in the World Cup.)

British League promoters realised that drastic action must be taken. So in November they offered John Berry the job of 'speedway supremo'. Regrettably the promoters lost their nerve and Berry turned the job down citing the unwillingness of the promoters to cede him sufficient authority[39].

Team: Jan Andersson 9.34, John Davis 8.72, Mitch Shirra 7.90, Per Jonsson 7.36, Peter Glanz 5.89, Malcolm Holloway 5.47, Dave Mullett 5.33, Gary Tagg 1.35, Billy Pinder 1.27

39 Notwithstanding his prickly relationship with the Reading promotion, Berry was an excellent promoter, with a deserved reputation for professionalism. I recommend his books *Confessions of a Speedway Promoter* and *More Confessions* (Retro Publications), which expand on this event, analyse the reasons for the decline of British speedway and much more. The second book also contains some interesting discussion of the motive for BSI's takeover at Smallmead – he predicted it would all end in tears!

1987 – 58.1 Seconds

The closure of Slough greyhound stadium in March meant an additional night of greyhounds at Smallmead. Bill Dore wanted to devote more of his time to the dogs, so at the start of the year he sold 50% of Allied Presentations to Thatcham motorcycle shop owner Brian Leonard. Born in Newbury in 1946, the new co-promoter had a 15-year speedway career. He made his debut in the second half at Oxford in 1962 and retired while riding for the Cheetahs in 1977. In between he rode for seven other clubs.

Leonard took over responsibility for team matters, including the team manager's role. Pat Bliss continued to look after the administrative side of the business. It turned out to be an unhappy marriage and soon after the season ended a very bitter divorce commenced, with both parties wanting custody of the Racers.

Also making a 'one year only' appearance were British League returnees Hackney. After a poor season brightened by the form of 16-year-old junior Mark Loram, the London team dropped back down to the National League. The final straw was the failure of British League promoters to put a team-building limit on heat leaders without which Hackney's chances of signing a top rider were limited.

An increasing number of British League tracks made noises about financial problems, although none were as severe as Swindon and Wolverhampton's 1986 woes. All teams struggled to complete their fixtures. As the season drew to a close Southern England experienced the worst storm since 1703[40]. Reading rode six of their eleven away league matches in October and the early season League Cup was not decided until November 1.

On that sad day Coventry won the League Cup at Belle Vue. The meeting marked the final time bikes would take to the track at the famous Hyde Road stadium. Few stadiums evoke as many memories as the sweeping bends, fine old wooden stands and the zoological gardens setting of Belle Vue. Along with the Sydney Showground and Pardubice, it was without doubt one of the world's greatest speedway tracks. And for Reading fans it provided them with the most heart-stopping race in their history – the 1973 Collins/Michanek cup final run-off.

The significantly better organised National League began to suffer too – Workington (in reality an exiled Glasgow team) and Boston both folded mid-season. At the end of the season Canterbury lost their Kingsmead stadium home, leaving Dave Mullett homeless.

Early in the season, Johnnie Hoskins passed away at the age of 94. Still promoting at Canterbury at the beginning of the decade, he was a larger-than-life presence in the sport that he is generally regarded to have fathered back in 1923.

Although provoking relatively little comment at the time, the most significant development in 1987 happened in Sweden. The Swedish League allowed foreigners to compete. Three Finns and two Danes including former World Champion Erik Gundersen took up Swedish team places. However, Vetlanda won the Swedish title without foreign help. Their number one Jan Andersson topped the Swedish league averages, with Per Jonsson (Getingarna) second and Gundersen (Vargarna) third. Like Britain, what started as a trickle eventually became a flood. A look at current Swedish teams shows that foreigners now predominate[41].

The world speedway scene remained predictable. Denmark completed a hat-trick of World Pairs crowns, provided the World Champion for the fourth year in a row and won their fifth consecutive World Team Cup. The individual final reached its nadir with a two-day event at the sparsely attended Olympic Stadium in Amsterdam. Hans Nielsen retained his title after Erik Gundersen and Sam Ermolenko had headed the overnight leaderboard.

---

40 Incidentally Michael Fish was right, technically it was not a hurricane.

41 For comparison in 2007 Vetlanda regularly tracked a top six consisting of Crump (Australia), Holta (Norway/Poland), Richardson (Britain) and three Poles.

Fifth place went to Reading's new number one – Per Jonsson. After doubts about his availability at the season's start due to national service, Jonsson lined up for his fourth season in Racers colours. After two years in which his progress had been gradual, he stepped up a level and challenged Jan Andersson for the number one position all year. In the early season League Cup Andersson held off Jonsson by 9.36 to 9.21, but in league matches Jonsson outscored Andersson 9.35 to 8.84. Jonsson also retained his national title with Andersson runner-up to his Reading team mate.

When Jonsson's availability was in doubt Reading looked to Sweden for a replacement. The unnamed Swedish target was probably Andersson's Vetlanda team mate Kenneth Nystrom. Racers other winter target Dave Mullett eventually stayed at Canterbury after a long and inconclusive wrangle between Reading and Canterbury over the fee. Mullett stayed put and Malcolm Holloway retained his Racers race jacket.

With Tony Olsson showing sufficient promise in the last month of the 1986 season to warrant a return, along with Glanz and Tagg, that left a heat leader spot up for grabs. Few expected John Davis to return after the spectacular falling out between Reading and Wimbledon that left him on the sidelines, but in late February Davis agreed terms with Reading for 1987. This left Mitch Shirra surplus to requirements. He moved to Swindon on loan, with an option to purchase that Swindon didn't exercise at the end of the season.

After completing a Bank Holiday double over Oxford (August 31) the Racers sat on top of the table. However, Coventry sat in second place with an unbeaten record. Winning the league already looked unlikely but runners-up seemed a realistic aim. Reading were themselves in the middle of a nine-match unbeaten run (of league and cup matches). This included no less than four 40-38 home league wins in a row. The first of these, against Cradley, was a classic meeting. Tony Olsson scored 13 paid 14, joining Jan Andersson for a final heat 5-1 over Erik Gundersen to steal the points from the Heathens.

1987 marked the first full season in Racers colours for Tony Olsson. He went on to become part of the Reading set-up for many years. Here he is pictured at his testimonial meeting in 1995. (DA)

The winning run ended at home to Swindon. Mitch Shirra registered a paid maximum against his former team as Robins won 41½ – 36½. The half point (only the second at

Smallmead) came from a Gary Tagg/Stephen Rose dead heat in heat 2. (New Zealander Rose averaged a negligible 0.63 from 21 matches for Swindon.)

In October, Racers dropped another home point when Coventry visited. The Bees went through the league campaign unbeaten, but needed a 5-1 in heat 13 to salvage a draw so perhaps it was a point gained. The meeting will be best remembered for Per Jonsson's performance. Not only did he record a maximum, but he opened the meeting with a new track record. Jonsson's winning time of 58.1 is still inscribed in the 2008 Smallmead programme as the current track record. Currently the next oldest track record is Berwick's – set by Sean Wilson in 1999. Prior to their closure Oxford's record dated back to 1988 – held inevitably by Hans Nielsen.

The record Jonsson broke belonged to Nielsen too. But there is some dispute over what that previous record was. The Reading programme listed Nielsen's 1985 time of 59.2, but earlier in 1987 the World Champion had recorded a time of 58.4. This took place in the Bank Holiday League Cup clash with the Cheetahs. Because of starting-gate problems the starts were off the green light. While some sources recognised this as the new track record the Reading management didn't.

The 3 league points dropped at home were balanced by five taken from away trips. A draw at Swindon, featuring a five-ride full maximum from Jan Andersson and wins at the league's bottom two (King's Lynn and Oxford) were their only rewards. Of the eight matches Racers lost, five were by 6 points or less. These included October near misses at Hackney, Cradley and Coventry – all of which were lost after the normally reliable Jan Andersson suffered engine troubles. Reading finished seventh out of twelve.

The League Cup campaign had been similar in many respects. They won at the bottom four teams, but lost three times at home. The net result was a sixth place finish in the League Cup table.

A promising looking line-up didn't quite deliver despite Jonsson's coming of age. The principal reason wasn't hard to identify. John Davis broke a bone in his leg riding in Germany before March ended. He returned three weeks later, but never managed to reproduce the form he'd shown in the previous two years in Racers colours. His season remained dogged by injury and ended prematurely when a hand injury picked up a month earlier forced him to sit on the sidelines. His final appearance for the Racers (on September 30 at Coventry) yielded just 3 points.

Peter Glanz – broke into the Danish national team in 1987. (DA)

Davis's final match saw Reading eliminated from the Knock-Out Cup by the narrowest of margins – 91-89 after a 3-all in the deciding heat. After a double over Swindon in the previous round Reading won a lively first leg by 4. Two 5-1s, both involving Tony Olsson put Racers ahead before a controversial last-heat decider. When Jonsson powered under Tommy Knudsen and the Dane fell the referee's decision was bound to upset one of the protagonists. The exclusion of Knudsen deprived Coventry of a draw and set up a tense second leg.

The dip in Davis's scoring meant that the much-improved Peter Glanz nearly replaced him as third heat leader. Glanz, an ever-present in the Racers team (the first since Bernie Leigh in 1981), made his international debut. Glanz scored paid 6 from six rides from three appearances in the England v Denmark series. Fifth place in the Danish Championship ahead of Tommy Knudsen and Jan O. Pedersen underlined Glanz's progress. Unfortunately his form tailed off towards the end of the season and he rounded off the year expressing a desire for a change of track.

Tony Olsson flourished once he moved down to the reserve birth, culminating in a maximum at home to Hackney in the Racers final home league match. Despite spending most of the season in the top five Malcolm Holloway had a good year. While finishing sixth in the Racers league averages he finished in the top 50 league averages, an indication of the Racers strength in depth.

At number seven Gary Tagg made modest progress, but still failed to hit a 3-point average. In the less demanding environment of the British Junior League he flourished. Among those who rode regularly at junior level only 16-year-old sensation Mark Loram bettered his average. The Rivets finished ninth in the British Junior League and sixth in the Junior League Cup. Rodney Payne (who deputised for Tagg when injured) and Nick Bates provided the main back up to Tagg.

For the first time in three years Reading hosted a major event – the British Open Pairs. On July 12, in front of a 3,000 crowd, Hans Nielsen and Andy Grahame took the title back to Oxford. The day before a rare crack in the Danish domination showed when Gary Havelock won the European Junior Championship[42] in Poland.

Team: Per Jonsson 9.34, Jan Andersson 8.99, John Davis 6.95, Tony Olsson 6.60, Peter Glanz 6.45, Malcolm Holloway 6.02, Gary Tagg 2.57, Rodney Payne 1.33

42 Still called the European Junior Championship despite including Steve Baker (Australia), Shawn Moran (USA), and Ron Preston (USA) among the winners. New Zealand also managed rostrum finishes with both Tony Briggs and David Bargh coming second. Finally in 1988 it became the World Junior Championship.

1988 – Year of the Vanishing Heat Leaders

As a consequence of the Dore/Leonard dispute, team-building plans for 1988 took a back seat. Leonard wanted to buy out Bill Dore's 50% stake in Reading and Dore responded with an offer to buy back Leonard's 50% holding. The legal wrangling continued until early March, with just days to go before the season's start, when Leonard agreed to sell his share in the club back to Bill Dore.

During this period both parties had been having tentative discussions with riders, but nothing could be finalised until the ownership position had been resolved. Dore represented Reading at the promoters' conference in January – possibly a clue to the outcome of the dispute.

The relationship between the British and National Leagues continued to be a rocky one, but there was much speculation about the sport's future and amalgamation of the leagues. In practice the main change introduced by the conference was fixed gate positions. Previously the top riders usually chose the best gates.

Sometimes this caused friction as acknowledged by Bob Radford in a 1987 programme piece: "The heat leaders have the main responsibility to help make the team tick, and that hasn't been much in evidence here for a few years." When he was team manager: "the Racers second strings begged me to let them ride with Mitch Shirra." Incidentally both Radford and Dore subsequently implied that they would have chosen Shirra over Davis in 1987, but that Leonard went for Davis. This confirmed the view articulated the previous year by Shirra that he would have been the choice of Dore and Bliss.

The conference also decided to abolish the League Cup and extend the league programme to two home and two away fixtures against each opponent. For the first time since 1969 the race format was changed. 1988 would see 15 heat matches culminating in a nominated riders heat. With the departure of Hackney the points limit increased to 48.

As expected Davis and Glanz left, with Shirra returning and Mullett finally signing. Davis moved to King's Lynn on a full transfer where he recovered some of his form. The highlight of his 1988 season must have been his unexpected appearance in the World Final, his first since 1980. He continued riding in the British League until retiring in 1992 after breaking a leg. Subsequent to leaving Reading he also rode for Swindon and Sheffield, finishing his career at the age of 37 with over 5500 points from 659 matches. Since the British League era commenced in 1965 only Chris Morton and Malcolm Simmons had made more BL appearances at the time of Davis's retirement.

Davis's transfer financed the purchase of Mullett who had been the target of at least six clubs. Shirra's return seemed inevitable once Swindon declined to exercise their option to purchase him, but there was a brief period of speculation about a swap with Sheffield's unsettled Shawn Moran. Incidentally Shirra returned to Reading as the reigning holder of the Golden Helmet. In May 1987 he won the helmet from Jeremy Doncaster in the last challenge before the competition fizzled out[43].

Although the compulsory junior had been abolished most clubs kept a junior to allow them to build a strong top six within the points limit. Reading were no exception. Obvious choice Gary Tagg went on loan to Eastbourne (where he had first learnt to ride). Unfortunately the preferred Reading line-up (including Tagg) came to 48.01. At 2.57 his average was too high (!) so second choice junior Rodney Payne (assessed at 2.00) took the number seven spot.

Another very significant personnel change took place on the other side of the safety fence.

---

43 How typical of the BSPA that they should let a competition with a fine history die such a pitiful death. The helmet itself had already been lost!

With Leonard gone the team manager's role needed filling. Dore resumed the role, with club statistician Tim Sugar becoming assistant team manager. In practice this paved the way for the handover of responsibility to Sugar as the season progressed. Although he had to wait until mid-September before getting a joint credit as team manager in the Reading programme he had been doing most of the work long before that. His elevation pleased many Reading fans, grateful to have a team manager who was passionate about speedway and understood every subtle nuance of the rulebook. Sugar had been present at Tilehurst's opening fixture way back in 1968.

Due to the control dispute the Racers fixture list had an unbalanced look to it. The Smallmead season opened on March 21, but Racers fans had to wait a month until April 16 for the first away match. The home season started with an international challenge against Getingarna. The club that Anders Michanek spent most of his career with were led by world finalist Jimmy Nilsen. Reading won comfortably as the visitors had a long tail. Bottom of the Swedish score chart was an unknown 17-year-old – Tony Rickardsson.

The most significant event of the 1988 season happened that week. Rye House promoter Ronnie Russell signed Jens Rasmussen and Peter Schroek. Up to this time, the 'Second Division' had survived 20 seasons without the use of non-Commonwealth riders. Plenty of Australians and New Zealanders, plus the odd Canadian, South African and Zimbabwean had appeared in the National League, but no Danes or Germans.

National League rules clearly forbade Russell's actions, but he went ahead anyway on the basis that the prohibition could not be enforced. As members of the European Union Rasmussen and Schroek were entitled to work anywhere in the EU. Although Exeter contemplated signing Peter Glanz other clubs did not rush to follow suit. Rasmussen topped the Rockets averages, but Schroek didn't last the season.

Racers league campaign started with a narrow win over Cradley despite an 18-point maximum from Erik Gundersen. Making the most of the easier rides at reserve, Dave Mullett top scored with paid 11 for the home team. The following week Gary Tagg replaced Mullett (who had injured himself while walking his dog)! Racers beat Belle Vue by six with Tagg picking up 7 points, his best-ever score for the Racers. Les Collins, Andy Smith and Mike Faria were among the riders he beat that night.

Both Cradley and Belle Vue ended the season in the top three, but Racers next opponents were eventual champions Coventry. Going into the final heat level the Bees rounded off the night with a 5-1. A modest 6 points from Per Jonsson didn't help the Racers cause.

Racers then opened their away account with two wins and two draws from their first four road trips. Both King's Lynn and Bradford were beaten with heat 15 5-1s from Andersson and Jonsson. At Oxford Jonsson beat Nielsen and Wigg in the final heat to secure the draw. Andersson and Mullett scored heavily in all four matches.

When Reading drew at Wolverhampton on May 2 they moved in to second place in the league with 15 points, but Coventry were already way ahead on 28. The highlight of April was the Diamond Jubilee Series celebrating 60 years of British speedway with an international tournament between England, Sweden, U.S.A. and Denmark. England finished top of the league after beating Denmark, but were easily beaten by the Danes in the final staged at King's Lynn in June.

The Swedes lost all three of their matches but Jonsson was on sparkling form with double-figure scores in all three matches. His team mates included Racers Tony Olsson and an unfamiliar youngster named Henrik Gustafsson. A Swedish emphasis on youth meant there was no longer a place for Jan Andersson even when the Swedes rode at Reading. Smallmead hosted its first international since 1984 – the score: England 58 (Wigg 14, Cox 11) Sweden 32 (Jonsson 17).

The tournament only featured the strongest speedway nations. At the time Australia didn't fit the bill. There were only two Australians riding in the British League (Stephen Davies and Steve Regeling), and they were both second strings. However, 1988 saw the British debuts of Craig Boyce, Leigh Adams and Todd Wiltshire. Adams came over briefly and only rode in second halves, but Boyce (at Poole) and Wiltshire (at Wimbledon) made a big impact on the National League.

The return to league action in May saw Racers lose ground as they lost all four away matches and at home to King’s Lynn. Good news came from Denmark where Peter Glanz qualified for the Nordic Final, earning himself a place in the Wolverhampton team.

In June Reading only had two away fixtures, and suffered defeats in both. At home they also lost again (to Belle Vue) after Per Jonsson crashed out of the meeting in his only ride. The month ended with Gary Tagg receiving a recall. In his first match back he managed a match winning 4 paid 6 as Reading pipped Oxford 46-44. Earlier in the month Tagg and his rival for the number seven berth, Rodney Payne, both rode in the British Under-21 Championship. Both scored 4 points in the Eastbourne-staged meeting won by Mark Loram. Later in the season Payne moved on to Wimbledon where he scored paid 9 from three rides on his debut.

When Tagg returned to the team it meant Reading were tracking a septet that clocked up over 60 years of service: Tagg 3, Holloway 6, Shirra 7, Olsson 8, Jonsson 9, Andersson 13 and Mullett 15 seasons at Smallmead.

Rain accounted for the centrepiece of the July programme. Jan Andersson's testimonial meeting, due to be staged on July 4, had to be postponed until later in the month. An Oxford/Swindon select led by maximum man Hans Nielsen beat a Racers Select 44-40. The two teams included veteran reserves: Anders Michanek and Bernie Leigh for Reading and Martin Ashby and Mick Bell for their opponents. Per Jonsson won the individual event that followed.

Jan Andersson in civvies after dislocating his shoulder jet-skiing. Putting on leathers once more for Andersson's testimonial meeting were (from left to right): Martin Ashby, Mick Bell, Anders Michanek and Bernie Leigh. (EP)

Unfortunately on the Thursday before the re-staging Andersson dislocated his shoulder – jet-skiing! The injury kept Andersson out for four weeks. The five meetings he missed prevented him from being an ever-present in 1988.

Before the injury Andersson stood seventh in the British League averages on 9.62, well ahead of Per Jonsson. In the matches after his return Andersson averaged well below 8 and surrendered top spot in the Reading averages to Jonsson. In October Jan appeared in his ninth consecutive British League Riders Championship. Later in the month he received a cheque for £12,000 presented by supporters' club stalwart Edna Chandler.

Andersson partnered Jonsson in the British Open Pairs, staged at Reading in mid-July. The Racers duo finished third as Nielsen and Wigg retained the title for Oxford. Later in the season Smallmead also staged a British Junior Pairs Championship. The Wolverhampton pair of Ade Hoole and Lee Edwards took the championship from runners-up Belle Vue. The junior Aces pair of Carl Stonehewer and Paul Smith (Andy's brother) made considerably more impact on the sport than the winners.

In August Barry Briggs's plans for a 'Golden Greats' meeting finally came to fruition. A packed Coventry crowd reminisced about Briggs, Ove Fundin, Ivan Mauger and the many other competitors. Anders Michanek came second to Peter Collins in his section, which also included former Racers: Terry Betts, Martin Ashby and Bengt Jansson. 45-year-old Jansson was still riding regularly for Rospiggarna in the Swedish League!

Inconsistency continued to characterize Racers fortunes. An away win at Sheffield in July was cancelled out by a home defeat against the same opposition in August.

September kicked off with the first staging of the World Final at Ole Olsen's Vojens track. Per Jonsson comfortably qualified for his second final where a first-ride exclusion prevented him finishing higher than fifth. The Danes continued to dominate, filling all the rostrum places. Gundersen regained the title with reigning champion Nielsen second and Pedersen third.

Jonsson had a good season internationally, marking him down as a serious candidate for future World Champion. Jonsson won his third Swedish championship in a row, a feat never achieved by Ove Fundin or Anders Michanek. The only rider to record a hat-trick before Jonsson was his Racers team mate Andersson (in 1979-81). The biggest meeting in speedway outside the FIM calendar went to Jonsson too. In the Czech Golden Helmet final he headed home Roman Matousek, Jeremy Doncaster, Armando Castagna, Tommy Knudsen and Zoltan Hadju. One of the less prestigious FIM events, the Champions Cup[44], also ended up in Jonsson's trophy cabinet.

The FIM's second ranked competition – the World Team Cup – took place a week after the World Final. Again Jonsson took a major role. With Jan Andersson overlooked, Sweden fielded a young team. At 23 Tony Olsson was the oldest team member. Despite their youth Sweden took third place after top scorer Jonsson beat England's Kelvin Tatum from the back in a run-off. Predictably Denmark ran out easy winners to complete a clean sweep of the three major events for the fourth year in a row.

Back in the league Racers improved their standing with 3 away points. Another win at King's Lynn followed a draw at runaway league leaders Coventry. In both matches Jonsson scored maximums.

Off track the season had begun to unravel. For the fourth year in a row the season ended on a low note. Doubts over the future of all three of Reading's heat leaders emerged. September started with a transfer request from Mitch Shirra. As the season ended Shirra's troubles multiplied. A routine drugs test at the World Pairs Final (Bradford, July 31) had shown up

44 A classic example of the pointless competitions invented to give 'important' meetings to minor speedway nations. It lasted from 1986 to 1994. The entrants were the national champions of 16 different nations. Jonsson had stiff opposition from the national champions of Bulgaria, Holland and host nation Yugoslavia. Subsequent winners included Jan O. Pedersen, Hans Nielsen and Tomasz Gollob.

positive for cannabis. In November an FIM tribunal banned him for two years. Before Shirra's case reached the public arena another positive test, this time at the British League Riders Championship, resulted in Gary Havelock facing similar charges.

The timing couldn't have been worse. Only a couple of months before Olympic Sprinter Ben Johnson had been caught with the steroid stanozolol in his body and stripped of his 100 metre sprint gold medal. The sports world was awash with talk about crackdowns on "drug cheats." Speedway officials felt obliged to talk tough. Despite the fact that cannabis is not performance enhancing, and the positive tests only provided evidence of use at some time within the previous six weeks, both riders faced punitive bans[45]. Shirra faced a two-year ban, and Havelock a one-year ban.

As speedway's profile shrunk big-name sponsors slowly drifted away except one. Sunbrite sponsored the Diamond Jubilee Series, most of the season's major events and Mitch Shirra. After backing Mitch for 11 years the drug charges came as a serious blow to both Sunbrite and the sport. At its peak Sunbrite's sponsorship was worth a five-figure sum to Shirra.

September ended with the news that Jan Andersson intended to quit British speedway. After ten years as a Racer, seven of them as captain, he seemed like a permanent fixture at Smallmead. Within days Jonsson indicated that he too was contemplating giving the British League a miss in 1989.

Reading rounded off the season on track with a home win over Coventry and three away defeats. Andersson scored 3 and 5 in what looked like his final two appearances for Reading. A further worry for the Racers emerged when doctors diagnosed Malcolm Holloway (absent for most of October) as diabetic.

An unexpected bonus in the shape of a cup final upped the interest level in October. The Rivets finished mid-table with Rodney Payne and Steve Chambers topping the score charts. Victories over Coventry and Oxford gave them a place in the junior cup final. Opponents Cradley won both legs. Troy Smith top scored at home and Chambers headed the score chart at Cradley.

In the end the Racers finished fifth with a team that could have done better. Too many points were dropped at home. All of the top four finished higher in the away league average rankings than the home ones. Had they performed a little better at home some of those five defeats could have been averted. Shirra's average dropped by over a point while Jonsson and Holloway slipped slightly. After a slow start Tony Olsson upped his average. Dave Mullett started the season with some big scores, but once he moved out of the reserve berth his scoring diminished. Mullett reserved his best performances for Reading's clashes with champions Coventry. Mullet's scored paid 15 at home to Coventry and paid 12 at Coventry.

Over in Suffolk promoter Chris Shears fell out with Speedworth (the owners of Ipswich stadium) and initiated a winter of turmoil in East Anglia. Shears wanted to promote in the British League at Mildenhall. John Louis wanted to take over at Ipswich, and drop them down to the National League. Elsewhere King's Lynn, Swindon and Sheffield all contemplated dropping down to the less-expensive environment of the National League.

With Reading potentially needing three new heat leaders many wondered if they too would join the stampede.

Team: Per Jonsson 8.98, Jan Andersson 8.93, Mitch Shirra 8.20, Tony Olsson 6.95, Malcolm Holloway 5.63, Dave Mullett 5.23, Gary Tagg 3.09, Rodney Payne 2.81

---

45 These points were amongst those in a trenchant letter published in *Speedway Star* supporting Shirra and Havelock. The author a Mr N. Dyer will re-appear later in this book. A similar approach to alcohol, arguably a more dangerous drug, would lead to near-permanent bans for 90% of speedway riders.

1989 – The Ipswich Invasion

On July 3 Racers beat King's Lynn (who finished bottom for the fourth time in five years). Ten weeks later Bradford (who finished one place above King's Lynn) also lost at Smallmead. In between, Racers rode 11 league matches, winning only one of them.

At home they suffered four defeats including a record thumping at the hands of Cradley. A 56-34 Heathens victory on September 4 replaced the previous entry in the record books – 46-32, a score registered three times in league matches: Cradley (79), Cradley (82) and Ipswich (84). The visitors were led by Erik Gundersen, scoring the last maximum of his career. Shawn Moran (guesting for Jan O. Pedersen) also scored a maximum while Simon Cross managed paid 14 and rookie American Greg Hancock racked up paid 10. Reading managed just two heat winners.

Many of the away matches during this run produced heavy defeats, including a 61-29 scoreline at Wolverhampton where Carl Blackbird top scored with a meagre 7. (While Racers were being trounced in the Midlands, Smallmead hosted an England v Australia sidecar international – won 46-43 by Australia in front of a crowd of over 1,000.)

This run characterized a very poor year. Reading finished seventh out of nine in the league, arguably their worst performance to date. Results in 1978 had been worse, but that year Reading struggled from the off. In 1989 a decent-looking team fell short. At first glance injuries played a major cause, but good scores from guests and favourable rider replacement rules suggest otherwise[46]. Nor could the weak tail be blamed. The poor form only manifested itself after Malcolm Holloway returned to the team in place of make-weight juniors.

Holloway and Mullett missed matches due to injury, but the main loss was that of Armando Castagna. The Italian scored double figures in three of his first five Racers appearances, but his form tailed off before a broken collarbone put him out for June. Then before July ended so had Castagna's season. A broken leg riding against (!) Reading kept him out of the saddle.

For the only time in their history Reading rode as a team abroad. On the weekend of 22/23 July the team travelled to Italy where they rode two matches against Italy's national team. In the first match at Lonigo Castagna top scored for Italy with 12. However, the Racers won comfortably by 72 points to 36. In the top scorers race at the end of the match Castagna crashed resulting in a badly broken leg. Racers won the second match at Udine 70-38.

Castagna arrived at Smallmead after a convoluted series of proposed moves eventually left Ipswich promoter Chris Shears with no track, but half a team. Andersson and Jonsson's departures left a huge gap in the Reading line-up, while Holloway and Glanz also looked to be moving on. Ipswich riders Jeremy Doncaster, Armando Castagna and Carl Blackbird filled most of that hole. All were originally named in the Mildenhall team that Shears intended to enter in the British League. To keep below the points limit (46 for 1989) junior Steve Chambers occupied the final slot.

After Shears's plans for Mildenhall fell through the track was saved from closure by a new consortium. Needing riders to make up their National League team Peter Glanz and Malcolm Holloway both joined. Gary Tagg once again found his average too high (despite being only just over 3) for a Racers team place and secured a berth in the National League with Hackney.

With Sheffield closing and Ipswich dropping down the top division had shrunk from sixteen teams to nine in the space of five years. In the end Swindon and King's Lynn stayed in the British League. Swindon tried unsuccessfully to tempt Per Jonsson back to England after

---

46 When Reading operated rider replacement for Armando Castagna, it meant extra rides for top riders Shirra and Doncaster. Reading used 20 guests, mainly for Castagna, but also for Olsson and Mullett. These guests averaged 6.43, a higher figure than all of the riders they replaced.

he had failed to agree terms with Reading.

At the start of the winter Reading's position looked challenging because as well as losing their Swedish spearhead Mitch Shirra would be unavailable due to his drugs ban. Despite originating in July of the previous year the case still hadn't been resolved at the end of 1989. At the beginning of February the FIM decided that due to procedural irregularities the case should be remitted back for a rehearing. Dates in April and then June were postponed before the hearing finally took place in Geneva on August 8 – over a year after the original positive test for cannabis. Shirra received a two-year ban, but appealed which meant he could continue to ride. Finally as the season wound down the FIM delivered its final verdict – a one-year suspended sentence.

Sadly the saga still had some mileage in it. The Speedway Control Board decided to charge Shirra with the all-purpose blanket offence of 'bringing the sport into disrepute'. A new date, for yet another hearing, was set for January 1990.

Despite his problems Shirra continued to receive the support of Sunbrite. The coal products firm extended their support for speedway and the British League became the 'Sunbrite British League'. Reading management demonstrated their backing for Shirra, appointing him captain to fill the position left vacant by Jan Andersson's departure. Given his fiery temperament this caused a few raised eyebrows. On track Shirra's form showed no noticeable decline. His ranking in the British League averages dropped from 17th the season before to 18th in 1989, but after missing out in 1988 he returned to the World Final where he finished sixth.

1989 saw the arrival of Armando Castagna (left) and Jeremy Doncaster (right) from Ipswich. Both were awarded testimonial meetings while at Reading. They are seen pictured here at Dave Mullett's first testimonial meeting – with Dave Mullett (centre). (EP)

Despite their dreadful team form the Racers fans had three of their favourites to cheer on at the Olympic Stadium in Munich. Jeremy Doncaster scored 12 points and finished third after losing a run-off to Simon Wigg. Tony Olsson, a surprise qualifier, managed a respectable eight. The meeting is generally regarded as one of the poorest finals in the history of the World Championship. A narrow track led to poor racing and a weak field resulted increased the sense of anti-climax as Hans Nielsen easily regained the world title.

With Ermolenko, Pedersen and Knudsen all sidelined by injury, defending champion Erik Gundersen fell by the wayside after a third-ride engine failure. Two weeks later Gundersen's career was over.

The opening heat of the World Team Cup Final at Bradford featured Gundersen, Jimmy Nilsen, Lance King and Simon Cross. All four riders charged into the first bend, and they all ended up on the track. Although a re-run with all four riders was ordered not a single one of them was able to take their place in the re-run. All four required medical attention, but Gundersen came off worst. As the Dane teetered between life and death the speedway community waited anxiously. Erik's recovery was a slow one, but more complete than many believed possible at the time.

England went on to defeat the devastated Danes, finally breaking Denmark's domination of the World Championships. Jeremy Doncaster top scored for England and third place Sweden included Per Jonsson and Tony Olsson in their team. England haven't won the World (Team) Cup since and if this hollow victory is discounted then 1980 is the most recent English/British win.

The coverage of Gundersen's injury far outweighed the space given to the season's one racing fatality. Oxford junior Paul Muchene passed away on July 4, four days after a crash at Hackney and just two weeks before the anniversary of Denny Pyeatt's accident at the same track. On the other side of the safety fence Reading lost Dick Bailey as a result of a car accident in Thatcham. The Clerk of the Course since 1973, Bailey had been team manager back in 1968 when the Reading team took to the track for the first time. Bailey's replacement as Clerk of the Course was John Hook who had been machine examiner in 1968.

Bailey's passing took place in April while Racers were competing for a place in the Gold Cup final. Reading finished second out of five to Oxford after losing their opening home match to the Cheetahs. Blackbird and Olsson started slowly, but Mullett (benefiting from a reserve berth) started strongly. When Doncaster crashed out in his first ride at home to Swindon (April 3), Mullett was the Racers saviour with 17 points. Reading won 46-43.

Hillsborough stadium is just a few hundred metres down the road from Owlerton, home of Sheffield Tigers. In April 1989 Liverpool and Nottingham Forest met there in an FA Cup semi-final. As a result of overcrowding 96 spectators lost their lives. This disaster and the fire at Bradford four years earlier have had a noticeable effect on all sporting venues. In Reading's case these sad events contributed to the closure of the back straight stand at Smallmead.

The league campaign showed initial promise, with away wins at Bradford, Coventry and Belle Vue on the plus side and just the one home reverse (to Bradford). Strengthened in June by the return of Malcolm Holloway after a torrid spell at Mildenhall, prospects looked encouraging. Then Reading's form collapsed with that run of one win in eleven matches.

Racers broke their losing run in mid September with a 10-point win over Bradford. Doncaster scored a paid maximum and went on to end a month that started with his World Final bronze medal by winning the Czech Golden Helmet. A crowd of 35,000 at Pardubice fêted Doncaster as he was joined on the rostrum by fellow Racer Tony Olsson.

As the season staggered to a conclusion Malcolm Holloway announced his retirement. An injury at Wolverhampton (in August) caused him to miss five matches and then a crash at Bradford sidelined him in October. A farewell meeting for Malcolm staged the following June turned out to be a bit premature. Holloway, who started riding at Swindon in 1976, made his final appearance in Racers colours as recently as 2004.

A regular habitué of the Geoff Curtis Bar, Holloway is one of the genuine characters of the modern era. His rapport with the fans at Swindon was demonstrated when he chartered an entire train for Swindon's cup tie visit to Edinburgh in 1981. Another great tale dates back to the 1982 attempt to stage speedway in Northern Ireland. Short of a referee at the last moment, the organisers asked Holloway along to impersonate a referee!

Although late in the season Racers searched for a new rider and announced the signing of Peter Karlsson. At 19 Karlsson had caused a major upset in September by winning the Swedish Championship. Delays in the paperwork meant that Karlsson didn't get to don the winged wheel, but Pat Bliss and Bill Dore maintained their interest in him over the winter team-building period.

The season ended with a home defeat against Belle Vue. The junior match that followed produced a memorable result. Belle Vue Colts dominated junior competition; led by Joe Screen and Carl Stonehewer the Colts came to Smallmead with a record of 27 wins from 27 matches. The Rivets surprised everyone by beating the visitors 19-17. Despite this performance the Rivets finished bottom but one in the British Junior League. Steve Chambers who started the season at number seven topped the Rivets averages. David Steen (who rode for the senior team when Holloway was injured) came next. Troy Smith and Lance Sealey completed the quartet who stopped Belle Vue. In October Chambers won the Dick Bailey Memorial Trophy with David Steen taking second place.

While Belle Vue Colts won the junior league by a massive margin, the British League race went to the wire. A three-way contest between Oxford, Wolves and Cradley was only resolved when Oxford beat Cradley on November 1. The close title race combined with a long hot summer and an overheating economy[47] boosted attendances. The BSPA reported that attendances had increased at all British League tracks, even quoting the remarkably precise increase of 21.4%.

Turning from commerce to more spiritual matters 1989 was the year that Jamie Luckhurst of Edinburgh found God. After telling him to retire God apparently decided it would be OK for Luckhurst to ride for Middlesbrough.[48]

Sweden's re-emergence continued in 1989. Per Jonsson (who became a father in April) and Jimmy Nilsen finished second in the World Pairs, a position Sweden last achieved in 1977. Sweden hadn't won an FIM gold medal in the individual, pairs or team events since their 1975 success. Surely a Swedish victory was long overdue? Anders Michanek won medals in both the 1975 and 1977 World Pairs. In 1989 he turned 46 and made an unexpected return in the Swedish Elite League, scoring 7 points for Rospiggarna. A dispute over his eligibility resulted in a suspension and no further appearances.

Jan Andersson and Per Jonsson continued riding in Sweden. While Jonsson lost his grip on the Swedish Championship (finishing third), his Smallmead track record remained unchallenged. Not a single rider came within a second of the 58.1 record. Fastest time of the season at Smallmead went to Hans Nielsen – 59.2 on August 28.

August was the month when the world began to change. In Poland Tadeusz Mazowiecki, formerly one of the leaders of the Solidarity movement, became the first non-communist prime minister in Central and Eastern Europe since the end of the Second World War. In the same week Hungary opened its border with Austria and East German holiday makers started disappearing to the West. Unable to 'hold the line' the East German authorities opened borders between East and West Berlin on November 9. The Berlin Wall, totemic symbol of the Cold War, ceased to have a purpose.

Revolution spread, Romania said goodbye to communism by executing President Ceausescu on Christmas Day while Czechoslovakia managed a more peaceful transition when Vaclav Havel became president on December 29 after the success of the 'velvet revolution'.

In their final years the communist regimes had become more inward looking, and this

---

47 House prices peaked in the autumn of 1989 before crashing. Six years later the average house still fetched 20% less than it did in 1989. High mortgage payments meant less disposable income, and a return to the downward trend of crowds in the following years.

48 A line shamelessly pinched from *NL '90* by John Callaghan, the funniest speedway book ever written.

applied to their speedway authorities as well. Only Roman Matousek (Czechoslovakia and Coventry) and Antal Kocso (Hungary and Bradford) represented the Iron Curtain countries in the 1989 British League. The most recent Pole to appear in the British League was Piotr Pyszny for Eastbourne in 1983. In September 1989 Piotr Swist won the Polish Junior Championship, with Tomasz Gollob third. Swist had been a target of Swindon for much of the 1989 season. 16 years later when he finally made his debut in British League speedway Polish fortunes, fuelled by the injection of capitalism, had changed beyond all recognition.

Another revolution that would have a profound effect on British speedway was also under way. In February 1989 Sky launched its satellite service. Sky's developing relationship with speedway would be a major influence on the sport over the following years.

Team: Jeremy Doncaster 8.64, Mitch Shirra 7.81, Armando Castagna 6.38, Tony Olsson 6.17, Dave Mullett 5.72, Carl Blackbird 5.30, Malcolm Holloway 4.38, (David Steen 2.56)

Jan Andersson keeps close to the white line – his unexpected return was a crucial ingredient in Racers 1990 year of glory. (DA)

1990 – It Can't Get Any Better Than This

History will record that 1990 was a momentous year. Tim Berners-Lee invented the Internet; German re-unification took place; Nelson Mandela left Victor Verster prison; and Mrs Thatcher resigned. But for anyone with a place for the winged wheel in their heart 1990 was the year – the glory season.

The headlines read:

- League champions
- Knock-Out Cup winners
- Per Jonsson crowned World Champion
- Todd Wiltshire: third in the World Final and voted SWAPA[49] rider of the year
- Jeremy Doncaster: Overseas Champion, top Englishman in the British League averages, winner of the Czech Golden Helmet

Even the junior team had their best-ever season finishing runners-up in the British Junior League.

Since the Lanning-inspired win of 1980 Reading had promised much, but delivered little. Only in 1983 did Reading finish within striking distance of the top three. In most years Reading looked much stronger than their final position suggested. Under Bill Dore and Pat Bliss team building tended to be very late and sometimes over-reliant on existing assets, unless there was a new Swede available for signing.

The shape of the 1990 team emerged very late in the day. The principle cause was Mitch Shirra's continuing legal battle over his positive drug tests in 1988. On January 29 the Speedway Control Board found Mitch guilty of bringing the sport into disrepute[50] and banned him for five years, three of them suspended. Shirra appealed and the RAC increased the suspended part of the sentence to four years. This left Shirra able to compete internationally in 1990 but out of the British League for one year. He continued to ride in Europe and represented his country in the World Pairs Final along with David Bargh. Mitch also reached the final of the Czech Golden Helmet.

In January Pat Bliss indicated that her preferred line-up for 1990 would be: Doncaster, Shirra, Mullett, Olsson plus recalls for Jonsson and Glanz, and promotion for Steen. Holloway (retired), Castagna (a gamble after his broken leg) and Blackbird (who wanted to leave) would be the missing riders.

An added complication came from Wimbledon's attempts to rejoin the British League. Realising that the BL needed them more than they needed the BL the Dons negotiated hard. Among their demands: the opportunity to sign a decent number one. With Jonsson likely to return to Smallmead the Wimbledon management (fronted by Russell Lanning, son of Dave) had their eyes on Jeremy Doncaster.

Shirra's suspension meant that there was no way Pat Bliss could let Doncaster go. In a very acrimonious atmosphere Wimbledon retreated to the National League. Peter Glanz joined Milton Keynes at the end of February leaving Reading with just one rider signed (Dave Mullett), and at least two more riders to find.

Among the possible signings were Lance King, Peter Karlsson and Todd Wiltshire. As press day approached the team remained a heat leader and a second string short. Then a solution came from an unexpected source; Jan Andersson was ready to don the winged wheel

---

49 Speedway Writers' and Photographers' Association.

50 Opinion on the SCB handling of Shirra's indiscretion is divided, but I'm firmly with those that believe the only people bringing the sport into disrepute were the SCB themselves. The one thing I can find to say in their defence is that the final outcome was consistent with the equally unjust treatment of Gary Havelock who also lost a year of his speedway career to this absurd witch hunt.

again.

In February, Jan had made what turned out to be his final appearance at the Telford indoor ice meeting. He signed off a phenomenal record on indoor tracks by winning the Euro Ice Masters after a run-off with former Racers junior Andy Campbell. Over the previous decade 13 appearances in indoor meetings at Wembley, Birmingham (NEC), Telford and Murrayfield netted 11 individual titles and 7 maximums in team matches.

With a reputation as a fast gater Todd Wiltshire attracted surprisingly little interest from British League clubs over the winter. Some said his decision to attend his sister's wedding at the expense of riding in the Australian Championship showed he lacked ambition and the mental strength to make it at the top level. Pat Bliss and Bill Dore paid £20,000 or thereabouts for the young Australian. Many thought that looked expensive.

Once Andersson and Wiltshire were on board there was no room for David Steen. At 2.56 his average was too high. Instead the final place went to Nathan Murray, a 23-year-old New Zealander who had attempted to break into the National League the previous year without much success. During the winter he attended a training school run by Mitch Shirra at Smallmead and did enough to catch the eye of team manager Tim Sugar. With Murray in the team the combined average of the Reading septet came to 46.00, exactly the points limit for the new season.

One piece of business on the team front remained outstanding – the destination of Carl Blackbird. Chris Shears's involvement at Smallmead was rather nebulous. When he brought Doncaster, Castagna and Blackbird to Reading he didn't join the promoting team and coverage at the time didn't make it clear who owned the riders: Shears or Allied Presentations.

When it came to finding a new home for Carl Blackbird, Shears demanded £12,000 for him and after deals with Peterborough and Mildenhall fell through negotiations with Edinburgh were finally completed. Then Poole approached Pat Bliss and Allied Presentations agreed a deal for Blackbird to go to the South Coast. After making his debut Blackbird missed his next Edinburgh match before the BSPA ordered him to honour his Edinburgh contract. Worn down by the long journey each week Blackbird had another very forgettable season. A better year at Long Eaton in 1991 followed. He stayed with the club until he retired in 1993 at the age of 28.

By the time Blackbird's destination was resolved, the Racers campaign was well under way and it already looked promising. Reading opened with away wins at King’s Lynn (in the Gold Cup) and Coventry (League). Wiltshire scored 9 and 16 points in these two matches, but the sceptics suggested that points would be tougher to come by once he moved up from the reserve berth.

In the return match against Coventry, Wiltshire scored paid 15 as the Racers managed a lucky escape. Using rider replacement for injured Doncaster, it needed a final heat 5-1 from Jonsson and Andersson to bring home a 2-point win. And that was only achieved after Coventry's Kelvin Tatum suffered an engine failure when ahead in the last-heat decider.

A poor result at Oxford (where Tony Olsson top scored) damaged Reading's chances of a place in the Gold Cup Final. The return match ended with Reading 40-26 ahead due to an electricity failure. Had that match reached its conclusion, Racers might well have snatched the bonus point that would have given them qualification. When re-staged Reading won, but Oxford easily held on for the bonus point they needed. Oxford went on to lose comprehensively to Bradford in the final.

A big win at Swindon (50-40 on May 26) put Racers top of the league after seven matches. Three away defeats in June, including one at King’s Lynn (wooden spoonists in waiting), left Reading's position at the top of the table looking more precarious. Then two away wins on successive nights stretched Reading's lead to 6 points. At Oxford Hans Nielsen was on the wrong end of a 5-1 in the last-heat decider and at Cradley Andersson dead-heated with Alan

Grahame in heat 5.

Then Reading undid the good work by losing at home to Cradley. (The match saw Nathan Murray's final appearance at reserve before David Steen replaced him.) A broken collarbone for Todd Wiltshire in the cup semi-final at Belle Vue contributed to a second home league defeat in July.

After nearly four years in retirement Phil Crump returned to Swindon on July 28. Two days later Reading used the race-rusty veteran as a guest for Wiltshire. With Crump scoring just two Reading lost to Belle Vue, their closest rivals, by a single point. The Aces drew level with Reading at the top of the table and only a better race point record kept the Racers ahead.

Seven matches without loss in August put Reading back in control of the title race. However, the month ended with two major injuries for Reading to cope with. After three consecutive double-figure scores Dave Mullett broke an ankle in heat 2 of the home draw against Wolverhampton (August 20). Five days later Tony Olsson broke his thigh and arm in a horrific smash while guesting for Cradley at Dudley Wood.

Despite these setbacks Reading completed a Bank Holiday double over Oxford with Wiltshire returning from injury with a paid 14 score at Cowley. Reading's lead over Belle Vue increased from 2 to 7, but the teams still had to face each other twice.

Racers management acted quickly to bring Armando Castagna back to fill one of the gaps left by injury. When Castagna scored paid 12 as Racers put Belle Vue to the sword in late September, Racers fans could sniff the title. The 61-29 win was the team's biggest of the season. By the time Reading travelled to Belle Vue on October 12 a bonus point looked sufficient to secure the title. 14 points from Doncaster and paid 9 from a recuperated Dave Mullett ensured that the bonus point was never in doubt. When news filtered through[51] of Wolverhampton's defeat at Oxford the title race was all but over. A defeat for Oxford the next day ended the remote mathematical uncertainty, and Reading owned the trophy[52].

That night Racers completed a league and cup double at Bradford. A 12-point first leg lead left the tie finely balanced. A 15-point Wiltshire maximum and paid 14 from Jonsson put Reading in with a good chance. But Bradford had beaten Reading by 16 in their first league encounter at Odsal so the outcome couldn't be taken for granted.

On a wet night, Bradford's chances plummeted when reserve (and Australian champion) Glen Doyle withdrew from the meeting after a heat 2 crash. The scores stayed close throughout the match, and the win on the night was a bonus. Wiltshire (13) and Mullett (11+1) headed the score chart in Racers 47-43 win.

Outside Reading there was a widely held view that it was a hollow victory. In the semi-final Reading only knocked Belle Vue out after an appeal led to the second leg's original result (57-33 to Belle Vue) being altered (to 51-38 in the Aces favour). With Reading winning the first leg 53-36 a 7-point aggregate defeat became a 4-point win.

After a dismal zero score at Wolverhampton (on July 23) Belle Vue's Peter Ravn quit. The programme for the cup tie against Reading the following Friday referred to Ravn as an ex-Ace and was extremely uncomplimentary about his Monmore Green performance. Crucially there was a blank space in the team sheet. Belle Vue used rider replacement for Ravn, on the

---

51 It would be several years before mobile phones became ubiquitous (as late as January 1999 barely a quarter of the population owned one). In those days finding out other results involved finding a (working) payphone, ringing the track staging the match concerned and hoping that someone answered the phone. Alternatively if you were prepared to wait a little longer a call to the phonesport hotline would give the information (at 25 pence a minute). Or a call home might elicit the information from Teletext – but it might be midnight or later before the results came through ... It's hard to credit in these days when heat-by-heat live updates are available, often from distant corners (can a sphere have corners?) of the globe.

52 Following 'amalgamation' a new trophy was awarded to the 1991 winners. Pat Bliss purchased the 1990 League Trophy, which went on display at Reading Museum during 2007.

understanding that they had permission from the BSPA. Racers team manager Tim Sugar objected, pointing out that the regulations required the name of the rider to be in the programme (explicitly stated in rule B14). Reading had their own problems: heavy traffic delayed the visitors' arrival and Todd Wiltshire broke his collarbone in his second ride.

The SCB upheld the protest thus eliminating the Aces who believed that they had qualified for the cup final fair and square. As a post script Peter Ravn returned to the Aces side at the end of August. Ironically Belle Vue had staged a testimonial for Ravn earlier in the season. This incident also started the annual pantomime that involved John Perrin announcing that he was fed up promoting Belle Vue and about to quit. And as each new season rolled round he was still there, until 2005 when Tony Mole took over.

Racers league programme finished with another win at home to Bradford and a 61-29 mauling at King's Lynn. The Bradford fixture was refereed by Chris Shears after the non-arrival of programmed official Reg Trott. The final league table showed Reading 5 points ahead of Wolverhampton and seven ahead of Belle Vue. On November 2 the Reading team and management received a civic reception in recognition of their achievements.

The spoils of victory – the honour-laden Racers team of 1990. Left to right, back row: Tim Sugar (team manager), Dave Mullett, Armando Castagna, Bill Dore (promoter), Tony Olsson, David Steen, Jan Andersson, Nathan Murray. Front row: mascot, Todd Wiltshire, Jeremy Doncaster and Per Jonsson. (BT)

The Rivets fared well in the Junior League. Their runners-up position (to Wolverhampton) was easily the Rivets best finishing position in the nine years (1984-92) that a junior league operated. The Rivets used only five riders: David Steen, ever-presents Troy Smith and Christian Howell, Lance Sealey (son of trackman Jeff) and Mark Seabright. Smith nearly upset the form book in the Junior League Riders Championship finishing second after losing a run-off with Belle Vue star Ritchie Musson. After a bad injury at Poole, the following year Seabright became more familiar as a mechanic for several riders including Andrew Appleton and Lee Richardson.

Reading staged the Dick Bailey Memorial as a second-half junior event. The trophy went to Rye House's Scott Humphries. Also competing was Poole junior Steve Leigh, nephew of Racers stalwart Bernie.

Poole's junior team that year also included 16-year-old Justin Elkins (much touted as a star of the future) and 17-year-old Australian Mark Lemon (experiencing British speedway for the first time).

Australia were beginning to re-emerge as a world force. In the World Pairs Final Todd Wiltshire and Leigh Adams went into the final race leading the field, but the Danes passed them to win the title for the sixth year in a row. Wiltshire produced the top score in the meeting: 25 points. This event was the final time six-man races were used in the World Pairs competition. A serious injury to Piotr Swist in the semi-final meant that it had already been decided that races would revert to four competitors the following year. Unfortunately the final produced another serious injury with Simon Cross hurting his back.

England fared better in the World Under-21 Championship, with Chris Louis taking the title ahead of Rene Aas and Tony Rickardsson. 1990 was a vintage year for English talent, the 1-2-3 in the British Under-21 Championship read: Joe Screen, Mark Loram, Chris Louis. Ex-Racer Gary Tagg finished seventh

England also came close in the World Team Cup finishing 3 points behind the United States. Jeremy Doncaster contributed 8 points to the English total. Denmark finished outside the top two for the first time since 1980 with only Hans Nielsen scoring well. Nielsen made history earlier in the season when he signed for Polish League club Motor Lublin. Economic liberalisation following the collapse of communism was injecting new money into the Polish economy triggering a speedway boom. On April 1, the opening day of the Polish league season, Nielsen was one of five foreigners to come to the tapes. Many more would follow.

Although failing to win the World Under-21 title Rickardsson did produce a shock victory in the Swedish Championship. Jonsson could only manage third. Runner-up position went to Erik Stenlund, the 1985 Swedish Champion, double World Ice Champion and (briefly) in 1996 a Reading Racer.

Hans Nielsen remained the best rider in the world. He headed the British League averages on 10.32, next were Jan O. Pedersen (9.25) and Jeremy Doncaster (9.05). However, the 'sudden death' one-off World Final was about who performed on the night, and there were several other riders in the field at Bradford who would be worthy World Champions come September 1.

Absent from the field were Doncaster and Shirra. After third place in the British Final and winning the Overseas Final, Doncaster fell at the final hurdle with a dismal display in the Inter-Continental Final. The New Zealand authorities declined to nominate Shirra for a Commonwealth Final slot denying him the opportunity of another World Final appearance. The Overseas Final at Coventry produced a Racers one-two as Todd Wiltshire achieved second place. While Wiltshire marched on, a number of other rising young stars suffered elimination at Coventry. Mark Loram, Billy Hamill, Greg Hancock and Leigh Adams would all fare better in years to come.

Castagna qualified from the Continental Final, a meeting he would have won but for an exclusion in his third ride. Wiltshire scraped through from the Inter-Continental Final taking the last qualifying place. Also through after finishing second in both the Nordic and Inter-Continental Finals was Per Jonsson.

On the big night, Jonsson opened up with a win from the back over Swedish rival Jimmy Nilsen, and by the interval Jonsson sat in equal first with outsiders Todd Wiltshire and Henrik Gustafsson. All had 8 points. Next time out Shawn Moran beat Jonsson to move into the lead – shared with Jonsson. Both won their final rides to finish on 13. Wiltshire's 12 points secured him an impressive third place, but the crowd waited, anticipating a run-off for the title.

The crucial gate went to Jonsson who never gave Moran a chance to recover[53]. After 16 years in the wilderness a Swede finally won speedway's ultimate prize. Following in the

53 Moran subsequently lost his silver medal, the result of taking painkillers prior to the Overseas Final.

footsteps of 'mighty' Michanek, Racers fans could now celebrate the success of 'perfect' Per. Jonsson literally dropped in on Smallmead for their next home meeting. He arrived by helicopter and then joined Wiltshire and the rest of the Racers for a lap of honour on a vintage fire engine.

Team: Jeremy Doncaster 8.98, Todd Wiltshire 8.56, Per Jonsson 8.24, Jan Andersson 7.35, Tony Olsson 6.47, (Armando Castagna 6.42), Dave Mullett 6.18, Nathan Murray 2.33, David Steen 1.98

Per Jonsson – World Champion. (DA)

1991 – The Threat of Relegation

For all Racers joy, their year of triumph turned out not to be the most important sporting news in Reading that year. In December 1990 John Madejski bought Reading Football Club for £315,000, at a time when they were heading for financial oblivion. Over the past 20 years speedway had competed with football for the headlines in the local media. Under Madejski the Royals fortunes would rocket and the Racers would become part of the supporting cast as the sports pages (nationally as well as locally) became more and more dominated by football.

Between 1978 and 1990 the combined strength of speedway's two leagues fell from 39 to 26. It had been six years since a completely new track (Arena Essex) opened. The British League struggled to function with five of its nine members racing on Saturdays and the FIM making greater calls on riders for weekend international events.

For several years relations between British League and National League promoters had been very poor. While the first Gulf War raged in the Middle East, peace finally broke out in promoting circles.

Mervyn Stewkesbury, promoter of 1990 National League champions Poole produced a 'blueprint' that would see a merging of the two leagues' management, and an expansion of the senior division. Four National League teams (Poole, Berwick, Ipswich and Wimbledon) joined the British League Division One. Eastbourne withdrew from British League Division Two, feeling that they deserved to be in the top league. At the 11th hour Sheffield re-opened to keep the number of tracks operating at the same figure as 1990.

Berwick, the surprise addition to the senior league, used a big fat chequebook to lure Jimmy Nilsen and Kelvin Tatum to the Borders. It later transpired that some of these cheques were of the rubber variety! At the end of the year they returned to Division Two. They did pick up a trophy on the way, winning the Gold Cup.

Newly crowned World Champion Per Jonsson spent the winter in Australia where he outshone all comers in a closely fought Test series. Sweden won 3-2 with Jonsson scoring 77 points, Gustafsson 50 and Nilsen 39. Todd Wiltshire topped the Aussie score charts with 63. Naturally Jonsson wanted a 1991 contract commensurate with his new enhanced status and asked for a 25% increase.

To make amalgamation work and allow the four new teams to build reasonable squads a very low points limit of 40 (including bonus points) was set. This left Pat Bliss needing to make tough choices about who to keep. Although Jonsson's demands were reasonable in comparison with other world-class stars it meant he ended up without a team place. The days when Reading maintained a reputation as one of the top-paying clubs were coming to an end.

Todd Wiltshire only finished fifth in the Australian Championship and had to rely on a seeded slot to continue his World Championship quest. He remained in Reading's plans along with Jeremy Doncaster. As he had never been formally transferred since making his debut for Ipswich in 1982 'Donkey' received a testimonial meeting. The event took place at the beginning of August. The meeting's main point of note was the return of Mitch Shirra, making his first Smallmead appearance since 1989.

Jan Andersson and Dave Mullett re-signed and David Steen retained a reserve berth leaving two spots to fill. With only 6.74 headroom below the points limit, options were limited. Extrovert Londoner Ray Morton joined on a 4.5 average leaving just over 2 points for the final position. At the start of March, Scott Humphries was announced as the final piece in the jigsaw. Born two days after Tilehurst opened its doors to speedway in 1968, Morton started his career as a King's Lynn junior. After switching to the National League he put in three solid seasons at Wimbledon. Humphries, a 26-year-old Australian and friend of Todd Wiltshire, came over to join Wimbledon in 1989, but spent 1990 on loan to Rye House averaging under 5 in the National League.

Reading's application for a work permit failed and Humphries's place went to Tim Korneliussen. The 22-year-old Dane had ridden for Hackney the previous year but a broken thigh ruined his season. It is doubtful if he was really race fit and after ten matches in which he scored just 8 points he was shown the door[54]. His younger brother Mads has had a considerably more notable career with Newport and Swindon.

The Racers season started off with a Premiership encounter against Poole. Both teams won their home legs by 12 points leaving the outcome unresolved. By the time Reading won the replay (July 8) their season had turned into a series of disappointments. In the deciding match at Smallmead Ray Morton scored his first Racers maximum as Reading outscored Poole 18-6 in the last four heats to win 95-85 on aggregate. Morton loved riding against Poole. And the rather unbalanced fixture list gave him plenty of opportunities.

8 July 1991 – The Racers capture the Premiership with a win over Poole. Lining up left to right, back row: Tim Sugar (team manager), Scott Humphries, Bill Dore (promoter), David Steen, Jan Andersson, Todd Wiltshire. Front row: Dave Mullett, Jeremy Doncaster and Ray Morton. (BT)

When the two teams met in mid August at Smallmead Reading's 55-35 victory turned out to be their biggest league win of the season. It was also the 14th time the two teams had met since March[55]. Morton made six appearances at Wimborne Road in Racers colours scoring 65 paid points for an 8.67 average.

The August Poole fixture also marked Mitch Shirra's first league appearance at Smallmead since 1989. After two double figures scores away his home return yielded a paid maximum.

The ubiquity of Poole was not the only problem with the fixture list. Reading rode no less than nine matches in 15 days (April 8-22). Most of these were early-season Gold Cup matches. Racers started well in the Southern group with wins at Poole and Ipswich. Wiltshire scored double figures in both matches, as he started the season in fine form. The other half of the spearhead Jeremy Doncaster fared less well, his maximum at former track Ipswich being a rare exception.

---

54 Candid as ever, Bob Radford's programme notes described his performances as "consistently awful".

55 Four premiership, two Knock-Out Cup, two Gold Cup, two league and four in the four-team tournament. Racers also met Swindon 13 times in 1991.

After those two wins, hopes on the terraces were running high, but Swindon brought Racers back to earth with a win at Smallmead (on April 15). When Oxford followed suit three weeks later, hopes of qualifying for the Gold Cup Final evaporated. A late win at Swindon lifted Reading to runners-up spot behind Oxford. Wiltshire and Doncaster both scored maximums, ominously neither managed to repeat the feat again during the season.

The league campaign began badly and by the end of July Reading sat in 11th place in the league, two places off the bottom. Three of the first five home matches went the way of the visitors. The victors were:

- Wolverhampton (Ronnie Correy scored 17 for the eventual champions),
- King's Lynn (benefiting from a Dave Mullett heat 1 fall that forced him out of the meeting), and
- Ipswich (with reserve Zdenek Tesar getting 16 points compared with two from the Racers reserve pair).

Against Ipswich and King's Lynn, Reading used rider replacement for Todd Wiltshire. On July 21 Reading travelled to the Peterborough-staged final after a convincing performance in the qualifying rounds of the Division One Four Team Tournament. Racers won three of the four rounds to win their group by 19 points. The day ended badly for Reading. A four-man pile up left Wiltshire with elbow and wrist injuries that would keep him out of the saddle for some weeks. Reading finished a distant third; Ipswich won the competition.

Promotion and relegation formed one of the main talking points of the amalgamation package. Reading were in a position that would have left the rest of the season anti-climactic in any other year. But everyone at Smallmead knew it was imperative to avoid bottom spot.

Guest rules were unusually restrictive in 1991. Only seven guests were used in the entire 156-match league programme. With rider replacement not looking an attractive proposition Racers replaced Wiltshire with the newly available Shirra. Failure to pay the fine levied by the SCB had extended his suspension until it was paid mid-season and the SCB gave him permission to resume racing in Britain from August 1.

Shirra returned two days after qualifying for his sixth World Final. After 15 years the lopsided qualifying competition got a makeover. The Continental Final, which had given a relatively easy path to the World Final for many Czechs and Germans (among others), got the chop. Instead, an open draw for two semi-finals replaced the Continental and Inter-Continental finals. All the Racers interest centred on the first semi-final at Rovno in newly independent Ukraine. Jonsson, Doncaster and Castagna all joined Shirra in the qualifying positions.

Shirra had already appeared in one world final that season, finishing fifth in the World Longtrack Championship. Winner Gerd Riss drew much comment with his unusual laydown machine. Shirra also rode regularly for Unia Tarnow in the Polish League, as did Jeremy Doncaster. In just the second season of foreigners in the Polish League, four of them filled the top five spots in the Polish averages. Ex-Racer Andrzej Huszcza being the lone Pole in the top five, which read: Hans Nielsen, Lars Gunnestad, Per Jonsson, Huszcza, Shirra.

The influx of foreigners highlighted how far Polish standards had fallen. In the World Team Cup Poland ended up in 12th position behind Hungary, Germany, Norway, Finland and the Castagna-led Italy.

In Sweden Nielsen could only manage second in the averages to Jonsson. Wiltshire also rode in Sweden and Poland, returning to league action in both countries at the beginning of September once his arm had healed.

Returning to Reading's league fight, Wiltshire wasn't the only rider to make way as Reading attempted to fend off relegation. David Steen lost his place and went on loan to Edinburgh in August. His replacement, Terry Mussett, became the fourth former Wimbledon rider to appear in Racers colours during 1989. Mussett fared even less well than Steen, who managed a respectable 5-point average for the Monarchs.

An unexpected away win for Eastbourne (at Coventry) on August 10 pushed Reading into the bottom spot. Racers stayed there for 16 agonising days until two Bank Holiday clashes with Oxford. A home leg gave Reading a 46-44 victory. Oxford, still in the relegation race themselves, relied too heavily on Hans Nielsen. An 18-point maximum at Cowley in the morning was overshadowed by his Smallmead performance – 21 points and the fastest Smallmead time (58.4) since Jonsson's 1987 record (58.1).

Five days later Nielsen lost out to Jan O. Pedersen in the Ullevi-staged World Final. In front of 25,487 spectators Nielsen beat Tommy Knudsen in a run-off for third. Second place went to the only non-Dane in the top four – surprise performer Tony Rickardsson. The night ended in disappointment for the Reading contingent. Jonsson (7), Castagna (6), Shirra (4), Doncaster (2) all finished in the bottom half of the field.

Earlier in the season Jonsson and Castagna had also appeared in the World Pairs Final, which was won by Denmark for the seventh year in a row. While Jonsson walked away with a silver medal, the big surprise was Norway's third place. Rising star Lars Gunnestad and one time Racer Einar Kyllingstad were the men celebrating.

Shirra and Doncaster returned to action for the Racers with a cup semi-final tie against Cradley. Reading went into the final heat of the second leg needing a 5-1 to level the tie, but Hamill and Hancock got the 5-1 ... for Cradley.

Wins at home to Swindon and away to Eastbourne followed, easing relegation fears. Jan Andersson scored a maximum against Swindon – the 66th and last of his Racers career. A Shirra/Andersson 5-1 broke the deadlock at Eastbourne after the teams went into the final heat level. The Eagles fielded Armando Castagna in the deciding heat, after signing him on loan from Reading as a replacement for John Davis. 'JD' had left struggling Eastbourne for Swindon, a team in even more trouble.

Another Reading loanee undid the good work of the previous week. Tony Olsson picked up 14 points for Belle Vue, who won 47-42 at Smallmead. Olsson had a difficult season. With doubts about his fitness at the start of the season he couldn't secure a team place in Division One. Dropping down to Division Two Hackney turned out not to be the solution. The Hawks went bust mid-season owing Olsson £2,000.

A new face in the Racers line-up added extra interest to the Aces fixture. Mussett lost his place to a new recruit. The debutant had only turned 16 six days earlier. Three days earlier he posted three wins and a tape exclusion in his junior league debut at Eastbourne. A maximum in the junior match against Belle Vue helped make up for the zero score in the senior match.

Phil Morris kept his place until the end of the season, and for 12 of the following 13 seasons. He

Just a few days after his 16th birthday and still studying for his GCSEs, Phil Morris became a Racers regular in September 1991. (EP)

remained part of the Racers set-up until a surprise transfer to Birmingham in December 2007. Morris did manage his first heat win at home to Berwick, but in 1991 points were hard to come by.

With Morris on board, the Racers won their last three home matches, while Swindon suffered two more home defeats making the wooden spoon an inevitability. The Swindon management made it clear that they didn't think competing in Division Two would be viable. Any question about the Robins continued survival became academic when Berwick's debts forced them down to Division Two leaving a space open for Swindon.

Berwick's place went to Arena Essex. Under new promoter Terry Russell the Hammers won 21 out of 22 league matches thanks to a spearhead consisting of Brian Karger and Bo Petersen. Both rode in the 1990 World Team Cup Final for Denmark. Karger also won gold as part of the 1991 Danish team that regained the World Team Cup by a huge margin. (Sweden were runners-up with Jonsson topping their score chart.) In the BSPA Cup, Arena met and defeated Division One opposition from Eastbourne and Coventry.

There were some positives in Reading's dismal season. Dave Mullett continued to improve, and reached his first British Final. Scott Humphries arrived with no great expectations, but produced some excellent results. He topped the Racers score charts twice at home, with 13 against Wimbledon and paid 10 against Cradley. As a result he found himself out of reserve in August and found life hard in the top five. The rider he relegated to reserve – Ray Morton – arrived with a 4.50 assessed average and finished the year with an average over 6, making him another success.

At least there was a sense of continuity at Reading. Their season started with a rained-off challenge against Swindon on March 18 and ended with the Thames Valley Triangle on October 14. Including one sidecar meeting and one more rain-off, Reading ran a programme of 31 meetings staged on 31 consecutive Mondays.

Barely 30 miles east of Smallmead another track fared less well. Speedway couldn't be made to pay at Wimbledon. Rain cut short the final meeting (June 5), a four-team tournament qualifying round. Victory in the last race at Plough Lane went to Reading's Jeremy Doncaster as rain put an end to the meeting after eight races.

One of the finest clubs in the sport's history left the stage in a lustreless manner. They won the league seven times in eight years (from 1954-1961) with Barry Briggs, Ronnie Moore and Bob Andrews among the team's leading lights. With Hackney following the same course a month later London was left without a speedway track. It is a fact of life that many parts of the media, whether consciously or not, take the view that: 'unless it happens in London it's not happening.' In the summer of 1991 speedway slipped off the radar. Its pleas for more coverage in the general media became increasingly forlorn.

Team: Todd Wiltshire 9.02, Jeremy Doncaster 8.43, Mitch Shirra 8.43, Jan Andersson 7.79, Dave Mullett 7.05, Ray Morton 6.55, Scott Humphries 4.60, Dave Steen 2.86, (Phil Morris 1.45), Terry Mussett 1.30

1992 – A Busy October

In the 17 weeks between 20 April and 16 August Reading rode 16 matches (excluding a woeful set of four-team tournament qualifying rounds). Racers schoolboy number seven Phil Morris (who finished sitting his GCSEs in June) probably appreciated the light fixture list. Despite being a full-time Racer he achieved eight grade A-Cs.

However, Phil Morris's academic success was overshadowed by the Racers on-track performances. As Reading advanced to the finals of three competitions and chased the league title the lack of activity in the middle of the season caused enormous difficulties.

Reading ended up riding 16 matches in the space of 24 days as October turned into a mad scramble to complete their programme.

When Arena Essex arrived at Smallmead on October 5, Reading stood fourth in the table with six of their twelve home league matches still to race, as well as two cup semi-finals. 48 hours after a comfortable win over the Hammers fans were passing through the Smallmead turnstiles again to witness a cup semi-final showdown with Cradley. In the previous 14 years the Racers had gone head to head with the Heathens seven times in the cup. Ominously the cumulative scores read: Cradley seven ties won, Reading none. For once, Reading mastered Cradley with a paid 16 contribution from Ray Morton giving Reading a 20-point lead to take up to Dudley Wood.

The following weekend (October 10/11) saw Reading in league action twice. A narrow defeat at title rivals Bradford (Jonsson picking up a questionable exclusion in the last-heat decider) and a win at Eastbourne (with Mullett and Morton grabbing double figures as Jonsson picked up his lowest score of the season) kept the title challenge on the road.

A double header on the following Monday gave Reading the opportunity to move to the top of the table. Reading recorded their two biggest wins of the year: 59-31 against Bradford (with maximums from Jonsson and Mullett), and 58-32 v Eastbourne. In heat 12 of the Eastbourne match Peter Nahlin beat fellow Swede Jonsson. Only later did this result achieve significance.

On Wednesday 14 October, the Racers suffered a set-back. Rain put paid to the return leg of the cup semi-final, adding to the fixture backlog. At Ipswich the following evening a Jonsson/Doncaster 5-1 in the deciding heat secured another win (48-41). Doncaster achieved a maximum at his former track, the only one of his season. Tony Olsson top scored for the Witches against his parent club.

After a couple of days' rest the Racers faced Ipswich again. Their next encounter was the BSPA cup semi-final at Smallmead. With Castagna riding in Italy, Racers reluctantly settled for the Sunday date. But with time running out the options were limited. Teams from both leagues participated in the BSPA cup, each tie being staged over a single leg. Racers reached the semi-final with wins at Stoke, home to King's Lynn and at home to Bradford. With Tim Sugar away, the Bradford match gave Pat Bliss a rare outing as team manager. Against Ipswich Racers won again, with a 5-1 in the last-heat decider. And again Olsson topped the Ipswich score chart.

24 hours later everyone was back at Smallmead. So too was the rain. After the previous Thursday's win at Ipswich a victory over Coventry would have given Reading the league title, but gratification was delayed.

Racers took on three away matches before the Coventry match was run the following Sunday (October 25). By then the league had been won. Cradley lost at Bradford on Tuesday leaving only Bradford in the race, and they needed Reading to lose all of their three remaining home matches by large margins. The Dukes loss at Arena on the Friday confirmed what already looked inevitable – Reading Racers league champions.

With so many matches, the Racers and their fans were perhaps too busy to take much notice of events elsewhere. On the Wednesday (October 21) the speedway world changed dramatically. The sport's international governing body, the FIM, voted to scrap the World Final and replace it with a Grand Prix event. It would be staged over six rounds, starting in Poland. This was all due to start in 1994, but organisational delays meant that it got put back a year. Most British promoters could see the threat to British speedway and there was plenty of mumbling about a breakaway from the FIM that never came to anything.

Wednesday also marked the start of a run of eight matches in eight days. Just 72 hours after the semi-final Reading went to Poole in the first leg of the BSPA cup final. Poole reached the final after three away ties – at Rye House, Swindon[56] and Eastbourne. The outcome, a 50-40 win to Poole left the tie finely balanced.

The day after, Racers secured another cup final slot losing 45-44 at Cradley for a 19-point aggregate victory. The bad news came in the shape of a broken collarbone for Ray Morton after a heat 2 fall.

Much to the annoyance of sponsors *Speedway Star*, the first leg of the final took place just 48 hours later when Reading travelled up to Bradford (October 24). With Doncaster only scoring 3 and Lance Sealey (replacing Morton) failing to trouble the scorers Reading tumbled to a 20-point defeat making the return leg a daunting proposition.

With the league title already won, Sunday's match at home to injury-stricken Coventry was a routine affair. With their top four injured the Bees made an excellent choice of guests, including Tony Olsson. The Reading-owned Swede took 16 paid 17 points from the Smallmead encounter. In 1991 guests were few and far between. Understandably Coventry were the exception, they accounted for 19 of the 26 guests used in league matches that year.

While Racers won comfortably, a last-heat decider win for Eastbourne (at home to Arena Essex) consigned Swindon to last place and relegation. The one consolation in Swindon's dire season was the form of Leigh Adams. Earlier in the season he became World Under-21 Champion in a meeting that produced the following top five: Adams, Mark Loram, Joe Screen, Lars Gunnestad, Tomasz Gollob.

After facing Coventry on Sunday the Racers returned to Smallmead on Monday for a cup final double header against Poole and Bradford. Ray Morton attempted a premature comeback against Poole. He lasted less than a lap and had to be replaced by Lance Sealey in the Bradford match. A Jonsson maximum and a 4-2 in the final heat gave Reading a 92-88 aggregate win in the BSPA cup. Reading comfortably beat Bradford, but the first-leg deficit was simply too large to pull back without a fit Morton. Mullett top scored (12+1) in the Knock-Out Cup final with Jonsson taking a paid maximum (11+1). Over 3,000 watched the two cup finals – an excellent crowd. With seven home meetings in 24 days many of the others were poorly attended.

Finally Racers wrapped up their season on Wednesday 28 October with another double header. It had proved difficult to agree dates with both the Ipswich and King's Lynn

---

56 The Swindon tie became one of speedway's classic farces. After the Robins and Pirates drew 45-all referee Mick Barnes ordered that the tie should be decided by a run-off. Swindon's Leigh Adams duly beat Steve Schofield leaving the Robins fans looking forward to the semi-final. Poole protested that the rules made explicit provision for a replay. The SCB upheld Poole's complaint and the Pirates easily won the replay. This added to the agony of Swindon's disastrous season. Hampered by a late start to team building they struggled to avoid the wooden spoon all season.

managements, but eventually they took to the track. Jonsson (full) and Mullett (paid) were unbeaten by an Ipswich rider, but Phil Morris crashed out of the match. This meant a surprise call up for junior Mark Sayer in the King's Lynn match.

Jonsson scored another maximum. Before the meeting Jonsson stood third behind Hans Nielsen and Sam Ermolenko in the league averages. His two Wednesday night maximums moved him to the top of the league averages. Jonsson ended the season with six maximums in a row at Smallmead. With a busy cup programme as well Jonsson ended the year with 643 points (including bonus) in official matches – a club record tally for a single season.

Although King's Lynn were only beaten 46-44 it still ensured that Reading ended the year with a 100% home record. In all competitions Reading won 27 matches at home. In no other year have Reading achieved this feat. 100% home league records in 1972, 1997, 1998 and 2004 were all spoilt by slip ups in other competitions.

The animosity with King's Lynn arose after the King's Lynn v Reading match was postponed unilaterally by promoter Buster Chapman on August 22. (The Stars would have taken to the track without their top two, Henka Gustafsson and Mark Loram.) A month later the SCB awarded the match 75-0 to Reading, causing much outrage amongst their title rivals.

Reading also received criticism over their fixture pile-up. Many took the view that Reading were the author of their own misfortune. With guest facilities almost non-existent any ambitious promoter was keen to avoid clashes with riders' overseas commitments and major international meetings. Much was made of a list of 63 dates, when Reading wouldn't race, that Pat Bliss gave to other promoters. In a robust defence Pat pointed out that 32 of these were on Tuesdays when no British League team normally rode, and a further 25 Wednesdays which only clashed with Poole, who were easily accommodated.

Reaching three cup finals required seven additional home dates, and rain-offs added another four dates to the diary.

The highlight of the season prior to October's hectic climax took place at Monmore Green in mid September. A double header between Reading and Wolverhampton combined the second legs of both the Knock-Out Cup tie between the teams and the Gold Cup Final. Both teams comfortably headed their Gold Cup qualifying groups. Racers started with seven wins in a row; Wolves did even better remaining unbeaten in ten group matches. Racers arrived with a 5-point lead from a wet Gold Cup Final first leg the day before and a 9-point lead from the August's cup tie first leg.

Reading's record at Wolverhampton was not good. Most recently they had been beaten 56-34 in May, the only time Racers lost a league match by more than 4 points during the season. However, both teams rose to the occasion and produced 30 heats of enthralling combat. In the first match Reading held a 3-point aggregate lead with only two races to go, but the Gold Cup went to Wolves. In the second half of the double header Doncaster (14+1) and Andersson (13+1) spearheaded a fightback to draw the match and go through on aggregate.

By this stage of the year it already looked as if Racers would win the league. Right from the start Reading carried the best record in the league. A win at Belle Vue (who finished sixth on 37 points, just one behind runners-up Bradford) got the campaign off on the right foot. Ray Morton's paid 13 was instrumental in Reading's 47-43 triumph. The following week Reading drew their second away fixture at Coventry, where Armando Castagna made a fine contribution. When Poole and Oxford beat Reading 46-44 in consecutive away matches during August it caused a few anxious moments, but in the end Reading topped the table by a convincing 12-point margin.

A settled team provided the foundation for Reading's success. Jan Andersson and Dave

Mullett rode in all 51 of Reading's matches. (Andersson finished his Racers career with a run of 120 consecutive appearances, a figure only surpassed by Bell, Humphreys and Leigh.) Per Jonsson, Jeremy Doncaster and Armando Castagna were ever-presents in the league campaign. Castagna missed four Gold Cup matches with a broken finger and Ray Morton's collarbone kept him out of five matches in October. The seventh member of the team – Phil Morris – missed only three matches.

Per Jonsson had a silver-themed year. As well as runners-up medals in the Gold Cup and Knock-Out Cup for Reading he also scored 11 points as Sweden finished second to the United States in the World Team Cup. A tight meeting saw England fade after leading with five heats to go. Jonsson collected a bronze in the World Pairs as Sweden finished one point behind America and England. After seven wins in a row the Danes finished a miserable fifth behind Italy. Castagna's 16-point haul made him the meeting's top scorer.

Between the pairs and team finals Jonsson attempted to regain his world crown in Wroclaw[57]. Surprise winner Gary Havelock relegated Jonsson to second. On the way to his first final Havelock won the British Championship, Overseas Final and came second (to Jonsson) in the semi-final.

During the year Jonsson also came second in the British League Riders Championship (the best performance yet by a Reading rider) and in the Swedish Championship – to American John Cook!

Racers strength came from the solid support given by the rest of the team. All bar Phil Morris finished in the top 50 of the league averages. Dave Mullett proved indispensable. He formed a fearsome opening partnership with Jonsson. Their 5-1 in the opening race at home to Ipswich on October 28 was the ninth time in nine league matches that the pair started the match with a 5-1 to the Racers. Mullett reached his second British Final, this time he qualified for the next stage. In June he made his international debut, top scoring as England beat Australia 55-53 at Smallmead. The team also included Doncaster and Morton. Also making his debut, Morton beat Aussie Shane Bowes for second place in the deciding heat.

On the training track – Per Jonsson gives advice to Mick Hester. Hester rode for the Ravens Conference League team in 1996 and went on to manage the Reading junior team. (BT)

Then in September the quiet

57 My first trip to Poland. Unfortunately British Airways sent my luggage elsewhere. Consumer choice was still a new concept in Poland and shopping for replacement clothes proved to be a novel challenge! Then came a downpour after heat seven.

Kentish farmer celebrated his testimonial by top scoring as Racers beat a Marvyn Cox Select 52-38. The meeting's main talking point came from the display of Jason Crump, replacing injured Ray Morton. The 17-year-old Peterborough rider achieved a paid 10 score. Mullett's testimonial season raised around £10,000, slightly down on the sums accruing to Jan Andersson and Jeremy Doncaster in their testimonial years.

Unlike the rest of the team Andersson and Doncaster saw slight falls in their league averages, but their experience added value to their contributions. Andersson's reputation as a remote loner underwent a reappraisal as he threw himself into the team's chase for silverware. After a strong start to the year in the Gold Cup he found himself at reserve. (The green sheets only included league matches, and after six he found himself lagging behind Ray Morton.) A 14-match spell at reserve yielded 13 double-figure scores. Captain Doncaster started the season slowly but by September he was back in the groove.

With Castagna and Morton delivering solid performances all that was required of Phil Morris was to beat the opposing number sevens and outscore his 2-point assessed average. At 2.91 his average put him ahead of other 'teenage sensations' of the time – Glenn Cunningham, Justin Elkins and Darren Pearson. Morris topped the Rivets averages in a Reading junior team that finished mid-table. Mark Tomlin and Lance Sealey provided the bulk of the support. The opening of Reading's new training track took place on April 26. Situated in the car park behind the first and second bends, it provided training opportunities for several years before a period of temporary disuse.

Over the 1991/1992 winter the possibility of returns for Jonsson and Tony Olsson gave Reading plenty of options. The choice for number one appeared to be between Todd Wiltshire and Jonsson. When Wiltshire fractured his pelvis in the Australian Championship the choice was taken out of Pat Bliss's hands. Told that he could not ride for at least a year Wiltshire turned to domestic matters, marrying Linda Hamnett (sister of Hackney rider Dave Hamnett) in July and then becoming a father the following year. His son's name – Anders. Wiltshire's changing priorities meant that his lay-off became a permanent retirement at the age of just 23[58]

When Jonsson re-signed at the start of February the full septet could be announced. With no place for Olsson he ended up at Exeter. Mitch Shirra went to Swindon and David Steen found a place at Milton Keynes. Shirra, now a veteran, managed one last World Final appearance and also finished second in the World Longtrack Final.

Olsson and Steen both had turbulent seasons, a by-product of the perilous state of British speedway. On 'black Wednesday' (September 16) interest rates rose to 15% before Norman ('Je ne regrette rien') Lamont pulled Britain out of the Exchange Rate Mechanism. Even before this the economy was already in recession, and crowds fell significantly. Many tracks reported falls of 20%. With bankruptcy looming, Sheffield and King's Lynn changed ownership mid-season. Other tracks showing signs of financial distress included Swindon, Rye House, Eastbourne, Berwick and Exeter.

Exeter responded quickly by cutting their costs and dispensed with Tony Olsson's services after one league match. In that match Olsson broke Scott Autrey's Exeter track record making him the new holder of the title of fastest man in British speedway. Such was Olsson's popularity in his short stay at the County Ground that he still won the vote for Exeter Supporters' Club rider of the year! After a month on the sidelines Olsson returned to Division One with Ipswich.

Exeter replaced Olsson with Frank Smart who had become available on the demise of

---

58 For the benefit of pedants he would have been 24 when he decided not to return to racing, but 23 when he broke his pelvis. And of course the retirement didn't turn out to be permanent.

Milton Keynes. Peter Glanz (who broke his leg at the end of May) and David Steen were also among the riders left without a team. Steen found a new home at Stoke. Later in June Mildenhall became the second track to pull out of Division Two.

At Ipswich Olsson replaced Jacek Rempala, one of three Poles appearing in the 1992 British League. They were the first since 1983, a sign of Poland's 'westward journey'. A further indication of the end of the Cold War came when the US Air Force left Greenham Common, scene of many protests against cruise missiles in the 1980s[59].

In 1992 Racers basked in the local limelight. As their successful run-in commenced Reading FC started the season in Division Two of the Football League. The launch of the Premiership meant that Reading were still a third-flight club. Their crowds were now two or three times the size of those at Smallmead, but success still eluded them. Over the next 15 years the trajectories of Reading's two leading sports teams would take very different paths.

Team: Per Jonsson 10.25, Jeremy Doncaster 8.15, Jan Andersson 8.05, Dave Mullett 7.73, Armando Castagna 6.87, Ray Morton 6.23, Phil Morris 2.91, Lance Sealey 0.73

1993 saw one of Reading's less successful Swedish signings – Kenneth Nystrom. (BT)

59 Speedway in the morning and a visit to the peace camp in the afternoon made for a perfect Bank Holiday day out.

1993 – Not a Bad Haul

After 1992's hectic finish the following season lacked excitement. Reading finished sixth out of eleven, about as average as you can get.

Over the winter, the promoters addressed two issues. During the previous year dissatisfaction with the reserve league grew. As a result the BSPA conference axed it, increasing teams to eight strong and matches to 18 heats. Many regarded this as a backward step and discussions about starting a third division for juniors gathered pace. Linlithgow, Buxton and Iwade were all identified as possible participants.

The biggest issue was that speedway was quickly going broke. Finally the conclusion was reached that riders' wages needed to be controlled. After years of increasing payments to riders (most of which was spent on their equipment) the time had come for a pay policy. Each team was allowed to pay its top two £40 a point, £30 for the next two and £25 for numbers five and six. Reading's crowds in 1993 averaged around 1300, and the adult admission charge was £5. Based on these figures riders' pay would have taken up just over half of the gate revenue. It would have been possible to balance the books[60] on the lower pay rates, but with overheads there wouldn't have been much of a profit at the end of the year.

Many riders prevaricated for a long time before accepting the new rates. Hans Nielsen stated that it would mean a pay cut from £60,000 to £35,000. Unable to meet his demands, Oxford couldn't put a team together and withdrew from the league. Coventry came up with a sponsor and signed Nielsen to replace the retiring Tommy Knudsen. Poole rode with guests for much of the season after number one Marvyn Cox decided to give the UK a miss. He took out a German licence, and even won the German Championship. Also in the field was ex-Racer John Davis.

Although Swindon reluctantly accepted relegation, they were not replaced because Division Two champions Peterborough decided that promotion would be too expensive. At the 11th hour Long Eaton promoter Tony Mole stepped in to keep speedway alive at Oxford albeit at second division level. The loss of local derbies against Swindon and Oxford certainly contributed to the flatness of the Smallmead season.

Although Division Two gained Reading's Thames Valley rivals it lost Berwick and Stoke. After arriving with a massive chequebook and forcing the cost of riders up for his rivals, Berwick promoter Terry Lindon's stint as a promoter ended with a disappearance after his company went bankrupt.

Like most tracks there was little news on the team front until the end of February. Then Jan Andersson, the master of Smallmead's inside line, announced his retirement from British speedway. Andersson called it a day after scoring 5,519½ points for the Racers from 544 matches, including 66 maximums. Only Dave Mullett can boast more appearances than Andersson, and nobody has ever bettered his figures for points scored or maximums. Like Dave Mullett he belonged to three title winning teams. He carried on riding in Sweden for another couple of years before finally retiring after a career spanning over 20 years.

With Tony Olsson keen to return Andersson's place was quickly filled. At least one other rider would go in order to keep below the 50-point limit. Ray Morton had been riding in Australia and proved difficult to contact. In his absence an old face returned to Reading. After

---

60 The crowd figures come from interviews with Pat Bliss quoted in 1994 *Speedway Star*. Most fans underestimate the scale of the overheads a promoter has to cover. Insurance, BSPA fees, rent or interest, and administration costs all mount up. I base this on my experience as an accountant (and I have acted for a speedway promotion).

some indifferent form in Division Two Peter Glanz wanted to come back to Reading for whom he had last ridden in 1987. Morton quickly found a new home at Poole, scene of several of his best performances.

With Jonsson, Doncaster, Mullett, Castagna and Morris returning the eighth spot went to Mick Tomlin.

Other close season news included the loss of Homefire as league sponsors. The Government programme of pit closures prior to privatisation of the coal industry caused hard times for Coal Products Ltd. Closer to home, Reading lost their most devoted fan – Joy Warne[61] – to cancer. Holder of various offices in the supporters/social club she seemed like a permanent fixture at Smallmead. Her ashes were scattered on the first bend, so in a sense she still is.

The Gold Cup no longer started the season, spectators wanted more meaningful fixtures and that meant league matches. Even Test matches struggled to draw as many people as an ordinary league match. The move to two home and two away clashes with each league rival proved popular, but longer matches didn't.

The longer matches made one sided matches into even bigger thrashings. Reading beat Poole 70-38 in August with Castagna scoring his first league maximum in Racers colours. The May 31 meeting with King’s Lynn made the Poole match look like a close encounter. Racers 75-33 victory remains their biggest-ever league win. The 42-point margin has only been exceeded in the Premier Trophy (v Trelawny in 2001) and the Knock-Out Cup (v Eastbourne in 1979 and Skegness in 1997). Wins of 40 points against Halifax (1973) and Berwick (1970) in just 13 heats could be regarded as more one-sided though.

One of the consequences was fewer away wins, even the eventual league champions only won four of their 20 away matches. Reading's season followed that trend with home wins balanced by away losses. At home three matches were lost, and only one other (against Ipswich) went to a last-heat decider. Away from home the Racers achieved three wins and a draw to end the year in credit by the narrowest of margins. Only at Poole did Racers lose after a last-heat decider.

All the away points came at the expense of the league's bottom four teams. April produced a draw at King’s Lynn. But as the Stars lost number one Mark Loram early in the match this felt like a point lost. A win at injury-hit Cradley in May featured 13 points from Armando Castagna and paid 10 from Peter Glanz. Wins at Ipswich (where Jonsson picked up a maximum and the track record) and Poole followed in August.

The win at Cradley came during a four-match spell when Per Jonsson was in dispute with the club. In the same week John Major's Conservative Government suffered the humiliation of losing the Newbury by-election to the Liberal Democrats. On May 3 Jonsson failed to turn up at Smallmead after claiming to have no transport, and that Pat Bliss had promised to provide a van for him. Pat Bliss struggled to find sponsors, but eventually help was forthcoming and Per returned with a maximum against Bradford.

An absent rider was the cause of Reading's unexpected home reverse against Arena Essex in April. Dave Mullett injured his knee in Reading's opening home league match (v Coventry) and missed three fixtures. Rider replacement yielded only 4 points against Arena.

The other two defeats were both against Eastbourne. In ten previous league matches at Reading (including two at Tilehurst in Division Two) the Eagles could only claim one draw to their credit. In 1993's 'A' fixture the Eagles had five riders in double figures as they won 59-

---

61 As a schoolboy I remember her lending me money to get in when I lost my wallet on a trip to Exeter. As Reading were annihilated 59-19 perhaps it would have been better if I had missed the match.

49. All Reading had to offer was Per Jonsson, he claimed 17 points and the fastest time of the season (58.6). In the second match a weakened Eastbourne team proved lightning can strike twice.

Yet when the league's top two teams turned up at Smallmead they were seen off. In mid-August, shortly after their second Smallmead defeat, Wolverhampton led the league by 11 points. Belle Vue languished in mid-table 15 points adrift without an away win in 12 journeys. Injuries decimated the Wolves and by the time of their final league match they were without four of their top five riders (Sam and Charlie Ermolenko, Ronnie Correy and Graham Jones). On October 25 Belle Vue travelled to Monmore Green knowing that a win would make them champions, but a draw would be good enough to crown Wolverhampton. In a thrilling encounter watched by nearly 5,000 the Aces won by a single point.

On the same night Reading wound up their league programme with a comfortable win over Arena Essex. It took four goes to run this match. Rain-offs on September 13, September 27 and October 11 made for a damp end to the season. (The September 20 fixture against Cradley also fell foul of the weather making it three postponements in a row.)

The line-up against Arena showed two changes from the one that opened the season. Junior Mick Tomlin only lasted a handful of matches before Lance Sealey replaced him. A hat-trick of race wins against Poole was the highlight of his season. The other absentee, Peter Glanz, quit at the beginning of July after failing to score as Racers went out of the Knock-Out Cup to Arena Essex. Glanz briefly resurfaced in Division Two at Oxford, but after 7 points from five matches retired again.

Just over a month later his replacement Kenneth Nystrom made his debut. On this occasion the 'when in need sign a Swede' mantra proved fallible. Nystrom failed to score more than 3 points in seven of his first eight matches. He did manage a couple of double-figure scores (at home to Ipswich and away at Cradley) after being relegated to reserve in October. It could have been different had Racers landed their number one target Mikael Karlsson (now Max).

Nystrom had returned to Sweden before the season sign off against Arena and junior Matthew Cross replaced him managing a respectable 5-point tally.

The remaining six members of the team experienced varying fortunes. Invigorated by a winter spent learning to bobsleigh, Armando Castagna upped his average, moving from 44th to 24th in the league averages. He picked up bronze in the Czech Golden Helmet and reached his fifth World Final.

The pivotal moment of the World Final came when Hans Nielsen and Sam Ermolenko clashed in heat 15. Ermolenko fell as Nielsen attempted to go underneath him. Nielsen's exclusion virtually guaranteed that Ermolenko would become champion. 'Sudden Sam' had shone all season, averaging 11.26 in the British League. Jonsson's 10.30 put him second to Ermolenko in the league rankings. Seven points and ninth place in the World Final equalled Per's worst final performance. Bottom of the field that day was World Final debutant Greg Hancock. Another first timer, Chris Louis did considerably better. Wearing the number 13 race jacket Louis emulated his father John and step-father Jeremy Doncaster by picking up the bronze medal.

Jonsson did regain the Swedish Championship and shared in Sweden's gold medal in the last ever World Pairs Championship. Sweden's win in the Pairs was their first since Anders Michanek completed a hat-trick of wins in 1975. In anticipation of the Grand Prix series the World Pairs was dropped from the international calendar.

Dave Mullett continued to raise his profile, reaching the Overseas Final of the World Championship and making two Test appearances against Sweden. The first Test at Exeter ended 56-52 to Sweden after Tony Olsson combined with Tony Rickardsson for a 5-1 in the deciding final heat. Jonsson (14) and Mullett (10) both acquitted themselves well. Olsson saw a slight drop in his average and at the end of the season expressed his desire to move to Division Two Swindon.

Reserve Phil Morris continued to make progress. He reached double figures twice and achieved two reserves maximums with 9 from three rides at Coventry and at home to Cradley. Morris also rode in the British Under-21 Final, won by Joe Screen who went on to become World Under-21 Champion.

In his fourth year as Racers captain Jeremy Doncaster endured a far worse season. His average plummeted, and at one stage it fell below 6. His form picked up towards the end of the season. His final eight matches yielded seven double-figure scores, but he contemplated retirement.

Perhaps the most trying season belonged to Racers promoter Pat Bliss. Father Bill Dore had reached 70 and Pat had become the sole promoter in all but name. In 1993 Pat continued to keep the show on the road while undergoing treatment for cancer.

The season did bring some reward for Pat and the Reading fans. It opened with a Premiership victory over Bradford and closed with Per Jonsson's win in the British League Riders Championship on October 31 at Swindon. The Premiership victory owed much to Armando Castagna who produced one of the greatest-ever performances in Racers colours by completing a paid 18-point maximum in the drawn second leg at Bradford. At the 24th attempt a Reading rider finally won the league riders championship. Mick Bell (way back in 1969) and Per himself (in 1992) had come closest with second places.

More silverware for the Racers; this time it's the British League Division One Fours. Phil Morris, Dave Mullett, Tony Olsson (back row left to right), Per Jonsson and Armando Castagna show off the trophy won at Peterborough. (BT)

At the season's mid-way mark in July Reading picked up the British League Fours title after a convincing display at Peterborough. Three bits of silverware – not a bad haul for a mediocre team in a largely forgettable season.

Team: Per Jonsson 10.34, Armando Castagna 7.88, Dave Mullett 7.39, Jeremy Doncaster 6.83, Tony Olsson 6.10, Phil Morris 5.66, Kenneth Nystrom 4.83, Peter Glanz 4.37, Lance Sealey 3.19

1994 – End of an Era

1994 marked the end of an era, both at Smallmead and in the wider speedway world.

On 20 August Ole Olsen's Vojens track staged the 49th and last World Final. It ranks among the most exciting. Greg Hancock and Craig Boyce lined-up in heat 19 just four laps away from the World title, but neither of them won the heat. Instead Tony Rickardsson's 3 points took him to the top of the leader board and an eventual run-off with Boyce and Hans Nielsen. Winner Rickardsson, runner-up Nielsen and England's Mark Loram all used laydown machines, which were not yet allowed in British League racing.

Another development was the lack of British League activity among the finalists. Only four of the top ten finishers were riding in Division One of the British League. A fifth rider, Long Eaton's Jan Staechmann, made history by becoming the first Division Two rider to reach the World Final since Ken McKinlay in 1956. Despite the success of Anders Michanek in 1974 the received wisdom of the last 25 years had been that to win the World Final a British League spot was a must. The World Final result suggested that this was no longer the case.

As the world stage prepared itself for the Grand Prix's start in 1995 Reading Racers were learning to live without their idol. The loss of Per Jonsson halfway through the season marked the point at which the future viability of speedway at Smallmead became a serious topic for discussion. Riders, management and fans alike all struggled on towards the end of the 1994 season in a thoroughly demoralised state.

Initially it looked unlikely that Per would line-up for the Racers as silence characterised the activity at Smallmead. At the end of February, Jonsson and Mullett both claimed to have had no contact with Pat Bliss over the winter. In the absence of any concrete news *Speedway Star* was reduced to reporting how many of Dave Mullett's ewes had given birth to twins – 27 apparently!

The new pay rates only showed small increases for inflation, and like a number of stars Jonsson showed little inclination to agree a new contract at these rates. The BSPA panicked and on February 20 reduced the previously agreed points limit from 44 to 40. Bradford (who had already splashed out £30,000 on Joe Screen) were furious. Within a fortnight the BSPA did a U-turn and Jonsson had indicated he would like a transfer.

Unhappy with the new pay rates Jeremy Doncaster made clear that he intended to retire. Tony Olsson got his wish to go to Swindon and Matthew Cross moved in the opposite direction to join Dave Mullett, Armando Castagna, Phil Morris and Ray Morton. On the eve of the season's start, Australian Shane Bowes joined the Racers on loan. After six successful years with Glasgow, Bowes (aged 25) had made it clear he wished to leave the Division Two champions and try his luck in the top league.

Reading started the season (at King's Lynn) with retired Doncaster as the notional number one and David Steen filling in. Shane Bowes top scored as Reading went down 36-60. But the good news was that Doncaster would help the Racers out for a couple of weeks, while Reading continued their search for a number one, provided he could then return to his home town track – Ipswich.

Doncaster's unexpected encore coincided with his best early-season form for some time and although weak on paper the Racers pulled off a surprise win at Coventry. Doncaster's departure was brief as his first match back in Ipswich colours took him to Smallmead (April 25). Four days earlier Jonsson had agreed to return. 'Donkey' scored 12 as Ipswich lost 49-47 after a last-heat photo-finish had gone against them. In the meeting Doncaster met Jonsson three times and beat him twice.

Although already 33, Doncaster carried on riding for the Witches until 2002 scoring over 5,000 points for Ipswich to go with the 2,238 he recorded for the Racers.

After his return against Ipswich Jonsson rode a further six matches at Smallmead, remaining unbeaten in all of them. Yet he only scored five maximums because against Wolverhampton he dead-heated with Peter Karlsson.

The day after (June 6) Per made his final league appearance for Reading in the return match at Wolverhampton. Despite losing Reading remained top of the league. Co-incidentally this meeting marked the debut of newly qualified referee Tony Steele. He earned the wrath of the Monmore Green crowd after failing to exclude Dave Mullett after a heat 8 clash with Patrik Olsson.[62]

5 June 1994 – Per Jonsson's last ever league ride at Smallmead. The legendary Jonsson/Mullett partnership records another 5-1. (BT)

With performances like the match at Odsal, where he stormed past the team riding pair of Joe Screen and Gary Havelock, Jonsson topped the league averages. His 58.8 winning time against Eastbourne (May 9) remained the fastest time of the season at Smallmead even though it was recorded using a dirt deflector. (Introduced at the start of the season, dirt deflectors were suspended in May after the threat of a riders' strike.)

Per also headed the Polish league averages where he rode for Apator Torun. On June 26 he travelled to Bydgoszcz, and won his first three rides (two of them against home idol Tomasz Gollob) in front of the 14,000 crowd. In heat 12, starting off gate four, he got caught in a first-bend melee and never got up.

---

62 At the time I sympathised with the home crowd, but watching the incident back on video later I realised that Mr Steele had called it correctly. However, not even he is infallible – I still can't understand how he excluded Phil Morris at Arena Essex in 2002.

With two broken vertebrae Jonsson spent the afternoon under the surgeon's knife in the Bydgoszcz hospital and was flown back to Sweden in an air ambulance two days later. As the weeks wore on it became apparent that the paralysis was not temporary, and that Per faced the rest of his life in a wheelchair.

Bob Radford set about organising a benefit meeting with the assistance of Pat Bliss and Jimmy Nilsen. Over 4,000 spectators experienced an emotional evening. After a last-minute go-ahead from his medical team Per flew over to witness the proceedings.

For the record Team Mullett featuring new World Champion Tony Rickardsson and Racers legend Jan Andersson won the meeting. Rickardsson dropped his only point to maximum man Peter Nahlin. Hans Nielsen (making his last Smallmead appearance) won the individual competition. Peter Collins, Barry Briggs and Anders Michanek appeared in a couple of 'Golden Greats' races.

Four World Champions (left to right): Anders Michanek, Ivan Mauger, Peter Collins and Barry Briggs turn-out for the Per Jonsson benefit meeting. (BT)

A month later the three principal organisers flew to Stockholm to present Per with a cheque for over £50,000. Further benefit meetings were staged the following year in Poland and Sweden. Simon Wigg won April's meeting at Torun, and September's Halstavik (home of Rospiggarna) meeting went to Peter Nahlin.

Reading's season simply fell apart after Per's accident. It would be a mistake to put this down to the loss of points from Jonsson. Racers used a guest for Per in all of the club's remaining 25 fixtures, and only when Jeremy Doncaster filled the role did the guest fail to reach double figures. Martin Dugard (five times), Jason Crump and Kelvin Tatum (four each) became very familiar with the winged wheel race jacket.

Jonsson's team mates, demoralised by his absence and dogged by injury, all saw their form drop off after Per's accident. Shane Bowes had a good spell in July and remained an ever-present but the rest of the team all missed matches. On the terraces despondency became the prevailing mood as supporters came to terms with the loss of Reading's finest stylist, and one of the most exciting riders of his generation.

The day after Jonsson's crash Reading went down 44-52 to King’s Lynn. A team including two guests and utilising rider replacement lost Cross in a heat 2 fall. The following night Reading went out of the cup after a second leg defeat at Coventry. Of the Racers regulars only Bowes, Morris and Morton rode.

Reading's casualty list included:

- June 19: Castagna injured at Italian Championship meeting, out for two weeks.
- June 23: Mullett picks up an arm injury in the fours round at Ipswich, also missing two weeks.
- June 27: Cross injured in his first ride.
- July 7: Both reserves injured in heat 2 at Ipswich. Already operating rider replacement Racers track only one rider in heats 4, 5, 8, 12, 14 and 15 (and none in the re-run of heat 2). Morton picked up an injury later in the match causing him to miss the next two matches. This match also produced an altercation between ex-Racer Mitch Shirra and referee Barry Bowles that resulted in a one-year ban, effectively ending Shirra's career.
- July 31 Morris breaks his leg grasstracking in France, bringing his season to a premature end.
- August 13: Morton out for three weeks after a foot injury at Coventry.
- September 12: The day after winning his ninth Italian Championship Castagna breaks a leg in the Czech Golden Helmet.
- September 17: At Eastbourne Mullett and Bowes crash out early in the meeting leaving Cross, Jan Pedersen and two guests to complete the match. Reading lose 33-63.
- October 2 The day before a planned return to the Racers team Castagna falls in Germany and rejoins the injured list.
- October 3: Morton makes his final appearance of the season after struggling to continue riding while not fit. A crowd of less than a thousand watches Eastbourne easily beat the Racers in their final home match leaving the wooden spoon a distinct possibility. David Norris scored an easy 15-point maximum for the Eagles that night.

In August, for the first time in their history, Reading lost three home matches in a row. By October 8 Reading had also set a new record for consecutive away defeats: 16.

On October 10 Reading visited Belle Vue, the only team below them, tracking guests Joe Screen and Jiri Stancl (son of the former Racer), using rider replacement and a stand-in junior (Anthony Barlow). After a season of adversity Racers dug deep and produced a great performance to ensure that Reading's trophy cabinet remained free of the wooden spoon. Mullett and Bowes both made double figures in support of guest Joe Screen's paid 16, but the real shock came from the reserve berth.

Jan Pedersen, a journeyman Dane with experience at Rye House and Arena Essex, arrived as cover for Phil Morris. After failing to average 4 in a dozen outings for the Racers he proved an unlikely hero. A massive paid 18 haul dwarfed his previous Reading scores.

The day before averting the disaster of bottom place Mullett made his first appearance in the British League Riders Championship, but failed to score. After winning the Reading staged semi-final he rode in the British Final on May Day, the same day as Ayrton Senna's death at Imola. The Formula 1 Champion had a base in Reading and is remembered by the naming of a road after him. Ayrton Senna Close in Tilehurst even has speed bumps!

Phil Morris continued to make progress, upping his green-sheet average from 3.13 to 4.99 and finishing seventh in the British Under-21 Championship. Unusually his away average exceeded his home figure. In contrast Ray Morton shed more than a point from his average – riding when far from fully fit contributed to his under-performance.

One Racer who had reason to be pleased with the season was Tony Olsson. Riding in Division Two for Swindon he finished second in the Division Two Riders Championship, second in the Division Two averages (behind world finalist Jan Steachmann), and won the Pairs Championship (with Tony Langdon).

Despite reservations from his medical team Per Jonsson travelled across the North Sea for his benefit meeting. Many top riders turned out for Per, including Greg Hancock seen chatting to him . (EP)

After a dreadful season Reading management openly hinted that Reading could be joining Swindon in Division Two. There were complaints about the track and even the design of their race jacket drew flak. (The wings were closed instead of open, and yellow!) Short of a win in the newly founded National Lottery[63] Reading's finances looked precarious. In sharp contrast Reading Royals won Division Two of the Football League and started well in Division One (now the Championship) in 1994/95.

One positive development did come about in 1994. After being mooted on many previous occasions a training league finally made it to the starting tapes. Originally named Division Three, it had four different aliases in its first four seasons – Amateur, Conference and Academy being the other three. However, it is still going strong as the Conference League and is now in its 15th season.

---

63 The first draw took place on November 19. In the interests of honesty in advertising it should have been advertised with the slogan: "Let's face it – it won't be you." One of its by-products was to hamper the ability of sports clubs to raise money through local lottery schemes.

The abolition of the reserve league in 1993 and the reduction from eight-man to seven-man teams in 1994 severely reduced the opportunities for juniors. England's already ramshackle approach to cultivating young talent appeared to be falling apart. In contrast Sweden and Denmark had extensive 80cc programmes for under-16 riders. The value of this approach can be illustrated by a quick look at the result of the 1993 Danish Under-16 Championship – Nicki Pedersen came first, future Racer Charlie Gjedde fourth, Bjarne Pedersen and Hans Andersen also made the top ten. (Now fast forward to 22 July 2006 at Smallmead.)

The tapes finally rose on the new league at the end of July with matches at Stoke and Berwick. Iwade, Linlithgow, Buxton and Mildenhall were the remaining starters. Various other tracks were mooted as potential starters including one at Swansea. Former Racer Malcolm Holloway was lined up as rider/coach, but the proposed Welsh track failed to receive planning permission. The rider/coach role at Berwick went to former Racer Glyn Taylor at the age of 40.

It may not have solved all of speedway's problems, but without the Conference League many fewer riders would have persevered to the point where they merited Premier League places. Furthermore three of the original six members are in the 2008 Premier League, along with the Isle of Wight, Rye House, Somerset and Scunthorpe all of whom opened as Conference League tracks.

Team: Per Jonsson 10.41, Armando Castagna 8.44,Dave Mullett 7.65, Shane Bowes 5.83, Ray Morton 5.15, Phil Morris 5.08, Jan Pedersen 4.43, Matthew Cross 2.61

15-year-old Lee Richardson practising on the training track in 1994. (BT)

1995 – The Decline Continues

Reading's doubts about continuing to run in Division One with its high cost base were resolved when the BSPA agreed to amalgamation of the two divisions. This created the Premier League – a single league of 21 teams, including newcomers Hull.

Per Jonsson was irreplaceable, but the lower points limit removed the need to search for an expensive new number one. Reading's existing assets (including Tony Olsson, looking forward to a testimonial) would provide sufficient strength.

As it turned out Armando Castagna, who was racing in Argentina, proved difficult to pin down; instead David Norris signed on loan from Eastbourne at the end of February. Norris made his Eastbourne debut in 1988 just a day after his 16th birthday. At the age of just 22 he had progressed to 12th position in the 1994 Division One averages. Although never matching the achievements of 1994, he completed 20 years in the sport in 2007, all but four of them with Eastbourne.

Mullett, Olsson, Morton and Morris returned as expected, but the signing of Petri Kokko meant Matthew Cross couldn't be squeezed in under the points limit.

David Norris – a broken leg cut short his 1995 season. (BT)

Other close-season news from the Promoters' Conference included a new scoring system for cup matches. Bonus points would be included in the match score, one of the wackier ideas to come out of the BSPA. It turned out to be a one-season wonder much to the relief of fans, tired of crossing out 5-1s in the programme and replacing them with 6-1s. However, later in the season Reading were involved in an even sillier scheme.

A Bank Holiday challenge (home and away) with Oxford incorporated a novel finale. Heats 15 and 16, the two nominated races, would be run simultaneously! Two separate races with four riders starting at the tapes and four on the back straight produced chaos. When Oxford's Martin Goodwin fell it became obvious that any fallen rider was at risk from the four riders in the 'other race' colliding with a stricken rider. Luckily Goodwin escaped safely, but the idea was abandoned before the evening leg at Smallmead.[64]

The first British-staged Grand Prix meeting was scheduled for Arena Essex, an announcement that caused much consternation, and on-track betting received the go-ahead.

---

64 How anyone could have failed to notice the flaw in this barking idea baffles me. In my view it remains the barmiest ever tried out. Not that it stops promoters coming up with ideas that merely tinker at the edges of speedway's problems without addressing the major challenges.

Sweden (plus Austria and Finland) finally joined the European Union meaning an end to work permit battles like those for Per Jonsson and Jimmy Nilsen.

Come press day at Reading the number seven berth went to Jason Gage. The first choice, a youngster not 16 until April, was revealed as Lee Richardson. Castagna joined Oxford, where Chris Shears had re-emerged as promoter. Within a month Racers asset Dave Steen had joined him in the Cheetahs team.

Reading's team turned out to be a solid one with a sound middle order. The problems were at the top and bottom of the team. In the weaker league Norris should have increased his average, but it fell and he dropped out of the top 20 in the league averages. Worse still, in June he broke a leg in the Overseas Final. It turned out to be slow healing and plans to return to the Reading team had to be abandoned.

In July, German-based Grand Prix rider Marvyn Cox signed for a month to cover for Norris. He made seven appearances, the last of them on August 21, the day after he regained the German National Championship title. Although his gating seemed a bit rusty he outscored Norris, the man he replaced, but the cost of flying him in from the continent made extending the deal too expensive. A plaintive appeal for sponsorship from Pat Bliss failed to yield anything. Bob Radford's programme notes (August 28) said of Cox:

> *"Quite simply we cannot afford him on the crowds we are getting ... Marvyn is quite shocked by how much crowds have gone down in the last three years since he last rode in Britain, not only here at Reading, but at other tracks too ... it is most depressing. Quite honestly I will be surprised if the promotion decides to open for the 1996 season and, yes it is that bleak."*

History records that Racers did survive, as did Lee Richardson's speedway career, which looked even more endangered than his club for most of the year. Lee's father had briefly ridden for Reading in 1975 early in his 12-year career with Eastbourne, Wimbledon and King's Lynn. Richardson junior had spent the winter learning speedway trackcraft on the Smallmead training track.

After making his debut within a week of his 16th birthday Richardson retained his place for the rest of the season. He missed half-a-dozen matches due to injury, but made 29 appearances. In 15 home matches he managed only eight third places, failing to better his debut score of 1 paid 2 all season. Away from home he picked up one second place (at Sheffield beating hopelessly outclassed Dutchman Rob Steman), and in the final match of the year took a victory from his first ride at Swindon. Weakened Robins fielded two Academy League second strings in that race.

As the year wore on he received an increasingly tough time from sections of the Reading crowd. Few could have imagined that he would be top of Reading's averages within three years, World Under-21 Champion a year after that and a Grand Prix regular by 2003 when he also won the Elite League Riders Championship.

Disappointing returns from the numbers one and seven berths meant mid-table mediocrity was the best Reading could aspire to. A mammoth league programme of 40 matches produced three away wins to cancel out three home defeats. In April Reading came away from their favourite hunting ground – Wimborne Road – with 2 points at the expense of Poole. A double-figure score from Ray Morton kept up his record of big scores down in Dorset.

Morton also played a key role in the next league victory away from Smallmead. The next ten away matches yielded just a draw at Exeter. (On May 29, a day more widely remembered for Stuart Lovell's penalty miss in Reading FC's 4-3 play-off defeat to Bolton.) Then King's Lynn surrendered to the Racers in September. Morton won heats 14 and 15 as Reading opened up an 8-point lead with two late 5-1s. A final away win at Swindon still left Reading an uninspiring 13th, two places below the Robins – who had acquired a new team manager part way through the season in the shape of Malcolm Holloway. Reading did finish above Oxford, for whom another ex-Racer, Mick Bell, took on team management duties.

The first of the home defeats, 57-39 to Ipswich in May, was Reading's second biggest home defeat in their first 28 years. It would have been worse had Norris not produced his best form of the year with 19 points. Later in the year, Eastbourne (comfortable winners of the League) and Wolverhampton (49-47 after a last-heat 5-1) took points away from Smallmead.

The Knock-Out Cup brought another home defeat against Ipswich. Elimination followed despite a win in the second leg at Foxhall Heath. Petri Kokko came up with 19 points, and Greg Hancock (guesting for Dave Mullett) registered an 18-point maximum. In June the Premier League Fours produced an even more disappointing performance, with Racers finishing no better than third in any of the four rounds.

The following month Tony Olsson's testimonial celebrated his ten-year association with the club. A 'Tony's Select' team won the meeting, although Tony rode in Reading colours against his own select. For the third time at Smallmead that season Chris Louis was easily the best rider on display. Tony's testimonial raised over £12,000 for the Racers sixth highest top division point scorer.

Tony was one of three riders to up his average by over a point in 1995. Olsson achieved this despite health problems (subsequently diagnosed as thyroid related) in the second half of the season. Petri Kokko flourished at reserve in the second half of the year, hitting double figures seven times in his last twelve matches, ending the season with a 5.97 average (compared to a 4.10 starting average).

Petri Kokko leads Oxford's Jimmy Nilsen. (BT)

The third rider, Ray Morton, also upped his game in the latter part of the year with seven paid double-figure scores in an eight-match spell during August and September. This included his first Racers maximum, paid 18 against Sheffield. Perhaps the most memorable event of Morton's 1995 schedule arose from an alarming racing incident at Cradley. Home rider Scott Smith[65] lost control and brought down team mate Steve Knott and Morton, sending a riderless bike careering across the centre green. It collided with a St John's Ambulance volunteer (who needed hospital treatment) before demolishing the starting gate.

Dave Mullett missed most of May and July due to injury which affected his late-season scoring. At the halfway stage Mullett held the number one spot, with an average above 9, ahead of David Norris. For once Phil Morris avoided injury to become Reading's only ever-present. At Ipswich Morris went to the tapes for his last ride in the British Under-21 Championship needing a win to give him a run-off for a rostrum place and progress into the

65 Born in Yorkshire; not the Australian of the same name who rode for Reading in 2003.

World Under-21 qualifying rounds. A first-bend fall, for which he was blameless, put him out of the re-run and dashed his hopes. Four Ipswich riders finished in the top six including winner Ben Howe and 16-year-old Scott Nicholls. Morris was rewarded with two caps for England under-23 in an entertaining series against the Czech Republic.

The track came in for much criticism, some of it from the Reading riders. In August track maintenance supremo Jeff Sealey walked out, exacerbating the problems. For the first time in their history Reading did not stage a meeting in October, finishing their season early on 25 September with a last-heat decider victory over Edinburgh.

Away from Reading the speedway world waited with interest to see how the Grand Prix would fare. It opened in May with Pole Tomasz Gollob winning on home shale. On the same night there were no less than four Premier League matches, including a Racers trip to Bradford. Hans Nielsen established a comfortable lead going into the final event, switched from Arena Essex to a newly refurbished Hackney. On a wet night, Greg Hancock became the first British Grand Prix winner and Nielsen held off Tony Rickardsson to win his fourth world title. What the 12,000 crowd and the Sky television audience will most remember about the night was Craig Boyce's ferocious punch that floored Gollob.

Marvyn Cox retained his Grand Prix place by finishing second to Australia's Leigh Adams in the Grand Prix Challenge. Earlier in the year Jason Crump won the World Under-21 Championship. All the evidence pointed to an Aussie return to the top level in international competition.

Crump's season ended with a transfer request from Poole. With Norris expected to return to Eastbourne, and Crump's liking for Smallmead a move to Reading seemed like a good fit. With poor crowds, no sponsorship and a limit to the costs Bill Dore was prepared to incur, a deal never looked like being concluded. Crump went to Peterborough where he joined Ryan Sullivan, another Aussie. Sullivan's dramatic progress included a win in the Overseas Final (now a qualifying round on the way to the GP Challenge). His form helped Peterborough to a top six place, making them the only ex-Division Two team to break the domination of the big name teams.

Overall the new league struggled to capture fans imagination. Many teams struggled with poor crowds, particularly Glasgow, Middlesbrough and King's Lynn. The stronger teams complained that the weaker teams were poor visitors, but they had refused to countenance rules that would make them release heat leaders and allow the weaker teams to strengthen. A secondary problem arose because without a second division the gap to the Academy League (1995's title for the Conference League) was simply too big. Lee Richardson, Jason Bunyan and David Mason were out of their depth in the Premier League, but didn't find the Academy League enough of a challenge.

Worse news came when one of speedway's big names fell to the dreaded developer. Cradley Heath were the glamour team of the 1980s and were still a big draw in 1995 tracking future World Champions Billy Hamill and Greg Hancock. Doubt was also cast over the future of Hackney when stadium owners Brent Walker went into receivership.

Team: (Marvyn Cox 9.44), David Norris 8.90, Dave Mullett 8.31, Tony Olsson 7.74, Ray Morton 7.01, Petri Kokko 5.97, Phil Morris 5.02, Lee Richardson 1.29

1996 – Rock Bottom

Ebullient second-string Ray 'the Ripper' Morton produced the main story of the year. He took over the captaincy from Tony Olsson at the start of the season and looked on course for his best-ever season.

The first sign all was not well came when Petri Kokko replaced Morton as captain for the June 3 defeat at home to Ipswich. Two days later Morton guested for Hull. The following week plans for him to take a two-week break were revealed amid speculation of a rift between Morton and the management.

"Racers shock as Morton joins Hull" proclaimed the *Evening Post* on June 17. Two days earlier Morton made his final Racers appearance in a fours round at Eastbourne. After a two-week delay Morton made his debut as a Hull rider. Both Morton and Pat Bliss denied the rumours of discord between them, and a Bob Radford programme column threw some light on the matter. The source of dissent was Morton's team mates, apparently four of them were unhappy with 'the Ripper.' A crash in the home fixture against Scottish Monarchs that left Dave Mullett injured and Morton excluded can't have helped.

The already under-strength Racers were further weakened by Morton's departure when the BSPA initially blocked the signing of Jorg Pingel from Exeter on the grounds it would leave Reading too weak. Pingel showed promise, finishing the season with a good run, but he could never be expected to fill Morton's shoes.

A final twist in the tale came on July 15 when Belle Vue arrived at Smallmead without Jason Lyons, his guest replacement stormed to a 15-point full maximum and helped the Aces to a draw. Morton never achieved a full maximum at Smallmead in five years with the Racers, but it took just one return visit for him to rectify that.

The biggest story of the year in international speedway had its origins in a dispute about 'solid block' tyres that culminated in a rider strike at the Overseas Final on June 9 at Coventry. Only three riders (Kelvin Tatum, Ryan Sullivan and Mark Lemon) were willing to ride on the tyres required by the FIM. Faced without a meeting and a full stadium the meeting went ahead (without FIM sanction) with riders using tyres of their choice. Ray Morton finished ninth, which should have ensured a place at reserve for the Inter-Continental Final.

The FIM threatened bans and fines. All 13 'rebels' were kicked out of the GP qualifying competition. Morton along with the others breathed a sigh of relief when the FIM climbed down in December and suspended the fines (£2,200 plus costs).

Morton's career continued for over a decade, much of it spent as a popular member of the Isle of Wight team although his testimonial meeting was staged at Hull in 1999. In 2005 a meeting to celebrate his 20 years in speedway took place at the Ryde track.

By the time Ray Morton left, Reading were already familiar with the lower reaches of the league, a situation that stemmed from the inability to sign a number one. Team-building news over the winter was non-existent. All of the 1995 team, with the exception of David Norris were available, and expected to re-sign. Instead there appeared to be a complete lack of activity leading to closure rumours. Mullett and Morton were among the riders going into print to reveal the lack of any contact from the Reading management[66].

A long list of riders had been floated as number ones, but cost meant that even if available a deal was never likely. Instead the promotion banked on the return of Armando Castagna at some unspecified date. Castagna was available following the end of Chris Shears's one-year tenure as promoter at Oxford. Even with Castagna the Racers would be close to the minimum

---

66 In a private conversation, just over a week before press and practice day, team manager Tim Sugar indicated that he doubted if any of the team had yet signed new contracts.

points limit.

On April Fools' Day, Racers kicked off their league campaign at home to Peterborough with a blank space in the programme for a new number one – Sweden's Erik Stenlund. A former team mate of Per Jonsson in Sweden, and Swedish Champion in 1985, Stenlund finished in the top ten of the Swedish Elite League averages in 1995. Born in 1962, his most recent British club was local rivals Swindon in 1988. However, his main claim to fame lay in his excellence on ice. Not once, but twice he broke the Russian stranglehold on the World Ice Speedway Championship – in 1984 and 1988.

Stenlund made a respectable debut with a paid 9 tally, but Reading lost a match that included nine drawn heats in a row by a score of 50-46. The following week Stenlund upped his score to paid 10, but this turned out to be his final performance. Announced as a temporary signing, his stay with the Racers was just eight days.

Blink and you miss it, ice speedway maestro Erik Stenlund's Racers career lasted just eight days. (BT)

With a weak top end Reading took the opportunity to strengthen the tail. A disappointed Lee Richardson made way for David Steen (returning from Oxford). A serious injury to Poole's teenage prospect Jason Bunyan created a vacancy at Poole, and within a fortnight Richardson had employment once more. At Poole he upped his average from 1.29 to 2.01.

When Stenlund left his place was filled by Jan Pedersen, a familiar face from 1994. Unsuccessful efforts were made to get a work permit for Pavel Ondrasik. A winter that started with (wishful) speculation about Jason Crump ended with Jan Pedersen as the replacement for David Norris. Only the most optimistic of Racers supporters believed that Reading wouldn't be fighting to avoid the wooden spoon.

In the end Crump went to Peterborough for £35,000. Doubts were cast over how long the transfer system would survive by the 'Bosman ruling' – a European Court of Justice judgment that effectively outlawed football's transfer fees as being a restraint of trade contrary to EU freedom of movement provisions.

The winter saw King's Lynn close and the stadium put up for sale, and Edinburgh enter the season without knowing where they would be riding. Eventually they moved to Glasgow (who had already folded) and became the Scottish Monarchs. League speedway returned to Hackney, but Arena Essex pulled out. With Premier League speedway looking too costly for some teams, moves were made to form a new league below the Premier League but of a higher standard than the Conference League. These efforts didn't produce anything concrete, but underlined the failure of amalgamation in 1995 and hinted at the way forward for 1997.

The BSPA conference voted to allow 'laydowns' into the Premier League and within two years they were ubiquitous. Little noticed at the time, but the Australian Under-16 Championship, held as the British season got under way, threw up some names that would feature in Racers teams. Kevin Doolan came third, but a run-off was needed to separate silver medallist Travis McGowan and winner Brendon Mackay.

Away from speedway, Berkshire became the centre of attention as protesters attempted to halt the construction of the Newbury by-pass.

Racers never managed to win more than two matches in a row at Smallmead during 1996. The average crowd, paying £7 a head (roughly £10 in 2008 prices), dipped below 1,000. Pat Bliss candidly admitted that the promotion had lost a lot of money.

In a season littered with lows the 56-40 cup thrashing by a modest London (Hackney's new alias) stands out. Yet after nine heats Reading were leading. The promotion endured another dismal night when Coventry visited. Rain left the track unrideable, and the meeting was abandoned after one race. The night ended with a large number of angry fans demanding their money back.

Away form didn't offer much consolation. A 67-29 loss at Belle Vue (in September) didn't even rate as the worst loss of the year. That came in April at Peterborough in a fixture delayed for a week after snow had put paid to the original staging after a single heat. Jan Pedersen topped the scorers' list with 7 out of 26. The Panthers stormed to 70. The 44-point losing margin is the largest-ever suffered by the Racers in a top division league match.

Inevitably the team spent most of the year at the bottom of the league. A May Bank Holiday double, against a Wigg-less Exeter lifted them off the bottom for a few weeks, but from mid-August onwards the Racers were firmly rooted at the foot of the table. Mullett missed the Exeter fixtures, but guest Paul Pickering made friends at Smallmead with two double-figure scores. These were also Pedersen's final Reading appearances as the following week Armando Castagna finally materialised.

Not a single maximum was scored in Racers colours in 1996. Tony Olsson did manage 18 points from six rides, but that was guesting for Swindon. However, Olsson did have an excellent season, and David Steen generally performed well, including double-figure returns at Eastbourne, London and Ipswich.

In contrast Morris and Kokko failed to progress and their contributions away from home rarely came up to the mark. Morris did well enough in the British Under-21 Championship to earn entry to the World Under-21 rounds. A 12-point return (one more than eventual champion Piotr Protasiewicz), put Morris through to the semi-final in Poland. Elimination followed after a disappointing single-point display there.

After disappointing for much of the year Dave Mullett and Armando Castagna produced their best form of the year in the closing matches. This was reflected in Reading's results; they won four of their last nine matches including a 49-45 victory at Oxford. A Castagna/Norris 5-1 in the last heat gave Racers the win. Norris made his return to a Racers race jacket as a guest after Tony Olsson broke a foot in the Czech Golden Helmet at the end of September.

Unfortunately it was too late; the wooden spoon was already guaranteed a place in the Racers trophy cabinet.

The Smallmead season ended with a second benefit meeting to raise money for a new wheelchair for Per Jonsson. Typifying the rotten season, the meeting succumbed to rain after seven races.

A few days later Castagna exceeded expectations in the Premier League Riders Championship, coming fifth. Sam Ermolenko finished eighth in the qualifying score chart but won the meeting after Chris Louis suffered an engine failure while leading the final.

Reading also fielded a team in the Conference League. Nicknamed the Ravens after a fans' competition they finished 11th in the 13-team league. Lee Richardson dropped just 2 points in the five Conference League appearances he made. Steve Targett was an ever-present, but it was Darren Andrews and Carl Checketts who contributed most points. Other riders included Lance Sealey, Roger Lobb and a Frenchman – Patrice Deloubes. The Ravens boasted just one away win, at Eastbourne. Curiously the Eastbourne team included no less than four future Racers: Bobby Eldridge, Shane Colvin, Tara O'Callaghan and Ian Clarke.

After a joyless season, rumours suggested that a change of promoter might be in the offing. Pat Bliss admitted that if the right offer came along she and her father might well sell up. Potential new owners named in the press included ex-Racers star John Davis, London promoter Terry Russell and Malcolm Holloway.

Did anything go right in 1996? Well, a victory over Swindon just when they looked capable of taking the league title for the first time in 29 years brought some temporary relief to the gloom that surrounded Smallmead. Swindon's challenge faded and Wolverhampton, spearheaded by the Karlsson brothers, did a league and cup double.

Team: Tony Olsson 8.12, Armando Castagna 7.69, Ray Morton 7.20, Dave Mullett 6.86, Petri Kokko 5.84, David Steen 5.02, Phil Morris 4.76, Jan Pedersen 4.55, Jorg Pingel 4.54

Destined for the wooden spoon – the Racers team of 1996, left to right: Dave Mullett, Tony Olsson, Jorg Pingel, Petri Kokko (on bike), Phil Morris, Armando Castagna and David Steen. (BT)

1997 – Dropping Down, A Good Decision

As widely predicted, the Premier League split into two over the winter. An Elite League of ten teams and a second division (confusingly called the Premier League) of 14. The lower cost base for the second division helped swell the number of tracks operating at the professional level. Arena Essex, Newcastle, Stoke and Berwick had not competed in the 1996 League. They were joined by new tracks at Skegness and Newport. While efforts continued (and still are over a decade later) to find a new home for Cradley Heath, a second year of operating without a home was not sustainable and they withdrew from the Elite League. (In 1996 Cradley competed for one last season based at Stoke.) At Hackney the receivers sold the stadium leading to the end of speedway there. After a season away King's Lynn returned with a new nickname – the Knights.

Innovation became the watchword of the winter. Dirt deflectors made a comeback after further tests in 1996. The Craven and Young Shields made their debut in 1997 as end-of-season play-off competitions. Teams were slimmed down from seven to six members to accommodate the increased number of tracks. In the previous 36 seasons a team had consisted of seven riders in every year except 1993 when eight was the norm. Under the new format teams had a reserve and a supplementary reserve, an arrangement that caused some confusion and re-drafting of the rules within a week of the season's start.

One suggested change didn't happen after an outcry from fans – a proposal to eliminate helmet colours! But another change did make it to the starting line. A "bold innovation that would modernise the sport" or "a barking mad idea that would put speedway on a par with *It's a Knockout*" depending on one's point of view, the "golden double" made its debut. On March 15, the opening day of the season, Swindon quickly fell behind at Coventry and Leigh Adams went into the history books as the first golden double. Starting off a 15 metre handicap, he finished third, on the wrong end of a 5-2 after an entertaining race with John Jorgensen.

Golden doubles were restricted to elite level cup matches in 1997. In both leagues the cup metamorphosed into the old League Cup competition with two mini leagues followed by semi-finals and a final.

Once the decision to have two leagues was made Reading were widely expected to opt for the lower division.

One of the brightest pieces of news in the last three years gave cause for second thoughts. Todd Wiltshire, a Racers star who burnt brightly and briefly at the beginning of the decade, wanted to make a comeback five years after he last rode. Still only 28 years of age Wiltshire's announcement delighted the Smallmead faithful. Pat Bliss flirted with the possibility of Wiltshire spearheading a Racers assault on the Elite League, but wisely opted for the more realistic cost structure of the Premier League.

Dropping down meant that after two winters desperately trying to put together a team Pat Bliss was spoilt for choice. Tony Olsson signed for Elite League Swindon, a move that everybody expected. At the end of 1997 he returned to Sweden and after a final season riding for Bysarna in the Swedish Elite League he hung up his leathers. Both Ray Morton and Petri Kokko found themselves teamless in 1997. Phil Morris was widely tipped to join Newport, but the deal fell through late in the day leaving him in the same position as Morton and Kokko. Newport took a leaf out of Reading's book by signing a Swede. Jan Andersson recommended Anders Henriksson who became an instant hit with the Wasps crowd.

Jorg Pingel had a short spell at Elite League Peterborough, but looked much happier in the Premier League at Berwick where he averaged over 7. Originally pencilled in for a spot in the Reading squad, the cost of air fares from Germany deterred Bliss from agreeing a deal. Instead she picked up Glenn Cunningham, a rider keen to move to the Premier League after stagnating at Swindon.

Dave Mullett (who started the season with the highest average of any Premier League rider), David Steen and Lee Richardson were pencilled in at an early stage. The other new face in the Racers team was Paul Pickering. With a fairly low average it was regarded as an astute move, the only reservation being the effect of travel from his base in Hartlepool.

Bliss also strengthened the off-track team, persuading Malcolm Holloway to take up a position described in the Smallmead programme as 'speedway administrator'. It turned out to be only a one-season appointment, and his next re-appearance at Smallmead was an even bigger surprise. The programme reflected changing times, with articles about speedway on the Internet. Although broadband was not yet commercially available, Internet usage was growing rapidly. Mention must be made of the memorably titled “It's Dyer 'Ere” column, which made the 1997 programme interesting reading. Nick Dyer's thoughts were far removed from the anodyne padding that usually fills up programmes.

The opening programme boasted that the Racers were fielding an all-British born team. This included Tara O'Callaghan, an Eastbourne junior with just five Conference League matches under his belt, who filled the reserve slot. Also listed was Zimbabwean David Steen, born in Maidstone according to all contemporary speedway reference books. Steen later admitted a certain 'economy with the truth'. Salisbury (now named Harare) had been replaced with Kent as his birthplace in order to ensure there were no questions about his eligibility at the start of his British career.

Reading started the season strongly fancied for honours. They opened with an aggregate challenge defeat against Oxford, another of the title pretenders. O'Callaghan provided the main talking point in the home leg. A fast starter he managed to fall four times and retire in his other ride. In heat 12 he led Oxford heat leaders Neville Tatum and Philippe Berge until the final bend before parting company from his machine.

It came as little surprise the following week when he fell in his first ride, breaking his leg badly. O'Callaghan will go down in the record books along with Bo Jansson (in 1977) for the brevity of his Racers career: just one ride in official fixtures. A year and a half later he still had no feeling in part of his foot as a result of the crash.

Fortunately for the Racers the regulations made provision for a 'track reserve' and rider replacement for the reserve. This meant the track reserve could take four of O'Callaghan's rides and the rider immediately above him in the averages could take the other one. Initially this extra ride went to Lee Richardson; later in the season Paul Pickering became the beneficiary of this rule.

All that was needed to make this work effectively was a suitable track reserve. Another Eastbourne prospect, Bobby Eldridge filled the position until July when Krister Marsh replaced him. In September Eldridge (representing Ryde) came within inches of being crowned Amateur League Riders Champion. A fast start in the title run-off saw him head Jon Armstrong until the diminutive Buxton rider passed him on the final bend. But Eldridge counter-attacked and a photo finish was followed by a long pause before the verdict was announced in Armstrong's favour.

Both Marsh and Eldridge picked up the odd point here and there, but it was the power of the top five that carried Racers to their season of glory. Racers topped the Southern group of the League Cup, despite a scare at home to Oxford. After a 46-44 defeat on track, team manager Tim Sugar slapped in a protest over Oxford's use of Krister Marsh instead of Jason Bunyan in the opening heat. Always renowned for his understanding of the rulebook, Sugar was proved right when the official result was amended to a draw. He knew the rules better than the Oxford management or the meeting referee Ronnie Allan!

Prior to the Oxford meeting Racers had already picked up three away wins in the cup competition, including one at Oxford[67] and a 53-37 victory at Skegness. Less than 500 watched the Skegness meeting and it came as no surprise when 'Skeggy' folded in June. Before taking on a new identity as Isle of Wight they completed their four-team tournament rounds with new signing Phil Morris settling in well.

Racers fours rounds didn't go well. Missing Pickering due to a broken collarbone (the only significant injury of the season for the top five), Reading finished a distant second to Oxford. The Arena leg of the competition is best remembered for the performance of Walford Lions and their new young star Ricky Butcher, as the BBC filmed for 'Eastenders'.

However, Reading were already setting the pace in the league so spirits were still high. Five league wins in eight days at the start of June including tricky trips to Hull, Sheffield and Newcastle made Racers the team to beat. A month of magical performances from the Racers coincided with the release of the first 'Harry Potter' book.

A fifth League Championship title finds its way to the Racers trophy cabinet. Celebrating are left to right: Dave Mullett, Paul Pickering, Tim Sugar (team manager), David Steen and Krister Marsh. Kneeling in front are Glenn Cunningham and Lee Richardson. (EP)

Further away wins at Berwick (where Steen top scored) and Oxford were accomplished in between the two legs of the cup semi-final against Edinburgh. Elimination from the cup after a last-heat decider left Racers to concentrate on the league. Reading's previous club record for consecutive league wins had already been surpassed. A win at Stoke (July 26) extended the run since the start of the campaign to 11 matches. Add two wins at the end of 1996 and the streak ran to 13 matches in its entirety. The previous record of eight matches, set in 1977, included four away wins. This record also fell; the Stoke victory made it seven away wins on the trot (including the win at Oxford at the end of the previous season).

The Stoke fixture marked the debuts of Krister Marsh (in Racers colours) and Phil Morris

67 I drove from St Ives in Cornwall to watch this match with only a couple of hours sleep the night before, after watching the General Election results flood in. After 18 years the Conservatives were out and Tony Blair entered Downing Street. Britain had the 'feel good factor' – magnified the next day when Katrina and the Waves won the Eurovision Song Contest. What a difference a decade makes!

(for Stoke). It also sent Reading back to the top of the table after a ten-day break, during which Long Eaton occupied the top slot.

All good things must end, and the following day Glasgow got the better of Reading after an exciting contest. Racers bounced back the next night with a 64-26 thrashing of Berwick in which Mullett achieved his third maximum in three days.

Wins at Arena, Newport (where Mullett established a new track record) and Exeter consolidated Reading's position at the top and compensated for a 46-44 defeat in an enthralling top of the table clash at Long Eaton. By now Edinburgh were the main challengers to the Racers, and a September trip up to Scotland would be crucial. The Monarchs stormed into a 38-28 lead which put them on level terms for the bonus point, but Racers fought back to guarantee the bonus point and force a last-heat decider. (Final score: Edinburgh 46 Reading 44.) Edinburgh couldn't really afford to drop the bonus point and their faint hopes evaporated 48 hours later with a defeat at Newcastle.

All Reading needed to do now was wrap up their home league programme by beating Newport. With the championship won the Racers wound up their away programme with a big defeat on an Isle of Wight track that came in for much criticism from the Racers camp. Incidentally Dave Mullett missed this meeting after falling off ... a haystack on his farm. It was the only match Mullett missed; Richardson and Cunningham went one better and were ever-presents.

Due to their move from Skegness, the Isle of Wight were in the middle of a spell of seven home matches in 15 days (including two double headers and one 'home' match ridden at Peterborough). Their efforts earned them eighth place in the league and a place in the Young Shield draw – against Reading.

Reading had already won the home leg 60-30 (in front of a crowd of under 600), when on a substantially better Smallbrook track Racers stormed to a 53-37 away win. This was the third time Racers had won away by 16 points during 1997: at Skegness in the League Cup, Berwick in the Premier League and Wight in the Young Shield. Not since 1986 had Reading raced to an away win of 16 points or more.

The semi-final tie against Exeter was lost in the first leg at Smallmead when Reading could only win by 4 points. A poor return from Paul Pickering left Racers with too much to do in the second leg in Devon. 48 hours later the Falcons travelled to Long Eaton for the first leg of the final. Sadly this turned out to be the last-ever meeting at Long Eaton. The Invaders couldn't go out on a high note losing the Young Shield Final. They had finished runners-up in the league as well, but did take home one title, the Premier League Pairs.

At Oxford in late September the Racers pair of Richardson and Mullett went into the final heat of the Premier League Pairs needing a 6-3 to take the title. Instead they conceded a 6-3 and had to settle for second. Richardson highlighted the progress he had made during the year by scoring 19 points to Mullett's 12.

Richardson started the year with a 3.00 green sheet average, and ended it with a 7.31 figure (for league matches only). A match-winning paid 15 at Sheffield and a maximum at home to Glasgow were the highlights. His startling improvement was assisted by the involvement of ex-Racer John Davis in the 'Richardson camp.'

He finished runner-up in the British Under-21 Championship after a marathon meeting at King's Lynn that ended at 10.40 p.m. Favourite Scott Nicholls won his first four rides and then suffered an engine failure when leading the last heat. Leigh Lanham took the title, but the 10 points from 15-year-old[68] David Howe attracted much attention. Racer Bobby Eldridge

---

68 In 1997 the rule prohibiting riders under 16 from competing (which was first brought in to stop Reg Fearman riding in 1948) was amended to allow 15-year-olds to compete in the Conference League and certain other meetings.

came up with a creditable 9 points. Richardson went on to reach the semi-final round of the World Under-21 Championship.

Mullett had started the year on top of the Premier League averages and stayed there all year. In league matches he reached double figures in every league match. In Reading's history only Anders Michanek has finished a season with a higher average (in official fixtures) than Mullett's 10.47 returned in 1997.

The Silver Helmet was re-established and Mullett started the season as the nominated holder. After defending it against Peter Carr (Edinburgh), his second defence ended in defeat to Robbie Kessler (Sheffield). Kessler's first defence was a successful one – against Glenn Cunningham, the only other Racers involvement with the helmet in 1997.

Mullett and Cunningham both featured in the Premier League Riders Championship. Mullett and Oxford's Neville Tatum were unbeaten in the qualifying heats, but unfortunately for them both went out in the semi-finals. Peter Carr (who qualified in eighth place for the final stages) won the final from Cunningham.

Cunningham had finished fourth in the league averages, his 10.06 return was over 3 points up on his starting average. He missed the Pairs meeting as it clashed with the final round of the World long/grasstrack Grand Prix. After winning the first round of the series Cunningham led the series for three rounds, and came away from the fifth and final round with a bronze medal.

Speedway's major international competition, the Grand Prix, produced a new World Champion. American Billy Hamill surrendered his title to compatriot Greg Hancock. Smallmead favourite Armando Castagna booked a place in the 1998 Grand Prix by winning the Continental Final.

Much attention was paid to the continental form of Todd Wiltshire. After Bradford were refused a work permit for him, Todd based himself in Germany and rode for Landshut. It didn't take him long to make an impact. He followed up an open meeting win in Prague (from Castagna and Tomasz Gollob) with the German Championship and a team spot at Gdansk in the Polish League. His good form continued when he returned to Australia for the winter. Wins in the final two rounds of the International Masters series gave him third place ahead of Jason Crump, and set him up for a storming return to British speedway in 1998.

Possibly the most extraordinary team name ever to appear in a league table made its appearance in the 1997 Amateur League. An extended league programme left Swindon and Reading unable to accommodate all the necessary fixtures, so they merged. Half the home matches were

In 1997 Reading and Swindon joined forces to track a combined junior team under the name "M4 Raven Sprockets". Ashley Holloway sports the blue-and-red halved body-colour. (BT)

ridden at Swindon and half at Smallmead. The chosen name: the 'M4 Raven Sprockets' hardly rolled off the tongue.

The juniors finished seventh in a 13-team league helped by an unusual double-header double victory at Buxton. In the first half of the meeting they beat Buxton, and in the second Belle Vue (nominally the home team) lost to the Raven Sprockets. John Jefferies and Gary Phelps both returned double figures in these two matches on their way to finishing first and second in the team's averages. Ian Clarke, Shane Colvin and Wayne Holloway (nephew of Malcolm) were among the other team members.

Peterborough easily won the Amateur League, tracking the finest team ever seen in competition at this level. Three new 15-year-olds: Simon Stead, David Howe and Ollie Allen took the headlines but the team also included Paul Clews, Ross Brady and Carl Wilkinson. Oxford Cubs came up with their own trio of lively looking 15-year-old prospects: Phil Ambrose, Lee Driver and Andrew Appleton.

This was the era of 'girl power', the Spice Girls chart career was less than a year old. Speedway reflected the trend when Angela McAlden made her debut for Lathallan (formerly Linlithgow) in June. Her second outing saw her line-up against the Raven Sprockets. Other female riders would follow, notably Charlene Kirtland and Jessica Lamb, both of whom were often seen at Smallmead.

While results were good, crowds continued to decline. Despite a reduction in admission charges (from £7 in 1996 to £6.50) attendances reached an all-time low, with average gates of well under a thousand. With the large asset base inherited from their Division One days the prospects on track still looked bright. But how much further could crowds fall before Pat Bliss and Bill Dore threw in the towel?

Bradford, facing poor crowds and redevelopment, withdrew from the Elite League during the winter. Oxford, bank-rolled by new promoter Steve Purchase, returned to the Elite League while Peterborough opted to drop down to the Premier League. The encroachment of Grand Prix weekends on their regular Friday race night was a factor.

Team: Dave Mullett 10.47, Glenn Cunningham 9.92, David Steen 7.75, Lee Richardson 6.73, Paul Pickering 6.50, Krister Marsh 2.43, Bobby Eldridge 2.00

1998 – A Cup Triumph

Nick Dyer described it as: "one of – if not the – greatest ever single display by a Reading team in their 30 year history."

The match in question took place at Peterborough in mid-September. By then pre-season favourites Peterborough had won every trophy on offer to them. Former Racers favourite Glenn Cunningham had moved to Peterborough and carried off the Premier League Riders Championship. At Newport he teamed up with Brett Woodifield to win the Premier League Pairs for the Panthers. As the hosts, a win in the Premier League Fours was probably the season's least surprising result.

Jan Andersson, a member of the 1990 cup winning team presents captain Petri Kokko with the trophy for Racers 1998 Knock Out Cup win. (BT)

With three 16-year-old talents – David Howe, Simon Stead and Ollie Allen – Peterborough romped away with the league. Defending champions Reading did well enough to finish second and provide a semblance of a challenge to the Panthers.

'Titanic' starring Reading-born Kate Winslet dominated the cinema screens in 1998, and, like the ship, Peterborough Panthers cruised through the season looking unsinkable. But in the cup final they met their iceberg in the guise of Reading Racers and Paul Clews.

Paul Clews started the year in the Peterborough team, but despite promising form found his team place taken by Ollie Allen. Racers had a vacancy at reserve, caused by events at Peterborough in the 60-27 cup defeat at Alwalton in May. Lee Driver, a talented 16-year-old, signed for Reading over the winter after showing promise at Oxford in the Amateur League. After five matches without a point his team place looked in danger. Then a surge of form earned him some rave reviews.

In the second heat at Peterborough the erratic Ross Brady ran into Driver sending him flying. A broken femur and damaged vertebrae ended Driver's season just as it was beginning to take off. Three years later he was still undergoing treatment. Driver never resumed his career. Initial replacement Ian Clarke (a Raven Sprocket in 1997) failed to make an impact before Clews arrived at the start of July. Although Clews scored in every match, he hadn't managed to top 5 points.

In the early stages of the Knock-Out Cup Peterborough did the double over Reading. However, because the cup's early stages were again run in qualifying groups, Racers lived to fight another day and face the Panthers again in the final showdown. The Panthers had not dropped a bonus point all year and had beaten Reading by 18-point and 33-point margins at Alwalton, so even the most optimistic of Reading fans struggled to predict a Racers triumph in the final.

Kokko and Richardson with four wins each led the charge in the first leg of the final at Peterborough. In an all-round display every one of the Racers picked up valuable points. None more so than Clews who beat Allen three times on the way to a 7-point tally. Racers came from 6 down to win 46-44, although the Panthers did have some bad luck when Cunningham crashed out while chasing Phil Morris in heat 10.

Peterborough crumbled in the second leg and Reading trounced the Panthers 57-33. Richardson won six races for an 18-point maximum, while reserves Clews and Krister Marsh returned 15 paid 16 between them.

Paul Clews became the hero of the hour in the cup final against Peterborough. Here he is pictured (second left) at Dave Mullett's second testimonial. Also pictured (left to right) are Armando Castagna, Mullett and Phil Morris. (EP)

October's Young Shield Final saw the Peterborough collapse continue with a last-heat defeat to the Isle of Wight – a team featuring Ray Morton, Jason Bunyan and 18-year-old newcomer Danny Bird.

Reading's Young Shield campaign ended at the first hurdle when Glasgow unexpectedly knocked the Racers out. A strong second leg performance at Smallmead climaxed in David Steen winning the last-heat decider to protect Glasgow's 3-point aggregate lead.

Glasgow were the unluckiest team of the year. In June, Stoke stood on the brink of closure. By the time they were back up and running, their League Cup results had been deleted from the records. In a bizarre statistical quirk Glasgow went from table toppers guaranteed a place in the semi-finals – to third place and elimination. The beneficiaries were Sheffield whose qualification hopes rested on a Stoke win at Berwick (one of the matches never ridden). Threats of legal action and a war of words followed. An RAC tribunal concluded that Glasgow were unfairly treated, but it was too late to undo what had already been done.

By the time of the appeal Sheffield had been eliminated on track after Racers drew at Owlerton in their semi-final tie, despite the late arrival of Lee Richardson. Salvation came from an unlikely source – Justin Elkins racking up paid 13.

Although David Steen missed out on cup progress with Glasgow he had a busy year. His testimonial took place at Smallmead in August. Marketed heavily under the title 'Bike Mania', Steen and his testimonial committee succeeded where many others have failed and managed to put together and market an event that attracted an audience beyond the regular speedway public.

A crowd of 3-4,000 watched motocross, sidecars, quad bikes, and 17 heats of speedway. Described in *Speedway Star* as five times the normal gate, this would imply average attendances of about 700. Dave Mullett beat GP rider Chris Louis in a run-off. Former Racers in the field included Armando Castagna, Ray Morton, Jeremy Doncaster and, in his first Smallmead appearance for seven years, Todd Wiltshire.

The Elite League continued to operate six-man teams[69] meaning that, although keen to return to British speedway, Wiltshire remained on the sidelines that spring. With one win in nine matches Oxford occupied bottom spot in the Elite League. After signing Todd they won more than half their remaining matches and climbed up to seventh place (out of nine). Highlight of Todd's return came in a match at home to Eastbourne (August 21). With Crump and Staechmann crashing out of the meeting early on, Wiltshire's six-ride maximum steered the depleted Cheetahs to victory. After retaining his German national title, he added the Australian Championship the following winter.

The Elite League itself was a one-horse race. Ipswich, boosted by the signing of Tomasz Gollob, began the season with 19 wins in a row. They also tracked Tony Rickardsson who went on to win his second World Title.

Returning to the Racers, the 1998 team was known before the end of February for the first time in several years. Mullett, Richardson and Marsh returned, but Paul Pickering joined Cunningham and Steen in moving on to pastures new. Although Pickering's efforts had been appreciated he hadn't lived up to expectations and a return to a more northerly base suited him. He signed for Stoke and served them well for a decade, not retiring until the age of 41.

Two of the newcomers were existing Reading assets Petri Kokko and Phil Morris. Kokko spent the previous season riding for Smederna in Sweden, while Morris returned from Stoke with a 6.53 official average. The final place went to Justin Elkins. Although only 23 he had already ridden for Poole, Exeter, Swindon, Coventry, Eastbourne and Long Eaton. Along the way he picked up a reputation for mechanical unreliability.

Elkins's year at Reading didn't change that reputation. Numerous engine failures (including three in three rides in May's cup loss at home to Peterborough), dogged him all season. Although reasonable at home, he failed to contribute much away from home. Krister Marsh started the year on an assessed average of 3 which he upped by over a point and a half. Both Elkins and Marsh rode in all Reading's league matches, and curiously they both returned their best away performance of the year at Arena Essex. Marsh (paid 12) and Elkins (6) steered Racers to victory after Dave Mullett could only complete two rides.

---

69 While the Premier League reverted to seven-man teams and introduced the format still in use today, the Elite League went for six-man teams, but used a formula designed for seven-man teams. This apparent contradiction was resolved by having four nominated slots in the programme for each team. Basically all teams operated permanent rider replacement for a non-existent rider!

Mullett remained a heavy scorer, but slipped down to fifth in the league averages, with team mate Kokko in seventh. In June the captaincy passed from Mullett to the more outgoing Kokko, and in an ordinary year these two would have been vying for rider of the year, but this was no ordinary season.

This was the year when Lee Richardson blazed a trail of glory in the Premier League. In Reading's colours he averaged 9.96 in league matches, a figure bettered only by Carl Stonehewer (Sheffield) and first-season sensation Nicki Pedersen (Newcastle). It could be argued he was the best rider in the league as his average in away matches was the highest in the league. A magnificent August Bank Holiday contributed to this result; Richardson posted two 18-point maximums in a single day, away and home to Exeter. He broke track records at Newcastle and Arena Essex and rode in all eight England under-21 Test matches, top scoring in the last six.

On the individual front he reached the World Under-21 Final, staged at Pila in Poland. His sixth place (shared with Scott Nicholls) was enough to win him a place in Pila's Polish Extraliga team the following season. In October, Richardson came home first in the Golden Ribbon, the junior version of the Czech Golden Helmet. He finished ahead of Krystof Cegielski, Nicki Pedersen and Ales Dryml in the final.

Andy Fuller, a keen Racers fan, lost his life in an electricity sub-station fire early in the season. A group of his friends instituted the Andy Fuller Memorial Award, to be given each year to the most improved Racer. It came as no surprise when Richardson became the first winner, or when he announced that he would be seeking an Elite League berth for 1999.

In contrast Phil Morris had a quiet season. Injuries sidelined him three times. The first two were done grasstracking, and the second kept him out for over two months. He also missed the second leg of the cup final after damaging his ribs in the first leg. His scoring failed to match expectations and this was very much a year for Phil to forget.

In summary Racers fielded an awesome top three, but didn't have quite enough support to hang on to their title. Defeats at Edinburgh by a single point and Hull and Sheffield by two could have been turned into wins and the title retained. At Hull and Sheffield the heat leaders all scored heavily, but the supporting cast managed just 5 at Hull and 3 at Sheffield. At Exeter in April the heat leaders all got double figures, while the remainder of the team managed a lone point between them.

As a result Racers only managed four away wins – against the teams that went on to finish in the bottom four: Stoke, Berwick (where Kokko got a full house), Newcastle and Arena. At home, Racers kept on winning: even beating title pretenders Peterborough by 8. The closest scrape came at home to Newcastle. Racers won by just 4 points after Kokko beat Nicki Pedersen in a last-heat decider. Immediately afterwards Pedersen retained his Silver Helmet against Kokko.

These results contributed to two record-breaking runs. Since losing at home to Bradford in September 1996, Reading had put together a streak of 26 home league wins in a row. After picking up all the bonus points available in 1997, the Racers continued to pick up the extra point for the aggregate win until out-pointed by the Isle of Wight in August. In league matches Reading clocked up 21 bonus points in a row.

Although they remained unbeaten in league matches at Smallmead, the Racers did lose three home matches. In the opening fixture Edinburgh won in the Premiership; next came Peterborough's cup win; and finally Newport won in a Honda challenge.

This was one of a number of experimental meetings that took place during the season, generating a marked lack of enthusiasm with both riders and fans. Most people were more interested in the football World Cup Finals. England lost to Romania that night. Host nation France carried off the trophy three weeks later. At least the Honda experiment indicated that somebody was attempting to address speedway's problems of escalating costs. Eric Boocock and Neil Machin deserved the credit for trying to control speedway's cost base.

By the end of the year Smallmead was a very different place. It ceased to be stuck at the back of an industrial estate, a new dual carriageway (the A33 relief road) drew near. A new structure loomed behind the third and fourth bends. In August this became a working building when the Madejski Stadium[70] opened. A crowd of 18,108 watched the Royals first match (against Luton Town) at their new home.

The changes at Smallmead weren't just physical though. In December, after a month in hospital, Bill Dore passed away (aged 76), just a month after Coventry supremo Charles Ochiltree. Although Bill had taken a back seat for some time, he was nominally still co-promoter. The promoters' piece in the programme still had both Pat and Bill's names on it, and he alone remained of the gang of four (Silver, Higley and Fearman being the others) who took the original gamble on building a stadium on a rubbish tip.

Dore never really won over the Reading crowds who saw him as remote and more interested in greyhounds. But it has to be acknowledged that by the time of his death Reading speedway was living on borrowed time, and only the goodwill of the Dore family kept the sport going in Reading. Bill shared the load with daughter Pat since she became co-promoter in 1984 and Ochiltree's passing made her the longest running promoter at a single track.

Pat's relationship with the Smallmead supporters had evolved considerably. After she emerged from her father's shadow the distance between her and the terraces gradually reduced. Three key factors caused fans to warm to Pat: her genuine delight at Reading's triumphs in 1990 and 1992, sympathy generated by her health problems and the depth of her concern for Per Jonsson after his tragic accident in 1994.

Bill Dore's death (and the increase in value of the Smallmead site created by the new road) generated more uncertainty than ever.

Team: Lee Richardson 9.86, Dave Mullett 9.46, Petri Kokko 9.46, Phil Morris 5.32, Krister Marsh 4.74, Justin Elkins 4.66, Paul Clews 4.04, Lee Driver 3.09

---

70 The new development cost in the region of £50 million – a bargain compared with London's Olympic Stadium, projected to cost £496 million (*BBC* , 11 October 2007). The Olympic Stadium will be just a few hundred metres from the site of Reading's saddest hour. The Olympic Opening Ceremony is scheduled to take place just 11 days after the 30th anniversary of Denny Pyeatt's fatal accident at Hackney.

1999 – A Bad Break for Dave Mullett

Evening Post reporter Dave Wright's career reporting on the Racers reached the 25-year mark. In 1995 Alan Hanson said of Manchester United: "You'll never win anything with kids." United won five titles in the next six years, and in 1999 the European Champions' League. Wright's report of 1999's opening meeting at Smallmead was similarly lacking in prescience, concluding with the forecast that: "things could only get better."

That night, fans faced a confusing journey to the stadium through the construction site that would become the A33 relief road. On reaching the track they waited for the late arrival of the track doctor and there was a further delay when the lights on the fourth bend failed and the match dragged on to 10.10 p.m. The result provided no redress for Racers supporters as a strong Newport side won 51-38. The Wasps (cheered on by their large band of travelling supporters) included Bobby Eldridge, Andrew Appleton and Chris Neath in their team. For Reading Justin Elkins started his season with an engine failure while Dave Mullett and Petri Kokko both delivered under-par performances.

Expectations were not high, winter team building left Reading more than 2 points under the limit. Mullett, Morris, Kokko and Clews returned and two new youngsters filled the reserve berths. Both Shane Colvin and Marc Norris gained their early experience at the Eastbourne training track. Colvin was 17 and had worn the Raven Sprockets race jacket in 1997. Norris (no relation to 1995 number one David) wouldn't be 16 until April.

This left Racers searching for someone with an average of 6.89 or less to fill the remaining spot. The names most frequently put forward were Jason Bunyan (who tried his luck with Ipswich in the Elite League) and Vesa Ylinen (too expensive). Whether Ylinen wanted pounds or euros is not recorded. (Finland was one of 11 countries participating in the launch of the euro at the start of the year.) With a shortage of riders in the right average range, Justin Elkins (average 4.79) got a second chance. Reading fielded a squad that looked like a candidate for a bottom three position.

After Christmas Swindon decided that the Premier League would be a more financially secure environment. Following a season without any local derbies this was welcome news at Smallmead. It did, however, mean the recall of Krister Marsh to his parent club. Glenn Cunningham also returned to Blunsdon. After his fabulous year in 1998 (including third place in the Overseas Final and two full international caps for England) Cunningham's career stagnated. His testimonial meeting took place at Somerset in 2004.

Poole won the contest for Lee Richardson's signature and were rewarded with a fine first season from the Bracknell-based youngster.

The Elite League returned to seven-man teams, Belle Vue flirted with a drop to the Premier League but stayed in the Elite. They were joined by Hull and Peterborough, whose elevation was enabled by an exceptionally low points limit – 40 including bonus points. The Premier League gained Workington, a track that had last seen action in 1987. The 'golden double' made its first appearance on Premier League tracks. Dave Mullett would become the first Racer to go off 15 metres; he picked up 6 points in a challenge match at Swindon.

At the end of February a fall cost Shane Colvin second place in the British Under-16 Championship. He ended joint fourth with Jason King, Chris Schramm and Glen Phillips. The title went to St Austell's Chris Harris.

At the start of the season neighbours Oxford staged a farewell meeting for Simon Wigg. Once a junior at Reading his illustrious career (including five World Longtrack titles) had come to an end after a series of blackouts. As the year progressed the medical prognosis became ever gloomier, and he passed away in November 2000. A wealth of talent turned up at Cowley to celebrate his career; Greg Hancock won the meeting from Jason Crump and

Armando Castagna.

Despite the gloomy outlook, Racers made a respectable start to the season winning all four home matches in the Premier Trophy. Morris and Elkins started well, but the real bonus came from Marc Norris's flying start to the season. Performances at Newport (9 points) and on the Isle of Wight (where he topped the score chart) suggested that he would prove to be even better than predicted. He only just missed out on qualification for the British Under-21 Championship, riding in the meeting as reserve. For the third year in a row Lee Richardson came second!

The landmark event of May took place at Coventry when their match with Wolverhampton became the first in the Elite League to be televised. The financial injection helped prop up the ailing Elite League, and the professional production values of the Sky coverage provided much welcome positive publicity for speedway.

Meanwhile the Premier League campaign got under way. Racers flew out of the starting blocks and amazed even the most optimistic of their fans with a draw and a win in the first two away fixtures. It may have been optimistic to talk about a title challenge but it looked as if Racers could end up nearer the top than the bottom. The draw at Workington was a classic encounter with home hero Carl Stonehewer passing Justin Elkins in heat 15 to save a point for the Comets. It was Elkins's paid 11 that nearly won the match for Reading. The following night Racers arrived in Scotland just three days after the first elections for the new devolved Scottish Parliament. Racers gained both points at Glasgow, with Paul Clews (paid 16) taking his turn to shine.

Two weeks later Reading returned to Glasgow and won again, this time in a cup fixture. However, it marked the start of the season's collapse. Marc Norris broke an arm on a poor track. It sidelined him for two months. Discarded by Belle Vue amid rumours of average manipulation, Jarno Kosonen stood in for Norris. The Finn scored 8 points in each of his first two home matches as Racers extended their unbeaten Smallmead league sequence to 29 matches.

A bizarre evening at Berwick (June 12) saw Petri Kokko absent for a month after a heat 13 fall when Berwick led 39-33. Tim Sugar, Reading's team manager, claimed the track was too dangerous and the match was called off. The referee then awarded Berwick three 5-nils, which were subsequently removed from the scoreline by the SCB. Although nobody realised at the time, the Racers had already embarked on a record run of defeats.

The next home meeting marked a new low. Looking for a win to go top of the league, champions-to-be Sheffield trailed by 4 points after nine races. Up-and-coming Sheffield star Andre Compton chased after Dave Mullett in the next race. The two raced into the first turn with Compton on the inside lifting slightly and ploughing into Mullett. Racers long-serving number one landed awkwardly by the hare rail on the outside(!) of the greyhound track, breaking a thigh, ankle and three toes. Racing was delayed for nearly an hour while Mullett received treatment on the track. The Yorkshire Tigers banged in three 5-1s to win the match. Sean Wilson (who ended the season top of the Premier League averages) raced to a maximum and then defended his Silver Helmet against Phil Morris.

Mullett's crash left Racers badly in need of a replacement, and Pat Bliss followed the tried and tested formula of recruiting a Swede. The signing came in the unexpected form of Per Wester, a 25-year-old in his sixth season at Valsarna. A steady 5- to 6-point rider in the Swedish Elite League he hadn't been on anyone's radar. He picked up 13 points from five rides on his debut (a 46-44 home win against Sheffield in the cup), and this was followed by a dozen at Sheffield. In his fourth match Wester blazed to an 18-point maximum from five rides, including a golden double win (the first by a Racer in an official fixture). He matched Mullett point for point (their 1999 averages were almost identical), but Mullett left a big gap that couldn't be filled simply by signing a new rider.

21 June 1999 – Dave Mullett's bike is removed from the track after his encounter with Andre Compton. Wearing a jumper that only a colour photo can really do justice to is Dave Robinson, now a referee. (BT)

Wester's debut also marked the exit of Justin Elkins. Three engine failures in three rides took his total for the season to 30 or so. Elkins had become a figure of fun on the terracing and when Bliss gave him his cards few supporters could be found to disagree with the decision. Marc Norris returned from injury making Kosonen redundant, but with no replacements for Elkins available Kosonen got a recall. Norris struggled to recover his early season form and Kosonen's point scoring tailed off too.

Morris hit form, but it wasn't long before another Racer joined the injury list. Shane Colvin came to grief in the home round of the fours.

Peter Collyer replaced Colvin and rode well enough to keep his team place once Colvin returned to the saddle. Collyer joined Morris in the spotlight as the central characters in a Channel 4 documentary on the sport, broadcast in November.

Colvin only regained his place when Norris was dropped after throwing a tantrum in the pits at Reading's penultimate meeting. In that match Reading lost 43-47 to Arena Essex. It marked their 17th league defeat in a row, no less than eight of them at home. Previous club records were three home defeats in a row (set in 1994), and seven for consecutive defeats (dating back to 1978). Reading's worst run of away defeats came in 1994. That record still stood (at 16) and it would need a bad start to the following season for that to fall.

Yet despite this terrible record Racers never lost heavily. After the Sheffield defeat the following seven home league matches were all lost by 6 points or less. Four were last-heat deciders and in a fifth guest Steve Masters (in for Kokko) crashed out in the first race. Phil Morris kept Racers in contention in this match (v Berwick) with the first maximum (a paid one) of his career. Kokko, Wester, and the much-improved Morris performed well enough to keep scores respectable, and only once (at Newport) did Racers lose by more than 20 points on their travels. Kokko's scoring away from Smallmead slipped a bit, but he remained in the league's top ten in the end-of-season averages. Paul Clews upped his average and provided some useful middle-order support.

By the time the final home match arrived, Reading had already confirmed their basement position in the league. The opponents were Edinburgh (who went on to win the Knock-Out Cup in October). A strong showing from the heat leaders steered Reading to victory and a final flourish of three 5-1s in the last three races even gave Reading the bonus point.

This match marked the final appearance of Tim Sugar in the team manager's role. He had reservations about continuing at the start of the year and intimated before the last meeting that he would not carry on in 2000. He was presented with a silver salver by the man who had ridden more races than any other under Sugar's guidance – Dave Mullett (walking with the aid of a stick) making his first return to Smallmead since his accident.

Phil Morris won the Andy Fuller Shield for most improved Racer, and a new award for Racer of the Year went to Per Wester. This was a result of a vote by users of the Reading Racers website. Launched and maintained by Andy Povey it has consistently been one of the best club websites in British speedway over the last decade.

1999 marked the total eclipse of the Racers, and the first total eclipse of the sun visible from the UK since 1927. Crowds at Smallmead continued to melt away and it came as a surprise to many that there were plans for major improvements to the stadium. Renovation was long overdue and the news did give more hope that speedway still had a future in Reading. The town centre had a new look too with the opening of the Oracle shopping centre in September.

From a Reading perspective 1999 was an unmitigated disaster, but there was much cause for optimism elsewhere. The Grand Prix produced a dramatic climax with Tomasz Gollob (leader with a round to go) pipped by Tony Rickardsson. Third went to Hans Nielsen, marking his retirement with a final flourish. Todd Wiltshire won the Inter-Continental Final to give him a Grand Prix spot for 2000. Lee Richardson became the World Under-21 champion. All three Elite League competitions produced last-heat deciders with Peterborough winning the league, cup and Craven Shield at the last gasp.

Speedway Star celebrated the end of the millennium by publishing the results of a readers' poll[71] to find the greatest riders of all time. Ten riders who had worn the winged wheel featured: Michanek 14th, Jonsson 17th, Wiltshire 50th, Ashby 61st, Betts 64th, Shirra 77th, Jessup 90th, Jansson 93rd, Eide 94th and Davis 98th. Future Bulldog Greg Hancock made the top 20 at number 19.

A glance through that list evoked memories of happier days for devotees of the winged wheel and the hope that a new era would spark further glory. Would 2000 see the Racers return to winning ways?

Team: Petri Kokko 9.42, Dave Mullett 9.04, Per Wester 9.00, Phil Morris 7.49, Paul Clews 5.70, Justin Elkins 5.59, Jarno Kosonen 4.51, Marc Norris 3.83, Shane Colvin 2.35, Peter Collyer 1.81

71 Mauger, Nielsen and Fundin filled the top three. As is usual with this kind of exercise, recent riders were probably over-represented at the expense of stars from the early days of the sport. My major complaint was simply that the poll was a year too early – the millennium didn't end until 31 December 2000!

2000 – Oh No, Not Again!

For the first time in many seasons the mood in British speedway seemed overwhelmingly positive. Hull returned to the Premier League, but otherwise the Elite and Premier League make-ups were unchanged. The Conference League expanded with a new track in Somerset and speedway returned to Rye House thanks to Len Silver. The Rockets had competed without a home track in 1999, tracking three Reading juniors: Simon Moon, Peter Collyer and Ian Clarke. The star of the homecoming meeting in May (apart from 'uncle Len') was a young rider called Chris Schramm.

Honours were shared around and both Elite and Premier Leagues produced close finishes. Eastbourne won the Elite League, aided by a solid contribution from Petri Kokko. They went into their final fixture needing to beat King's Lynn to stop the Norfolk team picking up their first league title.

King's Lynn did have the consolation of winning the Knock-Out Cup. Beaten finalists Coventry picked up the Craven Shield. The Norfolk team regularly featured five Australians, and when Adam Shields guested for them in July they tracked six! One of them was Travis McGowan. He started the year by winning the Australian Under-21 title (with Scott Smith third and Brendon Mackay ninth) and ended it with the biggest improvement in average of any rider in the Elite League.

The destination of the Premier League title depended on bonus points. For the first time since their introduction, the team with most match points did not win the title. Thanks to their massive home advantage Exeter picked up all 13 bonus points available, but only two away wins. It was enough to clinch the title on race points two days after Swindon lost a bonus point run-off against Newcastle (September 28).

Although Swindon remained without a league championship since 1967 they did win the Knock-Out Cup and the Young Shield, their first trophies for 33 years. Hull won the Premier Trophy.

To add to the sense of euphoria Britain had a speedway World Champion. Despite not winning a single round Mark Loram relieved Tony Rickardsson of his crown. And the British GP did have a British winner with wild card Martin Dugard storming to victory.

After 1999 Racers fans needed cheering up. And although their league record may have suggested otherwise there were several things to celebrate:

- Armando Castagna's return after a three-year gap
- Dave Mullett's recovery
- Phil Morris's best-ever season in his testimonial year, and
- the progress of Paul Clews.

Phil Morris celebrated the New Year by taking the New Year Classic title at Newport. Morris took over the captaincy from Petri Kokko. Morris held the position for five seasons – only Jan Andersson filled the role for a longer period. The unusually rapid completion of team building provided further encouragement. The possibility of Castagna's return first emerged in November, and by January Pat Bliss was in a position to confirm that five of the survivors from the traumas of 1999 would be lining up with Castagna. They were Wester, Morris, Clews, Colvin and Norris.

The final spot turned out to be another old friend. Krister Marsh completed the team in February after a year at Swindon with a green sheet average just over 5. This left Reading just under the team-building limit of 45. There have been few finer sights than physically imposing Armando Castagna powering round the Smallmead bends and his return was keenly anticipated. However, some reservations were expressed about the weakness of the tail, necessary in order to accommodate his 11.00 starting average. Nevertheless it looked like an attractive team with plenty of scope for improvement from the supporting riders. *Speedway Star's* pre-season preview predicted the number 11 spot (out of 14) for the Racers.

Early results suggested that might be an accurate assessment. An opening-night defeat to the Isle of Wight made it five losses, one draw and just one win from the first-night meetings between 1994-2000. While Castagna looked rusty, Islanders Ray Morton won the last-heat decider.

Two further Smallmead defeats (against Swindon and Stoke) were cancelled out by two away wins (at Stoke and the Isle of Wight) in the Premier Trophy campaign.

Morris, Clews and Colvin were all going well. Although Wester was the only Racer to record a maximum in the Premier Trophy (at home to Exeter), his form gave cause for concern.

The Reading team pose at press and practice day. They are (left to right): Dave Mullett (team manager), Shane Colvin, Paul Clews, Phil Morris (on bike), Marc Norris, Per Wester and Krister Marsh. Missing is number one Armando Castagna. (BT)

Racers tracked a settled team, only Clews missed a Premier Trophy match. In his British Under-21 semi-final he qualified despite a last ride fall that put him out of the final. Incidentally ex-Racer Lee Richardson came second in this event for the fourth time in a row! Richardson did have the consolation of making his Grand Prix debut (as a wild card at Coventry) later in the year. Another early-season disappointment came in the form of rain that washed out an international challenge against a Sweden under-23 team managed by Tony Olsson.

In June, Reading's interest in the Knock-Out Cup was quickly extinguished by Swindon. Despite losing the home leg the Racers pushed the Robins hard at Swindon nearly pulling off a shock victory. The home leg turned out to be Wester's last appearance in Reading's colours. A fall sidelined him, and with his confidence draining away he didn't return. He had four undistinguished outings for Eastbourne later in the season, before going back to Sweden to concentrate on riding for Valsarna.

After using guests for the next month Racers re-shuffled their named seven, replacing

Wester with Matt Read. Only 18, but already with 2½ years' experience at Arena, Read had been rather unfairly dropped by struggling Arena. After a colossal paid 18, from the reserve berth when Arena visited Smallmead the previous autumn, expectations were high.

Read managed just 3 points from two matches. Initially injured, but subsequently retired, Racers used rider replacement for him for the rest of the year. Read did resume his speedway career on the Isle of Wight in 2002 before becoming a very popular member of the Somerset team. Sadly a serious crash competing in the 2004 World Longtrack Championship in France initially left him confined to a wheelchair.

Reading tentatively negotiated their unbalanced league programme. There were no away matches in May and only one between July 3 and August 23. Read's debut at the start of the second quiet period marked Reading's fifth home league match. At this stage they remained unbeaten; however a draw and wins of 2, 4 and 5 points suggested that a better team would leave Smallmead with the points soon.

That happened in Read's second (and final) match two weeks later. Bottom of the league Newcastle won after first-year sensation Bjarne Pedersen raced to four wins. Reading's season exhibited as much stability as the 'wobbly' bridge over the Thames opened and closed within two days in the week before the Diamonds fixture.

The following Monday the visitors (Glasgow this time) won again. Racers ended July occupying the cellar position in the league. They spent the rest of the year in the bottom two.

After the Glasgow match, Pat Bliss revealed that Dave Mullett would be making a racing comeback in the struggling team. Many who witnessed his horrific accident the previous year didn't think he would ever ride again. Mullett had remained intimately involved at Smallmead in his role as team manager, and had donned his leathers once more in an after-meeting spin in May. Still riding with pins in his leg, the following Monday's event presented an ideal opportunity to race in front of the Smallmead crowd once more.

8 May 2000 – A post match spin for Dave Mullett marks the start of his return after the previous year's horrific crash. (BT)

At the age of 24 Phil Morris became one of the youngest riders ever to receive a testimonial. A healthy crowd witnessed Newport's Craig Watson beat old favourite Todd Wiltshire, Morris and Castagna in the final. Mullett's 8 points, including two race wins nearly put him in the final. Jeremy Doncaster, Ray Morton and Petri Kokko were among the other familiar faces helping Phil celebrate his first decade with the club.

Several changes were needed to accommodate Mullett. Tim Sugar returned to his old role as team manager as Mullett and Lee Herne replaced Colvin and Marsh in the named seven. Marsh soon found a slot in the Newcastle line-up and returned to Smallmead on many occasions, mainly in the colours of Exeter and Isle of Wight. Colvin's season unravelled after an impressive start to the year. He continued to pull on the Mildenhall race jacket in the Conference League. Lee Herne, son of Aussie World Team Cup winner Phil, made little impact. His best score (of 6+1) came at Newport, the club he rode for until they dropped him.

Mullett's return lifted spirits, but produced mixed results. Three ducks away from home suggested his return might be premature, but two double-figure returns in his four home matches made more encouraging reading. It left Mullett with a 4.39 average, a gift for the following year's team-building plans.

In his last outing Mullett dropped just one point as Racers beat champions in waiting Exeter 46-44. After this he went into hospital to have the pins removed from his leg and missed the final month of the season.

Mullett's other double-figure score coincided with Reading's biggest win of the season 57-33 against Arena Essex. This match also saw Phil Morris achieve a career first, just two weeks after his testimonial – his first full maximum for the Racers.

However, Mullett's presence didn't guarantee better results. Just a week after Arena came to town, Swindon arrived looking for their third Smallmead victory of the year. The outcome still makes those who witnessed it shudder to this very day. Defeat in a local derby is painful, but to lose 58-32 was just an embarrassment. So dominant were the Robins that reserve Mark Steel came away from Smallmead with a maximum. The 26-point gap between the teams still stands today as Reading's biggest home defeat.

Racers experienced further humiliation on their travels. For the first (and only) time in their history Reading failed to pick up a single point from their away league programme. In the process their losing streak grew to 23 matches breaking the previous longest losing streak (16 matches in 1994). This included a 67-22 mauling at Exeter, an even worse result than their Premier Trophy defeat in April. However, that 66-24 drubbing looked quite respectable a month later after Exeter ran up scores of 75-15 (Arena Essex), 74-16 (Glasgow) and 72-18 (Newport) in consecutive home matches during May!

By September the wooden spoon looked like it was staying put. The Sydney Olympics filled the sports pages, and the fuel protests dominated the news pages. These threatened to disrupt the climax of the speedway season and petrol shortages made life difficult for travelling riders and fans.

Reading's opening fixture in September featured a 'blast from the past'. After coming out of retirement to ride for Conference League Somerset in July, Malcolm Holloway, an old friend of the Racers, filled in for Lee Herne. 'Mad Wellie' fell while leading heat 2 and had to withdraw from the meeting hurt. His one-night-only return, 11 years after his last Racers appearance, wouldn't be the last time Malcolm would feature in the Reading story.

A seven-match Test series between Young England and Young Australia drew to a conclusion at Smallmead. The Aussies were beaten 49-39 on a night so wet that heat 2's winning time was 19.5 seconds outside the track record. Clews appeared in four matches along with Andrew Appleton, Chris Neath and Danny Bird. Current Racer Lee Herne and future Racer Travis McGowan donned the Roos race jacket in most of the meetings.

The credibility of the series was undermined when Phil Morris rode for Australia (without renouncing his Welsh nationality)! Short of riders at Newport, an emergency call was put in to the Morris residence and the start delayed for 45 minutes while Morris sprinted to the track. A paid 13 return justified his effort.

A week earlier Morris had represented Reading in the Premier League Riders Championship, another sign that he was finally realising his potential. In the end-of-season rankings Morris's efforts yielded the 13th highest away average in league matches. Morris finished the year with the Reading website rider of the year award. The Andy Fuller Award for the most improved rider passed from Phil to Paul Clews.

Castagna reached the completion of Reading's official fixtures without a single maximum, but still carried a healthy average that put him in the league's top ten. He won the Italian Championship for the first time since 1995 bringing his tally to 11 national titles. He announced his intention to return in 2001, but declared it would be his final year of competitive speedway.

Four of the seven riders who started the season in Racers colours survived for the whole season. While Castagna, Morris and Clews all received good end-of-term reports, the fourth – Marc Norris – failed to live up to expectations. Despite paid 11 in the final home match he still ended with an average of less than 4, fractionally down on the previous year.

Reading entered a team in the Southern Junior League. They won two out of six matches, finishing third out of four. Riders featuring in the team included Steve Targett, Matthew Tutton, Jessica Lamb, David Haddock and Dan Warwick.

The lights went out at the end of the season with a challenge against Newport (October 1). The air of dereliction that hung over Smallmead accelerated as the season wore on. At the final meeting a substantial number of track lights were out, even replacing the bulbs appeared to be too much effort.

This state of affairs wasn't entirely negative. After a year of speculation, none of which left anyone better informed about the stadium's future, repairs were being deferred in expectation of a redevelopment of the existing stadium. With new partners (on the greyhound side) waiting in the wings to rebuild the stadium, negotiations with Reading Borough Council crept forward.

The new dual carriageway had opened up the land to redevelopment. Thames Water were building a new sewerage treatment works, with the aim of getting rid of the 'Whitley whiff' once and for all. Commercial developers moved in, notably the Prudential owners of Green Park, and the land Smallmead stadium stood on looked ripe for re-development. With three landowners (Thames Water, Prudential and the council) the situation was complex and with local government not noted for its speed the situation seemed bogged down.

Pat Bliss and brother Martyn Dore (the Smallmead stadium manager) attempted to use lease renegotiations[72] to push the council into making a decision. A stream of press releases indicated their increasing frustration, but then in October the council publicly floated the suggestion that relocation to a brand new stadium was the way forward.

A somewhat grander stadium reached the end of the line later in the month. Wembley signed off with a football friendly (result: England 0, Germany 1) before demolition in December. Due for completion in 2003, its replacement finally opened in 2007. As a speedway venue the old stadium had been home to many fine occasions: Lloyd Goffe's World Final appearance, the controversial Michanek-Collins clash, Dave Jessup's mechanical nightmare and Penhall's sublime win in speedway's final appearance at the Twin Towers.

Team: Armando Castagna 8.88, Phil Morris 8.44, Per Wester 6.96, Paul Clews 6.25, Krister Marsh 5.61, (Dave Mullett 4.39), Shane Colvin 3.93, Marc Norris 3.61, Lee Herne 2.67

---

72 Although originally granted a 99-year lease, at some time in the previous decade the bulk of this period was surrendered to the council and replaced with a shorter lease.

2001 – A Cause For Optimism

Speedway's mini-boom continued. The sport enjoyed a good year at both international and British levels. At Reading too, the recovery from two wooden spoons began.

It was undoubtedly a better year, but it ended up as the season of near misses and 'if onlys'.

If only Charlie Gjedde hadn't touched the tapes at Workington, Reading could have captured the Premier League Pairs Championship. After a barnstorming display in the qualifying heats Reading went out in the semi-final after Gjedde's misfortune. With Phil Morris only dropping one point in five rides the Racers pair provided a real threat to the home winners.

The Premier Trophy started the season, and Racers topped the Southern group with two matches to ride. If only they hadn't lost at home to the Isle of Wight. Ray Morton hit his old club with a 17-point haul as the Islanders won 46-44. A draw would have been enough to see Racers through instead of the Islanders.

After eliminating Arena Essex in the first round of the cup, Reading faced Exeter in July. They were eliminated by just 2 points, largely due to poor returns from the reserve berth. If only they'd managed a couple of points more. Incidentally anyone choosing to give the home leg a miss could have watched a brand new television show – 'The Office' – starring Redingensian Ricky Gervais.

Exeter also cost Reading a place in the league's top eight, and entry into the Young Shield. An August Bank Holiday win at Smallmead from the traditionally poor travellers came as a surprise. A paid dozen from ex-Racer Krister Marsh, occupying a Falcons reserve berth, did the damage. If only Racers had won, then they would have finished seventh and Exeter would have been the team missing out on the Young Shield.

Reading would have been much closer to the top if it wasn't for the biggest disaster of the season. If only Paul Clews hadn't been injured. It is often easier to cover the loss of high-scoring number ones than that of second strings. In this case the record shows the impact of Clews's loss. With Clews the Racers won twice and drew once away from home and were unbeaten at Smallmead. Without him they lost three times at home with only an away win at wooden spoonists Newport to compensate.

Despite averaging over 7 Clews sat fifth in the Racers averages. Earlier in the season he achieved a hat-trick of home maximums – three in a row. At Sheffield in July he celebrated his birthday by topping the Reading score chart. Unfortunately he picked up a thumb injury in his last ride that would keep him out for two months.

With weak reserves, rider replacement wasn't an attractive proposition and Reading's management sought a replacement. If only they hadn't found Brendon Mackay! The young Aussie came from Northern Territory, not the strongest speedway outpost but his performances in the Australian Under-21 Championship made him a possible candidate. After receiving a work permit in double-quick time (ironic given events just a few months later) Mackay made a pointless debut. In the space of a month he made 11 appearances, averaging 0.94. All but one of the points he scored came from beating non-finishers. Tom Brown, a rider with a Conference League average below 6, provided Mackay with his sole won point.

If only Per Wester's employer had looked kindly on the Swede's request for time off to resume his Racers career. Clews had improved so much that Wester would come in on a lower average than Clews, and this made him an ideal replacement. A deal was done, in principle, but Wester couldn't reach an accommodation with his employer.

Clews eventually returned to the Racers line-up and in his first match back a paid 9 contribution enabled Reading to draw at Arena Essex. The combination of poor gating and an abundance of passing made him an exciting rider to watch. The award of the Andy Fuller

Shield (for the second time in a row) came as no surprise.

Clews's spell on the injured list exposed Reading's weakness at reserve. If only Shane Colvin and Marc Norris had stayed and fulfilled their potential. Instead both left the club abruptly without warning. Colvin did have one good pay night (paid 13 against Trelawny) and carried a respectable average (5.38). But although Norris rode in the British Under-21 Championship Final he still couldn't lift his average over 4.

Norris went first in late April. He quit his job with Chalfont Coaches (owned by Chris Shears) and left the club, further enhancing his reputation for being difficult to deal with. Norris left the sport, although he made a brief re-appearance in the Conference League with Wimbledon three years later, but was soon in trouble again. Colvin followed in June, but unlike Norris he hoped for a new team.

Chris Schramm, still only 16, had little experience at Premier League level, but clearly possessed potential. He became popular on the terraces and despite failing to maintain a 3-point average (due to a late-season dip in form) many hoped to see him return in 2002. Tommy Palmer (aged 30) was a journeyman recently dropped by struggling Newport. His spell in Racers colours was largely forgettable.

With Colvin and Norris departing, Racers looked overly reliant on loaned riders. Schramm (Peterborough), Clews[73] (Coventry), Gjedde (Swindon) and Palmer were not Reading assets, while Castagna and Mullett were reaching the end of their careers. That just left Phil Morris as the only asset with a long-term future. Chris Shears (who had joined the management team, but not in the capacity of promoter) contributed to a more active team-building strategy. For example Kim Jansson (yes another Swede) was given a try out in 2001's end-of-season pairs meeting.

Beauty and the Beast – Racers mascot Roary the Lion gets friendly with Charlie Gjedde. (BT)

The 2001 team was assembled in a more professional way than in many previous winters. Five of the previous year's team returned and were signed up fairly quickly – Mullett, Castagna, Morris, Clews and Norris. An active search for another heat leader threw up the names of Andrew Appleton and Scott Swain, before Charlie Gjedde signed. After two years in the Elite League a pre-season car accident resulted in him losing his team place at Wolverhampton in 2000. The last signing couldn't have an average much over 4 – after looking at David Mason the Reading management plumped for Shane Colvin.

Gjedde's season started well with three maximums in April, but he suffered a slump in

73 Clews was subsequently purchased from Coventry.

June. He missed a few matches due to international commitments (including a call up for Denmark's World Cup squad). His best performances both came at Swindon (18 in the Premier Trophy and paid 18 in the league fixture). The perception that he wasn't a team man meant that his return to Swindon at the end of the year surprised nobody.

Castagna just pipped Gjedde for number one spot in the averages. Having announced his plans for retirement, Castagna celebrated his career with a testimonial at Reading and a 'Castagna day' at Lonigo. He reached the final of his testimonial but finished behind Jason Crump, Phil Morris and Steve Johnston (unbeaten in the heats). The Italian meeting suffered from rain; Castagna did slightly better coming third to Sam Ermolenko and Billy Hamill. Racers duo Morris and Palmer joined in the festivities.

Armando enjoyed his visits to Trelawny, establishing a new track record on his first visit, and lowering it again on his next trip to Cornwall. Castagna retained his Italian Championship, making it his 12th and last national title. Coincidentally the same number of national championships as Czech Racer Jiri Stancl achieved. On current form, it is possible Matej Zagar may reach a similar tally of Slovenian Championships.

Phil Morris's career continued to develop. After a couple of weeks on the sidelines in August he returned with double-figure returns in all his last seven matches. He expanded his horizons by signing for Swedish side Getingarna – a move provocatively announced on the Reading website with the headline "Phil is a Wasp". There was much relief when on reading the story it became apparent that he had signed for Getingarna Wasps in Sweden, not his local team the Newport Wasps.

Farmer Dave Mullett completed a powerful top five. As hoped, he massively outscored his false starting average. He lifted his starting average (4.39) to nearly 7 in the early season Premier Trophy and in league matches only came in at over 8. An early-season scare when the foot-and-mouth outbreak threatened his availability melted away and in September he staged his double testimonial meeting. Only Barry Thomas (Hackney) and Michael Coles (Exeter) can make a similar claim. Racers favourites past and present filled the top four places: Lee Richardson, Jeremy Doncaster, Morris and Castagna.

Racers tracked a good team. Although they only won three away matches (at the teams who occupied the bottom three positions in the final table), they never dropped below 35 points on their travels. Glasgow (where Schramm was a match winner), newcomers Trelawny and Newport (an 18-point win without Clews) provided Reading with the taste of away success.

At home Reading chalked up three massive wins: 64-26 v Exeter (trophy), 68-22 v Trelawny (trophy) and 63-27 v Trelawny (league).

League champions Newcastle were one of the three teams to take the league points away from Smallmead. The five major trophies were shared around: the trophy went to Sheffield, the cup Hull, the Young Shield ended up on the Isle of Wight and Workington were victorious in the fours. If only Lady Luck had been kinder to the Racers, their name could have been on at least one of the trophies.

In October, Tim Sugar announced his retirement for the second time. In the same week Greg Hancock won the Grand Prix Challenge to retain his GP place after a poor year. The major development for the Grand Prix in 2001 was the introduction of Cardiff's Millennium stadium to the race schedule[74].

The other big development in world speedway came from the revamp of the World Team Cup. Relaunched as the World Cup it consisted of five meetings in seven days, all in Poland. The final two meetings produced some of the best speedway ever seen. An injury ravaged

74 Given that BSI always have an eye on the bottom line, the suggestion that Phil Morris should get the wild card, as speedway's leading Welshman, received an airing. Stranger decisions have been made.

England fought valiantly but missed out on a final place after Greg Hancock (the star of the meeting) beat Mark Loram in a run-off. In the final, Poland went into the last heat one ahead of Australia. When Pole Jacek Krzyzaniak fell, referee Tony Steele made the bravest decision of his career and excluded the Pole, much to the anger of the partisan Wroclaw crowd. With the aid of five-rider races and the 'tactical joker' (both controversial innovations) Tomasz Gollob scored 27 points (4, 3, 8, 4, 4, 4).

Poland provided the big headline in the Elite League, relatively unknown Krzysztof Cegielski's British debut season made an impact not seen since Bruce Penhall over 20 years before.

Peterborough hosted the World Under-21 Final. The Poles dominated with seven contestants (plus Polish-born Canadian Chris Slabon). Poland's David Kuwaja was the surprise winner, and Matej Zagar came sixth in his first British appearance. Zagar could only make the reserve berth in the European Under-19 Championship, but one rider who qualified was Danish Under-21 champion Sabrina Bogh.

Reading Ravens competed in the 2001 Southern Junior League. Line-up left to right: Andre Cross, Steve Targett, Dan Warwick (on bike), Mick Hester (manager), Matthew Tutton and Jessica Lamb. (BT)

Reading entered a team in the Southern Junior League, and they too had a female flavour. Jessica Lamb was one of five riders who rode regularly for the junior team. Dan Warwick headed the list of point scorers as the team finished fourth in the five-team league.

The year ended on an optimistic note: at international level with plans to expand the Grand Prix to ten rounds including a trip to Australia; at domestic level with the intention of Rye House and Somerset to join the Premier League and plans for new tracks in the Conference League at Carmarthen and Wimbledon; at Reading with the revelation of Island Road as the site for a new stadium.

Team: Armando Castagna 9.05, Charlie Gjedde 8.94, Phil Morris 8.42, Dave Mullett 7.77, Paul Clews 7.39, Shane Colvin 5.38, Tommy Palmer 3.51, Chris Schramm 2.82, Brendon Mackay 0.94

2002 – Dave Mullett Bids Farewell

On July 22 Dave Mullett lined up against Workington at number one. The meeting is best remembered for a bout of fisticuffs that resulted in Carl Stonehewer receiving a £1,000 fine and four-match ban (both suspended) after an attack on Reading's Anders Henriksson. The lasting significance of this match is that it marked the night Jan Andersson's name was removed from the record books. His 544 appearances (in official matches) surpassed the previous record holder (Bernie Leigh) by over a hundred.

On that night, Mullett made his 545th appearance as his Racers career drew to a close. Before the year started Mullett made it clear that 2002 would be his swansong. Dave had a fine final season, away from home he topped the Racers averages, and he bowed out by winning the final meeting of the year – the Winged Wheel Pairs (partnered by Chris Schramm).

Mullett first rode for Reading in September 1985, and after a couple of years as their number eight moved up full-time from National League Canterbury – his only other team in a 22-year career. His final tally of 561 appearances for Reading yielding 4,766 points (including bonus), puts him second in the list of Racers point scorers. That record is one that Jan Andersson still possesses. Mullett heads the bonus-point chart and at the time was the highest point scorer for Reading at Division Two level. That record has since passed to Phil Morris.

7 October 2002 – Martyn Dore (stadium manager and brother of Pat Bliss) presents Dave Mullett (left) and Chris Schramm (right) with the Winged Wheel Pairs Trophy. This victory marked the end of Mullett's career. (BT)

Mullett's career included five British Final appearances (1993's Overseas Final being his best year in the World Championship), several Divisional Riders Championship appearances and England international appearances. However, it is Dave's role as a team man that will mark him down as a Racers great. The unassuming Racer rode in three championship winning teams (1990, 1992 and 1997). As a reserve he was a hero of the 1990 cup final victory and in 1997 as number one he posted the highest average in the whole league. In between he featured in the legendary opening heat partnership with Per Jonsson that provided the foundation for 1992's title success.

Another member of the 1990 side hung up his leathers in 2002. When Kim Jansson replaced Jeremy Doncaster in the Ipswich side at the end of August, it marked the end of a career that started in 1982. His five (and a bit) seasons at Smallmead were the only part of his career that wasn't spent in Suffolk.

Although sad to see Mullett's retirement, the mood at Smallmead was more buoyant than it had been for sometime. With Reading Council publicly committed to a new stadium, and the likely site revealed, the prospects for the future looked positive. Allied Presentations unveiled in January that Gaming International were the company lined-up to fund the redevelopment. The owners of Swindon and Poole stadiums had already invested a substantial amount at Poole. Martyn Dore continued to manage on the greyhound side while Pat Bliss remained speedway promoter.

At the time it was hoped that the new stadium could be ready by 2003, although by the end of the year the target date had already slipped to 2005. In the meantime Gaming International set about making a few superficial improvements to keep the stadium going. These included a new turnstile area and new floodlights. However, Gaming International's most noticeable change sparked the 'great food rebellion'. In June, security guards strictly enforced a new policy that spectators could not bring any food or drink into any area of the stadium. Dave Wright wrote in the *Evening Post:*

> *"Even a woman carrying sweets for team mascot Roary*[75] *to distribute among the kids during the meeting was stopped. She was allowed to take them in but was warned by the guard he may not be so lenient next week. In all my 20 years*[76] *of following the sport I have never known Racers fans to be so uptight as they are this week".*

Threats of demonstrations, boycotts, and sponsorship withdrawal soon resulted in a climb-down.

Although Pat Bliss continued as promoter, Chris Shears's profile grew. Although not credited in the programme as promoter, he played a significant role and was often credited as co-promoter when speaking on Reading's behalf.

In a further change Nick Dyer and Pat Bliss shared the team manager's role. Bliss did away matches while Dyer took on home meetings. Like his predecessor Tim Sugar, Dyer was a die-hard Reading fan who knew his way round the rulebook and had graduated from programme contributor to team manager.

The optimism at Smallmead in the spring was shared by *Speedway Star* which celebrated its 50th birthday. Hopes for the new season were high, but by the end of the year the mini-boom had bust. In the Grand Prix, early leader Ryan Sullivan faded leaving Tony Rickardsson already crowned champion when the circus set off for Australia. It contributed to the huge financial loss (reportedly over £300,000) suffered by the Aussie promoters. The World Cup came to Britain, rain and Britain's failure to reach the final took the edge off the event. Reports of clubs in financial trouble once again featured in the *Speedway Star* and Britain experienced its first racing fatality in nine years – King's Lynn junior David Nix coming to grief in a Conference League match at Saddlebow Road. Laurence Hare, a popular and entertaining rider also suffered permanent injury.

Sky television's money had financed the mini-boom, but the expansion of the Grand Prix and the allure of armchair viewing meant the squeezing of gate revenues. Elite League

---

75 Roary the Lion, the *Evening Post* mascot, first appeared at Smallmead in 2001. In case you are wondering how a Lion gets to be a mascot for the Racers, the answer lies in Afghanistan. The iconic Maiwand Lion statue in Forbury Gardens is used by the *Evening Post* (and Reading FC) as a symbol of the town. It commemorates the 328 soldiers of the 66th Berkshire Regiment who lost their lives in 1880 at the battle of Maiwand during one of Britain's many ill-advised military interventions in Afghanistan.

76 Dave was reporting on the Racers when Smallmead opened in 1975, making 20 years a bit of an underestimate!

promoters attempted to mitigate the problem by restricting the number of GP riders that teams could field. The highest profile casualties – Greg Hancock and Todd Wiltshire – survived without a British team. For the fourth year in a row Elite League fixtures weren't completed and barely a dozen British riders featured regularly in the top league.

The big innovation of the season – the introduction of play-offs for the Elite League title – ended in controversy when Coventry travelled to Wolverhampton (racing on an off-night to accommodate Sky) without three Americans because of a clash with the American Championship. Wolverhampton progressed to the final where they beat table toppers Eastbourne.

The Conference League struggled to maintain credibility. The title was decided on October 30 at Stoke in a bizarre double header featuring Mildenhall, Peterborough, Sheffield and Newport. A young Peterborough team, spearheaded by Chris Schramm and Daniel King, came out on top. Wimbledon experienced a turbulent season on their return to speedway. Eleven years after Reading's Jeremy Doncaster won the final race at Plough Lane before closure, Glen Phillips (also of Reading) won the first race at the re-opening meeting. The Dons used 31 riders – including Justin Elkins who still hadn't sorted out his mechanical demons. When he returned to Smallmead with the Dons for a Conference level challenge against Reading Ravens he packed up three times!

The new venue at Carmarthen provided Conference League berths for no less than four riders with Reading connections. Matthew Cross (a member of the 1994 Reading team), Shane Colvin, Peter Collyer and Stuart Williams all appeared in the Dragons team. Williams returned to speedway after a 16-year break and joined Collyer and Colvin in the Reading back-up squad.

The Racers needed plenty of back-up in 2002. The phrase 'injury ravaged' immediately springs to mind when attempting to describe Reading's season. Every single one of Reading's starting line-up spent a portion of the season on the injury list.

They lost their first rider before the team even reached the tapes for the first match. In an unheard-of development Reading were able to announce a complete team before Christmas. Five riders returned. Morris, Clews, Schramm and Mullett were all expected, but the retention of Brendon Mackay was regarded as a bit of a gamble. At least this time he would start at reserve.

The gaps left by Castagna's retirement and Gjedde's return to Swindon were filled by riders that had proven track records. Jason Bunyan (on loan from Poole) and Tomas Topinka (a King's Lynn asset) had both found the Elite League tough going the previous year and were attracted by the opportunity of a Premier League team berth.

Topinka made his British debut in 1993 for King's Lynn and rode in the top division every year up to 1999 when he averaged nearly 6.5 points for Ipswich and King's Lynn. After missing 2000 he made a brief return to the Elite League in 2001 averaging 4.74 for Belle Vue. This gave him an average that made him an attractive proposition to a Premier League team looking for a new number one. But it also meant that he fell below the 5-point threshold required for a work permit. Given the element of discretion that had seen several other riders just below the cut-off receiving permits and Topinka's previous record, few anticipated any problem.

At the end of February the Department of Employment turned down Topinka's application. Reading immediately lodged an appeal, but within a week signed a replacement. After five seasons at Newport (including two years as their number one) Anders Henriksson had decided to give Britain a miss. As a result he was slightly under prepared, but still looked capable of filling the gap.

In March, Topinka's work permit appeal fell on deaf ears, but by the end of April the Czech had a work permit to ride for Elite League Coventry! After a reasonable year at

Coventry, Topinka returned to King's Lynn. Five high scoring seasons for the Stars in the Premier League followed. He would have been an excellent number one for the Racers and his removal from the Reading team sheet left them as the weakest team in the league on paper, with a combined average 1.5 points below the limit.

Then the season started and the Racers began to fall – literally. First to go down was Brendon Mackay. Paid 5 and a race win in a challenge at Newport suggested that Mackay might repay the faith shown by the Reading management. In the following day's return leg Mackay broke his arm. By the end of May, Mackay was practising after the meeting, but he never regained his team place. He rode in a few meetings at Somerset in the autumn and the following year appeared for Trelawny in the Conference Trophy averaging 7.

Glen Phillips, a tall 19-year-old, was snapped up before the end of the week. After being left without a team place he quickly established himself as a solid performer. He reserved his best performance (paid 12) for the visit of his former team – the Isle of Wight. Although nearly dropped after a mid-season dip in form he only missed one official match all year. That came at the beginning of July when he toured Sweden with the England under-21 team.

Phillips's reserve partner Chris Schramm became the next injury victim. A damaged wrist at the start of May put him on the disabled list for two months. After scoring paid 8 as a Conference League stand-in, Gavin Hedge was signed to cover for Schramm. Son of 1970 world finalist Trevor Hedge, Gavin started his career quite late and at the age of 31 had yet to establish himself as a Premier League regular.

Reading were grateful for Hedge's efforts, but he once again concentrated on his Conference League commitments as soon as Schramm recovered. Schramm lifted his average from below 3 to over 4 and his efforts earned him the Andy Fuller Shield for the most-improved Racer.

On June 24, the last match before Schramm's return, the injury jinx paid another visit. In a disastrous first race at Newcastle Bunyan (shoulder) and Mullett (ankle) both sustained injuries. Mullett was fit enough to resume racing the following Monday, but Bunyan was expected to be out for 12 weeks. Effectively Bunyan's season was over.

Bunyan's career started with spells as mascot at Milton Keynes and Peterborough. On turning 16 he won a team spot at Poole. He struggled and his career never quite took off. His aggressive style made him an exciting rider to watch but also an injury prone one. After three years at Ipswich he settled in well at Smallmead, easily outscoring his opening average and proving a gregarious team member.

Shears and Bliss quickly found a replacement for Bunyan. Ambitious Andrew Appleton had surprised many with his decision to go Elite in 2001. Although he ended the year with a league champions medal, he had failed to hit a 3-point average at Oxford. He continued to struggle in 2002 and just two days after asking for a move, Appleton signed for Reading (on loan from parent club Newport).

Born in Burghfield (18 June 1982) Appleton had the potential to be the best Berkshire-born speedway rider since Lloyd Goffe. Astute watchers of the speedway scene such as Nick Dyer had long championed Appleton and regarded his signing as very overdue.

He arrived at Smallmead as the New Zealand champion (beating ex-Racer Nathan Murray in a run-off). His impact was immediate and immense. Against Stoke Appleton dropped just a single point in six rides, and won the last-heat decider. With rider replacement (for Paul Clews) and Mullett crashing out of the meeting in heat 1 (again) Racers were really up against it. Appleton and Schramm (paid 11) saved the day.

He continued to score heavily. In four days at the end of August he ran up 64 points in four matches, and finished the season with maximums in his last two league matches at Smallmead.

By replacing Bunyan (starting green sheet 5.60, actual average 6.82) with Appleton (final average 8.95) the Reading management saved the season.

By the time Appleton arrived, Paul Clews was sidelined by injury. He reached double figures in three of his first five home matches but only managed to repeat that feat once during the rest of the season. His two weeks out with an arm injury just added to the disappointment of his season, which saw his average drop by over a point.

Henriksson was sidelined twice; he damaged a thumb against Trelawny and suffered a concussion riding in Sweden. Three of his four lowest scores came in September after his second spell out of action. Prior to this he had been a consistent and entertaining contributor to the Racers effort without pulling up any trees. Without him, Reading's season would have been fatally holed by the loss of Topinka; with him the Racers ship continued to float.

August marked Phil Morris's turn to fall under the spell of the injury jinx. He came away from Newport with bruising to the back and kidneys, and aggravated the injury with another fall on his return to the track in Sweden. This did not prevent Morris from experiencing the best summer of his career. In mid-July he sat in second place in the league averages (ahead of Grand Prix rider Carl Stonehewer). In September he climbed onto the rostrum at the Premier League Riders Championship after finishing third to Adam Shields and Craig Watson. Then in October he made his first (and as it turned out, only) British Final appearance finishing a respectable tenth.

Dave Mullett reached the August Bank Holiday with only one match missed, and that was due to an off-track injury. But at Exeter he became the seventh and final member of the starting septet to be struck down by the injury hoodoo. Mullett missed five matches after aggravating a back injury at Exeter in the traditional holiday morning fixture.

Andrew Appleton receives the rider of the month award for August 2002.On the left is Reading webmeister Andy Povey, and there are no prizes for guessing who John Alexander is supporting! (BT)

His absence left Racers woefully understaffed for the evening return. With Morris and Henriksson already out, and an extensive Bank Holiday programme, Reading couldn't find a guest. After approaching over 30 riders, the Racers ended up with former reserve Shane Colvin, recently discarded by Workington after scoring just 14 points in nine matches. His return had a happy ending: riding at number one he became the match-winning hero, opening with two race wins on the way to an 8-point haul.

Despite all the injuries, Reading's end-of-term report showed better results than the previous year. An away win at Isle of Wight (where Glen Phillips got paid 10 on his former track) ensured Reading topped their group and reached the Premier Trophy semi-final. There they lost out to Trelawny after a disappointing display in the home leg. In the final Trelawny defeated Sheffield in the battle of the Tigers and thus restricted Sheffield to just three trophies (the league, cup and Young Shield)!

Reading got to compete in the Young Shield after finishing one place higher than the previous year. At the end of June only race points kept Reading off the bottom, and only a late spurt after riding seven matches in 11 days to complete their schedule before the cut-off date allowed them to scrape inside the top eight. The crucial meeting came at home to Arena Essex when, after a night of brilliant racing, Reading salvaged the bonus point after a 54-36 win and a run-off. Appleton beat Hammers number one Leigh Lanham in three consecutive races: heats 14, 15 and the bonus point run-off.

The late run also featured an away win (only the second of the league campaign) at Workington. In a classic match Racers came from 39-29 down to win 47-45. Three late 5-1s (all featuring Phil Morris) and 17 points from Andrew Appleton were the key to Reading's unexpected victory.

The previous away win came from Reading's second visit to Cornwall. Morris top scored and won the last-heat decider, just a week after Trelawny demolished Sheffield in the first leg of the Premier Trophy Final.

At home Racers only failed to take the league points once. An early-season loss to the Isle of Wight could be put down to the absence of Dave Mullett and a first-race crash that put Phil Morris out of the meeting. The feature that characterised Reading's league itinerary was the closeness of most of their matches. Out of 34 league matches no less than 15 were decided by 6 points or less. For every near miss on the road there was a narrow escape at Smallmead.

Having reached the Young Shield, Reading failed to surmount the first hurdle. Racers official season ended acrimoniously at Smallbrook when the referee called off the second leg with the tie delicately poised at 82-80 to the Isle of Wight. Reading had called for an abandonment earlier in the meeting (when still ahead on aggregate), but the referee insisted on soldiering on until heat 12 when he called off the meeting after a track inspection at the request of the Islanders.

Life without Dave Mullett was about to begin. The announcement of the first two signings for next year (Phil Morris and Shane Colvin) before the Young Shield tie signalled that the Racers meant business.

Team: Andrew Appleton 8.95, Phil Morris 8.68, Dave Mullett 8.56, Anders Henriksson 7.54, Jason Bunyan 6.82, Paul Clews 5.96, Chris Schramm 4.32, Glen Phillips 4.29, Gavin Hedge 2.97

2003 – Welcome to Euphony and Janusz

Pat Bliss described it as: "the season from hell"; co-promoter Chris Shears came up with an even snappier summary: "crap!"

The close season gave no hint of what was to follow. The Premier League expanded to 18 teams as King's Lynn dropped down from the Elite League. No winter would be complete without some questionable innovations coming out of the Promoters' Conference, and this winter gave us green helmets (instead of white) and the 'tactical joker'. Subsequently renamed 'tactical ride', the tactical joker would be restricted to Premier League cup matches, where a team 8 points down could nominate a programmed rider (without handicap) who would score double points. The points limit stayed at 45 and Racers team building progressed to the point where they could name five riders before Christmas.

The early signings of Morris and Colvin were followed by confirmation that Paul Clews and Andrew Appleton would be returning. The fifth signing was a brand new name from Sweden.

Jonas Davidsson already had an impressive pedigree stretching back to 1997, when aged just 13 he won the Swedish 80cc title. Brother Daniel, Peter Ljung and Fredrik Lindgren were among his rivals that day. At 16 he qualified for his first European Under-19 Final and in 2002 was an ever-present in the Swedish Elite League for Rospiggarna. Davidsson's presence in the team provided concrete evidence that Reading were attempting to replenish their asset base and looking to the future.

Both Chris Schramm and Jason Bunyan remained in the frame for a team place. Enquiries to Peterborough about purchasing Schramm yielded an exorbitant price tag that frightened Reading off and he ended up on loan to Newport. Bunyan made an unexpected return to the Elite League at Coventry.

The final two slots in the line-up were filled by an unlikely pair. Scott Smith, an Australian with two years' experience at Newport (not to be confused with Scott Smith – an experienced Yorkshireman mainly associated with Cradley and Sheffield) and Stuart Williams would don the winged wheel.

In Williams's case this would be a mere 17 years after being named for the 1986 team. On that occasion a falling out resulted in his being dropped at the last hour. Shortly afterwards he drifted out of the sport and after successfully establishing himself in the engineering business took up the sport once more. At the age of 37 he re-emerged in the Conference League during 2002. His comeback looked doomed when in the autumn a traffic accident resulted in fatal injuries to Somerset junior Paul Gladwyn and hospitalisation for Williams. Contrary to initial expectations he made a quick recovery and won the chance to finally establish himself as a Racer.

Reading entered the season with a new team manager; Ivan Shears (son of Chris) had deputised on a few occasions the previous year – notably at Workington where his astute management contributed to a dramatic win.

The pre-season preparations were completed by the news that Euphony, a Reading-based telecommunications company owned by Racers fan Dave Faithful would sponsor the team. Not since the ban on alcohol sponsorship put an end to the 'XXXX Racers' in 1991 had the team been in such a favoured position.

Racers warmed up with the M4 Trophy, a tournament between Reading, Swindon and Newport. An opening win at Newport provided an encouraging start with Scott Smith looking like a good signing. On the downside Phil Morris hit the deck and missed the return leg 24 hours later. Racers could only draw the return fixture, a meeting marred by an injury to Stuart Williams. By the time he regained fitness he no longer had a team place. He briefly resurfaced at Newport, but once again fate had conspired against him.

Before Swindon could provide the next opposition the hubristically named 'operation shock and awe' signalled the start of the Iraq war. The Swindon encounter yielded another draw, and a third double-figure score for reserve Shane Colvin.

The Premier Trophy had been replaced by the British League Cup. It embraced all Elite and Premier League teams in a single competition. While a laudable idea in principle it proved to be an unworkable mess. Complex and inconsistent rules on rider eligibility undermined a competition that limped to completion. The omission of Arena Essex from the knock-out stages further damaged its credibility. The Hammers finished top of their group but had failed to win enough matches before the cut-off date.

The Racers failed to win a single one of their eight fixtures, a draw at home to Swindon in June was all they could manage. In the first match Andrew Appleton beat Mark Loram on the way to a 17-point haul as Eastbourne chalked up a comfortable win by a 51-42 margin.

Daniel King, signed to replace Williams, made his debut against Arena Essex in the first league encounter of the Smallmead programme. The match produced a 46-44 home win as maximum-man Appleton and Morris delivered a 5-1 in the final race. King settled in very quickly and registered double figures in his third match (at Newport on April 20).

A damaged knee in the Newport fixture marked the end of Morris's season in Britain. The Welsh skipper did recover sufficiently to make a comeback in June for his Swedish club Lejonen. It turned out disastrously as a cruciate ligament injury picked up in his first and only ride left him with his right knee in plaster. And that finished his season after just four league matches for Reading.

Appleton was the star of the comeback of the season as Hull were beaten 50-40 at Smallmead from 36-30 down. He scored 17 points. His overall form provided some cheer. Appleton finished fourth in the British Under-21 Championship (a meeting that Colvin and Daniel King also contested) and went on to reach the World Under-21 semi-finals. In contrast Clews, Colvin, Davidsson and Smith were all failing to live up to expectations.

Trelawny fielded a powerful spearhead of English star Chris Harris and first-season sensation Matej Zagar. They demolished Reading when the teams met in the cup during May. Racers couldn't provide a single race winner in the 65-30 second leg defeat in Cornwall.

May also marked Todd Wiltshire's first competitive meeting at Smallmead for 12 years. After an easy League Cup maximum, the Oxford star chose Smallmead to announce his plans to retire at the end of the year. A few days later Oxford became the subject of ridicule when they tracked Grand Prix veteran Andy Smith in a Conference League fixture.

Two home league defeats provided concrete evidence that Racers were struggling, although the month ended with the only away league win of the year. However, the 46-44 win at Stoke came from a team that included guests Danny Bird (15), Chris Mills (9+2) and Jason Bunyan. Unusually Smith and Clews both returned good scores too. Morris and Colvin were injured, while Appleton competed in the World Longtrack Final and Davidsson was qualifying for the World Under-21 Final. Racers climbed to 13th in the 18 team league.

Colvin became the latest addition to the injury list in the League Cup encounter at home to Swindon (June 23). Although Racers could only manage a draw, the match marked one of the few bright spots of the year. Signed on a one-match trial, little known Pole Janusz Kolodziej won the hearts of Racers fans with an exciting display that included a win in the deciding heat.

King meanwhile found transport a difficulty. Still only 16, he relied on his father who also provided support for Daniel's brother Jason, an Arena Essex rider. In July King left Reading, and (after a two-week ban for withholding his services) signed for Arena.

King's departure gave more opportunities to Joel Parsons, an Aussie junior who acquitted himself well in Racers colours.

King made a very quick return to Smallmead, appearing for England in an under-21 Test match against Sweden. Tony Olsson returned to his old track with a team including Antonio Lindback, Freddie Lindgren, Peter Ljung, Jonas Davidsson and brother Daniel. After a last-heat decider England won by 8 points. Ollie Allen (15) and Andrew Appleton (10+3) top scored.

7 July 2003 – Sweden under-21 are beaten 49-41 by their British counterparts. On the back row left to right: Fredrik Lindgren, Antonio Lindback, former Racer Tony Olsson (team manager), Peter Ljung, Daniel Davidsson. And at the front: Eric Andersson, Mattias Nilsson and Jonas Davidsson. (BT)

Two more home defeats followed before the month was over – to Newcastle and Berwick. The Bandits victory can be attributed to the phenomenal performance from reserve Josef Franc who stormed to a paid 19 tally. In between these two matches Danny Norton joined the team as a replacement for King.

Norton's statistics tell a very stark story: 19 matches, 60 rides, no wins and one second for a 1.27 average.

The death of Lord Shawcross in July (at the age of 101) provided an opportunity to reminisce about the golden era of British speedway. Shawcross was chief prosecutor in the Nuremberg war crimes trials, but in speedway circles he is remembered for his report in 1964 which ushered in the third golden era of British speedway. It proposed the formation of the British League, and within four years a second division was up and running, and the Reading Racers story had begun.

By 2003 it was hard to remember what such an atmosphere of optimism felt like. There was precious little of it to be found at Smallmead that year. The exception to the general mood was the signing of Janusz Kolodziej. News that a work permit had been received in late July led to speculation about whom he would replace.

Scott Smith drew the short straw. He bowed out in the Berwick match with a modest paid 4 score. His disappointing form, mechanical problems and (it appeared) lack of motivation had become too much for management to put up with. Smith moved on to Stoke where his potential remained unfulfilled, and the direction of his subsequent career was mainly downwards.

Nick Dyer heralded Kolodziej's arrival with the caution that: "I don't think he'll average anywhere near his (assessed) 9 points a meeting[77]". Between signing and making his league debut Kolodziej won the Polish Bronze Helmet (a competition for riders under 19), the best result of his career to date.

His debut against Sheffield (August 4) heralded 15 days of magic. Although Sheffield went on to finish runners-up to Edinburgh in the league, they lost at Smallmead. Four unbeaten rides from Kolodziej before a last-heat fall were a major factor in the defeat of the Tigers.

All six of Kolodziej's appearances produced a double-figure score including 17 at Berwick. Racers fans marvelled at Kolodziej's exciting style, and the variety of lines he used as he explored every opportunity to pass his opponents.

It soon became clear that dealing with Tarnow, Kolodziej's Polish club, would be a difficult challenge. His many Polish and international commitments meant that Reading decided to let him go. It was with great reluctance, and the hope that he would return remained strong.

Janusz Kolodziej's brief spell with Reading was the highlight of a traumatic 2003 season. (BT)

Results over the remainder of the season further boosted Kolodziej's reputation. Silver medals in the European Under-19 Championship and the Polish Silver Helmet indicated that he could compete with the best young riders in Europe. The top four from the European Under-19 Championship read: Bjerre, Kolodziej, Lindback, Lindgren. Lower down the order another Pole, Krzystof Buczkowski, finished on 5 points.

While all eyes at Reading were focused on Kolodziej during August the wider speedway community looked towards Scandinavia. Pundits' predictions proved to be wide of the mark when Sweden won the World Cup in Denmark. Weakened by the absence of reigning World Champion Tony Rickardsson, the Swedes found an unlikely hero in Peter Ljung. His win in the penultimate heat gave Sweden the lead. Discarded by Eastbourne after scoring just a point in four Elite League matches, Ljung's performance in the World Cup caused a re-awakening of British interest in the rider.

Ljung followed this up with another good showing in the Scandinavian Grand Prix at the Ullevi stadium on August 30. The meeting should have been run the previous week, but due to poor track preparation it had to be abandoned. Racers legend Jan Andersson (in Peter Karlsson's corner of the pits that night) said: "You cannot send a crowd of nearly 30,000 people home early on a sunny evening like that. This will set the sport back years."

---

77 Few would have disagreed with his comments in the Reading programme. I wouldn't have. Newcomers who succeeded in reaching the 9-point average they were assessed with in their debut season were few and far between. Bjarne Pedersen at Newcastle in 2000 had been the last rider to do so. Matej Zagar managed it in 2003.

Between these two stagings, Ljung returned to Britain as a Reading Racer. Although Racers went down to Swindon a paid 14 return provided satisfaction to Ljung and to the Reading faithful. Next time Ljung put on the Reading race jacket 38 days had elapsed. Ljung's diary read as follows:

- 25/8 Reading debut
- 30/8 Grand Prix
- 31/8 burns injury picked up riding in Poland
- 9/9 rides in Sweden for Luxo Stars
- 13/9 World Under-21 Final – aggravates injury, scores 6 (the same as Jonas Davidsson)
- 27/9 wins Golden Ribbon at Pardubice
- 2/10 makes second Racers appearance, aggravates injury and pulls out after three rides.

During this period Colvin made a brief re-appearance, and a big row blew up over the non-appearance of Andrew Appleton. The meeting at Workington on September 20 fell victim to the weather, but Appleton had taken a grasstrack booking instead. He earned a £500 fine and considerable displeasure from sections of the Smallmead crowd. It didn't help that his form had dropped off. Ironically the exception came in the re-staging of the Workington match where his trip up north yielded paid 17 points.

Partial compensation came from an improvement in the form of Jonas Davidsson. After reaching double figures just once in the first half of the Racers programme, a further nine double-figure pay days followed in the remainder of the season. He signed off the year with 16+1 in a 44-all draw with King's Lynn. His improvement also gave him the Andy Fuller Shield.

Euphony's support as team sponsors proved to be substantial, and one of the few positives of 2003. The Euphony Classic at the end of September gave Racers fans a chance to see old favourite Armando Castagna. The four riders competing in the final all went on to become Bulldogs! They finished in the order: Charlie Gjedde, Travis McGowan, Danny Bird and Mark Lemon.

Three days earlier a defeat for Hull guaranteed them bottom spot in the league. Racers ended 16th out of 18 with only eight wins in 15 home matches. Racers used at least one guest in every match from 21 April onwards, mainly for Morris and Colvin. Guests made a combined total of 57 appearances, including eight from Paul Pickering and an astonishing fourteen by Garry Stead.

The constant use of guests, the loss of Colvin, Williams and above all Morris, made for a turbulent year. Poor form elsewhere in the team didn't help. Late arrivals Daniel King, Janusz Kolodziej and Peter Ljung ultimately brought disappointment as a result of their stays being all too brief.

While King and Ljung were just bit players in the Racers story, Kolodziej's brief stint not only illuminated an otherwise dark season, but provided a key component of future hopes for glory.

Team: (Janusz Kolodziej 8.95), Andrew Appleton 7.67, (Phil Morris 7.09), Jonas Davidsson 6.19, Scott Smith 5.80, Paul Clews 5.30, (Daniel King 4.32), Shane Colvin 4.25, Joel Parsons 3.79, Danny Norton 1.27

2004 – Phil and Danny: A Pair of Champions

From 1999 to 2003 Reading recorded only seven league victories away from Berkshire, but allowed the visitors to leave Smallmead with the league points on 24 occasions. After five years languishing among the also-rans the Racers rediscovered the higher reaches of the league.

Better results were accompanied by better crowds, optimism about the move to a new stadium and the substantial support of Euphony Communications whose sponsorship underpinned the Racers revival.

A Premier Trophy Final appearance at the start of August brought back memories of past glories. Five coach loads of Racers fans trekked down to Exeter (thanks to a subsidy from co-promoter Chris Shears). Although Reading were hungry for success the fates were against them. Neutral sentiment sided with Exeter. Long-time promoter Colin Hill had kept the unfashionable club afloat for many years. Terminally ill at the time of the final, he was not well enough to attend. He passed away at the end of October. The hyped-up Falcons team, determined to win the trophy for Colin, found that luck was on their side.

Reading beat Exeter by 19 points on aggregate when the teams met in the qualifying round of the Premier Trophy in May and later in the season won by 21 points over their two league encounters. But Exeter took the honours in the Trophy Final.

With rider replacement operating for injured Danny Bird, Appleton and Zagar came to the tapes for the first heat at Smallmead. After just a lap Exeter were heading for a 5-nil lead. Appleton shed a chain at the start and Zagar fell after an ungainly challenge on the third bend. The Falcons were still 5 up after heat 7. A long delay followed during which it emerged that Zagar was on his way to hospital. The remaining Racers rallied round and scraped a narrow win in a last-heat decider.

Despite the vocal support, under-strength Racers couldn't mount a serious challenge to the Falcons at their County Ground fortress. The 59-35 reverse was their biggest defeat of the season.

Popular Chris Mills in action during the Premier Trophy Final against Colin Hill's Exeter. (EP)

Reading had reached the final after knocking Glasgow out in the semi-final. In the early-season qualifying group a draw on the Isle of Wight and a 20-point mauling of Newport in Wales got the season off to a good start.

Over the winter Reading lost a local rival as Swindon (under new owner Terry Russell) and Arena Essex moved up to the Elite League. The senior division benefited from the introduction of compulsory air fences. The Premier League also lost trackless Trelawny. Reading snapped up Zagar in December causing an initial fuss as Trelawny objected to the 'poaching' of their rider.

Franc Zagar was crowned Slovenian champion in 1985, when it was still part of Yugoslavia. His son Matej won his first Slovenian title in 2002 as well as the European Under-19 Championship. By 2003 he had already made his first Grand Prix appearance, marking him down as one of the hottest prospects of the new century.

A five-figure cheque (courtesy of Euphony) secured Isle of Wight heat leader Danny Bird to give Reading a devastating spearhead. Still relatively young at 23, Bird arrived at Reading with six years in the sport - all spent on the Isle of Wight. Two years doubling up in the Elite League at Ipswich had further enhanced his reputation.

Oxford asset Chris Mills rode with Bird on the Island in 2003 and followed him to Reading when he was signed to fill one of the reserve berths. After a year at Newport, Chris Schramm returned along with Reading's Welsh wizard Phil Morris.

That left two vacancies, one for a heat leader and the other for a reserve. After his falling out with the management the previous autumn Andrew Appleton seemed unlikely to return. Jonas Davidsson clearly had the capacity to improve his average after a strong finish to the season and would have made a good addition to the team.

However, negotiations with Davidsson didn't proceed as expected and Appleton got the nod. In the end Davidsson joined Oxford. Also moving out, after six years at Smallmead was Paul Clews. Originally signed on loan, but subsequently bought outright, Clews now went out on loan to Stoke. At second division level he held the record for most appearances for the Racers. In 2006 Clews received a testimonial meeting, staged at Stoke where he was still riding.

The first opportunity to win silverware came on June 20 in the Premier League Pairs. With Zagar and Bird both averaging over 10 their prospects looked good. The choice of Smallmead as the venue for the event raised hopes even further. Not since the 1988 British Open Pairs had Smallmead staged a major pooled meeting.

Expectations were adjusted downwards when Zagar damaged his ribs in a crash that ruled him out for most of June. In came Phil Morris. A 7-2 in the final over the Stoke pair of Paul Pickering and Alan Mogridge gave Bird and Morris the title.

Although this was the highlight of Morris's season a 21-point maximum (from six rides) at home to Hull warrants a mention. Best of all after the injury-blighted 2003 he only missed two matches in 2004, and during the season he overtook Paul Clews to assume the mantle of the rider with most appearances for the Racers at second division level.

By late June, Hull were already running away with the league. The Vikings opened their league campaign with a 46-44 win at home to Reading in April. Perhaps the season would have panned out very differently if Reading had managed to sneak a win at Craven Park.

Both Reading and Hull finished the year with 100% home records in the league, but whereas Hull won the majority of their away matches, Reading could only manage three wins away from Smallmead. The victories came at Newcastle, Somerset and Stoke. Nine of the eleven defeats were by 7 points or less. The final league averages show the power of Reading's top four. Zagar, Bird, Appleton and Morris finished second, third, twelfth and seventeenth respectively in the final league rankings. Morris would have been number one in the Hull averages! Simon Stead (Workington) beat Zagar to the top spot. Away from home the figures were even more impressive: Zagar (first), Bird (second) and Appleton (seventh).

While the top four had taken most of the headlines, Schramm's improvement did not go unnoticed. His end-of-season win of the Andy Fuller Shield for most-improved Racer was a popular one on the terraces.

The Achilles heel in the Reading line-up was at number seven. Steve Braidford (a Wolverhampton junior) and James Cockle (a Rye House youngster) were originally given a share of the second reserve position. After some early promise Braidford became the regular pick and Cockle moved on to Glasgow. Braidford suffered from an accumulation of minor injuries and off-track problems that led to him being dropped at the end of August. The replacement of Braidford by Jamie Westacott didn't manage to eradicate the Racers weak spot. Westacott made his Racers debut in May scoring 3 paid 4, a tally that wasn't topped once he became a regular.

Westacott first came to public attention three years earlier when, as a 13-year-old, the Phil Morris protégé rode in an under-16 Test series against Germany. During 2004 Westacott rode in the inaugural British Under-18 Championship (along with James Cockle) and toured Sweden in an under-21 Test series. Top scorer for the young Brits was Daniel King. The ex-Racer also won the British Under-18 title.

Danny Bird lost a month of racing due to a shoulder injury, but as this period coincided with two of Reading's three away wins it would be misguided to use Bird's absence as an excuse for Reading's failure to mount a stronger challenge to Hull.

Injury notwithstanding, Bird enjoyed the best year of his career. Eight points in the British Championship, and a 6.5-point average doubling up for Ipswich contributed to a call-up for the Great Britain World Cup squad. Bird represented Reading in the Premier League Riders Championship, finishing sixth after falling in the semi-final race.

Zagar, the other half of Reading's dynamic duo had an even busier year. In consecutive weekends Matej won the European Championship[78], appeared as a wild card in the Slovenian Grand Prix and took bronze in the World Under-21 Final.

Former Racer Jonas Davidsson finished well down the Under-21 Final field with 6 points. The line-up for the meeting sparked fears for the future of British speedway – not a single Brit qualified. Robert Miskowiak, one of four Poles in the field, won the event. It would have been five had Janusz Kolodziej not broken his arm in the European Championship Final. July saw Kolodziej win the Polish Under-21 title and in August he reminded British enthusiasts of his talent by top scoring for Poland in the World Cup Final staged at Poole. The entry of Poland into the European Union on May 1 meant that Poles no longer needed work permits to ride in Britain. Although it is hard to imagine anyone arguing against Kolodziej's impressive record.

With hindsight the 2004 European Under-19 Final makes interesting reading for Reading fans – three future Racers appeared in the meeting: Matt Tresarrieu, Krzysztof Buczkowski and Zdenek Simota.

Another international competition with Racers interest was the World Longtrack championship. Held over five rounds (including one in New Zealand), it featured Andrew Appleton among the leading contenders. He finished fifth overall. Appleton's Reading record included three maximums in a row during July.

Appleton's domestic season ended with a dislocated shoulder during the Young Shield Final. Reading easily beat Sheffield and then followed up with a nail biting 96-95 aggregate win over the Isle of Wight in the semi-final. In both legs the Islanders found themselves 8-up

---

78 A remarkably pointless competition, as the best riders in Europe don't enter. Britain ignores the competition completely and other major speedway nations enter riders of varying abilities. The winners are all good riders, but none could be described as anywhere near the best, or even the best not competing in the Grand Prix. The Roll of Honour reads: 2001 Bo Brhel, 2002 Magnus Zetterstrom, 2003 Krzysztof Kasprzak, 2004 Matej Zagar, 2005 Jesper Jensen, 2006 Krzysztof Jablonski, 2007 Jurica Pavlic.

only for the Racers to employ tacticals to narrow the gap. In the away leg Zagar even won off the 15-metre handicap, storming round Ray Morton on the final lap.

Despite carrying a 100% home record in all competitions Reading lost their home leg of the final 51-42 to Hull. It was a meeting where everything went wrong. As well as Appleton's injury, Bird, Morris and Schramm all suffered bike problems. Only Chris Mills, on his return from a broken collarbone, held out against the league champions. His paid 16 tally was easily his best of the year. After the first leg disaster the second leg was a formality, but Racers put up a respectable show losing by 8 in the away leg.

After a wet summer that caused considerable fixture disruption, October continued in a similar vein. Hull only won their Young Shield semi-final tie four days before the first leg of the final was rained-off at Smallmead. Another October victim of the weather was the Todd Wiltshire farewell at Oxford, abandoned after 12 races.

Over the winter another rider joined the ranks of the retired when 48-year-old Malcolm Holloway called it a day. His final season principally consisted of a Conference League rider/coach role at Swindon but he also made two appearances for the Racers including a match-winning paid 10 haul at Somerset.

Phil Morris poses with a neighbour from the Madejski Stadium – Reading FC goalkeeper Marcus Hahnemann. (BT)

Continuing the theme of departures, the opening in March of the new sewerage treatment centre (those bulbous constructions behind the second bend) promised an end to the 'Whitley whiff'. Nearby in Bracknell the Met Office workers packed their bags for Exeter. Unfortunately they didn't take the rain with them. At least with the harnessing of the Internet more accurate and more immediate weather information is now available to the travelling fan.

For the Racers, one departure had a significance that outweighed any other. Their third place finish in the league, two cup final appearances and the Premier League Pairs win made 2004 one of the most enjoyable seasons at Smallmead. Much of the credit for that has to go to the support of Euphony Communications. At the beginning of September a private equity buy-out of Euphony cast doubt on the future of their links with the Racers. Once Managing Director and Racers fan Dave Faithful left the company, the announcement that the sponsorship was over came as no surprise.

Dave Faithful's farewell message left no doubts about his fondness for the Racers:

> *"I'd like to give particular thanks to Phil Morris who is quite simply the best Team Captain in British Speedway and the hardest and most passionate worker for the sport I've ever met; to Paul Hunsdon, a good friend without whom it would have all been too hard; and to Pat Bliss who, is a downright nice person who cares passionately for Reading Speedway and its future."*

The 2004 Euphony Racers embark on their best season since 1998. Back row left to right: Steven Braidford, Chris Mills, Phil Morris, Jamie Westacott, Matej Zagar, Andrew Appleton, James Cockle. Front row: Danny Bird, David Faithful (Euphony MD – on bike), Martin Davidson (mascot) and Chris Schramm. (BT)

The season, and the Euphony era, finished with the 'Euphony Classic', an individual meeting with a £2,000 first prize won by Adam Shields (Eastbourne) after a run-off with Danny Bird.

Team: Matej Zagar 10.02, Danny Bird 9.67, Phil Morris 8.18, Andrew Appleton 8.10, Chris Schramm 5.01, Chris Mills 4.51, Steve Braidford 2.46, Jamie Westacott 1.83

2005 – A Season That Ended in March

A tumultuous 24 hours in the middle of the year left the strongest imprint on the year. In the space of 20 hours London won the Olympic bidding race and the 7/7 bombers struck. The first aroused memories of Hackney Wick stadium, now in the heart of the Olympic site, and the latter would have knock-on effects for the many frequent flyers in the speedway world.

In speedway Tony Rickardsson equalled Ivan Mauger's six world titles. He completely dominated the Grand Prix series, winning six of the nine events. Rickardsson's class and professionalism contrasted with the events at the World Under-21 Final in Austria. The competitors (including former Racers Daniel King and Jonas Davidsson) faced a quagmire, and officials called a halt to proceedings after 12 races. Krzysztof Kasprzak then became World Champion on the toss of a coin, making runner-up Tomas Suchanek one of the unluckiest losers in speedway's history.

A team competition for riders under 21 made its first appearance on the calendar. A Great Britain team featuring Chris Schramm and Daniel King trailed in behind Sweden and hosts Germany in their qualifying round. The final (staged at Pardubice) was won by Poland from Sweden, Denmark and the Czech Republic.

All four teams tracked a rider with Reading connections. Patrick Hougaard, barely 16, rode in the Danish team. At the end of the season he came over to Britain, riding in the Brent Werner Testimonial and Malcolm Holloway's 'Mad Wellie' Farewell. While Hougaard represented the future Racers, the current Racers standard bearer was Zdenek 'Sam' Simota.

Jonas Davidsson (Sweden) and Janusz Kolodziej (Poland) were both ex-Racers, and although hard to envisage at the time would return to Smallmead in the future. Kolodziej topped the winners' score chart, just one of many accomplishments in a splendid season. Kolodziej and Poland also won the European Pairs Championship (a competition even more pointless than the European Individual Championship). But it was on the individual front that Kolodziej's finest triumphs came. In Poland he won the Silver Helmet (for Polish riders under 21) and the Golden Helmet. In between these he was crowned Polish Champion with a 15 point maximum after beating Tomasz Gollob from behind.

Although the return of speedway to Scunthorpe and the sparkling Conference League form of Weymouth's Lewis Bridger provided some good news for British speedway, the predominating emotion was one of sadness as three venues reached their end. Hull left with a whimper. After leaping from wooden spoon in 2003 to title winners in 2004, their final year was dogged by disputes with their landlord and petered out with two home matches unridden.

Wimbledon closed in early October. The level of rent expected by stadium owners, the GRA meant speedway wasn't practical. The economics are simple: with land in London worth millions to developers for commercial or residential use sporting stadiums just aren't a viable land use. Existing venues are being picked off one by one. Redevelopment rumours suggest both Wimbledon and Walthamstow (a former speedway venue) may disappear and greyhound racing may follow speedway in being exiled from the capital.

A few days after Plough Lane passed into speedway history, Exeter's County Ground followed suit. With plenty of advance notice all the stops were pulled out. Reading junior Danny Warwick received a late call-up and performed well against more experienced opponents. A packed stadium (almost certainly in excess of the maximum permitted capacity) soaked up the emotion as Ivan Mauger performed the final four laps of the track and Honey Sanford laid flowers on the first bend in memory of her father Tony, who lost his life there.

In the Premier League Rye House's young and mainly English team dominated until King's Lynn bested them in two October cup finals to win the Young Shield and Knock-Out Cup. Much of the joy in Norfolk evaporated when just a fortnight later their young Australian

Ashley Jones met with a fatal accident in his home country.

In the Elite League table toppers Belle Vue lost the play-off final to Coventry. The Bees languished at the foot of the table after seven matches, but with some astute team changes became league champions. At the other end of the table Oxford avoided the wooden spoon with a narrow victory in their final match. The crucial factor in that win was an unexpected heat 14 victory by stand-in Chris Mills. He featured in the Oxford Conference League team that pipped Wimbledon to the title. Then to complete an eventful year the club went spectacularly bust.

For the Racers 2005 was a season to forget, followed by a close season to remember.

After a strong showing in 2004 the mathematics of the points limit meant that one of the powerhouse top four was destined to leave. Phil Morris made an early decision to sign for Newcastle, preferring certainty and the long trip up north to the risk of being left teamless in March. He experienced a disappointing year, but his Elite League appearances for Arena Essex showed he could still compete at the senior level.

Bird, Zagar, Appleton all agreed to return, keeping the top three intact, along with second-string Chris Mills. The occupants of the reserve berths were unknown until press and practice day, a situation reminiscent of the previous decade. Chris Johnson and Matt Tresarrieu both arrived from the Isle of Wight. Frenchman Tresarrieu, the youngest of three racing brothers, made just a handful of appearances for the Islanders. Johnson (aged 17) averaged just over 3 before losing his place in the Island team mid-season.

That accounts for six of the places in the Racers named seven, the final spot proved to be problematic. Looking for a second string, initial rumours suggested that Jonas Davidsson might be returning. However, negotiations failed and the club looked elsewhere. In mid February a new and unknown Czech joined Reading. Zdenek Simota (aged 19) was expected to join Racers on a 5-point average, but after a couple of weeks it emerged that his average would be assessed at 8, making it impossible to squeeze him in the team.

Reading returned to the Czech Republic for an alternative rider. The more-experienced Richard Wolff included three seasons at Trelawny on his CV and came with a 5.07 average that fitted Reading's requirements. Wolff's 2004 form in the Czech Republic showed that he was (at that time) a better rider than Simota. But because of four appearances in the Czech Extra League as a 17-year-old junior for Mseno (from which he gained a 1.00 average) Simota was assessed at the punitive 8-point level.

Over the course of the season Reading rode 23 official fixtures at Smallmead. For all practical purposes the season's hopes died less than halfway through the first match. In heat 6 Danny Bird pulled off a Houdini-like pass squeezing between Wight's Jason Bunyan and the back straight fence. Desperate to regain the lead, Bunyan badly misjudged his drive up the inside of Bird and left him sprawled on the track. A broken 'fib and tib' meant a lengthy recuperation period. The evening before, Doctor Who returned after a 16-year break. How Racers fans wished for a TARDIS so they could go back and start the season again.

Without Bird the Racers went down by a single point to the Islanders despite a 20-point haul from Zagar.

From here on, efforts to cover the gap left by Bird became the central theme that dominated the narrative of 2005.

After using rider replacement for three weeks, Reading introduced Zdenek Simota into the team. It represented a considerable gamble, as Simota couldn't be expected to come anywhere near matching Bird's scoring power. Paid 5 in his debut at Exeter and a paid 13 haul in his home debut indicated that the move was justified. As the season progressed, double-figure returns became more frequent and Simota transformed from unknown Czech Zdenek to popular Racer 'Sam'.

The next change caught everybody by surprise. Despite being promoted from reserve to the main body of the team where he faced more difficult rides, Chris Mills (aged 21) had upped his average since the start of the season. Suddenly he found himself replaced by Steve Masters (34). Originally announced as a temporary move, it became permanent a couple of weeks later. Mills declared "I'm absolutely bewildered", as were supporters on the terraces. Mills later found a berth in the Somerset team. His first match for the Rebels must have been satisfying – paid 11 at Smallmead.

Steve Masters had been an entertaining visitor on many occasions over his 15-year career, but after managing just 7 points in eight matches lost his place in the Belle Vue team. A drop down to the Premier League didn't help his fortunes, just 11 points in six matches didn't endear him to the Reading faithful.

Masters made his debut at Workington (May 14) where Racers were team managed by Eric Boocock. Ivan Shears's absence soon became a permanent one and Tim Sugar started his third spell as team manager.

After an injury at Hull sidelined Masters, rider replacement returned to the Reading team sheet. Racers desperately needed Bird to return and redeclared to include him in the team for the July 11 match at home to Edinburgh. Unfortunately celebrations were premature and Bird wasn't yet ready to ride. The BSPA refused permission for rider replacement. The dispute over the make up of the Reading team, problems with track watering and a faulty starting gate meant a delay of nearly an hour before the match started. Racers drafted in Jamie Westacott, who failed to score, and Reading went down 47-46 to complete an agonising night.

For the next match Reading redeclared their team again with Masters returning. Reading won by 12 points at Newport as Masters came up with a respectable 8 points.

Danny Bird leads team-mate Matej Zagar. In 2005 they combined to form a potent spearhead – but injury to Bird wrecked Racers season. (BT)

Finally on August 8 Danny Bird returned. Quoted[79] beforehand, Pat Bliss warned: "We ask the supporters to be patient and not to expect maximums straight away." Danny chose to ignore her warnings and went out and took maximum points from both his first two matches back. The long-awaited return came in a cup tie against Bird's previous team – the Isle of

79 http://www.readingspeedway.com – 4 August 2005

Wight. A comfortable victory was marred by a heat 14 accident. Wolff lost control and collided with Johnson, and a stray bike careered across the centre green hitting track-maintenance man Eric Colvin (father of Shane). A dislocated shoulder kept Johnson out for a month, but after a trip to hospital Eric was given a clean bill of health.

Just as Racers were beginning to feel good about the remainder of the season Bird returned to the casualty list. An encounter with Exeter's infamous steel fence left Bird with dislocated elbow, dislocated shoulder, broken nose and cracked knee. Disconsolate, Reading trudged on to the end of the season using rider replacement for Bird.

The rules at the time meant that any team running with a strong top two would be very vulnerable if they lost their number two rider. Without access to guests, prolonged use of rider replacement couldn't make up for Bird's absence. While the team changes made in an attempt to overcome this handicap brought Simota into the team, they also caused Mills to be discarded and enabled Masters's miserable spell in Racers colours.

In their pre-season preview the *Speedway Star*'s pundits named Reading among the title favourites. Without Bird they never had a hope. The Premier Trophy campaign in spring saw Reading finish bottom of the Southern group. Their final match in the Trophy was a real thriller. Racers beat Exeter 46-44 after a gripping last-heat decider in which Zagar twice re-passed Exeter star Mark Lemon.

The League campaign didn't see any improvement in Racers fortunes. Reading lost at home to Newcastle despite Zagar (paid 21) and Appleton (paid 15) both scoring maximums, and Berwick won at Smallmead on June 20 with ex-Racer Chris Schramm hitting Racers for paid 9.

The next day, a win for the Isle of Wight put Reading into the basement position. The following Monday, a convincing performance against Sheffield lifted Reading off the bottom, Tresarrieu (paid 17) and Wolff (paid 13) making crucial contributions.

Two further home defeats in July – to Edinburgh (as already mentioned), and Rye House – forced Racers back to the bottom. The Rockets did enjoy some luck at Smallmead, with unbeaten Simota falling in the last-heat decider.

Despite their poor league form, Racers found themselves in the semi-final stage of the Knock-Out Cup. Eventual wooden spoonists Newport were easily disposed of and Isle of Wight followed. This gave Reading a semi-final tie against the formidable Rye House team. After the Rockets won the first leg at Smallmead the bitter row over dates for the second leg seemed rather pointless.

Len Silver, no stranger to rows with Reading, insisted that the Racers should visit Hoddesdon when missing Simota, Zagar and Wolff (as well as Bird). When Silver got his way, Reading mischievously booked three King's Lynn riders who got some practice in ahead of their cup final visit to Rye House. After conceding 5-1s in each of the first five heats the final score of 65-25 in favour of Rye House almost seemed respectable!

As the season drew to an end, Racers clawed their way up to tenth. Away wins at Newport and Stoke, with contributions of paid 12 and 16 respectively from Simota, and five home wins on the trot meant that dire predictions of another wooden spoon in mid summer failed to materialise.

Zagar, Simota and Tresarrieu all flourished despite the struggles of their team. Zagar picked up three 20-point hauls, was never paid for less than double figures, and topped the Premier League averages. His increasing international profile caused him to miss a few matches, including three matches in 32 hours at Edinburgh, Berwick and Newcastle. His stand-in for these matches – Travis McGowan – notched up 51 points in the three fixtures. The highlight of Zagar's year, a third place in the Slovenian Grand Prix, added to the inevitability of a 2006 move to the Elite League. But who would it be with?

Simota's successes included third place in the Czech Championship, but he was shaded out by Matt Tresarrieu for the Andy Fuller Memorial Shield awarded to the most-improved Racer. Tresarrieu reached his second European Under-19 Final and appeared in the final round of the World Longtrack Grand Prix.

In 2005 the Andy Fuller Shield went to Matt Tresarrieu. Presenting the shield are Alex Fuller (left) and Bryan Horsnell (right). (BT)

Tresarrieu's weak spot was his mechanical reliability, a characteristic shared with Richard Wolff. The experienced Czech lifted his starting average, scoring freely in July when relegated to reserve, but could have contributed more.

The same could be said for Andrew Appleton, who slipped from 12th in the 2004 Premier League averages to 48th in 2005 (based on all official fixtures). His results were particularly disappointing when riding at number one and he did regain some of his potency when switched to the number three race jacket for the last two months of the season.

Final member of the team, Chris Johnson, was plagued by minor injuries, one of which was picked up at the British Under-21 Final. Later in the year he finished a respectable fifth in the British Under-18 Championship.

Racers completed their season before September ended. While most of the major trophies were decided elsewhere, in Berkshire there was little to do but speculate about Reading's future. By November 24, when 24-hour drinking became legal, Racers fans were raising a toast to a new era.

Team: Matej Zagar 10.43, (Danny Bird 9.38), Andrew Appleton 7.32, Zdenek Simota 6.41, Mathieu Tresarrieu 5.60, Richard Wolff 5.52, (Chris Mills 5.29), (Steve Masters 3.39), Chris Johnson 2.96

2006 – Who Let The Dogs Out?

30 January 2006 – the Day the Racers Died. Reading's new management were nothing if not bold. Aside from irritating supporters of the defunct Bristol team, the choice of 'Bulldogs' and the childish cartoon logo that accompanied it set off a storm of protest. The first[80] of many letters opposing the change of nickname appeared in that week's *Speedway Star*:

> *"So with one stroke of his marketing team's pen, Mr. Postlethwaite has consigned 38 years of proud history to the bin ... Word has it that (he) feels he can't market a product called the Racers. If one can't market a speedway team called Racers, I would suggest that it's time to pursue a new career."*

While many were prepared to give the new owners the benefit of the doubt, the name change remained a bone of contention. Throughout the 2006 season Racers fans were seen sporting 'T' shirts with anti-Bulldog slogans. (In the early weeks no Bulldogs merchandise could be purchased from the track shop, rather undermining BSI's claims about bringing a professional approach to Reading speedway.) That year the Reading programme regularly featured a fans fantasy league table featuring team names that demonstrated hostility to the change. Names like 'Racers Yes Bulldogs No', 'Bring Back Pat Bliss', 'The Famous Winged Wheel', and 'Never Forget the Racers' littered the listings.

Ever since 2002 when Gaming International moved in to take the lead role in the proposed stadium re-development, speculation and rumour suggested that a change of promoters and elevation to the Elite League were in the offing. BSI (Benfield Sports International) made an approach to Pat Bliss over the winter of 2004/05 but were rebuffed. A year later, after a traumatic season on track, the enthusiasm of 2004 had evaporated and Pat was ready to reconsider.

The official announcement on November 18 followed weeks of speculation. BSI would be the new owners with BSI supremo John Postlethwaite and Jim Lynch co-promoters. The Elite League welcomed them with open arms and Racers fans looked forward to a new era.

The Dore family involvement stretched back to the construction of Smallmead stadium more than 30 years earlier. Pat first helped out with her father's business because he was short-handed in the bar. Her role quickly developed via administration to co-promoter. When she stood down Pat was the longest-serving promoter in British speedway. Her habit of declaring the Racers starting line-up at the last possible moment and an insistence that Reading speedway would not live beyond its means did not always endear her to the Reading crowds. However, all but the most economically illiterate could see that just keeping the Racers going represented a considerable commitment to the club for which they were grateful.

Ambition had been noticeably lacking for a decade or more, excepting the Euphony sponsorship triggered revival of 2003-04. Even many of those who respected Bliss for her commitment to the Racers accepted that it was time for a change. Her departure meant that John Campbell (Edinburgh promoter since 1985) took over the mantle of Britain's longest-serving promoter.

Postlethwaite made his name in speedway when his company, BSI, acquired the rights to run the Speedway Grand Prix from the FIM in 2000. With no background in speedway he relied on his experience in other areas of motor sport (he was commercial director at the Benetton Formula 1 team) to 'professionalise' speedway's leading event. Despite some

80 The author of this letter – Mick Napier – takes the view that the 2006 chapter in this book is best represented by an empty page. In the interests of completeness the events of 2006/07 must be chronicled.

setbacks the Grand Prix series had expanded. Most of the traditionalists who originally opposed the GP series in 1995 now accepted that it was here to stay, but wondered if it could co-exist with Elite League speedway.

In contrast, Lynch had graduated from the terraces at Coventry in the early 1960s, via sponsorship of individual Peterborough riders, to becoming Panthers promoter. After five seasons (1998-2002) promoting he sold out and had spent 2005 at Oxford.

In the wake of all this upheaval the long-awaited grant of planning permission for a new stadium almost slipped under the radar. With a recommendation for approval from the council officers and little opposition, the Council's planning committee approved the plans for the Island Road site on December 7. The potential for promoting the sport at a brand new stadium must have increased the attractiveness of the deal to Postlethwaite. However, it remained to be seen how Postlethwaite would deal with conflicts of interest between his two investments.

The new promotion demonstrated a professional approach to team building. The entire team was announced in a single press release just before Christmas (although news of Charlie Gjedde's plans to rejoin Reading did leak out on his website beforehand). Faced with a low points limit (40 excluding bonus points), it was important to build a team that included riders with the potential to increase their averages substantially.

Reading possessed two such riders – Matej Zagar and Janusz Kolodziej. After a tremendous 2005 season, that earned him adulation from the Racers terraces and a 2006 GP nomination, Zagar's inclusion in the new Racers team came as no surprise. Despite his potential, nobody had succeeded in tempting Kolodziej back to Britain since his initial brief spell with the Racers in 2003, making his signing a real bonus. Danny Bird and Sam Simota were retained leaving the final two spots for newcomers to the Reading team.

Greg Hancock and Travis McGowan both arrived at Oxford in 2003 where they had developed a rapport over the previous three years. Hancock, at 35, may have been past his peak but was still a world-class performer. McGowan arrived in the UK at King's Lynn in 1999 and was well regarded as a solid middle-order rider. Approaching his 25th birthday McGowan was a three-times winner of the Australian Under-21 title in his earlier days and hadn't missed an official match in his three years at Oxford.

Zdenek 'Sam' Simota in action. (BT)

An eighth rider completed the line-up – but not in a riding role. Sam Ermolenko's appointment as sporting director indicated that the new boys in town were determined to make their mark. Ermolenko finished his British career at Peterborough the previous autumn, but had already agreed to ride for Rospiggarna where his 2006 team mates included Hancock, Kolodziej and McGowan.

As Racers fans nipped down to the bookies and placed their money on Reading the first problem emerged. The Internet discussion forums went into overdrive debating Danny Bird's average. Due to his injuries he never obtained a 2005 average, hence his 2004 green sheet would be used. Because he doubled up with Ipswich, he had two green sheet averages from that year. Lynch had used the PL one (the lower of the two), but his interpretation of the rulebook was open to question. As is so often the case in these situations the published rulebook seemed less than conclusive.

Rather than wait for a BSPA decision on Bird's average a new signing was unveiled in the first week of the New Year. Nearing 40, Andy Smith's reputation rested on three British Championship wins (1993-95) and a remarkable ability to retain his place in the GP competition despite poor performances in the event itself. He also spent some time riding on a Polish licence. He made his debut for Belle Vue at the end of 1982 and had three spells with the club. His other teams were Bradford, Coventry, Swindon and Oxford. Towards the end of 2006 Smith benefited from a testimonial meeting held at Belle Vue. On the rostrum were: Simon Stead, Jason Crump and Reading's Travis McGowan.

Smith would become the eighth rider to regularly carry the colours of all three Thames Valley teams. Bobby McNeil, Malcolm Holloway, John Davis, Glenn Cunningham, Krister Marsh, Charlie Gjedde and Jonas Davidsson are the other seven.

Bird attracted interest from several PL teams and ended up at Glasgow, with the intention of flying to home meetings. Bird went on to win a second PL Pairs Championship. Like the first (at Smallmead in 2004) it was held on his home track, now Ashfield in Glasgow.

Joining Bird in the northern reaches of the Premier League would be Matt Tresarrieu who signed for Premier League newcomers Redcar. 2005 Racers reserve Chris Johnson returned to Isle of Wight and also rode in the Conference League for newcomers Plymouth (who also tracked Jamie Westacott).

Andrew Appleton announced his intention to concentrate on longtrack racing, but did put in a brief and unmemorable spell with Eastbourne. Chris Mills returned to the Reading fold in the number eight role, and became a Reading asset when BSI purchased a job lot of Oxford juniors after Oxford had gone bust. The other riders included Craig Branney, Ben Barker, Sam Martin and Kyle Hughes. The move didn't go down well at Cowley and caused disappointment at Reading when it failed to lead to the setting up of a Conference League team.

In its pre-season preview the *Speedway Star* predicted Peterborough and Coventry for the top two positions. So when the fixture list revealed that these would be Reading's first two opponents, it seemed as if there would be an early opportunity to measure the new team's potential.

Not surprisingly, when Reading opened with two away wins, expectations reached stratospheric heights. A 6-point win in a last-heat decider at Coventry was followed by a convincing victory at the Showground. Zagar and Kolodziej shone as Reading cruised home 52-41. The last time Reading won back to back away wins at the senior level Per Jonsson and Jan Andersson were in the team.

The loss of the return fixtures against both teams introduced a note of caution to those hopes of replicating the triumphs of 1992. Zagar performed poorly in both fixtures, the second (against Peterborough) was just three days before the first of the GP series. This affliction became known as GP-itis and would trouble Zagar more and more over the next two seasons. In 2006 he averaged 7.02 in the nine matches he rode for Reading immediately before GPs, in his remaining 34 appearances his average came in substantially higher: 8.40.

Notwithstanding these defeats the Smallmead spectators were enjoying Elite League action. At Easter, Oxford came visiting and were crushed 67-28. Only King’s Lynn (in 1993) had come away from Smallmead with a bigger losing margin in a top division league match. The significance of the fixture was the downbeat departure of six-times World Champion Tony Rickardsson from the British scene. After Rickardsson refused to ride in the nominated race, Oxford promoter Aaron Lanney made his disappointment clear over the PA.

On May 8 Reading won an unexpectedly close encounter with Arena Essex after Andreas Jonsson came agonisingly close to his namesake's record. Since Per Jonsson recorded 58.1 seconds in October 1987 the record had looked increasingly invulnerable, but with the return of Elite level competition the permanence of Per's record could no longer be taken for granted. Andreas's 58.2 turned out to be the fastest time of the season and Per's record survived another year.

The previous Monday's match was called off for a most unusual reason. A parade to celebrate Reading FC's Championship League title, and their first-ever promotion to the Premiership, provided too much of a counter-attraction.

By the end of June, four more away victories propelled Reading to the top of the table. These were:

- Ipswich, which followed on from Peterborough and Coventry to make it three out of three on the Bulldogs travels (all seven Bulldogs were heat winners in this match).
- Eastbourne – despite missing Hancock, Zagar and Kolodziej. McGowan, Simota and guest Hans Andersen (with a maximum) rallied round.
- Oxford, where a 15-point win in the 'B' fixture provided revenge for an unexpected loss on an atrocious track in the 'A' fixture. McGowan took the starring role with paid 13.
- Swindon, beaten just 24 hours after the Cowley victory.

Kolodziej started spring with some brilliant form, benefiting from a spell at reserve. In his first 16 matches Janusz never dipped below 8 points; at the other end of the scale a paid 18 tally helped defeat Ipswich at Smallmead. Then he broke his collarbone riding in Poland (May 21). He returned to the saddle at the start of July, and after an undistinguished month re-broke his collarbone, this time while riding in Sweden.

Smith joined Kolodziej on the injured list at the end of June when he fell at Smallmead while riding against Poole. Smith made two brief returns, the first lasted just one ride (v Peterborough July 31) and the second a match in mid August at Swindon was followed by further injury when riding in Poland. Smith's contributions were under-valued. His Smallmead performances didn't warrant much comment, but away from home he returned several very useful scores including double figures at Oxford and Swindon in the back-to-back away wins.

The only rider who hadn't met expectations was Charlie Gjedde. His starting average of 8.08 (excluding bonus points) had turned into 5.68 by mid-June. However, he finished June with paid scores of 14, 12, 12, and 11.

Speedway's World Cup started in Poland on July 16 just a week after the football World Cup (and another England disappointment). Speedway crowds suffered from competing with football's World Cup. As the Swedish and Polish leagues became increasingly cosmopolitan, the British Elite League struggled to keep up with its continental rivals. Poland started scheduling some Extraliga matches away from their normal Sunday race day. Greg Hancock based himself in Sweden, making his itinerary even more complicated.

Mysterious absences[81] became a regular feature of League matches and undermined big events. In an effort to find a date clear of Swedish and Polish clashes, the Elite League Riders Championship moved from October to April. It turned into a fiasco as for the second time in a week rain won out. Five days earlier a Test match against Sweden (at Swindon) lasted just one race. Would either meeting even have started had Sky not been broadcasting?

---

81 Not to say that they never happened in earlier days. Certainly Anders Michanek missed a large number of fixtures in the Tilehurst era. The big difference now is that if a promoter says "rider X is on international duty and will miss Saturday's league match", it will be a matter of hours before a posting appears on the Speedway Discussion Forum pointing out that he is actually due to compete in a German league match – and a few hours later we even get the match report!

Since its inception in 1960 the Speedway World Cup had been staged in fine speedway venues such as Gothenburg, Pardubice, Wembley and Wroclaw. In 1973 a crowd of 80,000 attended the Katowice staging of the event. But the competition suffered a downgrading with the introduction of the Grand Prix and in 1996 just 2,000 witnessed the final at Diedenbergen in Germany. The 2001 revamp with the final four or five rounds staged over a single week helped to revitalise the competition.

However, the announcement over the winter that Reading would host the 'last chance' play-off and the final of the event caused a few raised eyebrows. It would not be unreasonable to suggest that had BSI not owned the Reading promotion, then the meeting would have gone elsewhere.

Australia and Sweden won the opening rounds in Poland and Sweden. The USA competed in the Mallila meeting, Hancock took 20 points more than half the Yanks total. Sam Ermolenko managed just 4 in what turned out to be the final competitive appearance of his career at the age of 45. Thursday's race-off was a bit of a non-event: Hancock took 19 of the 28 points credited to the USA team and Poland disappointed with Kolodziej achieving just 2 points on his home track. A slick dry track gave the 2,800 crowd poor value as Denmark and Britain cruised through to the final.

For the final two days later, a bigger crowd (4,500) witnessed better racing and a closer contest on a better track. With just four races to go only 5 points separated the four nations. Denmark (including Charlie Gjedde) finished strongly, winning with a race to spare. Australia (tracking Travis McGowan) slipped from joint first to last over those four heats.

The World Cup comes to Smallmead – American Greg Hancock leads Bjarne Pedersen (Denmark) and Scott Nicholls (Britain). (EP)

However, the defining incident of the meeting took place in heat 18 when Hans Andersen dived inside Chris Harris. Harris fell and Andersen's exclusion light came on. Andersen's reputation as an over-zealous rider probably caused the exclusion. The Danish contingent did not take the referee's decision well and their displeasure caused a reaction from some sections of the crowd. The victory parade passed off against a background of boos and a hail of bottles.

To accommodate the large (by 21st century standards) crowd the back straight stand re-opened for business, after earlier plans for its demolition were abandoned.

As the Elite League took a breather for the World Cup, disturbing news came from M4 neighbours Swindon. Stadium owners Gaming International unveiled plans to redevelop Swindon stadium, without a speedway track. The potential loss of long-standing local rivals would be a disaster in itself, but as Gaming International (and parent company Stadia UK) would be leading the redevelopment of Reading's stadium it gave cause to wonder whether speedway would be migrating to the Island Road site.

These fears were given added validity by the concern being expressed by the management over poor crowd levels. This reinforced the widely held belief that BSI was haemorrhaging money. After the season ended, sporting director Sam Ermolenko revealed that in August he was offered the choice of leaving or taking a pay cut. Ermolenko took the second option and continued to use his expertise to further Reading's quest for the league championship.

The title trail resumed with a brace of encounters against Wolverhampton. Defeat at home was doubly disappointing as Reading had drawn at Monmore Green after a thrilling encounter. In the home match a Gjedde fall in the last-heat decider and a poor return from Zagar (three days before the Italian GP) helped explain the shock result.

Wins at Arena Essex (where Gjedde shone) and Poole helped regain the momentum. At Poole the Bulldogs came from 10 down to win. McGowan starred, featuring in three 5-1s – two with Simota and the last-heat decider with Hancock. Displays like that at Poole resulted in Simota receiving the Andy Fuller Shield at the season's end.

Controversy surrounded yet another home defeat at the start of September when Coventry ran out winners by just 2 points. Hancock missed the match after returning to the States for the first round of the national championships. Billy Hamill rode for Wolves on the same night, yet he also rode in the Stateside meeting. Hancock went on to retain the title, bringing his number of wins in the event to a record equalling seven. (Mike Bast won seven titles between 1971 and 1979.) Bobby Schwartz had recently turned 50, but still finished 11th in the event which he had rarely missed since making his debut 30 years earlier.

After switching from Chris Mills to Glenn Cunningham to fill the number eight spot, a further change in August turned out to be an inspired move. Experienced Mark Lemon, a Poole asset riding for Stoke in the Premier League, took over the role. With Smith still injured he became a regular team member, and an instant hit after double-figure scores in two of his first three matches.

A strong finish from Swindon left Peterborough and Reading fighting it out with the Robins for the top two spots that would guarantee a home tie in the play-offs. Reading returned to the top after a remarkably powerful display at Alwalton where Reading stormed into a 43-29 lead on the way to a 6-point win. McGowan topped the score chart and reserve Lemon knocked up another double figure return.

Reading couldn't now finish out of the top two. Peterborough met Swindon in their final fixture. The Panthers win left Reading needing the bonus point from their final match, a trip to Belle Vue, to top the table. A miserable 25-point licking put paid to hopes of taking the top spot. Kolodziej failed to score and Hancock and Zagar both appeared to be suffering from that mystery illness – GP-itis.

Peterborough topped the table on race points after both teams finished on 64 match points. Four home defeats and seven dropped aggregate points (five by 4 points or less) provided ample opportunities for indulging in 'if onlys'.

Peterborough only lost two home league matches – both to Reading. Joining them in the play-offs were Swindon and Coventry. Both of these teams posted a home record showing one loss – and in both cases it was Reading who inflicted the home defeat.

Between the Belle Vue match and the play-off semi-final the Grand Prix reached its anti-climax. The title was already won, after Jason Crump achieved four wins and two seconds in the first six rounds to establish a commanding lead. The race for second went to Greg Hancock, in his best performance since becoming World Champion in 1997. Hancock was unlucky not to win the Cardiff GP, he was duelling for the lead with Jarek Hampel but ended up with an exclusion. He did win the penultimate round, the first GP ever staged in Latvia, after passing the mercurial Antonio Lindback in the final.

Lindback and Zagar both exceeded expectations in their first year as GP regulars. Zagar comfortably finished in the top eight to give him automatic qualification for 2007. His best result came in Prague where he finished runner-up to Hans Andersen.

The other big story of the GP came from the unexpected decline in Tony Rickardsson's form. At the beginning of August he announced his retirement, withdrawing from the series. This left Hancock as the only rider to have ridden in every single Grand Prix since its inception in 1995.

The spotlight returned to the Elite League play-offs and Smallmead, where the Bulldogs faced their local rivals from Swindon. On the news that Hancock would be missing due to food poisoning Reading fans awaited the contest nervously. For nine heats the two teams were evenly balanced, and then Swindon folded. Three wins over Leigh Adams in the last five races by Zagar made him the hero of the hour.

For the fourth time in five meetings gate one failed to provide a single heat winner. (In fact over the last eight meetings at Smallmead in 2006 only 7.5% of races were won from the inside gate.) This perplexed long standing fans as gate one had traditionally been the gate of choice.

On the eve of the play-off final Hancock mounted the rostrum in third place in the Elite League Riders Championship. That good news was tempered by the news from Hungary where Zagar's attempt to regain the European Championship resulted in a first ride crash. Reading used rider replacement for him in the play-off final.

Greg Hancock and Peterborough's Hans Andersen pose before the start of the 2006 Elite League play-off final. (EP)

Peterborough put up a strong performance at Smallmead and aided by two 6-point tactical rides and a final heat engine failure by Hancock restricted Reading to a 2-point win. Most of the 2,500 crowd left expecting that Peterborough would complete the job the following week. A few optimistic souls believed that Reading could record a third win at the Alwalton Showground, despite the absence of Zagar.

Kolodziej shone with paid 10 including the scalp of Hans Andersen. And this despite two punctures. Lemon's paid 13 included a controversial spill with Richard Hall that earned the Bulldog an exclusion. Their contributions propelled Reading into a 10-point lead on the night (12 on aggregate) with just three races to go. Then Reading's dreams were shattered as the Panthers finished with a 7-2 and two 5-1s. It couldn't have been any closer – Reading lost 95-94 with nine of Peterborough's points coming from exploitation of the tactical ride rule.

Speedway Star was flooded with letters condemning the tactical ride rule that gave a nominated rider double points without any handicap. Most of the neutrals sided with the aggrieved Reading fans. In a poll subsequently conducted by the Star 92% voted to scrap the rule. This overwhelming vote left promoters in no doubt about fans' views – so at their Conference they decided to keep the rule, with just a little tinkering.

But all that Reading were left to show for their exhilarating season was an award for the best club programme.

Team: Greg Hancock 9.28, Matej Zagar 8.13, Janusz Kolodziej 7.60, Charlie Gjedde 7.52, Travis McGowan 7.01, Mark Lemon 6.39, Andy Smith 5.52, Sam Simota 5.43

On May 18 the Bulldogs achieved a sensational draw at Coventry. Paid 13 from Sam Simota helped Reading to a last-heat decider. Needing a 5-1 for a draw, Scott Nicholls split the Reading pair (Hancock and Zagar) until a sublime cutback by Zagar on the last lap gave Reading the result they wanted. Given that Coventry went on to win a league, cup and Craven Shield treble, this was an outstanding result.

But in the context of everything else that happened in 2007, it bordered on the miraculous.

Nine days earlier the Bulldogs had imploded. Black Wednesday saw the Bulldogs world rocked by three pieces of bad news. The previous week Travis McGowan had picked up a shoulder injury in Poland. The initial prognosis suggested that no bones were broken and that Travis would soon be back on track. On Black Wednesday it emerged that there was a broken bone and McGowan would be out for a month or more.

Public confirmation of the news from Poland that Tarnow were not happy with the form of Janusz Kolodziej and wanted him to concentrate on their Polish commitments, dismayed Reading supporters. The announcement did at least leave open the possibility that Janusz might return later in the season.

And as if the loss of two riders wasn't bad enough, the day yielded a third casualty. The seeds of disaster number three were sown on April 20 when Reading thrashed Ipswich 60-32 at Smallmead in a fairly routine match. At the time comment focused on Kolodziej's first maximum and the pre-meeting withdrawal of McGowan after he aggravated a back injury in the pits. However, UK Sports Council Doping Control Officers were taking samples from three randomly selected riders. One of them – Danny Bird – tested positive. Bird was suspended pending testing of the 'B' sample. Once this also proved positive, a hearing was arranged. Bird's samples revealed traces of benzoylecgonine, an indicator of cocaine. He did not attend the tribunal held in July and received a two-year ban and was ordered to pay £1150 costs.

Although Reading were three riders down, at least their top two – Hancock and Zagar – could be relied upon to carry the team through the difficult times that beckoned.

But that belief didn't last for long. The Bulldogs faced embarrassment and humiliation when they fulfilled a league fixture at Ipswich (May 24). McGowan (still injured) and Simota (riding in the Czech League) were covered by rider replacement and Premier League guest Cory Gathercole. Then Hancock, who was based in Sweden, missed his flight while Zagar was delayed. His flight from Ljubljana, due in at Stansted at 6.15 p.m., didn't arrive until 7.30 p.m.[82] Ipswich magnanimously allowed Rory Schlein (booked as a guest for Mark Loram) to swap sides and help out the Reading team. Bulldogs received the expected hammering, and without Schlein's paid 15 it would have been a massacre.

Hancock donned Reading colours once more the following Monday as Reading left Cowley with a 6-point victory. Hancock recorded a maximum, surprisingly the only league maximum of his Reading career, and Simota shone in support.

To put that win in perspective, the Cheetahs had lost six out of nine league matches at Cowley including a 64-28 drubbing in a televised match versus Coventry. Since then, number one Jesper Jensen had bailed out and replacements looked hard to come by.

The full extent of just how bad the situation at Oxford had become was soon revealed. The following Wednesday afternoon's announcement that the return match at Smallmead (scheduled for Friday) would not take place was quickly followed by the news that Oxford had

82 Given that AA route planner recommends 90 minutes for the 54-mile journey from the airport to Foxhall stadium, Zagar would have missed the meeting's start, even if his plane had arrived on time. Commentators also remarked on the co-incidence that these events occurred just 48 hours before the Swedish Grand Prix.

pulled out of the league. Not since Ipswich in 1962 had a team pulled out of the senior division mid-season. The devastating news for Oxford supporters hit Reading by removing two of their three away wins from their league record at a stroke.

A subsequent rescue preserved Oxford's membership of the Conference League, but the Cheetahs departure from the Elite League alarmed all but the most complacent members of the speedway community. Some wondered which other tracks might be in financial difficulty.

They didn't have to wait long. BSI supremo John Postlethwaite came out into the open and admitted that Reading had proved to be a money pit. He claimed that in less than a season and a half, losses amounted to a staggering half a million pounds. Crowds in 2007 were down 29%, and the switch of race nights hadn't worked. His interview (*Speedway Star*, 9 June 2007) contained the admission that: "In hindsight, we shouldn't have changed the name from the Racers to the Bulldogs." Reading were not alone, later in the season Eastbourne and Peterborough both reported financial difficulties.

There had been two other major developments on the business side at Reading. In April IMG (which describes itself as "the world's premier and most diversified sports, entertainment and media enterprise") bought the rights to the Speedway Grand Prix from BSI. The deal included a role for John Postlethwaite, but did not include the Reading Bulldogs. Later in the month a further planning consent was granted for a new stadium. This one differed from the previous permission in that it incorporated a casino, described in the application as a 'racino'. Approval came despite opposition from other parties interested in running casinos. It made the new stadium more economically attractive and increased the likelihood of it ever being built.[83]

How would the sale of the GP rights affect Postlethwaite's commitment to the club? Observers wouldn't have to wait long before the denouement of the Bulldogs adventure, but first a recap of the team's on-track accomplishments.

The team that finished 2006 (i.e. including number eight Mark Lemon in place of Andy Smith) returned in 2007 with just one change. The single newcomer was a familiar face. Denied a 2006 place by the minutiae of the rules on averages, Danny Bird returned to replace Charlie Gjedde who moved back to Swindon. The complete team, including number eight Phil Morris, was unveiled to supporters at a fans' forum in January. In addition Morris finally signed (on loan) for his local track Newport, a full decade after negotiations with Newport promoter Tim Stone originally broke down.

The team came in at just a hundredth of a point below the team-building ceiling.[84] After downbeat comments from the promotion during the autumn, a weaker lower-cost team seemed a more likely path for BSI to pursue, but despite rider shortages inflating the cost of rider contracts BSI stuck with the high-cost option.

A further change came in the shape of a new race night – Fridays. Monday meetings faced competition from Sky and were vulnerable to airport delays with riders often en route from a Polish league match on Sunday to a Swedish Elitiserien fixture on the Tuesday. However, as Reading chose to run on Mondays when the weekend included a Grand Prix, the fixture list included almost as many meetings on Mondays as Fridays.

The racing season started with a big bang: the lavishly staged Sam Ermolenko Farewell meeting at Wolverhampton featured Bruce Penhall, with some of the coldest weather ever seen at a British speedway track during the regular season, and a superb display from Travis McGowan.

---

83 After the season ended, supporters were told at a fans' forum that Reading Borough Council wanted to see the speedway operation relocated to the Island Road site before the end of the 2008 season. Given that talk of a move had been in the air since 2000, this was greeted with a considerable degree of scepticism.

84 Reading would have been unable to field this team had they scored the extra points needed to secure the bonus point at Belle Vue the previous September. This fortuitous state of affairs led some cynics to suggest that average manipulation may have been a contributing factor to that poor display.

Four days later Ipswich's season started with a bang of a different kind; after less than half a lap number one Mark Loram's season was over. An unfortunate collision with Reading's Sam Simota left him with a badly broken leg. After a long delay the match limped to a conclusion, with the final races taking place in silence as at Foxhall a curfew applies to the PA, but not the racing! Mark Lemon piled up the points as Reading ran out unconvincing winners against the depleted and devastated Witches.

A busy Easter kicked off with a Good Friday double over Oxford, McGowan taking 33 (paid) points off his former team and propelling Reading to the top of the league. On Easter Sunday Reading were brought back down to earth by title favourites Swindon. The Robins repeated the double they had already achieved in March's warm-up challenge matches. They did so by a margin that can only be described as humiliating. Swindon won by 37 at Blunsdon, having earlier in the day bested Reading by 15 at Smallmead. The aggregate result for the bonus point (119-67) has only ever been worsened once – a 60-point margin in 2000 when the opponents were also Swindon.

In the pits – Travis McGowan prepares for another Smallmead encounter. (RM)

May brought further home defeats to Poole and Lakeside. The renamed Arena Essex team could thank number eight Chris Neath (a paid 16 contribution) for their victory.

These matches took place either side of 'Black Wednesday', and by the time Lakeside won at Smallmead the Bulldogs team contained replacements for Bird and Kolodziej. Both were familiar faces. Proving that old habits die hard, Sweden provided Jonas Davidsson, and closer to home Andy Smith agreed to wear the Bulldogs colours again. Smith only made half-a-dozen appearances, but Davidsson stayed to witness Reading's trials and tribulations for the remainder of the year.

Reading's problems were becoming more pressing. Following Oxford's demise, Postlethwaite and Lynch sought an emergency meeting with the BSPA. They emerged from the meeting with two conflicting messages: "business as usual", and that the club was up for sale. In reporting on the club's woes, journalist Dave Wright asked: "What more could go wrong for the Reading management?"

The answer came a few days later. After a 19-point haul at Wolverhampton (June 11) Hancock informed Reading management that he wouldn't be available for the Bulldogs next two matches. This turned into a short-term break, and it soon looked doubtful that he would ever return. In an interview at the start of the season (*Speedway Star*, 7 April 2007) Hancock observed of his winter negotiations:

> *"I told these guys I really wasn't sure I wanted to do a whole season. There's no way they're going to allow you to do half a season, and I understood if they didn't want me. I guarantee that if I ride for Reading speedway, you're going to get 100% Greg Hancock, but it's so much racing."*

What became apparent was that BSI had indeed allowed Hancock to ride for part of the season. It appeared that he only signed up until the end of May. Dave Wright had the answer to his question.

Hancock's next British appearance was in the Cardiff Grand Prix (June 30) where he led the final until passed by British speedway's new idol Chris Harris. Hancock continued to ride for Rospiggarna (Sweden) and Częstochowa (Poland) and, in September, added Russian club Togliatti to his CV. Rumours about large amounts of money being pumped into the Russian League had already increased worries about Britain's ability to attract top line riders. Ryan Sullivan missed Britain in 2007; instead he rode three matches in Russia.

After several poor Grand Prixs, Hancock ended the season on a high finishing runner-up (for a record 13th time) to Andreas Jonsson in the 'richest race in speedway' at the German Grand Prix. Having appeared in all one hundred Grand Prixs, Hancock qualified for 2008 by finishing sixth overall.

Back at Smallmead the situation looked dire in June. Any new owner would have to pick up existing contracts entered into by BSI – for example the expensive provision of mechanics to the team's contracted riders. Although the possibilities offered by a new stadium might attract interest, it seemed hard to imagine any prospective buyer emerging, and if one did then the likelihood of them remaining interested after due diligence seemed slim. Claims by various riders later emerged that they had been owed money.

The postponement on Saturday (June 16) of Reading's Monday clash with Coventry due to ongoing negotiations left all Reading fans on the edge of their seats. New owners were promised within days.

2007 – Phoenix

The name that most often cropped up in speculation about a new owner was Swindon promoter Terry Russell. On Tuesday June 19 came the announcement that everyone had been waiting for. Not only would the owners be changing, but so would the name. **The Reading Racers were back.**

The club's new owner Mark Legg, a Swindon-based businessman and father of Conference League rider Billy, planned to leave the running of the club to Malcolm Holloway – a man who needed no introduction to Reading fans.

The new management team exhibited a very sure sense of Reading's history, demonstrated by:

- The immediate announcement of the reversion to the Racers name.
- The appointment of Tim Sugar as new team manager. (This would be Tim's fourth spell in the role.)
- Plans to stage a Denny Pyeatt memorial meeting (unfortunately rained-off in July),
- Per Jonsson's September invite to Smallmead.
- And the decision, after the season ended, to revert to regular Monday race nights.

Just 24 hours after the takeover, the Racers roared in to action for the first time since September 2005. A makeshift team came away from Lakeside with the bonus point after a gritty display from Simota.

The Bulldogs have been put down and the Racers are back. Pictured left to right: Tim Sugar (team manager), Jonas Davidsson, Travis McGowan (on bike), Sam Simota, Matej Zagar, Mark Lemon, and kneeling at the front Janusz Kolodziej and Krzysztof Buczkowski. (BT)

The home meeting on July 9 ended a gap of 48 days without a wheel being turned at Smallmead. Three postponements due to rain, one due to Oxford's demise and the Coventry match postponed due to the sale negotiations explained the break in the schedule. Later that month even more rain followed and parts of Reading succumbed to flooding. The postponement of another home match (v Swindon on July 23) was the least of the town's problems.

Eastbourne provided the opposition when the Racers returned to the Smallmead track. The pleasure from an entertaining win was enhanced by the return of Janusz Kolodziej to the Reading side. Further changes followed. Chris Neath replaced Phil Morris at number eight. Later in the year Morris also changed his Premier League club with a sudden move to Birmingham. After extensive efforts to find a replacement for Hancock, a new signing finally materialised. Young Pole Krzysztof Buczkowski failed to score on his debut, but he did lead Chris Harris at Coventry until a last-lap fall deprived him of an impressive scalp. Within a month he hit double figures for the first time in his British career. The highlight of his season occurred when Poland won the Under-21 World Cup and Krzysztof topped the Polish score chart.

However Buczkowski couldn't fill the gap left by Hancock, and unfortunately another gap appeared with increasing frequency. After his moment of glory at Coventry in May, Zagar only completed one more away match for Reading. A variety of international commitments, illnesses, short-term injuries and travel problems kept him out of the Reading line-up.

Patience finally wore out when Zagar missed a Wednesday trip to Belle Vue, apparently due to sickness. The following night he 'recovered' sufficiently to ride in a Polish league match. But he should have been representing Reading at the Elite League Riders Championship. McGowan replaced him (and did well on an initially atrocious track). Zagar received a 28-day ban from the BSPA.

After the ban ended, Zagar's scheduled return was put on hold after a fall in Poland gave him concussion. Early in the week following this fall he informed Reading that he would not be fit for the next Monday's home cup tie with Swindon (Oct 15). This turned out to be a truly remarkable concussion, as it disappeared for long enough to allow Zagar to ride in the Grand Prix on the Saturday, but had laid him low again by Monday. Holloway made his disgust known in no uncertain terms. Sentiment on the terraces hardened against the Slovenian star. From Smallmead idol to persona non grata took less than a year for Zagar. Much as fans thrilled to his fence-scraping swoops, they had grown tired of his excuses.

For all that happened during the year, it seems quite remarkable that Reading were still in the Knock-Out Cup in October. After defeating Wolverhampton and Ipswich, a semi-final tie with Swindon looked like no contest. Reading had little hope of progressing after Swindon led for much of the second leg, held in mid September the day after an 18-point defeat at Swindon in the first leg. Then in heat 11, race leader Travis McGowan lost control and brought down Leigh Adams and Andrew Moore. The accident, one of the worst ever seen at Smallmead, resulted in the abandonment of the meeting. While Adams and Moore recovered in time for the Elite League play-off final McGowan had broken his shoulder for the second time in 2007.

Although many people expected the tie to be awarded to Swindon (at the time of abandonment Reading required a string of 5-nils to go through), a re-run was ordered. Swindon duly made it eight wins out of eight against Reading in 2007 when the tie was completed on October 15.

With McGowan out for the rest of the season, Reading made another signing for the final month of the season. At 18 Patrick Hougaard, the Danish Under-21 Champion and bronze medallist in the European Championship looked to be a fine prospect.

Over the course of the season Reading lost eight out of eighteen league matches at Smallmead. Despite this Reading never looked remotely like finishing bottom. Belle Vue and Ipswich always looked destined to finish in the bottom two. Even squandering a 10-point lead at home to Belle Vue couldn't prevent the Aces from picking up the wooden spoon. In this match, the final one of the home league programme, Davidsson excelled with paid 14 from the number two berth. And he was watched by none other than fellow Swede Per Jonsson. Per's appearance commemorated the 20th anniversary of his record-setting ride in October 1987. In July, nine weeks before his visit, Per's track record nearly fell. Lee Richardson (guesting in place of Hancock) clocked 58.27, less than a fifth of a second outside the record.

Davidsson's form partially dispelled his reputation for under-performing in the Elite League, but he still produced his best results on other stages. In July he managed 16 points riding for Sweden in a World Cup round at Coventry. In September he finished runner-up to Andreas Jonsson in the Swedish Championship and then came seventh in the Grand Prix Qualifying Final.

Jonas Davidsson – returned unexpectedly for a second stint at Smallmead. (BT)

Kolodziej, Lemon and McGowan all turned in good seasons despite the chaos going on around them. Kolodziej did better after his break from club duties and boasted five double-figure scores in a row in August. He ended the season as the holder of the Andy Fuller Shield, awarded to the most improved Racer. McGowan's average dipped a bit, but he saw his best two scores deleted from the records when Oxford folded. Lemon started the year well, and finished it on a high, winning the season finale.

Malcolm Holloway decided to have a second go at holding the Denny Pyeatt Memorial meeting. A Premier League calibre field acted as a tester for the possible change of leagues in 2008. Lemon won the final from Stojanowski (Isle of Wight), Sitera (Czech Republic) and team mate Hougaard. The field included veteran American Shawn McConnell (aged 48). There is no doubt that had he been available Bobby Schwartz (still riding at 51) would have joined him. The mere mention of his name instantly evokes memories of the glorious 1980 season. Instead Schwartz sent a deeply personal message.

He thanked the club for holding the meeting, and the fans for supporting it and signed off:

> *"Denny I know you are looking down on us all, we think of you often. You will always be a racer and great inspiration, we will never forget you. God bless you Denny."*

Team: Greg Hancock 9.54, Matej Zagar 8.00, Janusz Kolodziej 7.21, Travis McGowan 6.29, Jonas Davidsson 5.71, Sam Simota 5.24, Mark Lemon 5.20, (Krzysztof Buczkowski 5.05), Danny Bird 4.81, (Andy Smith 3.43)

Denny Pyeatt

15 November 1957 - 17 July 1981

always remembered

(EP)

Appendix 1

Reading Career Records

	Yr	Mtch	Rides	Pts	BP	TP	CMA	F max	P max
Roger Abel	1978	14	45	37	8	45	4.00	-	-
Colin Ackroyd	1981-82	12	41	37	5	42	4.10	-	-
Jan Andersson	1979-92	544	2435	5212.5	307	5519.5	9.07	46	20
Josef Angermuller	1971	8	23	14	5	19	3.30	-	-
Andrew Appleton	2002-05	163	815	1475	134	1609	7.90	2	9
Martin Ashby	1980	24	80	81	25	106	5.30	-	-
Mick Bell	1969-76	221	796	1041	182	1223	6.15	2	3
Terry Betts	1979	34	143	256	21	277	7.75	-	-
Danny Bird	2004-07	63	288	582	47	629	8.74	3	5
Carl Blackbird	1989	43	185	213	32	245	5.30	-	-
Eugeniusz Blaszak	1976	8	24	18	4	22	3.67	-	-
Ian Bottomley	1968	10	35	38	5	43	4.91	-	-
Kevin Bowen	1978-79	12	30	14	3	17	2.27	-	-
Shane Bowes	1994	42	212	273	36	309	5.83	-	-
Steve Braidford	2004	23	83	41	10	51	2.46	-	-
Pierre Brannefors	1983-84	87	324	422	92	514	6.35	-	1
Tony Briggs	1980-81	60	222	218	59	277	4.99	-	-
Krzysztof Buczkowski	2007	9	38	40	8	48	5.05	-	-
Jason Bunyan	2002-07	19	78	110	19	129	6.62	-	1
Armando Castagna	1989-2001	245	1199	2260.5	141	2401.5	8.01	5	2
Steve Chambers	1988-89	12	29	6	2	8	1.10	-	-
Ian Champion	1968-69	30	121	185	20	205	6.78	-	-
Mark Chessell	1985	12	39	16	4	20	2.05	-	-
Ian Clarke	1998	8	24	5	1	6	1.00	-	-
Paul Clews	1998-2003	208	922	1096	247	1343	5.83	-	4
Peter Collyer	1999-2003	19	61	21	6	27	1.77	-	-
Shane Colvin	1999-2003	86	327	266	54	320	3.91	-	-
Marvyn Cox	1995	7	36	83	2	85	9.44	-	-
Matthew Cross	1994	37	135	69	19	88	2.61	-	-
Glenn Cunningham	1997-2006	47	240	527	35	562	9.37	3	6
Geoff Curtis	1971-73	116	458	780	92	872	7.62	2	10
Jonas Davidsson	2003-07	62	290	375	59	434	5.99	-	-
Dene Davies	1968-70	82	310	380	58	438	5.65	-	1
John Davis	1975-87	331	1393	3007	108	3115	8.94	32	10
Jeremy Doncaster	1989-94	223	1093	2071	167	2238	8.19	3	5
Lee Driver	1998	12	35	20	7	27	3.09	-	-
Reidar Eide	1979-80	19	69	76	16	92	5.33	-	-
Bobby Eldridge	1997	17	62	25	6	31	2.00	-	-

	Yr	Mtch	Rides	Pts	BP	TP	CMA	F max	P max
Justin Elkins	1994-99	64	276	284	59	343	4.97	-	-
Jason Gage	1995	7	28	18	3	21	3.00	-	-
Andy Galvin	1986	6	18	18	2	20	4.44	-	-
Charlie Gjedde	2001-06	79	380	713	71	784	8.25	2	2
Peter Glanz	1983-93	221	810	881	201	1082	5.34	-	-
Ian Gledhill	1976-81	39	113	83	14	97	3.43	-	-
Henryk Glucklich	1978	20	64	41	6	47	2.94	-	-
John Grahame	1982-83	70	196	138	30	168	3.43	-	-
Steve Gresham	1982	36	140	186	9	195	5.57	-	-
John Hammond	1970	28	99	106	19	125	5.05	-	-
Greg Hancock	2006-07	59	293	643	42	685	9.35	-	1
Gavin Hedge	2002	10	39	23	6	29	2.97	-	-
Anders Henriksson	2002	36	165	292	19	311	7.54	-	-
Lee Herne	2000	10	42	25	3	28	2.67	-	-
Malcolm Holloway	1984-2004	229	829	927	187	1114	5.38	-	1
Bob Humphreys	1975-79	168	637	763	135	898	5.64	-	4
Scott Humphries	1991	33	133	127	26	153	4.60	-	-
Tim Hunt	1982-85	161	605	624	164	788	5.21	-	-
Andrzej Huszcza	1981	5	18	10	5	15	3.33	-	-
Alan Jackson	1969	17	60	94	18	112	7.47	1	1
Bengt Jansson	1975-77	87	351	526	76	602	6.86	2	2
Dave Jessup	1976-78	116	502	1261	31	1292	10.29	27	9
Uno Johansson	1982	7	23	12	4	16	2.78	-	-
Chris Johnson	2004-05	36	130	75	20	95	2.92	-	-
Per Jonsson	1984-94	343	1565	3152.5	230	3382.5	8.65	31	18
Daniel King	2003	9	38	35	6	41	4.32	-	-
Petri Kokko	1995-99	141	675	1192	95	1287	7.63	9	6
Janusz Kolodziej	2003-07	64	300	498	72	570	7.60	-	1
Tim Korneliussen	1991	8	23	6	0	6	1.04	-	-
Jarno Kosonen	1999	16	55	53	9	62	4.51	-	-
Einar Kyllingstad	1985	5	16	5	2	7	1.75	-	-
Bernie Leigh	1969-81	431	1633	1982	350	2332	5.71	-	2
Mark Lemon	2006-07	52	236	290	35	325	5.51	-	-
Mark Leslie	1980-82	7	14	3	3	6	1.71	-	-
Dag Lovaas	1971-73	112	458	952	73	1025	8.95	16	3
Brendon Mackay	2001	11	34	6	2	8	0.94	-	-
Krister Marsh	1997-2000	87	386	370	63	433	4.49	-	-
Steve Masters	1994-2005	10	36	27	4	31	3.44	-	-
Richard May	1969-75	204	770	1182	126	1308	6.79	7	7
Steve McDermott	1980-83	14	41	35	7	42	4.10	-	-
Travis McGowan	2006-07	74	358	534	68	602	6.73	-	-
Bobby McNeil	1973	7	25	27	6	33	5.28	-	-

	Yr	Mtch	Rides	Pts	BP	TP	CMA	F max	P max
Anders Michanek	1971-81	121	497	1292	22	1314	10.58	47	11
Neil Middleditch	1985-86	14	49	42	14	56	4.57	-	-
Jack Millen	1973	12	40	28	4	32	3.20	-	-
Chris Mills	2004-06	57	251	226	51	277	4.41	-	-
Phil Morris	1991-2007	434	1868	2697	350	3047	6.52	4	6
Ray Morton	1991-96	173	805	1116	174	1290	6.41	-	1
Geoff Mudge	1971-72	54	207	325	44	369	7.13	-	-
Dave Mullett	1985-2002	561	2526	4269	497	4766	7.55	12	19
Nathan Murray	1990	18	55	22	10	32	2.33	-	-
Terry Mussett	1991	13	40	12	1	13	1.30	-	-
Chris Neath	2007	5	19	15	3	18	3.79	-	-
David Norris	1995	19	111	237	10	247	8.90	1	2
Marc Norris	1999-2001	72	305	229	53	282	3.70	-	-
Danny Norton	2003-04	23	73	17	3	20	1.10	-	-
Kenneth Nystrom	1993	15	58	62	8	70	4.83	-	-
Tony Olsson	1986-96	278	1311	1977	270	2247	6.86	-	3
Tommy Palmer	2001	27	115	86	15	101	3.51	-	-
Joel Parsons	2003	16	58	44	11	55	3.79	-	-
Rodney Payne	1987-88	30	88	39	14	53	2.41	-	-
Jan Pedersen	1994-96	26	126	115	26	141	4.48	-	-
Glen Phillips	2002	43	181	159	35	194	4.29	-	-
Paul Pickering	1997	39	202	293	35	328	6.50	-	2
Billy Pinder	1986	22	66	18	3	21	1.27	-	-
Jorg Pingel	1996	18	78	76.5	12	88.5	4.54	-	-
John Poyser	1968	23	102	230	7	237	9.29	5	1
Cec Platt	1970	20	59	52	10	62	4.20	-	-
Phil Pratt	1968-70	58	197	225	44	269	5.46	-	1
Boleslaw Proch	1976-77	42	155	169	33	202	5.21	-	-
Ashley Pullen	1978-82	77	239	198	43	241	4.03	-	1
Scott Pulleyn	1989	6	18	3	0	3	0.67	-	-
Denny Pyeatt	1981-82	79	307	314	70	384	5.00	-	-
Lee Richardson	1995-98	102	494	762	60	822	6.66	5	1
Pete Saunders	1968	5	11	9	3	12	4.36	-	-
Chris Schramm	2001-06	123	494	414	98	512	4.15	-	-
Bobby Schwartz	1980-83	157	695	1573	78	1651	9.50	19	9
Lance Sealey	1992-93	47	151	81	19	100	2.65	-	-
Mitch Shirra	1983-91	261	1156	2335.5	102	2437.5	8.43	20	7
Zdenek Simota	2005-07	113	520	656	84	740	5.69	-	-
Andy Smith	2006-07	33	136	142	31	173	5.09	-	-
Graeme Smith	1972	11	35	28	5	33	3.77	-	-
Scott Smith	2003	25	120	161	13	174	5.80	-	-
Troy Smith	1988-90	9	21	6	1	7	1.33	-	-

	Yr	Mtch	Rides	Pts	BP	TP	CMA	F max	P max
Ted Spittles	1968	23	94	146	11	157	6.68	-	1
Jiri Stancl	1979-82	68	266	353	62	415	6.24	1	1
David Steen	1989-97	139	593	618	127	745	5.03	-	2
Bob Tabet	1969-70	38	128	150	29	179	5.59	-	-
Gary Tagg	1986-88	82	237	111.5	30	141.5	2.39	-	-
Glyn Taylor	1977-83	13	32	17	1	18	2.25	-	-
Melvyn Taylor	1978-79	45	167	176	45	221	5.29	-	-
Mike Tomlin	1991-93	6	18	3	1	4	0.89	-	-
Mathieu Tresarrieu	2005	40	200	244	36	280	5.60	-	-
Dave Trownson	1980-83	27	98	97	22	119	4.86	-	-
Doug Underwood	1977-79	61	203	192	34	226	4.45	-	1
Stanislav Urban	1983	25	84	57	11	68	3.24	-	-
Mike Vernam	1969-70	62	254	498	34	532	8.38	8	-
Paul Walch	1968	6	21	19	5	24	4.57	-	-
Jack Walker	1973	5	13	6	2	8	2.46	-	-
Stuart Wallace	1968	20	78	103	18	121	6.21	-	-
Hans Wassermann	1977-78	52	194	223	53	276	5.69	-	-
Joe Weichlbauer	1968	13	50	74	12	86	6.88	-	-
Jamie Westacott	2004-05	22	80	29	6	35	1.75	-	-
Per Wester	1999-2000	30	133	253	11	264	7.94	1	1
Vic White	1968	5	27	54	4	58	8.59	1	-
Todd Wiltshire	1990-91	59	296	607	41	648	8.76	1	3
Richard Wolff	2005	42	203	248	32	280	5.52	-	-
Peter Wurterle	1981	8	21	6	2	8	1.52	-	-
Bob Young	1970	26	104	141	18	159	6.12	-	-
Matej Zagar	2004-07	147	740	1634	81	1715	9.27	12	8

Notes:

1 *Minimum qualification 5 matches*

2 *Guest appearances are not included. The definition of what counts as a guest appearance has varied over time. This table follows the categorisation used at the time*

3 *All official fixtures are included: .i.e. League (inc. 2006 play-offs), Cup, League Cup (1981-87), Gold Cup (1989-92), BSPA Cup (1991-92), Premier Trophy (1999-2002 & 2004-05), Inter-League Cup (2003), Young Shield (1997-98, 2002 & 2004); but not the Craven Shield, Midland Cup, Premiership or Spring Gold Cup*

4 *Since 1999 double points have been available in various circumstances. These rides are counted, and points scored are counted as normal, not at their doubled value.*

Appendix 2

League Record – by Year

Year	*Lge*	*Team*	*Pos*	*M*	*W*	*D*	*L*	*W*	*D*	*L*	*race pts for*	*race pts against*	*BP for*	*BP again*	*MP*
1968	BL2	10	8	18	6	1	2	0	1	8	675	725	-	-	14
1969	BL2	16	2	30	13	1	1	6	0	9	1221	1103	-	-	39
1970	BL2	17	9	32	14	0	2	3	0	13	1278.5	1211.5	-	-	34
1971	BL1	19	6	36	15	2	1	3	2	13	1438	1361	-	-	40
1972	BL1	18	2	34	17	0	0	8	1	8	1454	1194	-	-	51
1973	**BL1**	**18**	**1**	**34**	**15**	**1**	**1**	**10**	**0**	**7**	**1494**	**1156**	**-**	**-**	**51**
1975	BL	18	6	34	16	0	1	5	0	12	1342	1308	-	-	42
1976	BL	19	6	36	14	2	2	5	1	12	1477	1325	-	-	41
1977	BL	19	3	36	16	2	0	9	1	8	1482	1323	-	-	53
1978	BL	19	14	36	11	2	5	2	1	15	1338	1462	-	-	29
1979	BL	18	7	34	14	0	3	3	0	14	1345	1305	-	-	34
1980	**BL**	**17**	**1**	**32**	**15**	**0**	**1**	**9**	**1**	**6**	**1434**	**1062**	**-**	**-**	**49**
1981	BL	16	11	30	7	4	4	2	3	10	1129	1208	-	-	25
1982	BL	15	9	28	11	0	3	1	2	11	1078	1103	-	-	26
1983	BL	15	4	28	13	0	1	4	0	10	1137	1044	-	-	34
1984	BL	16	4	30	14	0	1	3	1	11	1202.5	1126.5	-	-	35
1985	BL	11	9	19	5	2	2	1	2	7	734	743	6	3	22
1986	BL	11	7	20	4	3	3	3	0	7	757	801	4	6	21
1987	BL	12	7	22	9	1	1	2	1	8	874.5	840.5	4	7	28
1988	BL	11	5	40	15	0	5	5	3	12	1857	1736	12	8	55
1989	BL	9	7	32	9	1	6	4	0	12	1356	1521	5	11	32
1990	**BL**	**9**	**1**	**32**	**13**	**1**	**2**	**6**	**2**	**8**	**1513.5**	**1360.5**	**13**	**3**	**54**
1991	BL1	13	11	24	8	0	4	1	0	11	1030	1123	3	9	21
1992	**BL1**	**13**	**1**	**24**	**12**	**0**	**0**	**7**	**1**	**4**	**1199**	**944**	**11**	**1**	**50**
1993	BL1	11	6	40	17	0	3	3	1	16	2181	2129	10	10	51
1994	BL1	11	10	40	12	2	6	2	0	18	1815.5	2018.5	6	14	36
1995	PL	21	13	40	14	3	3	3	1	16	1876	1959	9	11	47
1996	PL	19	19	36	9	1	8	2	0	16	1590.5	1859.5	2	16	25
1997	**PL**	**14**	**1**	**26**	**13**	**0**	**0**	**9**	**0**	**4**	**1323**	**1011**	**13**	**0**	**57**
1998	PL	13	2	24	12	0	0	4	0	8	1130	989	10	2	42
1999	PL	13	13	24	4	0	8	1	1	10	1004	1140	2	10	13
2000	PL	14	14	26	7	1	5	0	0	13	1075	1262	2	11	17
2001	PL	15	9	28	9	2	3	3	1	10	1272	1250	6	8	33
2002	PL	17	8	32	15	0	1	2	0	14	1427	1448	7	9	41
2003	PL	18	16	34	8	2	7	1	0	16	1404	1653	2	15	22
2004	PL	15	3	28	14	0	0	3	0	11	1389.5	1228.5	12	2	46
2005	PL	15	10	28	10	0	4	2	0	12	1281	1310	4	10	28
2006	EL	11	2	40	16	0	4	9	1	10	1934	1756	13	7	64
2007	EL	10	8	36	10	0	8	1	1	16	1497	1779	3	15	26
	Totals			**1203**	**456**	**34**	**111**	**147**	**29**	**426**	**52045.5**	**50878.5**	**159**	**188**	**1428**

League Record – by Opponent

		Home			Away			BP	BP		
	M	W	D	L	W	D	L	W	L	Pts	%
Arena (Lakeside)	34	14	0	3	4	1	12	10	7	47	55.3
Belle Vue	72	22	2	12	4	2	30	7	14	63	38.2
Berwick	26	10	0	3	4	0	9	4	6	32	51.6
Birmingham	16	8	0	0	3	1	4	-	-	23	71.9
Bradford	33	13	2	2	4	0	12	10	6	46	56.1
Bristol	4	2	0	0	0	0	2	-	-	4	50
Canterbury	6	1	0	2	0	0	3	-	-	2	16.7
Coatbridge	2	1	0	0	0	0	1	-	-	2	50
Coventry	68	21	5	8	7	3	24	5	16	69	43.9
Cradley	59	20	0	9	7	0	23	7	9	61	45.5
Crayford	6	3	0	0	0	0	3	-	-	6	50
Crewe	4	2	0	0	0	0	2	-	-	4	50
Doncaster	4	2	0	0	1	0	1	-	-	6	75
Eastbourne	40	14	1	5	7	0	13	5	7	48	52.2
Edinburgh	22	8	0	3	0	0	11	4	7	20	36.4
Exeter	40	18	1	1	2	2	16	7	4	50	54.9
Glasgow	24	10	1	1	3	0	9	6	4	33	56.9
Hackney	28	11	2	1	4	0	10	1	1	33	56.9
Halifax	28	14	0	0	2	1	11	1	0	34	59.6
Hull	34	14	2	1	3	0	14	5	5	41	52.6
Ipswich	62	21	1	9	7	2	22	7	10	66	46.8
Isle of Wight	18	6	0	3	0	0	9	1	8	13	28.9
King's Lynn	68	25	4	5	9	3	22	10	9	85	54.8
Leicester	24	12	0	0	5	1	6	-	-	35	72.9
Long Eaton	10	5	0	0	2	0	3	1	2	15	65.2
Middlesbrough	10	4	1	0	1	0	4	1	1	12	54.5
Nelson	5	2	0	0	0	0	3	-	-	4	40
Newcastle	20	6	0	4	3	0	7	3	6	21	42.9
Newport	28	11	1	2	5	0	9	4	5	37	56.9
Oxford	42	16	0	5	9	1	11	10	6	61	61
Peterborough	16	6	0	2	2	0	6	3	4	19	48.7
Plymouth	4	2	0	0	0	0	2	-	-	4	50
Poole	50	18	3	4	12	2	11	9	3	74	66.1
Rayleigh	6	3	0	0	0	0	3	-	-	6	50
Rochdale	2	1	0	0	0	0	1	-	-	2	50
Romford	4	1	0	1	2	0	0	-	-	6	75
Rye House	8	3	0	1	0	0	4	2	2	8	40
Sheffield	58	23	3	3	8	0	21	8	8	73	55.3
Somerset	8	4	0	0	1	0	3	3	1	13	65
Stoke	18	8	0	1	5	0	4	6	3	32	71.1
Swindon	70	24	3	8	9	4	22	11	11	84	51.9
Trelawny	6	2	0	1	2	0	1	2	1	10	66.7

		Home			Away			BP	BP		
	M	**W**	**D**	**L**	**W**	**D**	**L**	**W**	**L**	**Pts**	**%**
Wembley	2	1	0	0	0	0	1	-	-	2	50
West Ham	2	1	0	0	0	1	0	-	-	3	75
Weymouth	2	1	0	0	0	1	0	-	-	3	75
White City	6	1	1	1	1	0	2	-	-	5	41.7
Wimbledon	26	13	0	0	3	0	10	-	-	32	61.5
Wolverhampton	62	23	1	7	5	3	23	4	17	64	44.1
Workington	16	5	0	3	1	1	6	2	5	15	38.5
	1203	**456**	**34**	**111**	**147**	**29**	**426**	**159**	**188**	**1428**	**51.9**

League Record – by Division

	M	*W*	*D*	*L*	*W*	*D*	*L*	*race pts for*	*race pts against*	*BP for*	*BP again*	*MP*
Division One	873	331	27	78	113	26	298	37565.5	36547.5	101	121	1042
Division Two	330	125	7	33	34	3	128	14480	14331	58	67	386
Totals	**1203**	**456**	**34**	**111**	**147**	**29**	**426**	**52045.5**	**50878.5**	**159**	**188**	**1428**

Notes:

1. *Division One record comprises 1971-1996 and 2006-07. Division Two record comprises 1968-70 and 1997-2005.*
2. *1985 home match v Cradley not ridden.*
3. *1992 match at King's Lynn not ridden. Match awarded 75-nil to Reading included in tables above.*
4. *Results of 2006 Elite League play-offs not included.*
5. *Excludes three matches against Oxford in 2007 that were deleted from the records.*
6. *Belle Vue and King's Lynn results include Division Two matches against second teams in 1968 and 1969.*
7. *Nelson and King's Lynn II switched tracks in 1970. Analysis includes away match at Nelson and home match with Bradford. Both fixtures against King's Lynn II were ridden before they relocated to Boston. Reading have never ridden against Boston.*

Conference League/Amateur League

Year		*Team*	*Pos*	*M*	*W*	*D*	*L*	*W*	*D*	*L*	*race pts for*	*race pts against*	*MP*
1996	Reading Ravens	13	11	13	4	0	2	1	0	6	477	508	10
1997	M4 Raven Sprockets	13	7	24	7	0	5	3	3	6	820	848	23
	Totals			**37**	**11**	**0**	**7**	**4**	**3**	**12**	**1297**	**1356**	**33**

Notes:

8. *In 1996 the competition was known as the Conference League, in 1997 the Amateur League. In neither season were bonus points awarded for an aggregate win.*
9. *1997 results include two matches awarded as 0-0 draws. The matches away to Berwick and Anglian Angels were raced over three laps instead of four, and the original results were expunged from the records.*

Appendix 3

Track Record – Tilehurst

Date	*Time*	*Rider*	*Meeting*
17.6.68*	72.4	Dave Schofield	for Nelson
24.6.68	72.2	John Edwards	Second half
15.7.68	72.0	Graham Plant	Stadium Trophy
22.7.68	72.0	John Poyser	v Middlesbrough
28.4.69	71.6	Martyn Piddock	for Canterbury
25.8.69	71.2	Mick Bell	Young England v Y Czechoslovakia
27.7.70	71.2	Tommy Johansson	Young Sweden v Y England
27.7.70	71.0	Richard May	Young England v Y Sweden
27.7.70	70.4	Tommy Johansson	Young Sweden v Y England
5.4.71	69.8	Ole Olsen	guest v West Ham
21.6.71	68.8	Bernt Persson	for Cradley
9.8.71	68.4	Anders Michanek	v King's Lynn
23.8.71	68.4	Jim Airey	for Sheffield
15.5.72#	67.4	Ole Olsen	for Wolverhampton

 # Fastest-ever time by a Reading rider - 67.6 by Anders Michanek on 1.10.73

** Fastest time in opening meeting. Records were previously established in heats 1,2,6 by Fred Powell, John Poyser and Ian Champion.*

Track Record – Smallmead

Date	*Time*	*Rider*	*Meeting*
28.4.75	64.6	Jim McMillan	for Hull
5.5.75	64.0	Anders Michanek	v Swindon
12.5.75	63.6	Anders Michanek	Golden Helmet v Crump Ht 1
12.5.75	63.4	Phil Crump	Golden Helmet v Michanek Ht 2
12.5.75	63.2	Anders Michanek	Golden Helmet v Crump Ht 3
16.6.75	62.0	Phil Crump	for Newport
30.6.75	62.0	Bengt Jansson	v Belle Vue
30.6.75	61.8	Anders Michanek	v Belle Vue
14.7.75	61.8	Ivan Mauger	for New Zealand: W Team Cup
19.7.76	61.4	Ole Olsen	Jubilee Trophy
25.4.77	61.4	Malcolm Simmons	for Poole
9.5.77	60.8	Dave Jessup	Nulli Secundus Best Pairs
18.9.78	60.0	Peter Collins	Manpower
28.9.81	59.7	Hans Nielsen	for Birmingham
14.6.82	59.4	Shawn Moran	for Sheffield
24.6.85	59.2	Hans Nielsen	for Oxford
25.5.87+	58.4	Hans Nielsen	For Oxford
12.10.87$	58.1	Per Jonsson	v Coventry

+ From green light start, not recognised in Reading programme

$ Fastest time since track record 58.2 by Andreas Jonsson (Arena Essex) – 8.5.06

Appendix 4

Miscellaneous Records

Points (including bonus) in Reading career

		total	*points*	*bonus*
1	Jan Andersson	5519.5	5212.5	307
2	Dave Mullett	4766	4269	497
3	Per Jonsson	3382.5	3152.5	230
4	John Davis	3115	3007	108
5	Phil Morris	3047	2697	350
6	Mitch Shirra	2437.5	2335.5	102
7	Armando Castagna	2401.5	2260.5	141
8	Bernie Leigh	2332	1982	350
9	Tony Olsson	2247	1977	270
10	Jeremy Doncaster	2238	2071	167
11	Matej Zagar	1715	1634	81
12	Bobby Schwartz	1651	1573	78
13	Andrew Appleton	1609	1475	134
14	Paul Clews	1343	1096	247
15	Anders Michanek	1314	1292	22
16	Richard May	1308	1182	126
17	Dave Jessup	1292	1261	31
18	Ray Morton	1290	1116	174
19	Petri Kokko	1287	1192	95
20	Mick Bell	1223	1041	182

Top Point Scorers 1968-70: *Mike Vernam 532, Richard May 497, Dene Davies 438*

Top Point Scorers 1971-96: *Jan Andersson 5519.5, Per Jonsson 3382.5, John Davis 3115, Dave Mullett 2890, Mitch Shirra 2437.5, Tony Olsson 2247, Jeremy Doncaster 2238*

Top Point Scorers 1997-05: *Phil Morris 2150, Dave Mullett 1876,Andrew Appleton 1609*

Top Point Scorers 2006-07: *Greg Hancock 685, Matej Zagar 663, Travis McGowan 602*

Points (including bonus) in a season

		year	*points*
1	Per Jonsson	1992	643
2	Jan Andersson	1981	603
3	Matej Zagar	2004	570 (58)*
4	Glenn Cunningham	1997	553
5	Dave Mullett	1997	539
6	Matej Zagar	2005	537 (52)*
7	Danny Bird	2004	532 (58)*
8	Bobby Schwartz	1981	510
9	Andrew Appleton	2004	507 (34)*
10	Jeremy Doncaster	1989	503

**Includes double points from tactical rides (as shown in brackets)*

Points in a single match

		match	*pts(rds)*
1	Bobby Schwartz	1980 @ Cradley	21(7)
	Phil Morris	2004 v Hull	21(6)^
	Simon Stead*	2005 @ Somerset	21(6)^
4	Matej Zagar	2005 v Newcastle	20+1(6)#
5	Matej Zagar	2005 v Isle of Wight	20(6)^
	Leigh Lanham*	2005 @ Rye House	20(6)^
	Matej Zagar	2005 @ Isle of Wight	20(7)#
8	Matej Zagar	2004 @ Exeter	19+1(6)^
9	Dave Norris	1995 v Ipswich	19(7)
	Travis McGowan*	2005 @ Newcastle	19(7)#
	Greg Hancock	2007 @ Wolves	19(6)^
12	Matej Zagar	2005 @ K Lynn	18+1(6)^
13	Petri Kokko	1995 @ Ipswich	16+3(7)

** Guest*
 # Includes double points ride off 15 metres
^ Includes double points ride from scratch

Bonus points in Reading career

1	Dave Mullett	1985-2002	497
2	Bernie Leigh	1969-81	350
	Phil Morris	1991-2007	350
4	Jan Andersson	1979-92	307
5	Tony Olsson	1986-96	270
6	Paul Clews	1998-2003	247
7	Per Jonsson	1984-94	230
8	Peter Glanz	1983-93	201
9	Malcolm Holloway	1984-2004	187
10	Mick Bell	1969-76	182
11	Ray Morton	1991-96	174
12	Jeremy Doncaster	1989-94	167
13	Tim Hunt	1982-85	164
14	Armando Castagna	1989-2001	141
15	Bob Humphreys	1975-79	135

Most bonus points in a season

		year	*bonus*
1	Dave Mullett	1992	81
2	Peter Glanz	1987	69
3	David Steen	1997	65
4	Andrew Appleton	2004	59
5	Tony Olsson	1993	57
6	Pierre Brannefors	1983	56
	Tim Hunt	1984	56
8	Paul Clews	2003	54

Maximums for Reading

		total	*full*	*paid*
1	Jan Andersson	66	46	20
2	Anders Michanek	58	47	11
3	Per Jonsson	49	31	18
4	John Davis	42	32	10
5	Dave Jessup	36	27	9
6	Dave Mullett	31	12	19
7	Bobby Schwartz	28	19	9
8	Mitch Shirra	27	20	7
9	Matej Zagar	20	12	8
10	Dag Lovaas	19	16	3
11	Petri Kokko	15	9	6
12	Richard May	14	7	7

Most maximums in a season

		tot	*full/paid*	*year*
1	Anders Michanek	26	22/4	1973
2	Dave Jessup	15	12/3	1977
3	Per Jonsson	15	8/7	1992
4	Dave Jessup	13	9/4	1976
5	Dag Lovaas	12	11/1	1973
6	Mitch Shirra	12	10/2	1983
7	Per Jonsson	12	7/5	1993
8	Anders Michanek	11	9/2	1975
9	Bobby Schwartz	11	8/3	1980
10	Dave Mullett	11	6/5	1997

Highest average in Reading career (minimum 10 matches)

1	Anders Michanek	10.58
2	Dave Jessup	10.29
3	Bobby Schwartz	9.50
4	Glenn Cunningham	9.37
5	Greg Hancock	9.35
6	John Poyser	9.29
7	Matej Zagar	9.27
8	Jan Andersson	9.07
9	Dag Lovaas	8.95
10	John Davis	8.94
11	David Norris	8.90
12	Todd Wiltshire	8.76
13	Danny Bird	8.74
14	Per Jonsson	8.65
15	Mitch Shirra	8.43

Highest average in a season (minimum 10 matches)

		year	*average*
1	Anders Michanek	1973	11.36
2	Anders Michanek	1975	10.91
3	Anders Michanek	1972	10.51
4	Dave Mullett	1997	10.47
5	Matej Zagar	2005	10.43
6	Per Jonsson	1994	10.41
7	Dave Jessup	1976	10.35
8	Per Jonsson	1993	10.34
9	John Davis	1979	10.32
10	Dave Jessup	1977	10.32

Appearances

1	Dave Mullett	1985-2002	561
2	Jan Andersson	1979-1992	544
3	Phil Morris	1991-2007	434
4	Bernie Leigh	1969-1981	431
5	Per Jonsson	1984-1994	343
6	John Davis	1975-1987	331
7	Tony Olsson	1986-1996	278
8	Mitch Shirra	1983-1991	261
9	Armando Castagna	1989-2001	245
10	Malcolm Holloway	1984-2004	229
11	Jeremy Doncaster	1989-1994	223
12	Peter Glanz	1983-1993	221
	Mick Bell	1969-1976	221
14	Paul Clews	1998-2003	208
15	Richard May	1969-1975	204

Consecutive appearances

1	Mick Bell	1971-1975	148
2	Bob Humphreys	1975-1978	132
3	Bernie Leigh	1978-1981	131
4	Jan Andersson	1990-1992	120

Andy Fuller Shield for the most improved Reading rider

1998	Lee Richardson	2003	Jonas Davidsson
1999	Phil Morris	2004	Chris Schramm
2000	Paul Clews	2005	Matt Tresarrieu
2001	Paul Clews	2006	Zdenek Simota
2002	Chris Schramm	2007	Janusz Kolodziej

Biggest wins (home)

1	Skegness (cup)	1997	68-21
2	Trelawny (PT)	2001	68-22
	Eastbourne (cup)	1979	77-31
4	King's Lynn	1993	75-33
5	Berwick	1970	59-19
	Halifax	1973	59-19
	Rye House (PT)	2002	65-25
8	Oxford	2006	67-28
9	Exeter	1973	58-20
	Berwick	1997	64-26
	Exeter (PT)	2001	64-26
12	Poole	1971	57-21
	Halifax	1977	57-21
	Bradford	1988	63-27
	Peterborough	1995	66-30
	Trelawny	2001	63-27

Biggest defeats (home)

1	Swindon	2000	32-58
2	Cradley	1989	34-56
	Swindon	2007	35-57
4	Ipswich	1995	39-57
5	London (cup)	1996	40-56
	Swindon (cup)	2007	38-54
7	Swindon	2007	39-54
8	Cradley	1979	32-46
	Cradley	1982	32-46
	Cradley (cup)	1983	32-46
	Ipswich	1984	32-46
	Oxford	1989	38-52
	Hull	2000	39-53
	Workington	2001	38-52
	Coventry	2007	39-53

Note: In 1996 Reading Ravens beat Sittingbourne 59-19 in a Conference League fixture. In 1997 the M4 Raven Sprockets lost 51-27 at home to Berwick (at Swindon) and 33-15 to Peterborough (at Smallmead)

Biggest wins (away)

1	Eastbourne	1980	52-26
2	Birmingham	1976	51-27
	Wolverhampton	1980	51-27
4	Long Eaton	1969	50-28
	Hackney	1973	50-28
6	Swindon (LC)	1984	49-29
	King's Lynn	1986	49-29
	Newport (PT)	2004	58-38
9	Coventry	1973	48-30
	Cradley	1973	48-30
	Oxford	1973	48-30
	Newport	2001	54-36
13	Leicester	1976	47-30
	Exeter (LC)	1984	47-30

Biggest defeats (away)

1	Halifax (cup)	1979	79-29
2	Crewe	1969	62-16
3	Exeter	2000	67-22
4	Peterborough	1996	70-26
	Sheffield	2002	67-23
6	Exeter (PT)	2000	66-24
7	Exeter	1977	59-19
	Rye House (cup)	2005	65-25
9	Belle Vue (cup)	1982	57-18
10	Halifax	1978	58-20
	Belle Vue	1996	67-29
12	Swindon	2007	65-28
13	Bristol	1977	57-21
14	Trelawny (cup)	2003	65-30

Note: In addition Reading were awarded a 75-0 victory in their 1992 away fixture at King's Lynn

Note: In 1997 the M4 Raven Sprockets won 50-26 away to Belle Vue in a meeting staged at Buxton

Promoters

1968-1973	Reg Fearman	Dunton, Silver, Littlechild & Wilson 20% stake in Allied Presentations
1975-1978	Reg Fearman	Dunton, Littlechild & Wilson replaced by Dore & Higley (Silver withdraws August 1976)
1978-1979	Brian Constable	Replaced Fearman in July 1978
1980	Dave Lanning	
1981-1983	Bill Dore & Frank Higley	
1984-1986	Bill Dore & Pat Bliss	
1987	Dore, Bliss & Brian Leonard	
1988-1998	Bill Dore & Pat Bliss	
1999-2001	Pat Bliss	
2002-2005	Pat Bliss & Chris Shears	
2006-07	John Postlethwaite & Jim Lynch	Until June 2007
2007-	Mark Legg & Malcolm Holloway	From June

Team Managers

1968-72	Dick Bailey	1972 home only
1972-73	Bob Radford	1972 away only
1975-78	Frank Higley	Resigned May 1978
1978-79	Mick Blackburn	From May 1978
1980-81	Mick Bell	
1982	John Smith	
1983-84	Bob Radford	Resigned May 1984
1984-86	Bill Dore	From May 1984
1987	Brian Leonard	
1988	Bill Dore & Tim Sugar	shared
1989-99	Tim Sugar	
2000	Dave Mullett	Until July
2000-01	Tim Sugar	From August 2000
2002	Nick Dyer & Pat Bliss	Dyer – home, Bliss - away
2003-05	Ivan Shears	Resigned May 2005
2005	Tim Sugar	From May
2006-07	Jim Lynch	Until June 2007
2007-	Tim Sugar	From July

Appendix 5

League Riders Championship Representatives

			points				*points*
1968	John Poyser	BL2RC	6	1989	Jeremy Doncaster	BLRC	5
1969	Mick Bell	BL2RC	13 (2nd)		Mitch Shirra	BLRC	0
1970	Richard May	BL2RC	7	1990	Jeremy Doncaster	BLRC	8
1971	Anders Michanek	BLRC	5		Todd Wiltshire	BLRC	5
1972	Anders Michanek	BLRC	9	1991	None	BLRC	-
1973	Anders Michanek	BLRC	11 (3rd)	1992	Per Jonsson	BLRC	11 (2nd)
1975	Anders Michanek	BLRC	8	**1993**	**Per Jonsson**	**BLRC**	**14 (1st)**
1976	Dave Jessup	BLRC	11	1994	Dave Mullett	BLRC	0
1977	Dave Jessup	BLRC	5	1995	Dave Mullett	PLRC	1
1978	Dave Jessup	BLRC	0	1996	Armando Castagna	PLRC	8
1979	John Davis	BLRC	4	1997	Dave Mullett	PLRC	12
1980	Jan Andersson	BLRC	10		Glenn Cunningham	PLRC	10 (2nd)
1981	Jan Andersson	BLRC	5	1998	Lee Richardson	PLRC	6
1982	Bobby Schwartz	BLRC	9	1999	Phil Morris	PLRC	5
	Jan Andersson	BLRC	8	2000	Phil Morris	PLRC	2
1983	Mitch Shirra	BLRC	8	2001	Armando Castagna	PLRC	2
	Jan Andersson	BLRC	7	2002	Phil Morris	PLRC	11 (3rd)
1984	Jan Andersson	BLRC	6	2003	Andrew Appleton	PLRC	5
1985	Jan Andersson	BLRC	5	2004	Danny Bird	PLRC	9
1986	Jan Andersson	BLRC	11	2005	Matej Zagar	PLRC	6
	John Davis	BLRC	5	2006	Greg Hancock	ELRC	12 (3rd)
1987	Jan Andersson	BLRC	10	2007	Travis McGowan	ELRC	6
1988	Jan Andersson	BLRC	5				
	Per Jonsson	BLRC	5				

Most Appearances: Jan Andersson 9 Anders Michanek 4

Venues: 1968-1970 Hackney, 1971-1987 Belle Vue (Hyde Road), 1988-1991 Belle Vue (Kirkmanshulme Lane), 1992 Bradford, 1993-1995 Swindon, 1996 Bradford, 1997 Coventry, 1998-2000 Sheffield, 2001 Coventry, 2002 Belle Vue, 2003-2005 Sheffield, 2006 Poole, 2007 King's Lynn

Note: since 1995 the top six/eight finishing positions have been determined by semi-final(s) and a final

International speedway comes to Reading. The Young England team (from left to right): Eric Broadbelt, Dave Jessup, Geoff Maloney, Peter Murray, Dickie May, Martyn Piddock, Mike Vernam and Mick Bell. (EP)

Happy times – Jeremy Doncaster during his 1991 testimonial season with promoter Pat Bliss. (BT)

Appendix 6

Major Meetings at Reading

Finals

	Competition	Opponent	Result	Aggregate result
14.10.68	Knock-Out Cup	Canterbury	L 44-52	L 80-112
1.10.73	Knock-Out Cup	Belle Vue	W 47-31	78 all – lost after run-off
24.10.77	Knock-Out Cup	King's Lynn	W 40-38	L 77-79
8.10.90	Knock-Out Cup	Bradford	W 51-39	W 98-82
13.9.92	Gold Cup	Wolverhampton	W 47-42	L 88-91
26.10.92	BSPA Cup	Poole	W 52-38	W92-88
26.10.92	Knock-Out Cup	Bradford	W 53-37	L 88-92
21.9.98	Knock-Out Cup	Peterborough	W 57-33	W 103-77
1.8.04	Premier Trophy	Exeter	W 46-43	L 81-102
25.10.04	Young Shield	Hull	L 41-52	L 85-104
2.10.06	League Play-off	Peterborough	W 49-47	L 94-95

Major Internationals

25.8.69	Young England 51 Young Czechoslovakia 57
27.7.70	Young England 69 Young Sweden 39
17.8.70	Young England 53 Young Czechoslovakia 55
24.5.71	Great Britain 78 Poland 30
10.7.72	Norway/Denmark 38 Sweden 40
9.7.73	New Zealand 43 USSR 34
14.7.75	World Team Cup Round: England 37, Australia 24, New Zealand 21, Scotland 14
23.5.77	England 46 Rest of the World 62
19.6.77	World Team Cup Round: England 42 Australia 33, Scotland 13, New Zealand 8
21.5.78	World Team Cup Round: England 43, Australia 21, USA 20, New Zealand 12
20.5.79	World Team Cup Round: New Zealand 30, USA 26, England 22, Australia 18
17.5.81	World Team Cup Round: England 36, USA 32, Australia 20, New Zealand 8
22.6.81	England 58 Denmark 50
15.5.83	World Team Cup Round: USA 38, England 27, New Zealand 20, Australia 11
4.6.84	England 54 Denmark 54
25.4.88	England 58 Sweden 32
15.6.92	England 55 Australia 53
7.7.03	Great Britain U-21 49 Sweden U-21 41
20.7.06	World Team Cup Race-off: Denmark 49, Great Britain 42, Poland 35, USA 28
22.07.06	World Team Cup Final: Denmark 45, Sweden 37, Great Britain 36, Australia 35

The Manpower

	Date	Winner	Runner-up	Third
1971	September 13	Barry Briggs	Anders Michanek	Reidar Eide
1972	September 18	Ivan Mauger	Anders Michanek	Ray Wilson
1973	September 10	Anders Michanek	Ole Olsen	Reidar Eide
1975	September 15	Phil Crump	Malcolm Simmons	Ole Olsen
1976	September 20	Peter Collins	Anders Michanek	John Louis
1977	September 12	Finn Thomsen	Gordon Kennett	Ole Olsen
1978	September 18	John Davis	Billy Sanders	Peter Collins
1979	September 17	Peter Collins	Bruce Penhall	Dave Jessup
1980	September 15	Chris Morton	Michael Lee	Bobby Schwartz
1981	September 14	*Rained off*	*not re-staged*	

Testimonials

12.8.79	Bernie Leigh
24.7.88	Jan Andersson (rained-off 4.7.88)
5.8.91	Jeremy Doncaster
21.9.92	Dave Mullett
23.7.95	Tony Olsson
3.8.98	David Steen
31.7.00	Phil Morris
15.7.01	Armando Castagna
16.9.01	Dave Mullett (double testimonial)

Other Events

17.6.68	Reading 41 Nelson 37 – First-ever meeting
8.10.73	Reading 45 Ole Olsen's United 7 33 – Last meeting at Tilehurst
28.4.75	Reading 48 Hull 30 – First meeting at Smallmead
20.6.76	Southern Riders Championship Final: John Louis
2.8.82	Denny Pyeatt Memorial Meeting
12.7.87	British Open Pairs: Oxford
17.7.88	British Open Pairs: Oxford
26.9.94	Per Jonsson Benefit Meeting
20.6.04	Premier League Pairs - Reading